WALKER'S
BRITAIN 2

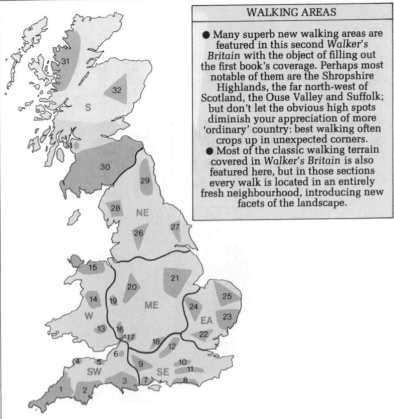

WALKING AREAS

● Many superb new walking areas are featured in this second *Walker's Britain* with the object of filling out the first book's coverage. Perhaps most notable of them are the Shropshire Highlands, the far north-west of Scotland, the Ouse Valley and Suffolk; but don't let the obvious high spots diminish your appreciation of more 'ordinary' country: best walking often crops up in unexpected corners.

● Most of the classic walking terrain covered in *Walker's Britain* is also featured here, but in those sections every walk is located in an entirely fresh neighbourhood, introducing new facets of the landscape.

(The sequence in which the areas are featured in the book corresponds to the Ordnance Survey's grid reference system, which works from west to east, and from south to north. Cornwall, furthest west and furthest south of the sections, comes first. Deeside and Speyside, furthest east and furthest north, comes last.)

WALKER'S BRITAIN 2

The complete pocket guide to 160 more walks and rambles

Pan Books/Ordnance Survey

First published 1986 by Pan Books Ltd,
Cavaye Place, London SW10 9PG
and Ordnance Survey, Romsey Road,
Maybush, Southampton SO9 4DH
Conceived edited and designed by
Duncan Petersen Publishing Ltd,
5 Botts Mews, Chepstow Road,
London W2 5AG
9 8 7 6 5 4 3

Pan ISBN 0 330 29141 6 (paperback)
ISBN 0 330 29652 3 (hardback)
OS ISBN 0 319 00072 9 (paperback)
ISBN 0 319 000915 (hardback)

Filmset, printed and bound in Great
Britain by BPCC Hazell Books,
Aylesbury, Bucks, England
Member of BPCC Ltd.

Just as with the original *Walker's
Britain*, a nationwide team of local
experts devised the routes, walked
them, then wrote the descriptions.
Among them we welcome back many
of the contributors to the first book,
and we are also pleased to introduce
several new names. All are life-
long walkers and ramblers, and most
are professionally or voluntarily
involved in the walking world,
countryside management or
recreation. A number have written
their own excellent local walking
guides, and these titles, with
publishers, are listed on page 288,
together with some biographical
details.
The editors and publishers thank
them for the enthusiasm and skill
– in all weathers – which has made
possible this second *Walker's
Britain*.

THE CONTRIBUTORS

Cornwall **David Platten, Jane Young**
and **Graham Holt**; South Devon **Liz
Prince** and **John Weir**; Dorset
Christopher Edwards; North Devon
and Exmoor **Brian Pearce**; Brendon
and Quantock Hills **Brian Pearce** and
C. Trent Thomas; Avon Region **Tom
Cairns** and **John Dent**; New Forest
Christopher Edwards; South Downs
Sheila and **Peter Burnie**; Wiltshire
Region **Christopher Edwards**; Surrey
Janet Spayne and **Audrey Krynski**;
The Weald **John King, George Mills**
and **Ben Perkins**; Chilterns and
Thames Valley **Nick Moon**; Brecon
Beacons and Black Mountains **Chris
Barber**; Mid Wales **Jim Knowles**;
North Wales **Jim Knowles**; Forest of
Dean and Herefordshire **Heather
Hurley, Susan Warren**; Cotswolds
Peter Heaton; Oxfordshire **Nick
Moon**; Shropshire Highlands **Neil
Coates**; West Midlands **Robert Kirk**
and **David** and **Janet Palmer**; East
Midlands **Brett Collier, Malcolm
McKenzie** and **Mike Statham**;
Hertfordshire and Essex **Harry
Bitten, Fred Matthews** and **George
Toulmin**; Suffolk **John Andrews**;
Ouse Valley and Fens **Trevor Noyes**
and **Janet Moreton**; Norfolk **John
O'Sullivan**; Yorkshire Pennines
Colin Speakman; The Moors and
Wolds **Betty Hood** and **Geoff
Eastwood**; Cumbria **Walter Scott** and
Roland Taylor; The North Pennines
Noel Jackson and **Janet** and **Cory
Jones**; Southern Scotland **Dave
Forsyth**; Western Scotland **Eilid
Ormiston, Sandy Cousins** and **Bill
Brodie**; Deeside and Speyside **Fred
Gordon**.

CONTENTS

The book is divided into 32 walking areas, which are shown, with page numbers, on the map on the preceding, facing page. For further ease of reference, the contents are also organized into seven regional sections, with page numbers as given below.

It is sadly impossible to produce a book as complex as this without room for improvement; in addition, the countryside changes – with surprising speed. Landmarks, particularly stiles and gates, disappear, are moved, or replaced in a different form. Dozens of users of the original *Walker's Britain* have written to us, in appreciation of the pleasure they had from the book, suggesting improvements or correcting errors. Through eight reprints of that title most of their suggestions have been incorporated. We very much hope that the same will happen again with *Walker's Britain 2*. Please address letters to Duncan Petersen Publishing Ltd at the address on the opposite page.

Using this Book

You can do the routes in *Walker's Britain* just by following the directions linked to the numbers on the maps. **However, some** understanding of maps and map-reading will greatly add to your enjoyment.

The map extracts featured in this book are made by Ordnance Survey, Britain's official surveying and map-making organization, usually referred to simply as O.S. O.S. maps are based on detailed surveys: accurate measurements of the ground combined with aerial photography. Few other maps of Britain are precision instruments in this sense.

The range of O.S. maps covers widely differing scales, for varying purposes. In this book are extracts from the 1:50 000 Landranger series.

To show the walking routes as clearly as possible, specially prepared, two-colour versions of the 1:50 000 sheets have been used.

1:50 000 maps are useful to walkers because, in colour, they show rights of way in England and Wales and are drawn to a scale giving enough detail for route-finding in most areas. For extra enjoyment of this book, use it with the relevant colour sheets.

As a beginner, start by getting to know the meaning of the map's symbols (see inside front cover). Contour lines are the only ones which are not entirely self-evident. They are surveyed lines showing the height of the ground above sea level: see map and photograph opposite.

Before starting to walk, set the map by pointing the top edge of it towards north. In featureless country, it is usually necessary to do this by compass, but remember that the sun can assist, too.

Next, get your bearings by singling out two or three features on the ground and identify them on the map. Check that the direction in which they lie as seen on the ground tallies with the direction as shown on the map. If it does not, rotate the map until it does: see map and photograph opposite, which are approximately aligned.

Next, understand the full implications of the map's scale. On 1:50 000 maps, one unit on the map represents 50 000 units on the ground. This is equivalent to 1¼ inches (3 cm) on the map for every mile (1.5 km) on the ground. An average walking pace is 3 mph (5 km/h) on the flat – a mile for every 20 minutes. In hill country, add up to 50%.

Finally, do not put the map away when you walk. Always know your position. Crosscheck it by observing landmarks as they pass.

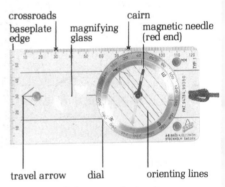

In poor visibility or on featureless ground, you need a compass. The 'Silva' type is the easiest to use with a map; here is one way in which it works.

Imagine being on moorland when the cloud comes down. Your present position is a cairn. You want to make for a crossroads. Place the compass baseplate edge on the map so it connects cairn and crossroads. Turn the dial so that the orienting lines on the transparent bottom are parallel with grid lines running N–S on the map, the arrow pointing N. Then turn the whole compass, plus map, until the red end of the magnetic needle points to N.

Look up and distinguish a rock or clump of grass that lies along the line indicated by the travel arrow. Eyes on the landmark, walk to it. Repeat the procedure.

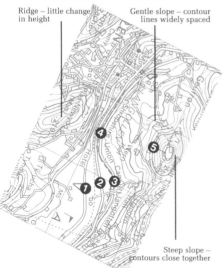

Ridge – little change in height

Gentle slope – contour lines widely spaced

Steep slope – contours close together

- The O.S. mapping used in this book does not show all rights of way, but the routes as marked are on rights of way or land with open access.
- The **sheet numbers** refer to the relevant O.S. Landranger sheet.
- The **six-figure number** following the sheet number is the grid reference of the walk's starting point on the Landranger sheet.
- **Mud after rain** means the route has a chance of drying out. **Mud** means suitable footwear must be worn.
- **The number of climbs** is a broad guide only. Remember **stiles** are of widely varying construction. **Path** usually means a narrow way – sometimes just beaten-down grass; **track** is usually broader and better defined.

Footwear and Clothes

You must have proper footwear for serious walking. Gum boots, gym shoes or kickers may be adequate for a stroll. Stout walking shoes will take you all day on country lanes. But if you walk regularly, and if you want to see the moorland and hill country – which means negotiating bogs and rough, stony ground, you need to protect your feet in leather walking boots.

Leather allows your feet to 'breathe' because it is porous. Ventilation is the key to comfortable feet because even if boots are sodden (as they will be – leather is no more than water-resistant), drying out can begin with the feet inside them. Rubber boots offer no such luxury: the feet are always slightly damp because the perspiration and condensation is trapped inside.

Only the stout construction of a walking boot can give the ankles the support they need to minimize risk of sprains. Only leather can mould itself to the feet providing the fit that allows you to walk all day comfortably.

A genuine pair of walking boots costs at least £40.00. Beware of other people's boots: they can never mould to your feet.

Wear in new boots on short walks – a total of about 30 miles (48 km) does the job. After walking, wash off the mud and let them dry naturally – direct heat distorts their shape. Wash them especially well after walking in boggy country: acids in marshy water can damage leather and stitching. While the boots are still wet, apply a dressing.

Clothes
When choosing walking clothes, remember that wind is potentially a serious problem. It reduces body temperature dramatically because of the heat loss in evaporation. A walk which starts in a light breeze in the valley can, on the hilltop, be a battle with a gale. Plan accordingly; have layers of clothing that can be shed or added to. Remember, too, that significant body heat is lost from the head: so wear a hat.

Waterproofs need choosing carefully because of the condensation problem: your body warmth causes water droplets to form inside a waterproof garment if it is tightly closed against the rain. Some new materials claim to minimize the slight dampness so-caused, but ease of ventilation is still important. The waterproof anorak that opens up the front allows this, whereas one-piece, knee-length cagoules do not. Capes give excellent ventilation, but blow around violently in strong wind and water dripping off will soak one's trousers.

Buying boots
• Go to a specialist who will let you take time over fitting • Try on boots before midday – later your feet may have swollen • Your big toe ought not to press against the boot's toe • When laced, the boot should hold the foot back, so that it does not slide forward when going downhill • Sides of the feet ought to be firmly held but not squeezed when boots are laced • The boot's heel should cup your own • Your heel will move slightly in a new boot, but soon the boot's heel and yours should move together • The back of the boot should be stiff enough to support your heel • The uppers should be one piece of leather – no seams to leak • A padded tongue and padded sides give extra comfort • The sole must have some flexibility and be at least ½ inch (13 mm) thick. 'Vibram' or 'Commando' composition soles are reliable • The welts should not stick out too far: this looks clumsy and if scrambling on the points of the toes long welts can lessen your contact with the ground, impairing balance. • Boots should have a scree cuff for gripping the ankle and keeping out small stones. • Hooks or 'D' rings are intended to be the easiest to tie with cold fingers • Two pairs of socks should be worn even with the perfectly fitting boot, a thin pair next to the skin, a thicker pair on top. The result is a cushioning effect and warmer feet. Most reputable dealers have thick socks at hand for the purpose of fitting.

Features of an efficient waterproof anorak

Zip can close to chin

Attached hood with drawcords

Elastic wrist bands in sleeves to keep out wind and rain

Large (map- or book-sized) button-down or press-studded pockets

Flap to protect zip from wet

Nylon gaiters to stop mud, stones and water from entering

Jeans, despite their popularity, are not ideal walking trousers. Wool or corduroy are warmer, and provide some protection against chilling wind; but corduroys, like jeans, are clammy when wet. The most comfortable combination for hill walking is knee-length breeches worn with long socks.

The rucksack should contain waterproof over-trousers. The most practical type can be put on without taking the boots off. Light, padded jackets give body warmth with freedom of arm movement which many appreciate.

The Walker, the Law and Safety

WALKERS' RIGHTS, AND DUTIES

Great Britain has more public footpaths than any nation on Earth. The network in England and Wales is more than 120,000 miles long; in Scotland, where the law is different, walkers theoretically enjoy even more open access to the countryside, though landowners may, and do, impose restrictions.

Moreover, in England and Wales, the right to wander in the countryside is supported by an interesting principle of law, itself an embodiment of many of the principles of social freedom we take for granted.

In law, public footpaths can be born at any time, on anyone's land, by the process known as dedication. Dedication can be 'presumed', in which case, if a path is in use without a break for 20 years, it is presumed to be a right of way. Or it can be 'direct', in which case it is negotiated, or even compulsorily ordered. A landowner can prevent presumed dedication by closing the path just once during the 20-year period; but the principle, and the possibility, of creating new paths always exists.

A right of way is just what it says: a right of passage across someone's land. The landowner may rightly object if the walker does damage, or leaves litter. But he may not complain – legally – if the walker pauses on the path to enjoy the view, or to eat lunch.

Trespass

If a walker strays from the right of way, he is trespassing. In this case the landowner ought to insist that the trespasser returns to the right of way, or leaves the land. Should the trespasser refuse, the landowner may use the minimum possible force to make the trespasser do so. In Scotland, the landowner may not intervene unless damage is done.

It is not an offence, in itself, to trespass; if you are taken to court as a result of trespassing, the landowner will sue for damages. If you, the trespasser, are found guilty, you would pay these damages. They may or may not amount to much in terms of cash; but you would also have to pay the landowner's legal fees: never cheap.

Maintenance

If a public footpath is blocked by wire, machinery, indeed by anything, the landowner is at fault and the walker may go round the obstruction, or climb it, making every effort to cause no damage. Generally, local authorities have a duty to keep the surface of paths in an acceptable condition.

A landowner may plough over a footpath if it is not along a field boundary or headland provided the path is returned to usable condition within two weeks of starting to plough, or as soon as practicable if weather prevents this being done. Sometimes farmers leave an unploughed strip; if they do not, the walker is still entitled to walk across, provided he or she keeps to the right of way. In Scotland, it is more usual for a right of way to be diverted as a result of ploughing.

Ploughing out and cropping over of paths perenially worry and confuse walkers. People instinctively feel that it is better to trespass, and thereby avoid damage than to keep to the footpath. But in legal and practical terms, the best course is to keep to the right of way. The damage to a field under crops is minimal if the walker(s) keep in single file; the consequences of trespass may be worse.

The Ramblers' Association

All these privileges, which are all too often abused and neglected (especially where ploughing is concerned) are protected on our behalf by the Ramblers' Association.

This is a privately funded lobby group, and if you care about going on country walks, you should support it, too. It has many local branches. The address of the head office is 1/5, Wandsworth Road, London, SW8 2LJ.

Bulls

Do not let your country walk be spoilt either by being unnecessarily frightened, or foolhardy when there are bulls or cows around. Cows and bullocks (castrated bulls) may rush up to you in a field, but they are rarely being aggressive.

If you see a bull alone in a field where there is a public right of way, it is probably there illegally; if it is with cows, it is probably there legally. If you encounter a truly aggressive (ie, charging) bull in a field where there is a right of way, tell the police and the Ramblers' Association.

Stallions, boars and cows with calves should be treated with due caution.

The Landowner

Remember the landowner's point of view, whatever your feelings about private ownership of land. Farmers, rich or poor, provide employment. Possibly their chief objection to walkers centres on dogs, which can upset livestock and kill game. After that, damage to crops and property are the main causes of friction. Share the countryside: you have a right to be there, but it is not exclusive.

SAFETY ON THE HILLS

Britain's mountains and hills are not high, but they are dangerous. Because they are near the sea, their weather changes fast.

Much about modern life makes us especially vulnerable to their treachery. We are unfit, because we sit all day. We arrive at walks in the comfort of cars, from which it is doubly hard to imagine the potential nastiness of the serenely inviting hilltops. Once out of the valley, a perfect summer's day can turn, in minutes, to wintry ghastliness.

Almost all accidents, and tragedies, can be prevented:

● Wear the right clothes and footwear (see pages 8-9). Take spare clothing.
● Be equipped. The lunch box should contain some emergency rations – chocolate, dried fruit and biscuits. There should be a flask containing a hot drink. The prudent take a first-aid kit, even on a day's outing. Learn first aid for frost bite, fractures, hypothermia and strains.

The same applies to a whistle, a torch and a spare battery. Know the distress signal: six blasts of the whistle, or shouts – of anything – followed by a minute's silence, then repeated.

Take a map. The O.S. 1:50 000 sheet for the area (better, 1:25 000 sheets or the 1:25 000 Outdoor Leisure Map as well) and a compass.

● Say where you are going; or at least leave a note on the car windscreen. Report any changes of plan by telephone. When you are home, report in.
● Plan the route. Make sure it is within the capabilities of the weakest member of the party. Allow enough time to be home well before nightfall. Allow an extra hour for every 1,500 feet (457 m) to be climbed. Take a watch. Know what the time of sunset will be.
● Ring the pre-recorded 24-hour forecast, or the local met. office for a weather report.
● Do not go alone. Three is the minimum safe number. In an accident, one can go for help; the other stays with the injured.
● Move at the pace of the slowest. Never straggle. Never split up, unless to get help.
● If the cloud comes down, walk in single file with 20 yards (18 m) between each of you. The last man – or woman – uses the compass, directing the leaders.

If you are caught in poor visibility, and cannot find the way down, stop until the weather clears, find shelter or build a windbreak from branches or rocks. Put on spare, dry clothing. Sit on something dry. Eat part of the emergency rations and drink something hot. Build an emergency bivouac from anything suitable – a groundsheet, a plastic mack, a cape. If cold, keep the limbs moving. Stay awake. Loosen laces and cuffs; huddle close to companions.

WHEREVER YOU WALK, KNOW AND FOLLOW THE COUNTRY CODE.

THE SOUTH-WEST

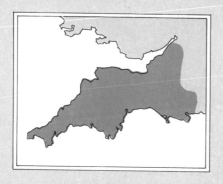

CORNWALL

The county unites an enchanting coast, nearly all walkable;
industrial landscape around St. Austell, where china clay
mining still goes on; a plateau of farmland; and the
moorland tracts of Bodmin (like its big brother, Dartmoor, a
dome of granite) together with the rather underrated high
ground that forms the spine of the extreme south-western
part of the county – the Land's End peninsula.

Most of these types of country are represented in this
section; there is the appropriate selection of coastal walks,
all different in nature to their counterparts in the original
Walker's Britain; and there are several ideas for inland
walking: one can tire of continual exposure on blustery
clifftops, and sheltered, secluded country such as the banks
of the Tresillian River makes a welcome change. For the
energetic, there is a route on the southern edge of Bodmin
Moor which involves some easy scrambling over rocky tors;
and for those in search of ancient, mysterious echoes, a
route south-west of St. Ives takes in the numinous Men-an-
tol stone, otherwise known as the Devil's Eye.

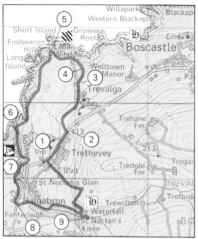

Ladies Window and St. Nectan's Cauldron
3¾ miles (6 km) Sheet 190 075894

Moderate Some of the best coastal scenery, combined, in typically Cornish style, with woodland and a traditional farm settlement close by. A diversion to Boscastle, either by foot along the coast, or by road, would complete the day's outing. *Fields, coastal path, woods and riverside; one steep descent into Rocky Valley; if field at ❷ is under cultivation, continue along road to Trevalga and turn left down track immediately before houses, then right at T-junction for ❸.*

Start Trethevy, 16 miles (26 km) SW of Bude. From Bude, go S on the A39, then take the B3263 through Boscastle towards Tintagel, until reaching Trethevy. Use the Hermitage Café **car park**, opposite Rocky Valley Hotel. Parking here is, however, reserved for customers of the café at the head of St. Nectan's Glen.

❶ Turn left out of car park and walk along road verge in Boscastle direction. Immediately after last bungalow on right, 100 yards (91 m) before large barn ❷ go left into field through a gate. Follow hedge to go through second gate in far right-hand corner. Turn right and follow track through Trevalga. After passing last farm, fork right at white gate ❸. In 75 yards

(68 m), cross small bridge over stream ❹ and turn left on to coastal footpath. To find Ladies Window ❺ leave path and bear right at top of rise. From there, keep left along cliff top to find main path down into Rocky Valley, otherwise some steep scrambling is involved to gain the valley floor ❻. Follow path across bridge and up valley to another bridge ❼. Recross stream here and walk round behind old hill to find rock carvings. From mill, continue along path beside river, and up through Halgabron. Just past last house ❽, turn left over stile at signpost for St. Nectan's Glen. Cross field towards trees and go through small gate on to path through woods. Access to waterfall ❾ is down private path from Hermitage Café. Retrace steps and leave café by main exit, going through a small gate, then up paths to a lane. This leads back to ❶.

Ladies Window is a natural hole eroded in an outcrop on top of the cliff, affording a spectacular view.

Behind the old mill ruins are two ancient Celtic labyrinth patterns cut into the cliff face. Their origin and purpose are obscure, one legend being that they were cut by shipwrecked Phoenician sailors. The same motif appears in the stone mazes on the Isles of Scilly and on numerous pieces of Celtic jewellery.

St. Nectan was a Cornish saint who settled by the waterfall. On his death, two of his female disciples are said to have diverted the stream above the fall, buried him in the river bed with a hoard of treasure, and allowed the stream to return to its old course. The treasure is supposed now to lie at the bottom of the 'keive', or cauldron – a deep, round bowl forming the upper tier of the waterfall – from where it has defied all attempts to retrieve it.

After visiting Boscastle in 1864, Swinburne wrote of ". . . the dark grey swollen water, caught as it were in a trap, and heaving with rage against both sides at once, edged with long panting lines of incessant foam . . ." Malory, Tennyson and Kingsley were among the many other poets who came here.

Cornwall
NORTH COAST

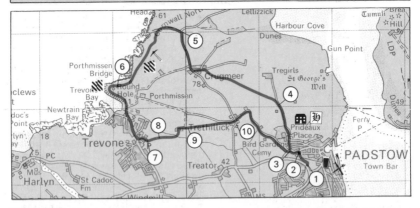

Trevone Bay
5 miles (8 km) Sheet 200 915753

Easy Explores some gentler aspects of Cornwall's northern coast, starting from the interesting old harbour town of Padstow. *Lanes, fields, open downland along coastal section.*

Start Padstow; use the town's main **car park**, alongside the B3276 at top of town.

❶ Leave car park on side opposite main entrance and turn left along footpath to church ❷. Turn left along road and right at small roundabout ❸. Continue past Prideaux Place and under bridge. On left, ¼ mile (0.5 km) beyond bridge, leave road by stile and signpost: Public Footpath – Crugmeer ❹. Follow the path, then the road into Crugmeer, turning right at the second road junction. Walk on for ¼ mile, then leave road by a stile into field, at sharp corner ❺. Follow the footpath down through 2 fields and then left along the cliff top to the Round Hole ❻. (Do not attempt to climb down into Round Hole, despite the many pathways: the side walls are treacherously unstable.) Follow the path along the cliff top and down to the beach. From beach, follow lane up to Trevone village and turn left past chapel of St. Saviours. Go through small gate at end of track ❼. Cross field diagonally towards stile ❽, go over it and cross next field heading towards buildings. Cross stream by footbridge and leave barn to left, following path over stile ❾ at end of track beyond house. Follow path along

hedge and across corner of field to next stile. Go over stile and head for gate and lane in far corner. Turn right along lane and follow it to crossroads ❿. Continue along lane, back to ❸. Retrace steps to ❶.

🏠 Prideaux Place was built in about 1585 on the site of a monastic grange belonging to Bodmin Priory. At the time of the dissolution of the monasteries in the reign of Henry VIII, there was some complicated and shady dealing between the Prior of Bodmin and the Prideaux family to keep the land out of the hands of the king. There is an underground passage linking it with Abbey House on Padstow Harbour. Some say it dates from when monks lived in the grange and Abbey House accommodated nuns.

⟋ The dark blue slate of Trevone bay dates from the Upper Devonian, 350 million years ago. The slate has been used for the font in St. Petroc's, Padstow, and for many local farmhouses.

⟋ Round Hole is a sea cave, the roof of which has collapsed. At low tide, the base is accessible from the beach.

🍺 The Old Customs House was once a grain warehouse, only becoming a pub/restaurant in 1975. Other pubs in Padstow include the Golden Lion and the Harbour, homes to the two 'Obby 'Osses: Old 'Oss and Blue Ribbon 'Oss, which are paraded through the streets on May Day.

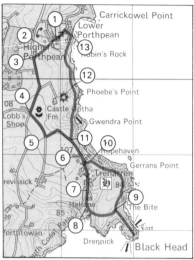

Around the Black Head
5 or 2 miles (8 or 3 km) Sheet 204
032507

Moderate Here is the pastoral S coast of Cornwall: sunken lanes with a profusion of wild flowers in the hedgerows; a peaceful beach with a waterfall; distant glimpses of industrial Cornwall. Altogether a varied and interesting day out. *Lanes, exposed headland, woodland and fields; 2 uphill stretches, the last mile very steep (the shorter version of the walk avoids this).*

Start One mile (1.5 km) S of St. Austell. On entering St. Austell, take the A390 towards Lostwithiel and turn right along unclassified road signposted Porthpean Beach. Follow signs for Lower Porthpean. (For shorter walk continue to Higher Porthpean, and then go on, following signs for Trenarren. Park at ❻.) On the right, at bottom of hill, there is a **car park** opposite the Porthpean Sailing Club.

❶ From car park, turn right uphill as far as telephone box, then turn left and immediately right through narrow alley between houses and on to footpath. Cross stile at end of path and walk round to left of toilets, on to tarmac road ❷ which crosses Youth Camp site (permissive path). Follow road to main entrance of youth camp ❸ and turn left along lane to Lobb's Shop ❹ (now a private house, but until recently a general store). Turn left here, along lane signposted Trevissick and Trenarren. At No Through Road sign ❺, also signposted Trevissick, turn left. Bear right at sign: Impracticable for Motorists. ❻ (Start here for shorter version of walk.) Continue along road, keeping right at entrance to Hallane House ❼ and follow path down to Hallane Mill and beach. From beach, return past mill to Coast Path signpost ❽ and turn right through gate up fairly steep hill. (There is no danger from the rifle range, which is given a wide berth by the coastal path.) Where another path goes off to right, follow it to Black Head for panoramic views. Retrace steps to ❾, turn right along path, and follow it round for ¾ mile (1 km). At fork in path, by bench ❿ go left, and at T-junction with track, turn right. Continue along track past ❻. A little further on, a footpath goes up steps and over stile ⓫ signposted Coast Path. Follow path to foot-bridge over stream ⓬ and then on, to emerge at back of Hideaway Restaurant ⓭. Walk through restaurant car park to road, turn left and walk downhill to ❹.

🌿 The hedgerows here contain an abundance of wild flowers including campions, stitchwort, herb Robert, primrose and hop trefoil.

✳ The area had a thriving population of Iron Age farmers, though their marks on the landscape have been largely worn away by time. At Castle Gotha Farm stood a fort – excavated once, but now ploughed over.

🏠 Trenarren is the home of the historian, A. L. Rowse.

👁 Black Head gives panoramic views of Cornwall's southern coast. To the S is Chapel Point, on the far side of Mevagissey Bay. Looking NE across St. Austell Bay, one can see the busy china-clay port of Par.

👁 Looking back here, one can see Ropehaven, a substantial house built in the 1880s by someone determined to 'get away from it all'.

Cornwall
LAND'S END PENINSULA

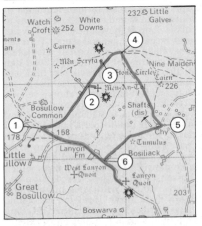

Ding Dong Mine and Lanyon Quoit
3 miles (5 km) Sheet 203 419344

Easy Samples some of the prehistoric monuments for which west Cornwall is famous, and provides a glimpse of 18th-C. tin mining. *Farm track, open moorlands; muddy in places; can be very bleak and exposed in bad weather.*

Start 7 miles (11 km) SW of St. Ives. From St. Ives, take the B3306 towards St. Just. After passing through Zennor, take third turning on left signposted Madron – approx. 5 miles (8 km) – and continue as far as telephone box (about one mile – 1.5 km). **Parking** in lay-by on left, at start of farm track, opposite Men-an-tol Studio.

① From lay-by, walk straight up track. Pass a driveway to an isolated cottate on the left, and 75 yards (68 m) further on ② turn off track to right, over an inconspicuous stone stile. Follow path through gorse to Men-an-tol. Return to main track, turn right and continue to iron gate on left ③. Go over stone stile beside it, and walk to Men Scryfa, visible in field beyond. Return to main track and turn left 50 yards (46 m) beyond ruined building ④. Turn right along a path and head towards mine chimney, visible in distance. 50 yards beyond mine chimney is an iron gate ⑤. Cross the stone stile beside it and keep to main track as it swings round to the right. Follow the track to the road. ⑥ For diversion to Lanyon Quoit,

turn left at road and walk on for ¼ mile (0.5 km). Then retrace steps from Lanyon Quoit and return to ① along road.

※ Men-an-tol Holed Stone, also known as the Devil's Eye, was probably the entrance to a Neolithic or Bronze Age tomb but has been moved from its original site and re-erected with 2 standing stones. It is said to have healing properties but the sufferer must crawl through the hole no less than 9 times.

※ Men Scryfa is one of a number of standing stones in the area. It has been suggested that they were erected at nodes of natural electro-magnetic energy and scientific measurements of such energy lend some support to this idea. The inscription, in Latinized Cornish, is a later addition dating from the 5th C.

↖ Ding Dong Mine, established in the early 18th C., was once the most hazardous tin mine in Cornwall. Men retired through ill health before they were 30 and most died in their early 40s. Cornish tin was traded with the Phoenicians but its real heyday was in the 18th and 19th C. Later, the discovery of tin in Malaya and Australia closed the mines. There are many collapsed shafts in the area, so keep to the track.

※ Legend has it that King Arthur once used Lanyon Quoit as a table, but in fact it is the remains of a Neolithic burial chamber, the covering of earth having been eroded away. After collapsing in a storm in 1815 it was reconstructed with only 3 of the original 4 supports.

Above and opposite, Men-an-tol Holed Stone, with its two standing stones.

Cornwall
NEAR TRURO

Tresillian River
7½ miles (12 km) Sheet 204 861457

Easy Cornwall's maritime heritage features prominently in this walk, although the throng of boats plying Tresillian's sheltered estuary are now mostly pleasure craft. The highlight of the walk is the historic rowing-boat ferry. *Bridleways along wooded river banks, then country lanes; path may be muddy between ⑤ and ⑥. Much of the walk skirts Lord Falmouth's estate of Tregothnan, where the public are not welcome, so keep to the lanes. The path between Merther Farm ⑤ and Tresawsan Farm ⑥ is private but may be walked with permission from either farm.*

Start 1½ miles (2.5 km) E of Truro. From Truro, take the A39 towards Tresillian. Shortly after the road reaches the river, there is large lay-by, with a Tourist Information Centre; **parking** in lay-by.

① From lay-by, cross road and turn left. (Although a busy road, there are wide verges and excellent views across the river.) Continue into Tresillian, turning sharp right, past Tregothnan Lodge ② along lane signposted St. Michael Penkevil. After ¼ mile (0.5 km) turn right down rough track past sign for Treffry ③. Keep to fenced track through farmyard, and beyond. Where the track rejoins the lane ④ turn right and continue as far as entrance to Merther Farm. (Call at farm and seek permission to walk next part of path.) ⑤ Leaving farm buildings to right, fork left through gate and across field to woods on far side, then cross stream and bear right through gate and up hill. Follow track between farmhouse and outbuildings to where it meets the road ⑥. Here turn right and follow the road, through Merther Lane village, to a T-junction ⑦. Turn left and keep straight on to visit St. Michael Penkevil and Tregothnan House (if open). Otherwise, turn right after 100 yards (91 m) over an inconspicuous stile and walk on to ferryman's house – the white cottage nearest the water ⑧. Ferry operates during daylight hours, all year, weather permitting. (If crossing from Malpas side, attract attention by ringing bell in slipway wall.) Once in Malpas, turn left for detour to the Heron Inn, otherwise turn right and follow the clearly defined bridleway to Pencalenick (signposted St. Clement Bar and Yacht Club). Turn right at the T-junction in St. Clement village. At Pencalenick, cross the river by causeway ⑨ and turn right along main road to ①.

🏠 The remote village of St. Michael Penkevil has an interesting church with Pre-Raphaelite windows.

❀ The Tregothnan Estate is closed to the public, but the house and gardens open 2 or 3 times a year.

🔟 The Malpas ferry used to be the main route into Truro from the E, carrying horse-drawn vehicles as well as passengers. The present ferryboat is over 150 years old. Legend says that Tristan and Iseult (Isolde) used the ferry on their ill-fated journey to Tintagel, and that the name of Malpas – from the French for bad passage – derives from the tragedy of their love affair. There may be a more mundane explanation for the name. The river currents here are quite strong, and in stormy weather the wind funnels up the estuary, making the crossing something of an ordeal.

🍺 The Heron Inn serves real ale and good lunches.

🏠 St. Clement's Church dates from 1259. It was extensively restored in the mid-19th C. In the churchyard is a pre-Christian standing stone thought to be over 1,400 years old.

Wigeon, one of several wild duck species which frequent the Tresillian River.

Cornwall
NEAR TRURO

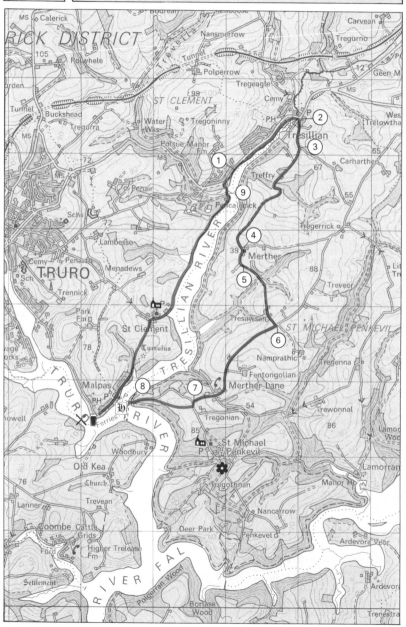

21

Cornwall
BODMIN

Devil's Jump and Treswallock Downs
7 miles (11 km) Sheet 200 097773

Moderate Unspoilt countryside on the W edge of Bodmin Moor; fine views.

Good walking routes on Bodmin, keeping strictly to public rights of way, are difficult to find. This route replaces one in the first edition which, unknown to the publishers, trespassed on private land. *Moorland, farm land; some sections very boggy, appropriate footwear essential.*

Start St Breward, off the A39, 5 miles (8 km) S of Camelford; **park** considerately near the church.

① Follow road uphill from church; past last house turn left on to footpath. Head downhill until, about half-way down, another path crosses; here ② turn right. Follow path to road junction, where ③ follow sign for Hamatethy. Pass through entrance gates and as drive leaves wood, turn left; go across fields, past sheep pens. ④ Continue straight ahead across fields, then follow stone wall. ⑤ At sunken track, turn right, uphill, and keep to this track until it joins road. ⑥ Turn left, and opposite entrance to Newton Farm climb over wall and fence. Go downhill to river, cross and head for shed painted green. Go through gate beside it, bear left and, in a straight line, head across fields to Tor Farm, seen in the distance, passing Devil's Jump on left. ⑦ Pass between farmhouse and barns, bear right over hedge, cross field to gate and follow hedge on left to Trewint Farm. Pass house, and where ⑧ drive bears left, go straight on over stile. Follow path to Advent Church, passing Cornish Cross. ⑨ After visiting church, leave by same gate and head towards stile on opposite side of field; continue uphill to road. Cross, follow track downhill to stream, over bridge, up to farm buildings and keep to the right, following stone wall on left, then path, across field to road. ⑩ The path continues on other side of road, down to streams, up on the other side, through farm buildings, across fields to road where ⑪, on other side, look for stile over stone wall, half right in distance. Head for this and follow footpath, keeping marsh on left, passing farm on right; cross track and one field. Take footbridge across stream and go

uphill through ⑫ Cargelly Farm. Keep house on right; follow track, then cross fields. At road turn left. Where road bends sharp right ⑬ go straight on, following track to open moor. Turn right, crossing moor to road where ⑭ turn left and follow road, over cattle grid until reaching entrance to Palmer's farm where ⑮, turn right, leaving road to follow path to ①.

🛐 The Advent Church gives visitors a taste of what it was like before motor cars and crowded roads. The congregation is drawn mainly from the neighbourhood's farmers and shepherds, a community relatively unchanged, even by the 20th C. The 9-pinnacled tower may be unique in Cornwall.

🦶 When a consortium of Cornish saints chased the devil out of the county he was forced to jump from this prominent tor all the way over to the other side of the valley; or so runs the legend of Devil's Jump.

🍺 The Old Inn: real ale, bar food, pleasant garden.

🏛 Across the stream on the right side of the entrance are the remains of a once-elaborate portcullis guarding the estate.

Sundew

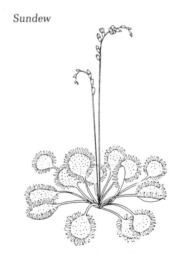

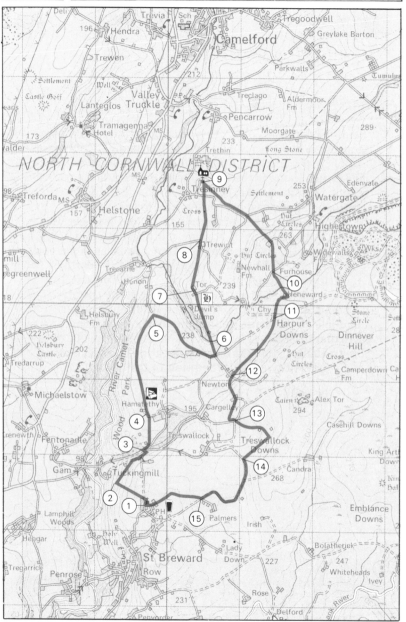

SOUTH DEVON

Semi-wilderness, contrasting with beautiful agricultural landscape, make up South Devon. Dartmoor accounts for the first; the South Hams the second.

The South Hams is the band of countryside, at its widest about 15 miles (24 km) across, which is bounded to the south and south-east by the sea; and to the north-west by the south-eastern flank of Dartmoor. In foul weather, these small, irregular hills offer safer, more sheltered walking than Dartmoor, and on fine days they can be as green and lush as any in Britain. If it were not for the dearth of footpaths, and the threats to those which do exist, this would be among the most ideal walking in the country. The name South Hams possibly derives from 'southern hamlets'; or perhaps from *homme*, a bygone term for a particular division of land. At the north-eastern end of the South Hams is the Exe estuary, location of a fascinating one- or two-day expedition in this section.

South Devon
DARTMOOR

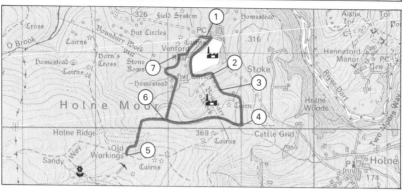

Venford Reservoir
3½ miles (5.5 km) Sheet 202 686712

Easy A short walk from a lovely little reservoir into country that looks deceptively unpromising from the road. From July–September the bilberry crop is an added incentive. *Reservoir enclosure, open moor, dry leat channel, valley; one climb.*

Start Venford Reservoir, 5 miles (8 km) W of Ashburton. From Ashburton (6 miles – 9.5 km – W of Newton Abbot), take the B3357 signposted Dartmoor, Two Bridges. After 3 miles (5 km), turn left to Holne. Go past village, then cross open moor to Venford Reservoir. **Car park** on far side of reservoir dam.

➊ From car park, cross the road and a few yards up, go through a little gate on to path. Follow path around reservoir. ➋ Leave reservoir enclosure by second stile, some yards after intake stream, and walk straight up moorland. ➌ Turn left at the second leat (water course) and follow for ⅓ mile (0.5 km) to right turning where a cart track cuts through bed of leat ➍. Follow track to Ringleshutes Mine ➎. Return by same track to where it crosses a stream ➏. Turn left down this valley. After ⅓ mile look out for a dry leat channel leading off to the left. This leads round the hill above the reservoir railings. ➐ Return to ➊ keeping reservoir below on right.

🖼 Venford Reservoir covers 33 acres and can hold up to 198 million gallons

(900 million l.) of water. The dam was built of Dartmoor granite between 1900–7, to supply domestic water to Paignton. The knobs on the top of the perimeter fence were added after the landowner of the time expressed concern that deer might be injured if they tried to jump the fence.

🖼 Holne Moor has several leats, 2 of which are still in use. Leats are man-made channels that take water from natural streams and carry it along the contours of the hills. Holne Moor Leat takes water from the O Brook on Holne Moor to another small river, the waters of which are used in Buckfastleigh. Holne Town Leat supplies water from below Ringleshutes Mine to several farms around the village of Holne. It is important not to block these leats or do anything that might break the banks down.

↖ The great gullies left here (called 'gerts' on Dartmoor) are the remains of Ringleshutes open-cast mine which dates from the 17th C. or even earlier. The miners in this period had to follow the tin seams up the hillside. The valley leading down to the reservoir has also been extensively worked.

🌿 The shrubby bilberry or whortleberry plants that cover the moorland here were once an important part of the local economy. Known as whurts, or 'urts, they were mainly harvested by the children, school closing for a week when the berries were ripe.

South Devon
DARTMOOR

Burrator to Siward's Cross
6½ miles (10.5 km) Sheet 202
568694

Moderate Starting in a beautiful valley, this is a relatively undemanding route to the high southern moor, with fascinating mining remains to be seen. *Woodland, open moorland; 2 climbs; mud after rain.*

Start Burrator Reservoir, 10 miles (16 km) due NW of Plymouth. From Yelverton, 9 miles (14.5 km) N of Plymouth, take the B3212. Turn right after 1½ miles (2.5 km) on to road signposted Meavy. After one mile (1.5 km), bear left to Burrator Reservoir. **Parking** at far end of reservoir near perimeter road.

➊ From car-parking area, walk along the road towards rounded hump of Sheepstor, following it as it swings right. ➋ After ⅓ mile (0.5 km), turn left on to track through plantation, passing ruins on left and emerging on to moor. ➌ Walk uphill beside wall and bear left, leaving wall as you gradually climb flank of the hill along sheep tracks. ➍ At the brow, head for a clump of trees in the moorland, about ¾ mile (1 km) away. (If following the leat — man-made water course — do not walk

Crossbill, now breeding on Dartmoor; the specialized bill is plainly visible.

directly on its banks.) Turn left at the trees ➎ and follow the stony track for 2½ miles (4 km). ➏ At Siward's Cross go straight on, following a rather eroded turf track. ➐ At next junction turn left on to clear stony track, and soon left again on track which crosses the Devonport Leat. Follow this to ➒.

🐦 Crossbills, which were once only visitors to Devon, found the conifer plantations of Dartmoor to their liking and now breed here. They are more often heard than seen, with their chip-chip, chip-chip call coming from high in the trees. They live on seeds extracted from pine cones by means of their specialized bills; those which accidentally fall save the forester the job of propagating seedlings.

🏚 Narrator Farm, along with about 10 others in the area, was evacuated and demolished either at the building of Burrator Dam in 1898, or when the water level in the reservoir was raised by 10 feet (3 m) in 1928. Burrator Reservoir supplies Plymouth.

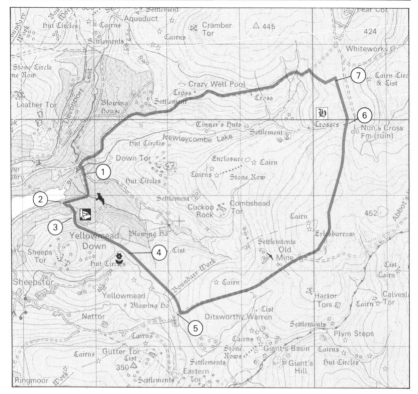

♣ S-facing stone walls around Burrator are too dry to be hospitable to plant life, but their N-facing sides are colonized by wall pennywort, stonecrop, and many species of mosses, lichen and ferns. One unusual little plant is the Cornish moneywort.

🔨 Ruins of the 19th C. Eylesbarrow tin mine. About 100 yards (91 m) to the right of the track are remains of the smelting house and the long horizontal flue which carried fumes from the furnace. Remains of the wheel pit and leat can also be seen. On the upper side of the track and running roughly parallel to it are the posts which supported a flat rod system, used to pump water from the mines. This method of transmitting power from a waterwheel to a pump in the shaft relies on a long line of rods supported on trestles and connected to a crank on the waterwheel. As the wheel turns, the rods are moved back and forth across the ground surface. At the shaft the horizontal motion of the rods is converted into a vertical motion which operates the pumps. All around this area are pits, tips, old shafts and adits. The most prosperous period of this mine was 1815–30; thereafter, yields steadily declined.

✝ Siward's Cross was first recorded in 1240. On one face are the words BOC LOND referring to Buckland and marking the boundary of the lands of Buckland Abbey. The cross was probably erected in the time of Edward the Confessor, when Siward, Earl of Northumberland, held 2 manors locally.

South Devon
DARTMOOR

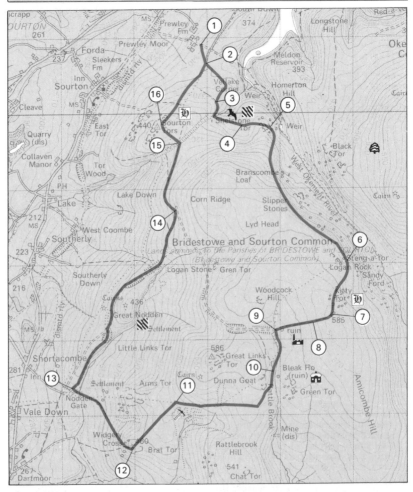

High Dartmoor
9½ miles (15 km) Sheet 191 549909

Moderate An adventurous ramble introducing the wilderness of northern Dartmoor. *Moorland, rocky outcrop, ridge, disused railway; 2 climbs; mud. Boggy patches after ⑩. From ⑧ to ⑫ keep to the right of red-and-white firing range boundary poles. Do not attempt in poor visibility. Strong footwear, waterproof clothing and a compass are recommended.*

Start Prewley Moor, 4 miles (6.5 km) SW of Okehampton. Take the A30 SW from Okehampton, then turn on to the A386 towards Tavistock. After ½ mile (0.8 km), take road on left leading to Prewley water treatment works. Go over cattle-grid and follow road for 200 yards (183 m). **Parking** on the common on the right, not more than 15 yards (14 m) from road. Do not park on road or obstruct access.

① From the road, walk up towards ridge

South Devon
DARTMOOR

following boundary fence around treatment works on left. ❷ Go through low banks and follow wall to left, then path. ❸ Take track to head of stream. ❹ Turn left half-way up col and continue to Shelstone Tor. ❺ From tor, walk to top of ridge, keeping West Okement Valley in view below on left. ❻ At Steng-a-tor, bear slightly right to avoid bog. Keeping right of firing range boundary poles, head for Kitty Tor. ❼ From tor, carry straight on to range notice-board and tall firing-range pole, then turn right. ❽ Keeping wide artificial drainage channel to right, continue to low-walled ruined buildings. ❾ Turn left along poorly defined path keeping marshy area on right. ❿ Cross stream below ruined Bleak House, turn left and follow track. Keep to right of range board and poles. ⓫ At end of extensive cuttings bear half-left, following well-defined path to Brat Tor (hill with cross on summit). ⓬ Turn right at summit in direction of furthest ford, identified by erosion either side of river. Head for ford to right of large enclosed field, reaching river at first of 2 prominent river bluffs. ⓭ Cross river, walk uphill and on reaching track, bear right and follow disused railway line. ⓮ At railway turning loop, turn left downhill. After 75 yards (68 m) turn right along another trackway and follow to head of valley. ⓯ Cross over cutting, then turn left off track and head for top of Sourton Tors. ⓰ At summit, turn right and descend to ❷, then return to ❶.

The rubble (known locally as clitter) from the severely weathered Shelstone Tor extends down into the West Okement Valley, and is home to stonechats and wheatears.

Beneath Black Tor to the E are the dwarfed, gnarled oaks of Black-a-tor Copse, one of the 3 fragments of ancient woodland remaining on Dartmoor. The rocky terrain and thin soil have stunted the growth of the trees.

Kitty Tor was the subject of controversy when, in 1882, the War Department established a training area and shooting range here. Deprived of their common grazing rights and access to the moor throughout the summer, the local people objected. Safety precautions were minimal and in 1893 a passer-by narrowly escaped death. As a result of protests, more public access is now permitted, and warning boards and posts have been erected to make the area safe.

Some authorities say 'tor' derives from the Welsh twr, meaning heap or tower.

The head basin of the Rattle Brook was once the scene of the largest commercial peat-cutting works on Dartmoor, involving great investment which was never returned. Started in the 1850s, it was worked intermittently for over a century. When the original workings gave promise of financial success, the manager was provided with the house here – then named Dunnagoat Cottage, but now a ruin known as Bleak House. The long scars of the peat cuttings are clearly visible to the E of the house.

The workings seen here are the evidence of tin streaming, first practised in medieval times. The silty deposits left by rivers and streams were picked over in search of the ore.

The valley floor to the E marks the boundary of the great granite mass of Dartmoor. This is volcanic rock, whereas the whale-backed dome of Great Nodden is made of metamorphic slate. Such rock was originally formed from fine mud and silt, compacted into sedimentary rock by centuries of accumulating deposits, then later transformed into much harder rock by the heat and pressure of volcanic activity (hence 'metamorphic').

The cool springs of Sourton Tors helped to produce a commodity in great demand in the 19th C. – ice. Sourton Ice Works operated in the 1870s and 1880s, preparing large blocks of ice in shallow ponds during winter. They were transported to Plymouth in spring and early summer – a slow journey by horse and cart, during which much of the product simply melted away. What was left was used in food preservation, particularly for fish. Undulations in the surrounding land mark the site of these ponds.

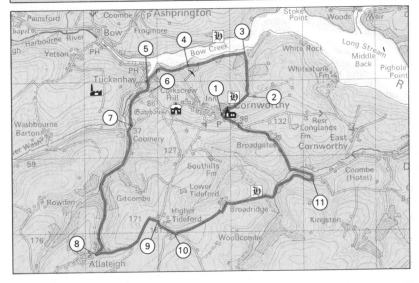

The Heart of the South Hams
5 miles (8 km) Sheet 202 828556

Moderate Pleasant rambling along green lanes, leaving a lasting impression of what is best about this Devon landscape – its farms and fields, combes, rivers and woods, all set in an unending rolling landscape. *Green lanes, riverside; one climb; very muddy in parts.*

Start Cornworthy, 5½ miles (9 km) SSE of Totnes. Take the A381 from Totnes towards Kingsbridge, and after one mile (1.5 km), bear left to Ashprington. At church, bear left to Bow, then turn left to Tuckenhay. Turn left to Cornworthy. **Parking** in village. Please do not cause obstruction.

① Facing church at E end of village, turn left following footpath through farmyard, turning right after Cornworthy Court and going straight on through gate. ② Where green lane divides, bear left. ③ On reaching Bow Creek, follow footpath to left. Follow well-defined path up creek bank, passing ruin on right and later crossing small footbridge. ④ Just past quarry, go through gate on left and turn immediately right, keeping creek in sight and walking parallel to it. ⑤ Turn left up track where path joins short road leading to small housing estate. Turn right at track junction. ⑥ Turn left on reaching road and, just past mill, bear left up green lane. ⑦ At barn, turn right along road and take first left. Go past Coomery, and follow track to Allaleigh, bearing left at wooden building frame. ⑧ Bear left along road. ⑨ Ignore first right turn, then at second road junction, bear right and follow road for 400 yards (366 m) to Broadridge Cross ⑩, then turn left. Follow green lane for over one mile (1.5 km), turning left down grassy track at ⑪, just before reaching road. Follow track to ①.

🏠 On entering Cornworthy from the W a solitary gatehouse can be seen in a corner of a private field. This is all that remains of an Augustinian Nunnery founded here in about 1205 and swept away in Henry VIII's suppression of 1536.

⛪ Cornworthy Parish Church is mainly 15th C. with an original rood screen, but its internal splendour is attributable to the Georgian period, when refitting took place during the tenure of the Reverend Charles Barter, who was vicar for no less than 71 years (1775–1846).

Cornworthy was originally an Anglo Saxon 'cornworthig' – a clearing for cereal growing.

The Domesday Book records 13 fisheries in Devon, most of which were salmon fisheries. The Dart was, and still is, a notable salmon river and at Cornworthy, Domesday records that fishermen had to pay 30 salmon a year to the lord of the manor.

The disued quarry here supplied basalts for the completion of Dartmouth Castle in 1481. On the creekside, the footpath goes by a small, rounded, grass-grown lime-quay and a kiln with a substantial outer wall. Adjoining it is the ruin of a small cottage ('Tin House') where the lime workers lived. Some of the local lime workings date from the 15th C. – most of this was used for mortar and it was not until the late 16th C. that lime was applied to the land. The practice greatly increased in the 18th C., and several large kilns remain near the Waterman's Arms in Tuckenhay. The success of the lime-burning trade in this area was largely due to an appreciable demand from the remote farms to the W of the River Dart.

The Dart at Hexworthy – in its infancy; it is a fine salmon river.

In 1850, the now-quiet hamlet of Tuckenhay was a hive of industrial activity. It had 2 paper mills, a corn mill, lime-burning kilns, a rope manufactory and cider presses, as well as being a considerable little port handling cargoes of roadstone. The silting up of the harbour brought this industry to an end. A wall was built in the Harbourne estuary to deflect incoming silt from the deep-water channels around the quays, but all in vain. The wall can still be seen at low tide. One of the smaller buildings just off the River Wash mooring point is the old gas-house, erected by Mr. Abraham Tucker, to provide lighting for the hamlet in 1806 – 4 years before gaslights came to London.

Most of the green lanes that the walk follows have their origins over 1,000 years ago. The arrival of the Saxons in the South Hams during the 7th–8th C. heralded an important phase in settlement and route patterns, and the increase in population meant that wooded valleys were cleared on a scale hitherto unknown.

South Devon
NEAR KINGSBRIDGE

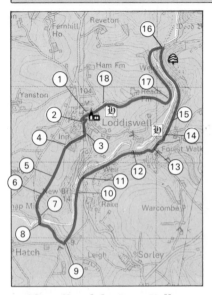

Loddiswell and the Avon Valley
6 miles (9.5 km) Sheet 202 721486

Moderate The South Hams is so well known for its coast that few visitors explore its green inland acres, which offer delightful countryside to the walker. *Fields, valley, disused railway, riverside, green lane; one climb. Path ill-defined between ⑯ and ⑰.*

Start Loddiswell, 3 miles (5 km) N of Kingsbridge on yellow unclassified road. Kingsbridge lies on the A379. **Car park** near church.

① From church gate, bear left down narrow lane to centre of village. ② With Loddiswell Inn on right, carry on downhill for 100 yards (91 m). ③ Turn right by New Bridge pub and walk up Town Lane. ④ At right-hand bend, turn left into field following waymarked path. Follow field boundary on left. ⑤ Cut across middle of field. ⑥ Follow hedge on right. At bottom of second field, go through *second* gate on right. Cut diagonally across field, following path above stream to stile ⑦. Climb, and turn left to bridge ⑧. Turn left and follow lane to junction. ⑨ Follow lane to left and after 25 yards (23 m), turn left

into field and follow waymarked path. Cross stream course, then head for stile. Climb and walk to bridge. ⑩ Go up steps, cross road, then go down other steps into field, keeping left to bridge. ⑪ Join lane, then bear left along lane. ⑫ At nurseries, turn left towards bridge, and cross over stile on right. ⑬ Rejoin lane, turn left and go under railway bridge, then bear left. ⑭ At former station (now a residence) go over stile to right of house and garden. ⑮ Cross stile on left, then turn right following course of old railway. ⑯ Leave track as it bends right and cross bridge. At end of bridge, go left down embankment, then left again to follow path between river and field boundary. After 30 yards (27 m), bear left and keep to riverside path. ⑰ At small stream, bear right, following waymarked footpath at edge of small wood to farm. Follow farm track to Ham Butts crossroads ⑱. Go straight on to ①.

🏠 Loddiswell (pronounced 'Lodzwell'). Church dates largely from the 14th and 15th C., but has a 12th-C. Norman font. This is in the same red sandstone which gives the soil in this area its characteristic ruddy colour. In the church porch are the old village stocks – unusual in providing accommodation for 3 occupants of varying sizes – man, woman and child perhaps.

🏛 Loddiswell station – once a halt on the Great Western Railway, Kingsbridge branch. This line ran for 12½ miles (20 km) from South Brent on the edge of Dartmoor to Kingsbridge, crossing the river valley 10 times. Opened in 1893, it was closed as part of the Beeching cuts, in 1963. At ⑬ there is a GWR boundary marker, dated 1899.

🌲 Avon Valley Woodland, owned and managed by the Woodland Trust, extends for almost 2 miles (3 km) along the Avon, N from Loddiswell Station. It forms one of the largest blocks of broad-leaved woodland in the South Hams.

🏛 The name Ham Butts derives from 2 Old English words. 'Ham' meant an enclosure, or meadow, and 'butts' refers to a place where oddly shaped fields abutt or join.

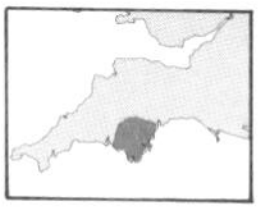

South Devon
NEAR KINGSBRIDGE

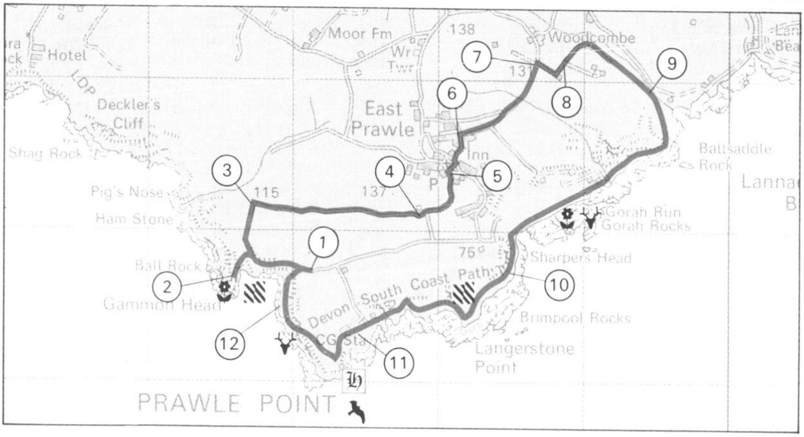

Around Prawle Point

9 miles (14.5 km) Sheet 202 771358

Moderate Explores Devon's southernmost tip, with its rocky cliffs, sheltered coves and beautiful wooded valleys. An outstanding area for bird-watchers. *Cliffs, fields, green lanes, wooded valley; one climb, one steep descent; mud between ⑧ and ⑨. Take care in wet weather on descent to coast path at ①.*

Start Prawle Point, 12 miles (19 km) SSE of Kingsbridge. From Kingsbridge (between Plymouth and Dartmouth) follow the A379 E. At Frogmore, turn S to South Pool and continue to East Prawle. Take lane between telephone box and bus shelter. Turn left, then right, and at sharp left bend, carry straight on into field. Private **car park** in field. (There is another car park around sharp left bend.)

① From car park follow track by wall (on left facing sea) down to coastal path. Turn right to Gammon Head. ② Retrace steps to cove, then bear left along narrow path, and left again after 100 yards (91 m). Follow path uphill, keeping enclosed field on left. ③ At track junction, turn right and continue along green lane. ④. At road, go straight on and continue straight uphill to East Prawle. ⑤ At village, cut across green on right (by bus shelter) to Pig's Nose Inn. Follow lane down to junction, then bear left and after 75 yards (68 m), take first right down narrow lane. Follow this to telephone box on right. ⑥ Turn right into narrow, surfaced lane, and go straight on at first 2 junctions. ⑦ At next junction, go through wooden gate and bear right along track. ⑧ At junction, go straight on and follow track, then path down to coastline. ⑨ On joining coastal path, bear right and follow for 1¼ miles (2 km). ⑩ In flat, broad field, keep to path on seaward side. ⑪ Follow path on seaward side of hedge in front of cottages and ascend to coastguard lookout point. ⑫ Cut back right, uphill to ①.

The sandy cove tucked under the eastern flank of Gammon Head is a superb place for swimming. Notice how the W side of the cove (facing the prevailing winds) is more weathered.

The coastal flora includes gorse, thrift, the little blue flower heads of spring squill, and the aromatic wild thyme.

Near Gorah rocks, the shore can be reached at low tide; rock pools full of marine plants and creatures.

The path here follows the edge of a series of raised beaches: one field inland are the former cliffs. Prawle means look-out hill.

The headland is an important migration watchpoint.

A good spot for sighting grey seals and, in summer, basking sharks.

South Devon
NEAR SIDMOUTH

Combe and Cliff
10¾ miles (17 km) Sheet 192
207881

Strenuous A little-used stretch of East Devon's Heritage Coast, and the leafy combes and peaceful villages that lie just inland. *Woods, cliff tops, beach; 3 climbs; mud between ❶ and ❼, and ❶ and ❾.*

Start Branscombe, 5 miles (8 km) E of Sidmouth. From Sidmouth take the A3052 E, and after 3½ miles (5.5 km), turn S to Branscombe. Follow signs to Branscombe Mouth from village. Buses from Sidmouth and Beer to Branscombe Mouth. **Car park** at Branscombe Mouth.

❶ From car park bear right following coastal footpath immediately behind café. Follow steep path up grassy flank of West Cliff ❷ and continue. ❸ Ignore footpath on right to village, and continue in same direction along track bordered by woods. ❹ At path junction, keep straight on, following finger posts to Weston Mouth. Keep to footpath through fields. ❺ Cross mouth of stream on beach. Go up winding steps on right, then follow grass path signposted Dunscombe ¾ mile. ❻ At upper edge of copse, turn right off main track to follow fence bordering woods. ❼

Pass through fields at Slade House Farm,, then turn left along narrow tarmac lane. Cross road ❽, then follow signed path to Salcombe Regis. Turn right along lane. ❾ Turn left down lane just after church. ❿ Go through gate with notice, Private Road to Coombe Wood Farm. ⓫ Just beyond farmhouse, take signposted path on left, heading diagonally up hillside. ⓬ At far end of Dunscombe Cliffs, take path skirting inland, around head of valley to coast at ❺. Retrace route to ❹ then take zigzagging path on left, down through steep wood. Cross stream and walk through churchyard. ⓭ Leave church, and turn right along village street. At road junction, bear right and go immediately right down lane. Where it swings right, follow footpath on left back to ❶.

✗ The Sea Shanty Café at Branscombe Mouth was once a coal yard, the coal arriving by sea. Lime burning and gypsum production were also important here, and the coastguard cottages (now the lookout) hint at a smuggling trade that was rife in the 18th and early 19th C.

↖ The small greensand quarries in the combe here were worked to provide quality building stone, some of which

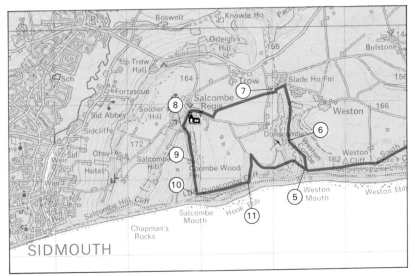

was used to build Exeter Cathedral in the 14th and 15th C. The quarries were reworked in 1930 for the building of the modern church of Woolbrook, at Sidmouth.

At Salcombe Regis the lich-gate leading into the churchyard is furnished with a large bolt made from the shaft of a 'resurrection corkscrew' – an implement used by body-snatchers to lever a partly unearthed coffin from its grave. This one was acquired in the early 1800s after Sidmouth doctors and a labourer were caught in an attempt to steal the recently buried body of a Salcombe boy. (A lich-gate is a roofed gateway.)

Branscombe's parish church is dedicated to St. Winifred, an obscure North Welsh saint who died c.650. Such a rare dedication suggests that a church may have existed here since that time, but the massive central tower and part of the nave are Norman. Inside there is an Elizabethan gallery, box pews and a rare 3-decker pulpit.

Queen Victoria ordered her wedding dress to be made of Honiton lace made at Beer and Branscombe.

One of Branscombe's great attractions is its working smithy, dating back possibly to the 15th C, operated now by one of the country's two female blacksmiths.

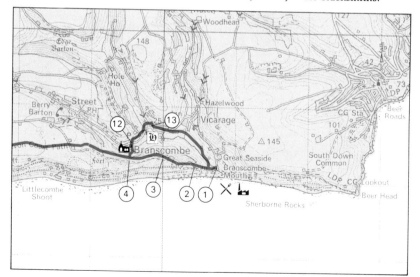

South Devon
NEAR EXETER

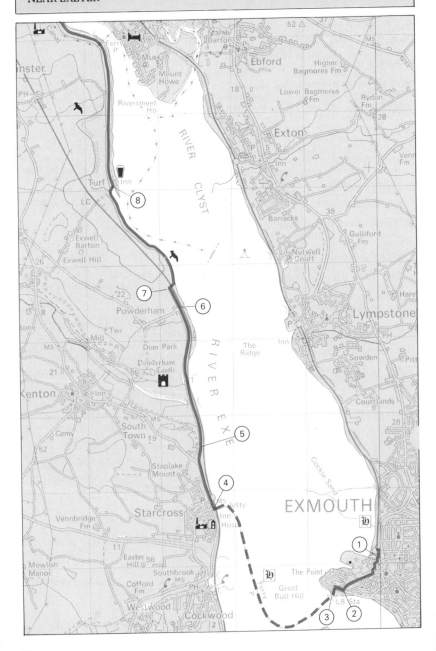

South Devon
NEAR EXETER

The Exe Estuary
9¼ miles (15 km) Sheet 192 000812

Moderate Along the length of the estuary, an area steeped in history – particularly transport history – and with many interesting viewpoints. If you wish you can start the walk with a train journey and a historic ferry crossing which combine to make such an unusual outing, that although the walk is just over 9 miles (14.5 km) there is a good case for taking two leisurely days on the route, stopping for the night in Topsham where there is a range of accommodation (see hints on this page). The route is perfectly feasible in one quite long day, but this does not leave so much time for lingering. *Parkland, estuary, canal towpath.*

Start Exeter, St. David's Station. From there take train to Exmouth, and ferry from ③ to ④. Ring Exmouth (03952) 72009 for ferry times. Alternatively, omit ferry crossing by taking train from Exeter to Starcross and start walk at ④. In winter, ferry does not run, so take train to Starcross. **Car park** at St. David's station.

① From Exmouth Station, bear right and follow road signs marked Seafront and docks, then continue following signposts marked Seafront only. ② At seafront turn right, and pass a small pier. Walk down road, keeping The Beach pub on right, to ferry boarding quay at end. ③ Catch ferry to Starcross (NB water taxis may take you elsewhere). ④ After disembarking, turn right at end of pier and cross railway line via footbridge on left. At road, turn left to visit Brunel's Atmospheric Railway, otherwise turn right. Go past the railway station then follow footpath running parallel to railway line. ⑤ Almost at end of grassed area, bear left to go through metal gate. Turn right along lane, signposted Powderham Castle. Do not turn left to castle, but continue along road. ⑥ At sharp left bend, carry straight on along track beyond painted, wooden gate. ⑦ At end of track, turn right to cross over railway line through small gates. Take care, as this is a busy line. Turn left on other side. ⑧ At Turf Hotel, keep to left of lock and follow towpath, keeping canal on right.

Continued on page 38.

🏠 Exmouth is Devon's oldest seaside town, frequented by Exeter people since the early 18th C. A railway from Exeter to Exmouth was first mooted in 1842 but the scheme became involved in the 'Battle of the Gauges'. A further attempt in 1854 failed for lack of capital but a line opened at last in 1861. The sea wall was built between 1841 and 1870.

🏠 The Exmouth Ferry has a long history. Sherborne Abbey, Dorset, possessed a manor from 1122 on the E side of the Exe and it developed a regular ferry across the estuary from the fishing hamlet of Exmouth to a landing-place now called Starcross. This enabled travellers to avoid a detour of 20 miles (32 km) through Exeter. A loss of tolls to the city caused concern so an agreement between the Abbot of Sherborne and the City was made by which a tax on the ferry was levied. Sherborne Abbey was suppressed in 1539 and the city acquired the ferry.

🗼 Still standing at Starcross, is the Italianate sandstone tower which housed one of the stationary engines built by Brunel, to power his experimental railway. Called the Atmospheric Railway, it removed the need for a moving engine to pull the carriages. The system cost £400,000 to install but proved unsuccessful, and became known as the 'atmospheric caper'. Normal locomotives ran on the line after 1848.

🏰 Powderham Castle, home of the Courtenay family since 1390, stands in beautiful parkland. It has a large herd of fallow deer. The castle building was started by Sir Philip Courtenay (Lord Lieutenant of Ireland and Earl of Devon) in the 14th C. and is really a fortified manor house.

🦢 Many species of wading birds visit the Exe estuary, and are seen in greatest numbers 2–3 hours after high tide. Winter sightings include as many as 10,000 dunlin, 5,000 oystercatchers, and 10,000 wigeon.

🍺 The interesting old pub at Turf is still accessible only on foot or by boat.

South Devon
NEAR EXETER

Exeter Docks
Continued from page 37.

Continued from page 37.

(In about another mile (1.5 km), there is a ferry into Topsham where you can find accommodation.) ❾ Cross over dual carriageway and continue to towpath. ❿ Turn right over road bridge leading to Country Park. Continue along towpath with canal now on left. ⓫ Just past Welcome Inn, cross over 2 swing footbridges. Turn right and continue straight on down road, keeping land-moored boats on right. ⓬ Follow road to left, then cut across grassed area to river and walk along towpath. ⓭ By old maltings building, continue along towpath at end of Shooting Marsh Stile (row of 5 terraced houses). ⓮ At Blackaller Weirs, cross over footbridge on right then turn left. Continue along towpath or follow river. ⓯ Turn right along Station Road, then level crossing to station ⓰.

🦅 Exminster marshes also boast many birds, including avocets in spring, and whimbrels, wheatears and sand martins in summer. Listen for the unbirdlike 'reeling' noise of the grasshopper warbler, and the harsh song of the reed warbler – rather like a demented, cackling laugh – coming from among the reeds.

⚓ The port of Exeter owes its early development to the drive and flair of the Elizabethan city leaders. They initiated the building of the first canal of any significance in England – the older stretch of the canal, between ❿ and ⓬, built by John Trew in 1556, the first in Britain to have 'pound' locks which have gates that lift, rather than swing. The 5-mile (8-km) canal linked the then seaport of Topsham with the trading centre of Exeter. Due mainly to a prosperous wool trade, Exeter became a major port and the canal was extended for ½ mile (0.8 km) across the Exminster Marshes. Further prosperity brought with it the need for canal improvements and in 1698 William Bayly was appointed to build a true ship canal. He absconded with the funds after leaving the canal in an impassable and ruinous state. Undaunted, the council raised loans and the work began again in 1700–24. The costs of this final extension, changes in ship construction and the development of the railways from the 1840s brought an abrupt end to the canal's profitability and by the 1960s its death knell as a trading waterway had been sounded. However, a new lease of life was given to both it and the Quay and Basin area with the opening of the Maritime Museum in 1969. Most of the quayside warehouse buildings date from the 17th and the 18th C.

🍺 Double Locks Hotel dates from the early 1700s and shows a strong Dutch influence: it is probably England's oldest canal-side pub.

🛏 Topsham (page 36) is better than Exminster for an overnight stop – the latter being close to the M5. Exeter Tourist Information Centre (0392) 72434 will advise on accommodation available in Topsham, but there are two pubs which offer beds for the night; The Globe, Fore Street, tel. (039287) 3471 and The Lighter Inn, The Quay, tel. (039287) 5439.

38

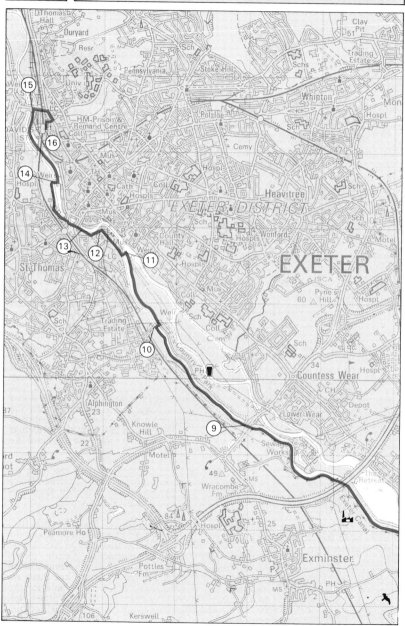

DORSET

Nowhere is Dorset crossed by a motorway; quite good
grounds for its reputation as one of England's least-spoiled
counties. Dorset addicts, however, have no need of rational
arguments to explain their enthusiasm: the rather bare
central hills, with their many traces of ancient human
habitation, have an inexplicable power to strike a chord.
They also have a character all their own: on the face of it,
they look like downland in Wiltshire, Sussex or Berkshire,
yet somehow they are not quite like anywhere else. But gut
feelings about Dorset hardly need justifying when Thomas
Hardy has done it so well already.

The five routes in this section will introduce not just the
pleasures of the Dorset downs (the route entitled *The West
Dorset Hills* is perhaps the best choice if you want a first
taste of these), but the other faces, too. A walk based on
Lulworth Cove shows some of the coast's many interesting
geological features, as indeed does another starting at
Abbotsbury, from where there are fine views of the
extraordinary Chesil Beach. The route entitled *Maiden
Castle* encapsulates, as well as any, Dorset's historical
associations. It starts at the well-known landmark, Hardy's
Monument: Hardy as in "Kiss me, Hardy", not the writer.

Sturminster Newton and the Blackmoor Vale
5½ miles (9 km) Sheet 194 788142

Easy Truly Hardy's Dorset, and much of it still as he would have known it, with lush river valleys, wooded hills and the old market town of Sturminster Newton. *Riverside, woods, fields.*

Start Sturminster Newton, 7 miles (11 km) SW of Shaftesbury on the B3091. Large **car park** off Station Road.

① From car park walk downhill in the direction of prominent hill-fort to path along dismantled railway. After 100 yards (91 m), take steps leading right and walk along river path to Fiddleford Mill. Follow road around mill, ignoring road leading right. At pink cottage ② take path by stream to Fiddleford Inn. At main road, turn right and then left along path marked Public Footpath ③ uphill beside trees. Turn right ④ through Piddles Wood along path marked with an orange arrow. Take first left along wide track to road ⑤. Turn right to junction ⑥, then turn left and right along footpath. At minor road ⑦ turn sharp right on footpath marked DCC Footpath. Cross several stiles to main road. Turn left and take first minor road on right for ½ mile (0.8 km). Turn right along footpath ⑧ leading to footbridge across river. Cross and turn right, then follow path along river to mill. Recross river and then cross again on stone road bridge ⑨. Turn right and pro-

ceed along river to church. Go through churchyard to village and car park.

🚉 This is part of the route of the Somerset and Dorset railway, which once ran from Bath to Bournemouth, but was closed in 1966.

🚉 Fiddleford Mill, once used for grinding corn, was also a hiding place for contraband liquor. Workers from Sturminster Newton came here for boisterous drinking evenings, and it was the scene of brawls and murders.

🍺 Fiddleford Inn: food and coffee.

🏰 Only the mound remains where the Saxon castle once stood. The ruins on top belong to a much later building.

🚉 Sturminster Newton Town Mill has been restored and can be seen in action. It is open to the public from 1 May–30 September, 11–5 on Saturdays, Tuesdays and Thursdays, and from 2–5 on Sundays.

🏠 Riverside Villa was the home of Thomas Hardy from 1876–8. Hardy described the time spent here with his first wife as "our happiest time", and here, too, he wrote *The Return of the Native*.

⌒ Sturminster Newton bridge is medieval and bears a grim reminder to vandals.

🏫 The Old Boys School claims as one of its former pupils, Dorset's much-loved dialect poet, William Barnes (1801–6).

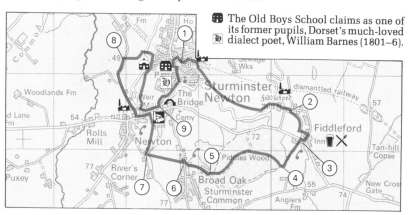

Dorset
LULWORTH

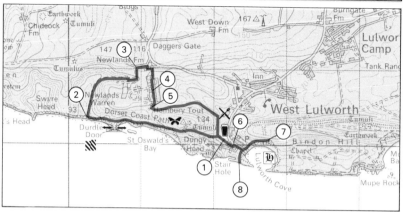

Lulworth Cove
4¼ miles (7 km) Sheet 194 821801

Moderate Dramatic cliffs and spectacular coves combine with gentle, grassy inland valleys to make this an excellent short walk. Specially interesting in summer for the butterflies, although Lulworth can be busy with tourists then. For a peaceful walk, winter is the best season. *Cliffs, valleys; 2 climbs. Rocks will be slippery after rain. Do not proceed E along cliffs beyond ⑦ unless firing range is open.*

Start Lulworth Cove, 8 miles (13 km) SW of Wareham. Large **car park** by the Cove.

① From car park follow wide track climbing steeply away from cove to edge of cliff. Follow cliff path for one mile (1.5 km) then, at bottom of dip, turn right, inland ② along signed path. As path bears right, keep to left of caravan site and turn left along farm track. ③ Turn right to road, then right again along main way through caravan site ④. When this bears right, turn left on path ⑤ which runs along side of hill, leading back to car park. The path around Lulworth Cove can be reached by following road ⑥ almost to the water. ⑦ This is the limit of the walk. Return by

Opposite: Durdle Door, popular destination for the casual stroller along the cliff path west from Lulworth Cove. Once you are past it, the crowds thin out. Some like it best whipped by waves in a south-wester.

same path via Stair Hole ⑧ at water's edge. Retrace steps to ①.

🦋 On summer days the grass is full of chalkhill blue butterflies. There are also graylings, marbled whites, and the dark green fritillaries. The rare golden-coloured Lulworth skipper was first seen at Durdle Door in 1832, and can still be found only in this area alone.

👁 Views to Portland in the W and St. Aldhelm's Head in the E.

🌊 Durdle Door is a natural rock archway caused by the waves flinging pebbles at the base of the rock, also by the immense compressive force of the waves enlarging cracks in the rock.

🍺 There are choices of pubs and cafés by the car park.

📖 Lulworth Cove is where the dashing but ruthless Sergeant Troy was thought to have drowned in Thomas Hardy's *Far From the Madding Crowd*, and it has another, less well known literary association: when Keats, dying of consumption, left England for Italy, never to return, his ship called in at Lulworth Cove. The poet is said to have come ashore for a few hours and been inspired to write his lovely last sonnet which begins: 'Bright star, would I were steadfast as thou art –'.

43

Dorset
NEAR DORCHESTER

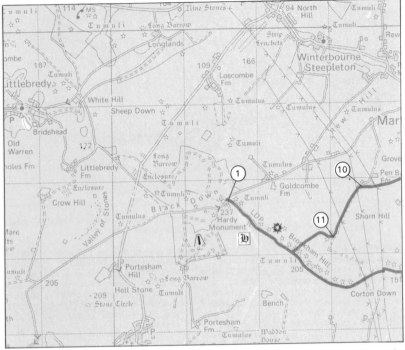

Maiden Castle
9 miles (14.5 km) Sheet 194 616877

Moderate Across the rolling green downland roof of Dorset, an ancient, windswept landscape guarded by Maiden Castle, the strongest hill-fort in Europe. *Downs, valleys, fields; tracks through the farms get muddy. Route indistinct between ② and ③: follow directions carefully.*

Start Hardy's Monument, 4½ miles (7.5 km) SW of Dorchester. Take the A35 W to Winterbourne Abbas, then turn S along minor road to the monument. Regular buses and trains to Dorchester. The walk can be picked up at Maiden Castle, ⑤ one mile (1.5 km) SW of Dorchester on the A354. Large **car park** at monument.

① From car park, turn right along road. After 200 yards (183 m), take path, signed with a blue arrow and an acorn, leading right. Walk for 2 miles (3 km). About 200 yards past 2 prominent tumuli on the right ② turn left, then bear right ③ towards the huge earthworks of Maiden Castle. Join track ④ and follow to road. Turn left and take right fork. When road bears sharply right, take footpath on left passing along left-hand side of Maiden Castle. Turn left along good track ⑤, and left again at crosstracks ⑥. Follow blue arrows through farm. At road junction ⑦ take track on other side of road leading down towards Martinstown church. Take road ⑧ opposite church, then turn left on to path ⑨ when road bears sharply right. Follow path across fields and turn left at second track ⑩. Follow for ½ mile (0.8 km) then turn right on to gravel track ⑪ (signposted Hardy's Monument) to ①.

🏛 The Hardy Monument – not to Thomas Hardy, but to Admiral Hardy, immortalized by Nelson's much-misunderstood death-bed cry "Kiss me, Hardy". The Admiral lived at Portesham, one mile S of the monument.

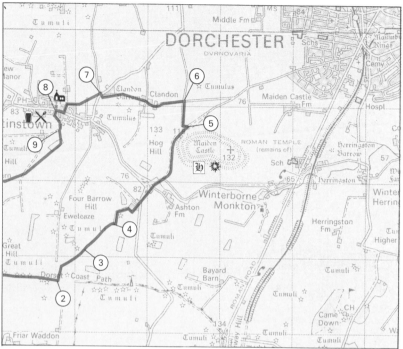

$\overset{1}{\mathbb{V}}$ The best all-round views of Dorset can be seen here. On a clear day the Channel coast all the way from Start Point in Devon to the Purbeck Hills in the SE can be seen, with the Isle of Portland, reaching well out to sea, in the centre.

✸ Bronkham Hill and Corton Down are strewn with barrows, the relics of ancient burial sites.

✸ Maiden Castle is the largest Iron Age hill-fort in Britain, covering an area of 115 acres. It was a secure fortress for 3,000 years, until taken by the Romans in 43 A.D. In the late 4th C., a Romano-British temple was built within the ramparts, and its square foundations $\mathbb{b}$ can still be seen. William Treves in his Highways and Byways in Dorset (1920) writes: "No man meddled with its walls, so that its great valla became merely shelters for sheep. Thus it is that Maiden Castle survives in perfect preservation, an astounding monument of the work of those busy Celts whom the Romans on their coming found in the occupation of England." Thomas Hardy used Maiden Castle as the setting for A Tryst at an Ancient Earthwork. Here, too, Henchard saw the return of Donald Newson, and watched Elizabeth-Jane meet Farfrae in The Mayor of Casterbridge.

🏠 Martinstown Church – St. Martin – has probably the best example of a barrel-shaped roof in the country. For 100 years this church had no bells because they had had to be sold to defray debts. In 1947 bells rang again when 5 were put in to commemorate those who died in the Second World War.

🍺 The Brewer's Arms serves food. ✕ Admiral Hardy thought the best beer in the world came from this part of Dorset.

Dorset
NEAR WEYMOUTH

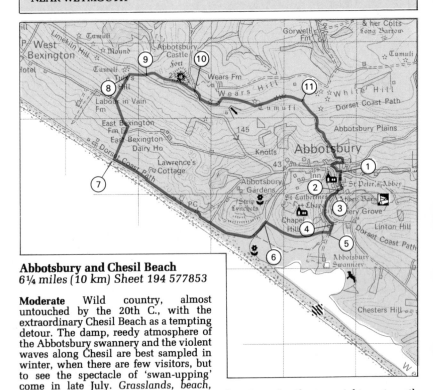

Abbotsbury and Chesil Beach
6¼ miles (10 km) Sheet 194 577853

Moderate Wild country, almost untouched by the 20th C., with the extraordinary Chesil Beach as a tempting detour. The damp, reedy atmosphere of the Abbotsbury swannery and the violent waves along Chesil are best sampled in winter, when there are few visitors, but to see the spectacle of 'swan-upping' come in late July. *Grasslands, beach, downs ridge; one climb.*

Start Abbotsbury, 8 miles (13 km) NW of Weymouth on the B3157. Large **car park** by Abbotsbury church.

❶ From car park, walk through churchyard and remains of abbey to Great Barn ❷. Follow road marked Pedestrian way to Swannery. At fork ❸ bear right. ❹ Turn right along path marked to Swannery. ❺ Take footpath to right signed To Tropical Gardens. ❻ Turn left and follow path signposted Chesil Beach and West Bexington for 1½ miles (2.5 km) along beach. ❼ Leave beach and take path signed To Abbotsbury Hill Fort. ❽ Turn right along Dorset Coast Path, signposted To Hardy's Monument. ❾ Cross road and rejoin path to hill-fort. At minor road ❿ turn right, then go left along footpath just before reaching main road. Continue along ridge for one mile (1.5 km). ⓫ At

junction of paths turn right on to path signposted To Abbotsbury. At road turn right, then go left at junction to ❾.

🚪 In the pulpit of Abbotsbury Church are bullet holes made in 1644, when the Royalists attempted in vain to keep the church from the hands of parliamentary forces during the Civil War.

🏛 The remains of a large Benedictine Abbey founded 1,000 years ago. It was destroyed during the Dissolution of the Monasteries, but the Great Tithe Barn beside it remains fully intact. This barn is 275 feet (84 m) long and is thatched with reeds from the Fleet. It stores thatching reeds today.

🚪 St. Catherine's Chapel is 500 years old and is built in the simple style of the Perpendicular period. It serves as a

Dorset
NEAR WEYMOUTH

landmark for sailors. The monks of Abbotsbury used to keep a fire burning here to warn ships of the treacherous shoreline.

Behind the natural sea wall of Chesil Beach, the Abbotsbury monks established a swannery to supply their tables. Those swans' descendants are still here, along with many other wild visitors, including the occasional osprey.

Chesil Beach is one of the geological wonders of the world, but how it was formed is still a matter of controversy. A marvellous assortment of seaweeds and marine animals can be found in the debris on the strand line.

On the shingle grow sea holly, with its prickly leaves and grey-blue flowers, the beautiful yellow horned

Abbotsbury, couched in downland not far from Chesil Beach. Save for low ground at Weymouth and Swanage, the coast from here to Poole Harbour is characterized by splendid bare downs.

poppy and the white-flowered sea campion.

Abbotsbury Sub Tropical Gardens are open from 10–6 daily from 17 March–13 October. It was among the first plant collections established in this country, and was supplied by early collectors who risked their lives in remote corners of the world to bring back beautiful plants.

Abbotsbury hill-fort, or 'Castle', dates from the Iron Age.

Magnificent view along Chesil Beach to the Isle of Portland.

Dorset
NEAR BRIDPORT

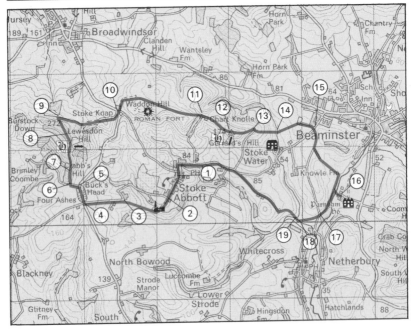

The West Dorset Hills
7¼ miles (11.5 km) Sheet 193
453007

Moderate/strenuous Hauling up to 2 hilltop viewpoints makes this route good exercise; Parnham House, open in summer, is the alternative attraction. *Fields, hills, valleys; 2 climbs; mud along the farm tracks.*

Start Stoke Abbott, 6 miles (9.5 km) N of Bridport. Take the A3066 to Beaminster from Bridport, then follow minor road W to Stoke Abbott. **Parking** along the roads in village.

① Take road S out of village but go straight on when road bears sharply right ②. In a few yards turn right across field on footpath. Continue passing wooded areas on right and left to join ③ minor road. Follow this straight on to main road ④. Turn right, and then go left along road marked Private Road ⑤. Take first footpath on right, through gates ⑥. Go through another gate ⑦ and follow edge of wood uphill. At fork on top of hill ⑧, bear right. Turn right again at junction ⑨ at bottom, and follow track then lane to the B3162. Cross over and take footpath ⑩ through farm, signposted To Beaminster. Walk beside Waddon Hill to building ⑪. Take path running along left side of building up to trig. pillar ⑫. Walk down hill along hedge on left ⑬ to stream. Turn right and walk along stream for 100 yards (91 m) to footbridge ⑭. Follow path from bridge to farmhouse and go down track to minor road ⑮. Take track opposite then follow second footpath on left leading across stream ⑯ to Parnham House. Retrace steps to stream, recross, and turn left, proceeding to good track ⑰. Turn right and then left across stile. Cross field to stile ⑱ then go over footbridge ⑲ and bear right across field to good track. This leads to minor road to Stoke Abbott and ①.

🏭 Fascinating secluded old mill, glimpses of the old machines through the windows.

\\!/ Lewesdon Hill gives magnificent

48

views. William Crowe, Rector of this parish from 1784–8 was author of a poem *Lewesdon Hill*, part of which is inscribed in the 16th C porch of his former church.

Waddon Hill is the site of a Roman fort, built during the invasion of 43 A.D. It was probably an advanced position during the invasion and most likely was held by a detachment of the Second (Augusta) Legion, though there is evidence of the presence of cavalry. It was abandoned in 61 A.D., demolition being carried out carefully and the site left in tidy condition. Finds from the excavations can be seen in the Bridport and Dorset County Museums.

Views of rolling Dorset countryside and Stoke Abbott nestled in its valley. The Dorset poet William Barnes wrote of this area:

> *Sweet Be'mi'ster, that bist abound*
> *By green an' woody hills all round,*

Stoke Abbott village, viewed from the church, and looking much as it has done for one hundred and fifty years.

> *Wi' hedges, reachen up between*
> *A thousan' vields o' zummer green.*

Beaminster Union Workhouse was built in 1836 under the Poor Law Amendment Act, at a cost of £5,000, and was situated near the eastern boundary of the parish. The inmates numbered between 70 and 100 from that year until 1939, when the premises were occupied by the army. After lying unoccupied for 2 years the building was purchased in 1975 and converted into flats.

Parnham House, now a school for furniture craftsmen, has a long and bloody history. During the Civil War, Lady Ann Strode was beheaded in the Great Hall by Cromwell's troops. The house is open to the public between April–October on Wednesdays, Sundays and Bank Holidays.

NORTH DEVON AND EXMOOR

The commanding attractions of North Devon and neighbouring North Somerset are the coast, the moors, and the streams and rivers, and one can experience all these in a day's walk. Dunes, sandy beaches and towering cliffs make the coast fascinatingly varied; and along it all runs The South-west Peninsula Coast Path.

Inland, the main block of Exmoor's heather moorland extends south to Simonsbath in the heart of the former hunting forest. Through the moorland, along deeply cut combes, tumble the streams. Exmoor is moorland at its most benign, but in bad weather, with poor map reading, it is possible to get lost. However, roads are frequent. Paths are plentiful. The Exmoor National Park has made a thorough job of signposting and there are a number of 'permissive' paths, opened in conjunction with landowners as a concession to supplement existing rights of way.

Watersmeet and the Cleaves
5 miles (8 km) Sheet 180 740477

Moderate Dramatic views of a beautiful river valley. *Wooded gorge, heathland, riverside; 2 climbs.*

Start Combe Park National Trust car park, 2 miles (3 km) SE of Lynmouth. Take the A39 from Lynmouth towards Barnstaple. At junction with the B3223 at Hillsford Bridge, continue straight ahead through gate into **car park**.

① Turn left out of car park and cross road. Use wide verge to walk up road to hairpin bend. Take signposted bridleway which leads into woods from bend. Go through gate and continue uphill. At fork ② continue straight ahead along path signposted to Lynton and Lynmouth. Continue for one mile (1.5 km) along valley side, descending and ascending zigzags along the way. Where path forks by rocky outcrop ③, take right fork signposted to Lynmouth. Descend over outcrop and continue downhill into Lynmouth. At road turn left. Turn right at road junction. Go over bridge ④ and turn right up Tors Road. Walk upstream, keeping on riverbank for ¾ mile (1 km) until river is crossed at Blackpool Bridge. Keep close to river on right bank for another ¾ mile to twin rustic bridges at Watersmeet. Turn left to cross first bridge, then turn right up steep path ⑤ which ascends river cliff between bridges. At top, turn right and continue on path to Hillsford Bridge; cross and return to ①.

❗ Myrtleberry Cleave: 'cleave' means a steep valley side and 'myrtleberry' is whortleberry or bilberry. From here there is a fine view over the East Lyn gorge.

A recent drop in sea level, or breaching of the valley by the sea, has caused the river to cut down rapidly and deeply. There are many rare plants growing here, including Irish spurge and Devon whitebeam.

Until the late 18th C., Lynmouth was a small, rather isolated fishing hamlet and port, but the 19th C. saw its rise in popularity as a tourist resort. Shelley's Cottage Hotel stands on the site of the temporary home of the poet. He came here in 1812, trying to avoid the authorities, after distributing leaflets critical of the government. He wrote many more pamphlets while staying in Lynmouth, even throwing them into the Bristol Channel in bottles to gain a wider audience.

By Lynrock Bridge is the ruin of the Lynrock Mineral Water works, where a spring issues from the rock. The works were destroyed during the disastrous flood of 1952, along with several old bridges: all those seen along the walk are replacements. Many of the originals were packhorse bridges, associated with the woodland industries of lime burning, charcoal making and tan barking.

Watersmeet House, now a National Trust Information Centre, was built about 1830 as a fishing lodge for the Halliday family, who owned much land in the area at that time. Teas are served during summer.

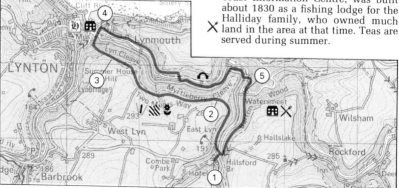

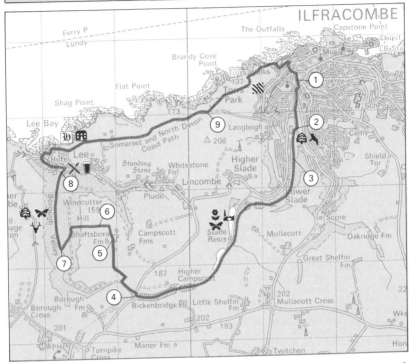

Lee Downs
8 miles (13 km) Sheet 180 515475

Moderate Starting in the area's largest holiday resort, but soon passing through an interesting range of landscapes, including some superb coastal scenery. *Disused railway line, farmland, woodland, coastal downland; 2 climbs; mud betweeen ❻ and ❼.*

Start Ilfracombe. At traffic lights near parish church, turn along road signposted to the sea front. **Parking** at the Wilder Road Car Park, or on street in Station Road between ❶ and ❷.

❶ From car park turn left into Wilder Road, then right at traffic lights. At War Memorial/shelter go left up Station Road (the middle of 3 forks). ❷ At top of Station Hill, take track to left from factory gates. Continue up hill, into woodland. ❸ Turn down to right on to former railway track.

Follow for 2 miles (3 km). At car park turn left on to road ❹. Go over bridge and turn left on to farm road. Continue along road to Allenders Farm. As road turns right into farmyard, take small path to left ❺. Take stile over hedgerow. Continue straight over next field, crossing stream. At signpost, turn left and take grassy and later muddy track along hedgebank on left-hand side of gorse-covered hill ❻. Drop down diagonally over hillocks in next field to bottom corner. Take path through plantation. Cross track down into next plantation. Turn right after stream at bottom ❼ and continue alongside stream to Lee. Go across bridge and through gate ❽ and cross field on right-hand side. Pass on to track, turn left and continue to sea front. Turn right along sea front and after right-hand bend, turn left up lane signposted Coast Path. Pass through gate at end of tarmac road and continue for another ¾ mile (1 km). ❾ About 200 yards (183 m) before gate at

North Devon and Exmoor
ILFRACOMBE

Butterflies to be seen on this walk: top is a marbled white; middle a dark green fritillary and bottom a pearl-bordered fritillary.

end of track, turn left and take stile across field. Keep to seaward side of small hill, then take stile and walk to summit of next hill. Descend on seaward side of hill. Follow track until it turns away from sea and into Ilfracombe. Turn left and keep downhill, crossing Torrs Park Road and turning left to junction with Wilder Road. Turn right to ⓪.

The Cairn is a mixed woodland nature reserve managed by the Devon Trust for Nature Conservation. Many of the Scots and Austrian pines planted on the W side of the hill early this century have now died, mostly through storm damage. This leaves patches where enough light reaches the woodland floor for the natural regeneration of broadleaved trees such as ash, beech and hazel. The dead wood provides insects for birds, such as woodpeckers – all 3 native species are to be found.

Once part of the Barnstaple–Ilfracombe line, the old railway track now forms an extension of the Cairn Nature Reserve. Built by the South Western Railway and opened in 1874, it reached its peak popularity in 1939, carrying thousands of visitors to Ilfracombe. This section of the track was famous for having one of the steepest railway gradients in the country – 2 steam engines were required to pull the train up the 1-in-36 slope. Its embankments now support a wealth of wild flowers and many buddleia bushes, that have escaped from gardens. Together, they attract more than 20 species of butterfly including the marbled white, dark green and pearl-bordered fritillaries.

Borough Valley contains a mixture of old broadleaved woodland and new coniferous plantation belonging to the Forestry Commission. The conifers, mainly spruce, have been planted close together to help them to grow straight. They exclude most of the light from the woodland floor, limiting the number and variety of plants which can live there, and providing few opportunities for wildlife. The broadleaved woodland is much more diverse, especially in its small clearings, where many butterflies are found in summer, including 3 species of fritillary. Red deer are also seen.

A diversion of 200 yards up the road to the right at ⓿ leads to the Grampus public house, a converted cottage.

Lee is a straggling hamlet infamous for its occupants' wrecking and smuggling activities in the 18th and early 19th C. The building next to the beach was originally a corn mill, but became a private residence in about 1890. It was much-painted in the 19th C.

The Torrs, also called the Seven Hills, along with Lee Downs, are National Trust property. The Torrs were purchased in 1967 with funds from Enterprise Neptune, set up by the National Trust with the aim of buying up stretches of the country's coastline and so protecting them from unsightly development.

53

Braunton Burrows
8¼ miles (13.5 km) Sheet 180
463351

Moderate A fascinating variety of wildlife habitats, interesting historical background, and the sandy beaches for which North Devon is famous. *Sand dunes, beach, estuary, marsh; mud in lane after point ⑤.*

Start Braunton Burrows National Nature Reserve, 6 miles (9.5 km) W of Barnstaple. Take the A361 from Barnstaple to Braunton, then turn on to the B3231 towards Saunton. After 1¼ miles (2 km), turn S on lane signposted Braunton Burrows, to Nature Reserve. **Car park** in Sandy Lane, where the hard surface ends. Buses to Braunton from Ilfracombe, Barnstaple and Croyde. If using public transport, join the route at ⑤. From bus stop on the A361, walk W along Caen Street to Second Field Lane.

① From car park continue down dirt road. Walk along road for ¾ mile (1 km) and just past flagpole ②, take track to right where there is a barrier to vehicles. Follow this winding track to beach, keeping M.O.D. range signs to right. At beach ③ turn left and walk along beach, keeping close to dunes but not on them unless tide is too high. After one mile (1.5 km), just past wooden groynes turn left into dunes at start of boardwalk ④. Follow boardwalk and keep straight on at end to metalled road at White House. Turn right at house ⑤ and take path which skirts around it. Follow crest of bank between marsh and estuary for 2 miles (3 km) to Velator Quay. Join road and continue towards Braunton. After about 200 yards (183 m) turn left ⑥ along lane beside pair of cottages. Cross stile and keep to right-hand edge of next 3 fields. ⑦ Turn left and go along lane past factory to housing estate. Continue straight up road (Field Lane) to main road. ⑧ Turn left down Second Field Lane. Continue straight across Great Field and go along lane at end of field ⑨. At road go straight ahead. Walk along road and at next junction turn left to ⑩.

♣ Braunton Burrows is one of the largest sand dune systems in Britain, covering 970 acres. Although leased to the Ministry of Defence, about two thirds of it is managed by the Nature Conservancy Council as a National Nature Reserve. Of the 400 flower species recorded here, several are found nowhere else in Britain. Rarer species include the sand pansy and the tiny sand toadflax.

🏠 White House was once known as Ferry House, as boats could be taken across the Taw estuary from here. It stands at the end of an embankment, built in 1857 to reclaim Horsey Island from the estuary of the River Caen. The marshy pond nearby was once an arm of the river.

🏠 Velator Quay was important in the 19th C. when sailing ketches came up Braunton Pill bringing coal, bricks, fertilizer and limestone. There were once 3 limekilns here. Farm produce was exported along with sand, taken from Crow Point and used as ballast. The traffic declined with the coming of the railways in 1874.

🏠 Braunton Great Field is one of the 2 remaining open fields in Britain. It is a huge field divided into strips with different owners producing different crops. There are fewer owners and larger strips than formerly, but it is essentially the same system of farming as practised here in Saxon times.

🏠 Braunton Marsh was formerly a saltmarsh, but became a freshwater marsh when the sea wall was built in 1815. It has been a popular area for the fattening of beef cattle from medieval times, and some of the linhays (cattle shelters) date from that time. Most, however, came with the 19th-C. reclamation. The drainage ditches constructed for this now support a rich fauna and flora, with a fine display of
♣ irises in June.

The marsh is also used by wildfowl – they can be a stirring sight flying in at dusk. The estuary of the Taw is a rich feeding ground for waders: in the autumn there is a chance of whimbrel and green sandpiper, and in the winter sanderling, greenshank and bar-tailed godwit; oystercatcher, turnstone and ringed plover all year.

North Devon and Exmoor
NEAR BRAUNTON

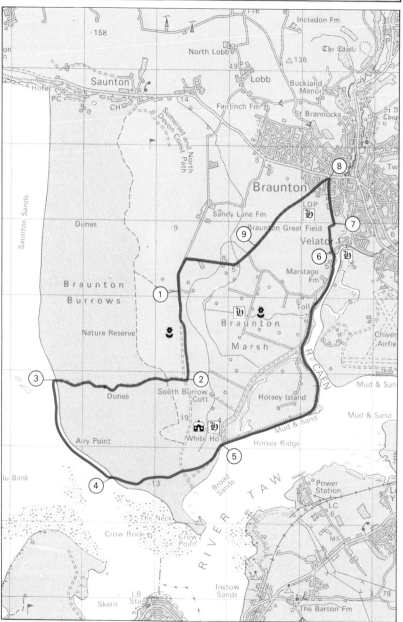

North Devon and Exmoor
NEAR LYNTON

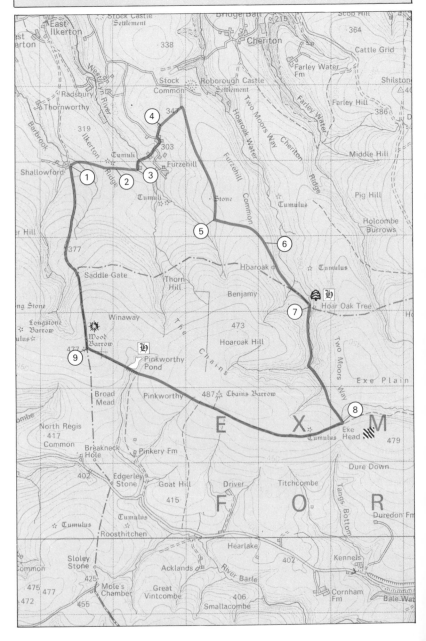

The Chains
9 miles (14.5 km) Sheet 180 714449

Strenuous A challenging walk through wild, remote country. *Heather and grass moorland, farmland; one climb; mud. Route ill-defined between ① and ③, and ④ and ⑥.*

Start Shallowford, 3 miles (5 km) S of Lynton. From Lynton, take the B3234 to Barbrook. Turn right along the A39 then take the left-hand turn just after the filling station, (signposted Ilkerton). Continue for 2 miles (3 km) to the end of the metalled part of the road at Shallowford Farm. Do not pass Shallowford. **Parking** on verge, but do not obstruct gates or farm entrance.
Do not drive more than a few yards on to moorland since this is illegal and vehicles can become stuck.

① Take track leading on to moorland opposite farm entrance. Cross small stream and continue straight ahead. Cross ridge at lowest point ②, to right of burial mounds, crossing ridge-tracks diagonally. Make for nearest building behind hedge on far side of ridge. Take gate ③ immediately to left of building and follow lane round next farmyard (North Furze-hill). Continue straight ahead at top of farm drive. Soon after left-hand bend, take gated green lane up to right. At top of lane ④, keep straight ahead and close to hedge on left. Take gate at far end of field and turn right in next field. Keep close to hedge on right and, after the corner, turn through gateway on right. Keep straight ahead across next field and then bear slightly left through gate on to open moorland. Take track straight ahead, keeping round edge of ridge, to gate in fence ⑤. Go through gate and bear left. Cross ridge on left, walking away from fence at same time. At hedge bank, take gate ⑥ where there is small bend. Pass diagonally down over field and take gated track past ruined farm. Continue straight along track beside hedge banks to gate above river ⑦. Follow main track upstream for one mile (1.5 km) and through gate to the signpost at Exe Head ⑧. Turn right and go through second gate. Follow bank on right-hand side straight ahead for 2 miles to Pinkworthy Pond. Cross dam and continue alongside bank on far side

to gate. Go through gate and continue straight ahead, across moorland to another gate ⑨ where 2 banks meet. Go through this, and walk straight ahead for ½ mile (0.8 km) and descend to another gate. Follow clear track ahead to ⑩.

🔍 Just across the river from the track is a small oak tree with a fence around it. Called the Hoar Oak Tree, it is an ancient boundary mark of the Royal Forest of Exmoor. There were few other trees in the forest, which was largely open-grass moorland. The original oak died in the 17th C., and this is the third on the site. When sold in the early 19th C., the Royal Forest was enclosed with the wall which runs alongside the tree. The new landlord, John Knight (see next entry but one), was responsible for planting most of the mature trees seen in the area today.
There is a chance of seeing red deer.

🐾 Exe Head is the source of the River Exe, which flows E along the main ridge of Exmoor, while other streams flow directly N or S from this watershed. Originally this was the source of Hoaroak Water but the Exe, in cutting its valley westwards, has captured the headwaters of the northward flowing river.

📷 Pinkworthy Pond (pronounced Pinkery) was constructed in about 1830 for John Knight, who had bought a large part of the Forest of Exmoor in 1820, with the intention of reclaiming it for arable farming. He was hampered in this by the acid soils in the area, and needed to import vast quantities of lime to fertilize the land. The pond and its channel (or leat) were probably planned to provide irrigation for the land between Pinkery Farm and Honeymead, with the aim of encouraging grassland.

🌿 Wood Barrow is one of a series of Bronze Age burial mounds along the Chains ridge, linked by a ridgeway track of the same age. About a mile to the W of the barrow stands the Longstone, a 10-foot (3-m) high stone which may have been put there to mark the track.

BRENDON AND QUANTOCK HILLS

Neighbouring ranges of gentle, bracken-covered hills, the Brendons and Quantocks adjoin Exmoor and are the last real upland before one reaches the sombre, misty flatness of the Somerset Levels. Between the gnarled and stunted oak woods (their trees bonsai'd by the thin soil) are areas of sunny heathland, and cool, dark conifer plantation. The latter can claim to be more attractive than the usual, with some fine stands of Douglas fir and hemlock showing how magnificent such trees can be in maturity.

Paths and forestry tracks are plentiful, but in the Quantocks you may find your peace spoiled by motor traffic. It is an ever more popular area for walkers and drivers alike.

Brendon and Quantock Hills
NEAR TAUNTON

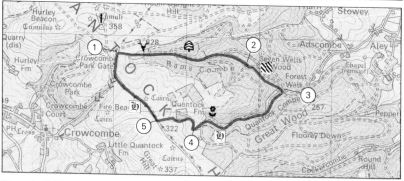

Quantock Forests and Heaths
3½ miles (5.5 km) Sheet 181 150378

Easy A relaxing stroll through changing countryside, with distant glimpses of the sea. *Moorland, woods; 2 climbs; mud.*

Start Crowcombe, 10 miles (16 km) NW of Taunton, off the A358. Take the road signposted Nether Stowey; go up steep hill and over cattle-grid; in 300 yards (274 m) on the left is Crowcombe Park Gate **Car Park** (no sign).

➊ From car park, cross road and go down wide track opposite, over heathland, through gate and down through Rams Combe woods. In 300 yards fork right and ¾ mile (1 km) from here take right fork again. A picnic area with lavatories is soon reached **➋**. Continue for ¾ mile (0.5 km) to a Forestry Commission hut **➌**. Here, turn right over bridge and go through gate. Take right-hand path, soon passing house on right. Continue up wide forestry track: Quantock Combe. Keep on main track in W direction, occasionally passing posts with red marks (forest trails). Bear right where path forks. Later keep straight ahead, ignoring wide forestry track which turns back, on right. Continue upwards, swinging to right, with a stream below on right. Where forestry track swings sharply left, keep straight on up narrow footpath. In 30 yards (27 m), on left of path, half-hidden, is St. David's Well. Continue up winding woodland path, soon emerging on to open heathland. Continue over heath for 200 yards (183 m) to road **➍** going to Quantock Farm. Turn right along this for

200 yards. Just before cattle-grid and gate leading to the farm, turn left up path to a metal gate. Go through gate, and turn right, along path between two wire fences, past farm. Go down past old beech trees, and through a wooden gate just beyond the farm. Turn left over stile, and walk alongside hedge at edge of field, up to trees at the top, and over gate on to Quantock Ridge Walk. **➎** Go right and continue to road. Turn right to **➊**.

⚐ 200 yards N of car park.

♈ Red deer may be seen almost anywhere on the walk and the herd here includes a rare white hind.

🌲 The plantation here consists of Douglas fir, with its dark drooping foliage, and hemlock – neat, soft foliage.

🗻 Notice the change in colour of the rock – up to **➌** it is the rich, rust colour of old red sandstone, dating from the Devonian Period, 400 million years ago, thereafter it is late Triassic.

🕍 St. David's Well, ancient and holy.

⚜ The charming area around the stream here consists of a curious mixture of vegetation. The majestic Douglas firs come from America's Midwest, while the rhododendrons on the stream bank originated in the Himalayas.

🕍 The route here follows an ancient ridgeway, running the length of the Quantocks. The strangely shaped trunks were originally a hedge.

Brendon and Quantock Hills
NEAR WEST QUANTOXHEAD

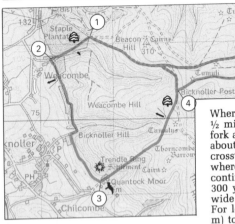

Beacon Hill
*3½ or 5 miles (5.5 or 8 km) Sheet
181 116410*

Moderate A short but invigorating walk which includes a marvellous vantage point with superb views of the Bristol Channel and surrounding hills. *Woodland, open moor; one climb; mud.*

Start Beacon Hill Car Park. From West Quantoxhead, take road S to Bicknoller and Taunton. After ¼ mile (0.5 km), at small crossroads with Staple Lane marked on right, go left up lane, leading over cattle-grid to **car park** marked with National Trust sign for Beacon Hill.

❶ Cross stile by left-hand gate in SW corner of car park, just above steep drop, and close to noticeboard describing area. Follow path down through wood, with stream on left. Go through gate **❷** to lane, turning left on plank over stream, opposite cottages. Follow path just inside wood, which opens out to give good views to right in about ¼ mile. Before entering woodland again, take path forking up to right. Soon drop downwards and follow wire fence to forest road. Turn right along road for 100 yards (91 m) to gate. Just before gate, turn left up track along path, winding round base of Trendle Ring. Go through small gate to three cottages **❸**. Turn left between cottages, through a gate and past old quarry on left. Go up grassy path with beeches on right.

Where trees and bank bear right, in about ½ mile (0.8 km), turn left, taking right fork along track over moor. Continue for about ⅓ mile (0.5 km), going straight over crosstracks until reaching a tall post where paths meet **❹**. For shorter route, continue straight along ridge track for 300 yards (274 m), then fork left along wide track. Follow this round hill to **❶**. For longer route, take track 10 yards (9 m) to right of post, and go left up over moor, soon passing tumulus on left. Fork right here and continue for one mile (1.5 km). At small grassy space, 200 yards (183 m) before small circle of trees, turn left **❺**, along track for ¼ mile to edge of woods **❻**. Turn left at crosstracks, and go uphill. In ½ mile, fork left, up to ridge. From there go straight ahead, round side of hill, to **❶**.

🌳 The rich mixture of trees in this woodland includes sweet chestnut, evergreen oak and larch.

〻 Views to the Brendon Hills and Exmoor, with Bicknoller village down to the left.

🌸 Trendle Ring, an Iron Age settlement, is balanced on a spur of Bicknoller Hill, commanding a fine view over the valley. In Old English, *trendle* means circle or hoop. The Quantocks are rich in prehistoric remains, and during the Iron Age were the territory of the tribe known as the Dumnonnii.

🐦 Green woodpeckers in the woods.

〻 Far-reaching views over the Bristol Channel to the cliffs of South Wales.

🌳 The weather-beaten hawthorns and hollies dotted along the moor have been shaped by the prevailing winds.

〻 Bridgewater Bay and the Mendips.

Brendon and Quantock Hills
NEAR MINEHEAD

Dunster Park
4 miles (6.5 km) Sheet 181 990433

Moderate Although close to the attractive but busy village of Dunster, this route passes through quiet woodland and over open heath, from which the views are excellent. *Mixed woodland, open heath; 2 climbs; mud.*

Start Dunster, 2½ miles (4 km) SE of Minehead on the A39. Take the A396 through Dunster towards Timberscombe. Turn left, just before the last houses in the village, along a lane with a small signpost to the **car park** near Gallox Bridge. Buses from Minehead and Taunton stop at junction of the A39 and the A396. Walk along the A396 for ¾ mile (1 km) to start.

➊ From car park turn left and cross bridge. Pass cottages on right and at crossways ➋, take track up into woods to right (signposted Timberscombe and Luxborough). Keep uphill on blue waymarked track, which eventually levels and descends to valley bottom. ➌ Go straight on along metalled road through plantation. About 200 yards (183 m) beyond plantation, take track into woods on left ➍. At top of hill, take track around side of cottage and go down hill to bottom of next valley. Where main track turns left, take field gate to right ➎. Cross field and take stile to track on far side. Turn right and follow track up and just over top of hill, ignoring right forks. Turn left through gate in wall ➏, and take track signposted to Dunster over crest of hill. Turn right at dip in hill ➐, and follow main track downhill. Turn left at next junction and continue downhill. Go through gate at bottom, then continue straight ahead to stile. Go over stile, turn right and return over bridge to to the car park.

⌢ Gallox Bridge is one of a number of
🏠 packhorse bridges built as a result of the wool trade which made medi-
🌲 eval Dunster prosperous. Originally known as Doddebridge, it was renamed in Tudor times after the gallows then at the crossroads on the far side of the bridge. It spans the River Avill, whose reaches were, in medieval times, tidal, allowing boats to come up to Dunster.

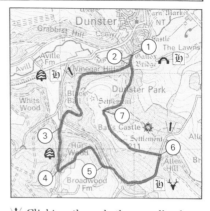

↯ Climbing through the woodland on
🏠 the side of Vinegar Hill (called Gallox Hill locally) there are glimpses of Grabbist Hill across the valley. It was here that Mrs. Alexander is reputed to have composed the hymn 'All Things Bright and Beautiful'. Dunkery is the 'purple-headed mountain', the Avill is the 'river running by', and the 'tall trees in the greenwood' are here, including giant redwoods.

🌲 Here in Broadwood is the tallest stand of trees in Britain. It is a 19th-C. plantation of Douglas firs, some of which are now approaching 200 feet (60 m). Some are labelled with the date of planting, plus vital statistics. This is 'Cathedral Walk'.

🏠 Withycombe Gate is one of the main gateways through the Deer Park wall.
↯ The Deer Park was created by the Luttrells of Dunster Castle in 1755.

✳ Bat's Castle is an early Iron Age hill-fort. It has a roughly circular rampart and ditch with an entrance on the eastern side and a further bank and
↯ ditch across the ridge to the SE. There are fine views all round on a clear day. Clockwise from the N can be seen the Welsh coast, the islands of Flatholme and Steepholme in the Bristol Channel, Hinkley Point nuclear power station, the Quantock hills, Blue Anchor Bay, Dunster Castle, Black Hill (to the S), Croydon Hill, the Avill valley with Dunkery beyond, and Grabbist Hill.

Brendon and Quantock Hills
NEAR WATCHET

The Mineral Line
10½ miles (17 km) Sheet 181
011364

Strenuous Revealing the rich variety of landscapes found in this little-known range of hills. *Farmland, woodland; 3 climbs. ⑦ and ⑧ may be overgrown.*

Start Treborough, 7 miles (11 km) SW of Watchet. From Washford on the A39, turn S on minor road signed Cleeve Abbey and Roadwater. From Roadwater, follow signs to Treborough. **Parking** on road or verge at Treborough in front of the cottages near the church. Do not obstruct entrances for farm vehicles.

① From Treborough walk back along road and turn left down towards Roadwater. After ½ mile (0.8 km), turn left into woodland over stile marked Treborough Woods ②. Descend through woods and turn right at junction. Join track and follow it through gate, back to road. Turn left downhill and after ½ mile turn right along farm track ③. At junction, turn left downhill to road. Turn right and follow road through Leighland Chapel and on downhill. Near bottom of valley turn left

after passing Pit Farm drive, cross course of old railway line, and follow path up into woods. Turn right at path junction ④. Follow path uphill through woods and alongside field to iron gate at the top. Cross lane and continue uphill to farm buildings at top. Walk around barn ⑤ to gate on to road. Turn left and after ¼ mile (0.5 km), turn right down path signposted to Nettlecombe ⑥. Follow edge of field to bottom then walk downhill to Nettlecombe Court. Pass in front of house, then turn left up drive behind church ⑦. Go through gate on rough track and turn left along path signposted to Roadwater. Keep close to left-hand side of field. Go through gate at top then walk diagonally up through trees following red waymarks. Cross road ⑧ and continue straight ahead following red waymarks for one mile (1.5 km). At road, turn left, walk downhill for 25 yards (23 m) and enter field on right ⑨. Follow path down between field and woodland to road. Turn right and walk downhill for 250 yards (228 m). ⑩ At first houses, turn left through field gate along path signposted Chidgley Valley Path. Follow path through woods and across a small valley to woods on far side. Continue along

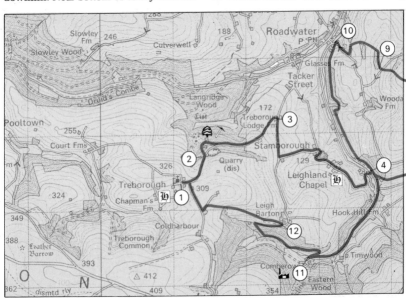

Brendon and Quantock Hills
NEAR WATCHET

A 19th C. steam goods train.

valley side to path junction ⑩. Turn right downhill, then left on to former railway track. Follow for 1½ miles (2.5 km) to Comberow Farm ⑪. Turn right beside farm buildings, cross stream and walk up into woods. Take first turn left and follow stream up to path junction at top of woods. Turn right and immediately before farm turn left ⑫. Follow top edge of field up valley side to lane. Turn left to road. Turn right and return to ⑨.

🏠 At 1,000 feet (305 m) above sea level,

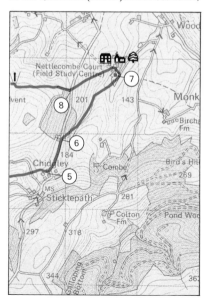

Treborough is the highest village in the Brendon Hills. In the 19th C. it supported a much larger population than today, with nearby slate quarrying and iron mining providing employment.

🐿 Treborough Woods Nature Reserve consists of mixed woodland and old oak coppice, as well as scrub, which is colonizing the spoil heaps from the slate quarries on the hillside above. Slate was quarried here from medieval times right up until 1938.

🏛 Leighland Chapel is named after a medieval chapel which served the nearby Abbey of Cleeve. The chapel was completely rebuilt in 1862 to accommodate the burgeoning congregation of iron miners.

🏠 Nettlecombe Court is a Tudor manor house containing a fine hall with a minstrels' gallery. It was originally the home of the Trevelyan family, but now belongs to the Field Studies Council. It is not open to the public, but parties may view it by appointment. The Church of St. Mary contains medieval monuments to the Raleigh family. In the nearby park are some large oak trees, planted in the 16th and 17th C.

〴 From Kingsdown there can be fine views N to the coast.

🚂 At Comberow is the base of the former incline on the mineral railway. In the 19th C. a steam railway linked the iron mines on the summit ridge of the Brendon Hills. The ore was passed down this incline to another railway which then took the ore down the valley through Roadwater to Watchet, from where it was shipped to South Wales. The incline was finished in 1861. It had a 1-in-4 gradient along which there were 2 tracks. Trucks dropped by gravity down one track and were winched up the other track by a large steam engine housed beneath the track at the top. The mines could not compete with cheap foreign ore and the incline closed in 1883, to be reopened briefly between 1907 and 1910.

AVON REGION

The walks in this section occupy but a corner of the county of Avon, indeed, one lies just over the border, inside Wiltshire; they are not representative of all the sound walking to be found, or perhaps sought out, in Avon; instead they are designed with the useful aim of giving local people and visitors alike an organized – even an ambitious – basis on which to explore the Avon Valley between Bath and Bradford-on-Avon, and its immediate vicinity. For, besides the Mendip Hills, this is probably the best-loved of local destinations for a day out, especially now that work to the Kennet and Avon Canal towpath has made the valley the most obvious choice for a family stroll near Bath. Between Bath and the Dundas Aqueduct the surface is all-weather, so expect cyclists and pushchairs.

That canal, and the industries which were its *raison d'être*, are themes which link all the walks except one. Don't be misled into thinking this is anything but rural walking; however, the routes have a stimulating way of bringing you repeatedly upon human habitation and activity, either present or past. The *Somerset Coal Fields* walk is a substantial day's ramble by any standards, and, between the villages, you will feel well away from it all.

Avon Region
NEAR BATH

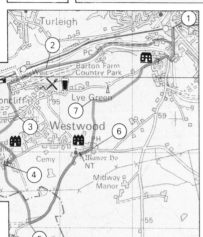

stile on to track. Continue on track, bearing left, before turning right up flight of steps bounded by iron handrail; cross stile into field. Continue up side of field and cross stile in corner, into lane in village ③ where turn right. Continue a few yards before turning left up track beside bungalow, signposted Lower Westwood. After emerging on lane, turn left and continue ¼ mile (0.5 km) to junction, where turn right down lane to Iford. Before bottom of lane, turn left along signposted footpath ④ along high stone wall. But short detour to Iford Manor is worthwhile. Continue until it emerges on to lane by bungalow ⑤ where turn left and follow lane into Westwood, passing manor and church. At junction, cross to pub and proceed up lane to left of pub. ⑥ Cross stile into field and head for far left-hand corner, to the left of the TV mast. Cross double stile and again head towards left-hand corner of next field, passing under wires and between the poles. The stile ⑦ is not visible until close up; cross it (buildings on Lye Green face you), turn sharp right and follow path across fields over 2 stiles to TV mast. Head between TV mast on left and line of poles on right towards stile by stones, then to stile 20 yards left of drinking trough in next field. From here head towards far left-hand corner of next field where there is a stile not visible until close up; keep to the right of the pole. Cross next field, and head left across field after that, towards hedge, passing between two airshaft buildings. Follow hedge down and over stile on to lane (Jones Hill), where turn right and continue to Bradford-on-Avon, bearing right at bottom to join Frome Road. Turn left to ①.

Bradford-on-Avon
5 miles (8 km) Sheet 173 825606

Easy Wool and water are the dominant themes of this part of rural Wiltshire, made rich by the 16th- and 17th-C. wool trade. *Riverside, canal, aqueduct, villages, farmland; one climb; mud.*

Start Bradford-on-Avon. Large public **car park** at Bradford-on-Avon Station, just off the B3109 (Frome) road; bus and rail services from Bath.

① From station car park, turn right and walk along the B3109 (Frome road), passing sports ground. Turn right down lane signposted Tithe Barn (parking is also available here). Cross stile in front of barn and go down to riverside walk by information board, turning left and continuing to second information board. Follow path as it bears left of electricity substation and continue along canal towpath which may be severely muddy where excavating machinery has been at work. Bear right and continue to Avoncliffe Aqueduct. Before crossing aqueduct, turn right ② towards the Cross Guns pub. Follow lane sharp left under aqueduct and continue along river past Avon Villa and The Old Court. Here turn left, past high wall of The Old Court and over gate into field where the wall ends. Follow up side of field, bearing slightly right to cross stone

The 14th-C. tithe barn was formerly a grange of Shaftesbury Abbey.

The aqueduct dates from about 1804.

The Cross Guns: real ale, pub food.

Iford Manor is 16th C. with a Georgian façade added in 1725. Built by Thomas Horton, leading Bradford-on-Avon clothier.

Westwood Manor, home of the Horton family, formerly of Iford Manor, is basically 15th C.; open to public.

65

Avon Region
NEAR BATH

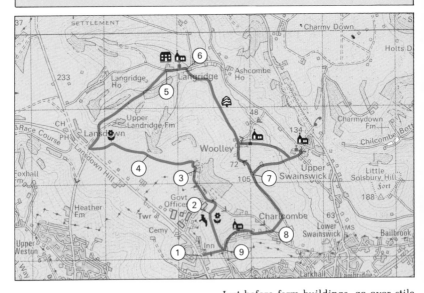

Churches of the Lambrook Valley
5–6 miles (8–10 km) Sheet 172
743670

Moderate 4 peaceful churches of great antiquity, combined with some fine wildlife habitats. *Rough pasture, quiet lanes; 2 climbs; wet in places.*

Start Hare and Hounds pub, about one mile (1.5 km) N of Bath on road to Lansdown. Where the road becomes less steep, look for the pub on the right. Bus from Bath Station to Ensleigh (about every hour) – alight at Hare and Hounds. Some **parking** space on main road opposite starting point, otherwise in Lansdown Park on W of main road. Please do not use the Hare and Hounds car park.
① Go down footpath beyond low building just S of Hare and Hounds, following hedge on right. Go over stile and turn left to waymarked post in field. Continue to far corner, and cross stile to follow hedge uphill for about 400 yards (366 m) towards government offices. Climb stone stile just in front of wire perimeter fence.
② Turn right following fence to tarmac lane. Go left, then right at junction, past cottages to ornamental gateway. Go over gate at left of this, and follow grassy track.

Just before farm buildings, go over stile on left ③. Climb steep slope to tree clump, then turn right over ladder stile, and bear diagonally left across field to a stone stile (waymarked). Bear slightly right across field to cross another stone stile. Continue to wooden gate, leading on to a broad dirt track with breeze-block buildings (Roman Lodge Farm) at right ④. Cross another stile straight ahead and follow the wall/hedge at right to a stone stile and playing field. Follow wall on right of field, past a gate to waymarked stone stile by lone tree. Cross stile to meadow and cross it half-left. At road double back along stony track for about 250 yards (220 m) to reach well-marked stone stile about 10 yards (9 m) N of track. Cross stile and head half-right towards waymarked post, then carry straight on across fields to a metal gate. Continue downhill to cross a stream. Go through gate at left, crossing stream again. Climb gently half-right, keeping stone barn wall on left, across field to right, to wooden stile. Go over stile and keep straight ahead across field. Go through metal gate on to road, turn right to Langridge Court Farm ⑤. Continue downhill past the church, and 100 yards (91 m) further is a gate on the right leading to a footbridge ⑥. Cross bridge and strike ahead uphill to some

Avon Region
NEAR BATH

Ash in winter, plus seed and flower – a common tree on farmland hereabouts.

trees. Keep on to corner of field and go through waymarked gate. Follow hedge on right soon going through (waymarked) gate on right. Clearly defined path bears left here, then swings right to follow contours along valley. It passes through 3 waymarked gateways, then over a stile to the road. Turn right and for shorter walk keep on along road to ⑦. To see Woolley church, or for longer walk, take next left. Cross stone stile (waymarked) at right of church, and go along enclosed path and into field. Bear right down to metal bridge. Over bridge turn right, continue over stile by stream, and then climb left to Upper Swainswick. Path to village goes up concrete steps through garden of old house with modern extension. Leave Upper Swainswick by the same path, but aim straight downhill for inconspicuous bridge which leads towards group of farm buildings on opposite hillside. Go through farm gate to left of farm then along metalled farm track to lane ⑦ and turn left. Follow this lane for ½ mile (0.8 km). Just past metal gate on right, cross a rough overgrown stile (waymarked) and head uphill to another stile. Keep straight on, to reach gate and stile, near bungalow at lane junction. ⑧ Follow lane ahead, and bear right at next junction. 200 yards (183 m) on, a rough track leads off half-right;

continue over stile, following old garden wall, to reach Charlcombe church. Track swings left past church to join road. Turn right, and follow road for 400 yards (366 m). On the right, opposite the old stone manor house, is an inconspicuous waymarked stile between a driveway and a farm gate. ⑨ Cross this and climb the hill, retracing steps to reach ①.

🌱 The hedge followed here contains a dozen different plant species, indicating considerable age. The plants include honeysuckle, dog roses, field maple and wayfaring tree.

🐦 Skylarks nest on the rough ground here.

🌱 Meadows full of flowering plants like this are now a rare find. Look out for yellow rattle, which resembles a yellow-flowered dead-nettle, though belonging to a different family. It gets its name from the way the seeds rattle in their pods.

⛪ Langridge has a Norman church standing next to the medieval courthouse, now a farm. There is a fine 13th-C. madonna over the chancel arch, a 1441 brass, and plenty of admirable local woodcarving on the pews.

🍃 Ash trees, with their feathery leaves and black buds, are common in these fields and hedgerows. They were encouraged to grow on farmland in the past as their exceptionally hard, resilient wood was useful for making handles for agricultural implements.

⛪ Woolley's unusual church was designed by Bath architect John Wood in 1761.

⛪ The Norman church of Upper Swainswick has a built-in tower, and fine later medieval ogival arches in the S porch and wall.

⛪ Charlcombe's tiny picturesque church is basically Norman, but much restored. Have a look at the remarkable amateur carvings of *fleurs-de-lis* on the font.

Avon Region
NEAR BATH

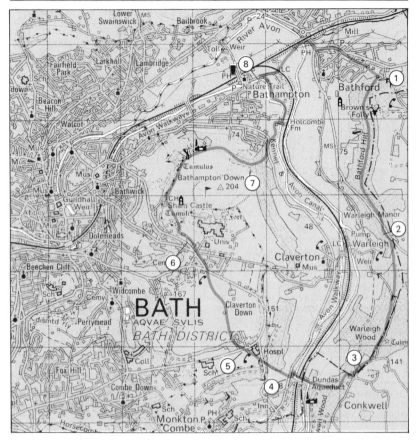

Brown's Folly
8 miles (13 km) Sheet 172 798664

Moderate The scenery, wildlife and industrial archaeology on this walk are all linked by a common theme: limestone. Quarried from several local sites, it not only went into the construction of the Kennet and Avon Canal, a major feature of the route, but was carried via the canal into Bath for its fine Georgian buildings. *Wooded valley, downland, woodland, river, canal; two climbs; mud after rain*.

Start the A4, going NE out of Bath and, in 3 miles (5 km), turning right on to the A363. Turn immediately left at the Crown Inn. Continue to top of hill, turn right up steep lane (Prospect Place); unsurfaced **car park** at top of lane on right by entrance to nature reserve.

Leave car park, cross lower stile and ① follow path along hillside. (Optional detour up stepped slope to Brown's Folly, then rejoin main path.) Continue through woodland, ignoring nature trail posts going off to right. Bear right in woods (path ill-defined in places). Continue on path out of nature reserve, but still in wood, until reaching the A363; cross, turn left and continue 250 yards (220 m) to Wiltshire County Boundary sign ② where turn right on to signposted footpath.

Where path forks, take upper path through scrub and woodland to Warleigh Lane. Turn left and continue along lane ½ mile (0.8 km) to junction where turn right to follow lane signposted Conkwell. Turn right at next junction (in village) – signposted Bath and Limpley Stoke. In 200 yards (183 m), past pig farm, turn right down signposted (but half-concealed) track ③ which leads to Dundas Aqueduct. Cross aqueduct and continue round to the right to cross canal bridge. Turn left and soon go right, up wooden steps beside small stone warehouse to reach the A36. Cross, and go over the stile ④ a few yards along the road, to the right. Follow path steeply up the fields. At top right-hand corner of second field, cross stile and follow path around boundary walls to reach lane. Cross lane; footpath continues opposite between high wall and metal fence. Go through kissing gate and follow path as it bears right, to emerge on road. Turn left, continue a few yards then take signposted footpath ⑤ on right. Pass woods and follow path as it bears right, keeping to the wall. Cross stone stile, and take path going diagonally left across field and then along hedge. Cross double stiles and keep straight on towards community hall building, emerging on road to right of it. Cross road and turn left along road with stone walls either side. Continue downhill, then turn down right-hand fork (North Road). In ¼ mile (0.5 km) pass University Medical Centre and ⑥ in about 100 yards (96 m), *after* bridleway signpost, join track and follow it to Sham Castle. Continue on footpath immediately below golf clubhouse. Cross wooden stile and follow track towards TV mast. Continue, keeping close to golf course fence. Passing metal gate on to golf course, head up near the fence and follow path around immediately to its left and through the woods. Path ends at a wooden stile ⑦; cross and turn immediately sharp left to descend steeply down rocky track (plateway) – slippery in wet weather – to the A36; cross road and turn right. Pass nursery gardens and take (hidden) signposted footpath on left, leading down to canal. Cross wooden canal bridge, turn left and follow towpath for ½ mile. Approaching Bathampton village, and road bridge, go through white gates across towpath ⑧. Cross grass verge and turn

right down lane which leads to level crossing. Cross stile opposite and follow path diagonally across field to metal stile. Cross and continue in direction of electricity pylon; beyond it climb with path via stile up side of railway embankment. Follow footpath over railway bridge and descend to the A363. Turn right, then keep right at the Crown Inn, following lane which becomes path across field. Turn right at road to return to ①.

🏰 Brown's Folly – and the nature reserve – get their name from the stone tower commissioned by Mr. Wade-Brown, local quarry owner, in 1849, partly to provide work for the unemployed; exceptional views over the valley towards Bath. The nature reserve is a mixture of woodland, scrub and limestone grassland grown over the remains of the quarries: a rich habitat for wildlife, including deer, badgers, birds and butterflies. Wild flowers include harebells, rockrose, wild thyme and orchids.

🛶 Dundas Aqueduct is named after Charles Dundas (later Lord Amesbury), who ran the Kennet and Avon Canal for 40 years until his death in 1832. The steep footpath down to the aqueduct was formerly a tramway which conveyed stone from quarries in Conkwell. Notice the old hand-operated crane for loading barges.

🏰 Sham Castle, perhaps the best-known of England's 18th-C. follies, was built for Ralph Allen, the 'builder of Bath' as an eye-catcher to enhance the view from his house in Lilliput Alley in the town centre.

🛶 Hampton Down gives fine views across Bath, and to Little Solsbury Hill. Stone quarrying was a major industry here in the 18th C. The plateway, dating from 1808, was built to take stone down to the canal near Holcombe Farm. Stone sleeper blocks, into which the cast-iron plates were fixed, are still visible; the whole structure passed over the A46 by means of an arch, now demolished.

🍺 The George, an attractive canal-side pub with real ale and good food.

Avon Region
NEAR BATH

Somerset Coal Fields
12 miles (19 km) Sheet 172 747613

Moderate Industrial archaeology in a rural setting; a Neolithic burial chamber and Second World War tank traps vary the interest. *Farmland, villages; three climbs; some particularly bad mud after rain; follow directions carefully from ❹ – don't turn off the green lane.*

Start Bath, taking the A367 S from the city centre and, on the outskirts, turning left on to the B3110 past hospital. At crossroads turn right (opposite Cross Keys) down lane signposted Southstoke. Lane bears right down incline into village. **Parking** at top or bottom of incline; frequent bus service to Cross Keys (Foxhill bus), which leaves about ⅓ mile (0.5 km) to walk to ❶.

❶ From church, join surfaced track to right of farm entrance. Soon bear left down track, go through metal stile on right into field and follow path down valley past ruined house to stream. Keep left of stream and disused canal and go under arch to meet surfaced lane where ❷ turn right and continue to Combe Hay. Pass church on S-bend and in 300 yards (290 m) go over stile on left on to footpath waymarked by yellow arrow. Follow it down to and across Cam Brook and then up towards lane, where turn left and continue to junction ❸. Take the unsignposted right turn up green lane (Upper Hayes): very muddy after rain. Continue, passing farm buildings, to junction of tracks where ④ turn left up narrower track (main track descends to White Ox Mead). Continue to crossing of tracks, go directly ahead over stile into field and follow hedge along to lane. Cross lane and take track opposite. Go through gate and follow hedge along to another lane. Cross, through gate, and follow track down to Shoscombe Farm ⑤. Turn right and walk up lane to junction. Turn right again, then left, to descend into Writhlington. As mine workings (possibly overgrown) come into view before the bottom, turn sharp left on to footpath running parallel with disused rail track. Continue via stiles to Paglynch Farm and along farm track to junction of lanes ⑥. Turn right down hill under disused railway bridge and over Wellow Brook. Climbing up hill past converted mills, cross half-concealed stile in hedge into field. (If this is impassable, continue up the hill, turning left at the lane junction to descend to ⑦.) Head towards farm building in distance, crossing spring. Emerge on Single Hill just below cottage and ⑦ turn left to follow lane down to brook. Before crossing, enter field on right by concrete tank trap. Follow path along brook but head up field to cross tributary brook at narrowest point. When farmhouse is in view, head to right of belt of trees to pass below farm and on to lane ⑧. Cross and take signposted bridleway opposite, through Stony Littleton Farm. Follow signs to Long Barrow. Path continues along hedge above barrow and across field, marked by dead tree stump. Go through gate opposite and follow track until it meets lane. Turn left and continue left again at next junction to cross Wellow Brook. Turn right into Wellow main street, passing Methodist church, and continue to parish church. Past this, turn left ⑨ (but immediately up side of churchyard); at end of churchyard, cross stile and turn right to second stile and into field, descending to cross the valley to a large stile under trees near junction of power lines. Cross stile, turn right, and follow hedge to emerge on lane where ⑩ turn right and continue to junction, where turn left by farm buildings (Twinhoe). Before last buildings, turn right down track. Bear left at junction with private track; follow narrow path between hedges – it broadens out near bottom. Go through gate and over footbridge ⑪. Turn right

over stile (yellow waymarks) into field 50 yards after crossing. Walk along brook for one mile until path terminates at embankment. Cross stile and turn right to follow path under disused railway bridge, past dilapidated outbuildings and on to lane (at stile with footpath sign). Turn left and continue, passing farm on right. After a steep climb, take next footpath signposted on right ⑫, cross stile and ascend brow of hill with hedge on left, entering an overgrown path in field corner. Continue with path across another stile, up side of field to stile in large stand of beeches. Continue down field, bearing left, through gap in second field and over stile in top left-hand corner, to emerge on to lane. Turn right and continue past The Packhorse; at top, turn left to church.

St. James's Church has a fine Norman doorway. Manor Farmhouse and The Packhorse are 17th C., the farmhouse has a 16th-C. tithe barn.

The Somerset Coal Canal was opened in 1810 to serve the local collieries. It ran 9 miles (14.5 km) up the Midford and Cam Brook valleys and connected with the Kennet and Avon Canal at Dundas Aqueduct.

The Wheatsheaf – real ale and bar food – a pub above Combe Hay lane.

Combe Hay Manor dates from 1730; gardens occasionally open to public.

Writhlington Colliery was one of the last Somerset collieries to close; it was still using steam winding engines in 1966. The poor-quality coal served in local power stations – and some is still salvaged from the spoil heap.

Stony Littleton Long Barrow can claim to be one of the finest and best-preserved in the country; key from Stony Littleton Farm.

The Fox and Badger; real ale, bar food.

Wellow's main street is lined with mainly 17th- and 18th-C. cottages.

The Packhorse is unspoilt pub dating from the 17th C.; real ale, scrumpy cider; bar food.

SOUTH-EAST ENGLAND

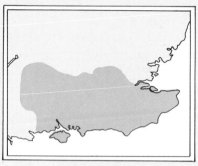

NEW FOREST

The Forest, as local people call it, is one of the most difficult walking areas in Britain for finding the way. Many paths and tracks are in a state of deterioration – returning to undergrowth; and many are added by the activities of the Forestry Commission year by year to an already large and confusing network. The problem is compounded because under the trees, one's sense of direction quickly diminishes, and the Forest has been lived and worked in for centuries. (It is not only a former royal hunting ground: there are traces of industry, and of settlement, all over.) The maze of paths and tracks cannot be shown in truly helpful detail by Landranger mapping at a scale of 1:50 000, and if you wish to improvise your own routes, the only satisfactory aid is the Ordnance Survey Outdoor Leisure Map for the area. It features the whole of the New Forest on coloured Pathfinder mapping (scale 1:25 000). The only disagreeable feature of this beautifully varied landscape is bog. Sited over impermeable geological deposits, so they cannot dry out, these occupy about 7,000 of the Forest's 92,000 acres. The best way to distinguish boggy ground is to look for cotton grass: in summer it has white, whispy tufts. Don't be tempted to take the bold course, wading through. You can sink in up to your neck.

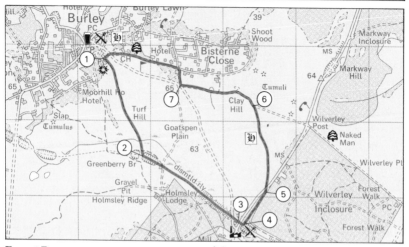

Forest Panorama
4½ miles (7 km) Sheet 195 214028

Easy Located in the SW corner of the forest – smuggler territory with a romantic past – centred on the picturesque village of Burley. *Heath, disused railway.*

Start Burley, 3 miles (5 km) SE of Ringwood. Take the A31 E from Ringwood and after one mile (1.5 km), turn S to Burley. Leave Burley on the road signposted Lymington–Brockenhurst. **Car park** in on the right in 200 yards (183 m). Regular buses to Burley from Southampton and Bournemouth; from Burley walk to the start.

① From car park take footpath, which initially runs parallel to road. Walk over Turf Hill to railway bridge, then turn left to walk along dismantled railway ②. Follow for one mile, then cross minor road and take track opposite Old Holmsley Station ③ which leads under bridge. ④ Bear left immediately and follow grassy track parallel to main road. Where track disappears ⑤, cross road (A35) and pick up track on far side. On joining a wide gravel track ⑥, turn left and follow to road ⑦. Turn right and then left along Colt Lane which leads back to ①.

▼ The Queen's Head serves real ale and food. It was once an important centre

✗ for the distribution of smuggled liquor
🏛 and other contraband. Daniel Defoe, writing in 1727, maintained that the New Forest port of Lymington had no foreign trade "except it be what we call smuggling and roguing; which, I may say, is the reigning commerce of all this part of the English coast". Convicted smugglers are said to have been hanged 2 miles (3 km) away, at Naked Man Tree, an old oak whose
🌳 remains can still be seen.

✻ A Bronze Age axe hoard was found here in 1926.

🚂 Old railway site with platforms and Holmsley Station. The railway was built in 1847 and dismantled in 1964. The Old Station Tea House serves
✗ cream teas.

🏛 The sunken ways used by smugglers can be seen here.

🌳 Coming back into Burley, one passes some magnificent pollarded beeches. (Pollarding is cutting off the tops, for fuel or fodder and it produces the large number of slim stems seen on these trees.) They must be over 280 years old, because the government banned pollarding of New Forest trees in 1698, during a fit of anxiety about dwindling supplies of ship timber.

New Forest
NEAR RINGWOOD

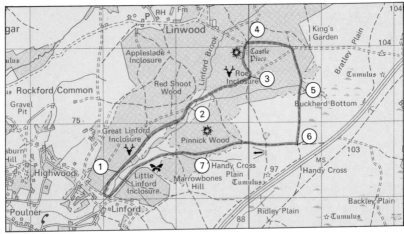

Linford
5 miles (8 km) Sheet 195 183074

Easy This part of the Forest could almost
have been made for the walker: mature
oak, hawthorn, willow and blackthorn
are interspersed with wide grassy lawns,
providing wonderful picnic places.
Despite these attractions, there are not
too many tourists and the tranquillity of
the ancient woodlands can be enjoyed.
*Valley, heath, woods. The path through
Pinnick Wood ⑦ is indistinct.*

Start Linford, 2 miles (3 km) NE of Ringwood. Take the A31 E from Ringwood and
after one mile (1.5 km), turn left to
Linford. Regular buses to Ringwood from
Southampton and Bournemouth, then
walk one mile along minor road signposted Linford. Large **car park** on N side
of the bridge at Linford.

① From car park walk along gravel track
which runs up the N bank of the brook.
Where it meets other paths ②, turn right
along another gravel track. About ½ mile
(0.8 km) further on, there is a wide cutting
on the left (not marked on the map).
Ignore this and take the turning just after
it ③, along a track with deciduous trees
on the left and conifers on its right.
Proceed through Roe Inclosure crossing
the prominent earthworks to a wide path
④. Turn right and take the first track on
the right which leads out of the woods on

to heath at gate ⑤. Continue in same
direction to junction of paths ⑥ just before
road. Turn right towards wood ⑦. Keep
walking downhill with stream on the left
for ¼ mile (0.5 km). Do not cross the
stream. The well-defined, wide path running down the Linford valley will then
be seen. Follow this path back to ①.

Ⓥ Stream life abounds in Linford Brook
which flows into the River Avon.

Ⓥ Herds of fallow deer can be seen in
Roe Inclosure and Pinnick Wood.

✳ This Iron Age fort is one of the few
accessible forts in the Forest. It is
covered with trees, but the embankments can be easily seen.

\⁄/ Views of the Avon Valley and the hills
of Wiltshire and Dorset beyond.

✳ There is an ancient pound in Pinnick
Wood, though it is difficult to find. It
is a small earth-banked enclosure,
probably dating back to the 11th C.
and was used as a secure place for
keeping pigs during the night.

🦋 Hornets nest in the fallen oaks. These
uncommon wasps are recognized by
their large size, loud hum and distinctive colouring: yellow and orange-
brown stripes. Their aggressive reputation is false – they rarely sting.

Bolderwood
7 miles (11 km) Sheet 195 240093

Easy A particularly fine ramble for an autumn day when the great beeches of Mark Ash Wood are turning. *Heath, scrub, woods. Bratley stream has no footbridge and boots are needed to ford it.*

Start near Bolderwood, 3 miles (5 km) W of Lyndhurst. From Lyndhurst, 5 miles (8 km) SW of Southampton, follow the Emery Down road, then take the first left, following signs for Bolderwood. Large **car park** on right in 3 miles, shortly before road goes under the A31.

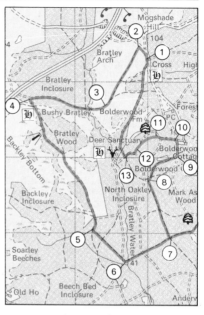

❶ From Canadian war memorial in car park, walk N along road for 200 yards (183 m), then turn left on to path ❷ which runs along left side of valley. After ½ mile (0.8 km) ❸, bear right towards gap in trees in bottom of valley. Just before reaching a gate and the A31, turn sharp left on to good track ❹. Follow this for 1¼ miles (2 km), then go straight on at sharp left-hand bend. Take the first path on the left ❺. At next path junction ❻ go straight on, following Bolderwood sign. At second junction ❼, cross over gate and walk to road to see the beeches of Mark Ash. Return to gate, cross it, then turn right along path. At second junction ❽, turn right then immediately left and follow track to road (Bolderwood Ornamental Drive) ❾. Turn left, then take the wide track ❿ opposite Bolderwood Cottage. At fork in track, bear right to pick up arboretum walk at ⓫. (Not shown on the O.S. map but marked with green-banded posts.) Where the walk curves sharply to right ⓬, go straight on to gravel track. Turn right, then right again at path junction ⓭. Bear right again at next junction; follow path to ❶.

🏠 The Canadian Memorial is a reminder of the great concentration of troops in the Forest just before D-Day, 1944. Forests were used as assembly points to conceal troop movements.

🏠 Charles Kingsley chose Bushy Bratley as the setting of one of his most romantic poems, *Ballad of the New Forest*, in which the young daughter of a gamekeeper falls in love with a poacher. The two men meet by the river in the twilight, fail to recognize each other, and in the ensuing fight both are killed.

⩔ All-round views of the Forest.

🌲 Mark Ash Wood is, for many, the most beautiful beech wood in the forest. It was planted in the 14th or 15th C. Trees at the limits of people's lands used to be marked, and the ash trees around the edge of this wood all acted as boundary markers, hence the name.

🌲 The route includes part of the Forestry Commission's Bolderwood Arboretum Walk which passes many fine examples of foreign trees, including eucalyptuses from Australasia.

⩔ At the deer sanctuary, wild fallow deer come and go unmolested.

🏠 When the New Forest ceased to be a royal forest, in 1851, the Deer Removal Act was passed. All the Forest's deer were, supposedly, killed, with the intention of improving grazing for other animals. But the deer soon re-established themselves.

New Forest
NEAR LYNDHURST

The Essential Forest
7 miles (11 km) Sheet 196
348064

Easy Encompassing all the characteristic New Forest features: beautiful stretches of heath, bogs and dense woods – and with many echoes of the New Forest's long history. *Heath, woods; mud. The paths through Denny Wood at ❸ and between ❻ and ❼ are indistinct.*

Start Beaulieu Road Station, 3 miles (5 km) SE of Lyndhurst. From Lyndhurst, 5 miles (8 km) SW of Southampton, take the B3056 to Beaulieu Road Station. Regular trains to Beaulieu Road Station from Bournemouth and Southampton. Large **car park** on right just before station.

❶ From car park, take the path running S, parallel to the railway at first. ❷ Turn right before the gate to walk through heathland and copses. At the second footbridge ❸, keep straight on into Denny Wood for 200 yards (183 m). The clearings and buildings of Denny Lodge and the wide path will be seen. Turn right on gravel track, then left at top of hill. When track bears left ❹, take the track straight on beside a fence. Bear right at clearing to meet collection of gravel paths. Cross these and continue in same direction along gravel path, then take second track on right. ❺ At the footbridge over river, turn round and look just left of where you have come. The route follows the gated track 200 yards away. At T-junction, turn left and follow path as it bears round to the right. ❻ Bear left before Little Holmhill Inclosure and then right. Take track bearing sharp left to minor road, then turn right. (If the route becomes confusing in this section, bear left to minor road,

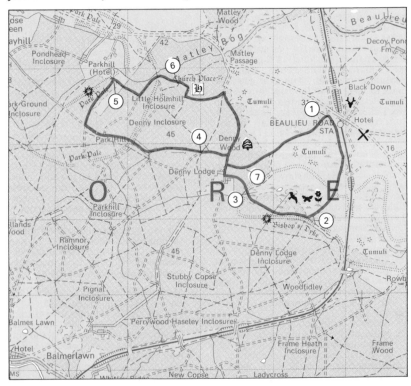

New Forest
NEAR LYNDHURST

To yield the massive oak ribs of a ship frame, the oak had to have grown in a certain way; and even then it supplied but a few. New Forest oaks were the principal supply for the Adams' yard at Bucklers Hard, about 4½ miles (7 km) SE on the Beaulieu River, which built a line of warships in the 18th and 19th C.

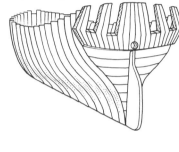

rejoining route by turning right at Matley Passage.) After ½ mile (0.8 km), turn left on path through Denny Wood. ⑦ Walk downhill, bearing left for ¼ mile (0.5 km) to heath, with railway station and car park visible in distance.

✕ The Beaulieu Road Hotel serves food.

Ϋ The ponies, which roam the New Forest, are sold here in April, August, September, October and November. The New Forest Scouts' regiment used Forest ponies, and they are known for their strength and jumping ability. The ponies are feral – descended from domestic stock – but they have been here over 900 years, so their exact origin is unknown.

♣ New Forest bogs harbour many rare species, including the marsh gentian (its blue flower appears in August) and the bog orchid. The bogs are also the home of specialized insects, such as the large marsh grasshopper, identified by bright red markings on its hind legs. In spring, lapwing, redshank, curlew, snipe and other marsh birds come here to breed.

✹ Bishop's Dyke marks an area said to have been secured for the Church in the Middle Ages by the Bishop of Winchester, who was promised as much land as he could crawl around on his hands and knees in one day. Why he should have picked this area, and such an uneven course to crawl, nobody knows.

✹ Park Pale embankments form part of a deer enclosure and date back to the 12th C.

🏛 Church Place was once a royal hunting lodge, and may formerly have been the site of a Saxon church. William the Conqueror is said to have destroyed many churches and villages to create good hunting terrain in the Forest. Forest laws, designed to favour game animals, set stringent limits on the activities of the human inhabitants, and were much resented by them.

🌳 One of the most beautiful of the Forest's ancient woodlands, Denny Wood has magnificent mature oaks and beeches. The poor clay soils of the New Forest, like those of the Weald, tend to produce massive, spreading oaks, rather than tall, straight ones, and such trees once had special value for shipbuilding.

SOUTH DOWNS

It is hard to walk the South Downs these days without being reminded that it is a landscape under threat. Here you may be walking what is described as unspoilt chalk grassland, but with the uncomfortable knowledge that ploughing will take another bite at it before long. There you will encounter a piece of wetland, prized as a scarcity. Somewhere else, you find yourself treading one of the last haunts of the great bustard. Once, the downs were chalk grassland, cropped short by sheep, from head to foot; now, cultivated fields creep far up the slopes and sometimes over the spine; paths are frequently obliterated. Still, it will take more than intensive farming to spoil the wide views and, outside holidays, the feeling that this remains some of the loneliest walking in south-east England. There are remarkably few human settlements actually on the downs.

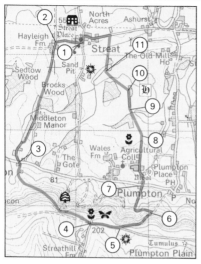

through gateway, and go past old quarry workings on left. The path then curves sharply right, downhill through a 5-barred gate into an unsurfaced lane between hedges. Follow lane to road **⑦**. Cross road and walk down lane signposted Plumpton Agricultural College. Walk along road into grounds, past an old barn on right, and continue on track, past football field, to gate **⑧**. Walk diagonally left across field, aiming for gate which marks culvert crossing stream. Head diagonally left again to another gate at muddy culvert in gap between 2 woods. **⑨** Go through narrow strip of woodland ahead with stiles at each end. **⑩** Bear left round field towards another wood. Walk round right-hand margin of wood to find line of bushes and small oaks. **⑪** Follow this downhill and cross it to footbridge. Walk uphill along clear path to unsurfaced lane. Turn left to **①**.

🏠 Streat Place, Tudor, built 1590.

🌲 This V-shaped plantation commemorates Victoria's golden jubilee.

🌿 The N slope of the Downs is virtually natural grassland, with typical downland flora. Unfortunately, cattle-grazing in winter has caused soil erosion, while the discontinuance of sheep grazing, and the reduced rabbit population (due to myxomatosis) have allowed some woody shrubs to establish themselves. But in places the downland flowers still flourish, and aromatic herbs, such as thyme and marjoram, are plentiful. Butterflies are still abundant, too.

🌸 Bronze Age settlements here yielded highly significant finds in 1934.

🌿 Many of the hedges in this area are over 400 years old, and the one on the W of the track past the football field is some 600 years old.

🏛 There is an unexcavated Roman Villa here, dating back to the mid-3rd C. Fragments of tile, plaster and pottery are frequently found on the surface.

🌸 A Mesolithic site, dating back to about 3000 B.C.: flint tools continue to be found here.

Streat and Streat Hill
5 miles (8 km) Sheet 198 351152

Easy A circuit at the foot of the Downs. Unspoilt chalk grassland survives here, and it blooms with wild flowers in spring. *Farmland, downs, woods; one climb; mud. Path ill-defined between ⑩ and ⑪, but stiles and gates indicate route.*

Start Streat, 7 miles (11 km) NE of Brighton. From Brighton, follow the A23 N. After 6 miles (9.5 km), take the B2112 to Ditchling, then the B2116 E, turning N after 2½ miles (4 km) along lane to Streat. **Parking** near Streat church.

① From the church, walk along unsurfaced lane past Streat Place. Do not follow Public Footpath sign through cemetery. **②** At Hayleigh Farm turn left along farm road, ignoring track on right. At end of road, continue in same direction along track between hedges, then beside woodland, to emerge through a large gateway on to road **③**. Follow signposted bridle path opposite. The track bears left over fairly steep, open downland, then crosses the top of a V-shaped plantation to meet the broad South Downs Way **④**. Turn left, crossing a farm road, and continue to junction of tracks **⑤**. Fork left, downhill, to first track on left (through gate) **⑥**. Walk

South Downs
NEAR ARUNDEL

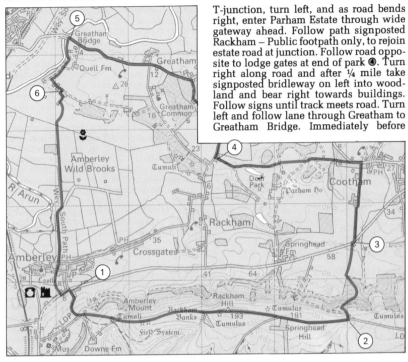

T-junction, turn left, and as road bends right, enter Parham Estate through wide gateway ahead. Follow path signposted Rackham – Public footpath only, to rejoin estate road at junction. Follow road opposite to lodge gates at end of park ❹. Turn right along road and after ¼ mile take signposted bridleway on left into woodland and bear right towards buildings. Follow signs until track meets road. Turn left and follow lane through Greatham to Greatham Bridge. Immediately before

Amberley Wild Brooks
9 miles (14.5 km) Sheet 197 032129

Easy A full day out, with something to interest everyone, particularly the naturalist. *Downs, woodland, park, marsh; one climb; mud – not recommended after rain.*

Start Amberley, 4 miles (6.5 km) due N of Arundel. **Parking** on roadside.

❶ From crossroads on the B2139, go uphill along Mill Lane. After ¼ mile (0.5 km), follow South Downs Way sign on left. Follow clear path for 2⅓ miles (3.5 km), over summit of Rackham Hill to car parking area where the Way is joined by a road on the left ❷. Turn left, and immediately take bridleway to right as road bends sharply left. Bridleway is signposted in 50 yards (46 m). Follow downhill through woodland. Continue along this road, then turn right. Turn left into Clay Lane ❸. At

bridge ❺, take footpath left, on near bank. After ⅓ mile (0.5 km) follow signposted track bearing left from river. Turn left at track junction towards farm buildings and go straight through farm. Turn right ❻ at signpost beside wood, and follow path down to low-lying area past Caution, Dangerous Marsh sign. Follow well-defined path through marsh, ignoring tracks to right and left, until it becomes broad farm track, meeting road in Amberley. Bear right at road, cross in 50 yards and follow signposted footpath back to the B2139. Turn left to ❶.

🗗 Chalk Pits Museum.

🏰 Amberley Castle, started in the 14th C.

☘ Amberley Wild Brooks is an outstanding piece of wetland, and traditionally used for grazing, peat and haymaking. The area has 86 species of water plants – over half the total found in Britain.

Cuckmere Haven

5¼ miles (8.5 km) Sheet 199 519995

Easy Traverses the South Downs to take in peaceful lowland forests on one side and exhilarating cliff tops on the other. *Forest, open downland, cliff tops; several climbs along the cliff top.*

Start Exceat, 7 miles (11 km) W of Eastbourne. Take the A259 from Eastbourne to Seven Sisters Country Park Centre. **Parking** Park Centre.

➊ From car park, cross the A259 to South Downs Way sign. Walk uphill, then go over stile in wall. Follow signposted path through wood towards West Dean. ➋ At village, turn right at bottom of steps along track signposted To A259 coast road. Ignore crossing track and, after 1½ miles (2.5 km), track bears left to T-junction. Turn right into lane and go past pumping station and cottages, then left at second T-junction ➌. At junction of 4 tracks ➍, take right fork, uphill, over stile in wall to road. Follow to main road ➎. Cross, then take track signed Crowlink and when it bears right, go straight on towards cliff edge. Turn left for diversion to Birling Gap Hotel, otherwise turn right along cliff path to Cuckmere Haven. ➏ Walk across ridge between lagoon and shingle

beach, then inland to ➊.

🏠 By the churchyard in West Dean is the former priest's house, dating from the 13th C., and claimed to be the oldest house in continuous occupation in the county.

🌲 Friston Forest was established in 1927, mainly as a beech wood.

〰 Speedy erosion of the chalk cliffs by the sea has left a shore platform, but unfortunately access is difficult and the incoming tide can be dangerous.

💡 Belle Tout, predecessor of the modern lighthouse at Beachy Head.

〰 The River Cuckmere is the only one in Sussex without a town or even a road at its mouth. It runs down a cut made in 1846, which left an area of saltmarsh around the old meanders. The area is a nature reserve, behind the shingle ridge, a lagoon has been dug to encourage water birds to nest. The area is cordoned off during the breeding season, but the nesting birds are easily seen.

⚓ Seven Sisters Country Park gives complete freedom of access to walkers.

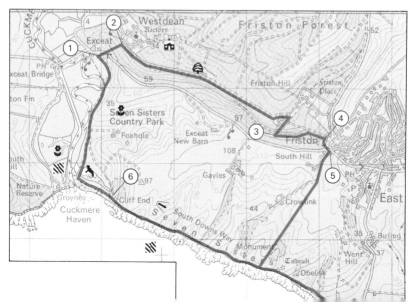

South Downs
NEAR SHOREHAM

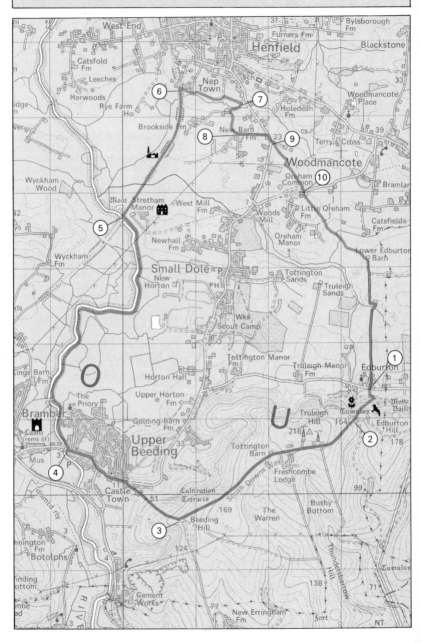

Truleigh Hill and the Adur Valley
11½ miles (18.5 km) Sheet 198 234114

Easy A varied walk, with high and low sections, giving an overview of the Downs and their complex history of human settlement. *Downs, dismantled railway, riverside; one climb; mud between ❾ and ❼. Follow signs carefully from ❻ onwards.*

Start Edburton, 10 miles (16 km) NNE of Worthing. From Worthing, take the A27 to Shoreham, then the A283 to Upper Beeding. At the roundabout, follow the A2037 and after 1½ miles (2.5 km), turn on to road signposted Poynings, Fulking and Edburton. **Parking** on roadside near Aburton Farm, next to church.

❶ Go through gateway opposite Aburton Farm, and follow path through field and gate. Turn left immediately and bear sharply right, uphill. Walk past 3-armed signpost through gate to join South Downs Way at junction of tracks ❷. Follow Way for 1¾ miles (3 km) to large signpost ❸. Take track signed Upper Beeding. At main road, turn left, then, at mini-roundabout, turn right into Bramber village street. ❹ At river bridge, take footpath upstream on right bank for 2½ miles (4 km). ❺ At steel girder bridge, turn right along dismantled railway for 1¼ miles (2 km). ❻ At gate across railway track, with footpath signposts on both sides, double back parallel to railway on downhill path to right. At next footpath sign, turn left. In 100 yards (91 m), go right over stile and follow garden fence over footbridge to second stile. Go ahead, keeping to left of fields and ignoring signposted side paths, to junction of tracks just past poultry farm and market garden. ❼ Turn right, then left at next footpath sign. Walk through field gate, and turn left, soon going through another field gate. Follow footpath sign to stile in corner of field. ❽ Climb stile, then bear left down well-made farm road facing New Barn Cottage. At main road, turn right, then take first lane on left. ❾ Go through signposted gate immediately on right, and walk to further signposted gate in far corner of field. Follow path over signposted stile into copse emerging into field. Walk diagonally to opposite corner and enter wood-

land. Keep to narrow path along left edge of wood to road. ❿ Cross and follow signposted footpath beside house called Woolvens. Cross signposted stile at end of garden into field. Cross 2 fields with signposted stiles. Continue in same direction towards farm buildings, crossing lane, small bridge and signposted stile. Follow farm track back to ❶.

🦅 Edburton Hill was one of the last places where the great bustard was found: hunting with greyhounds speeded this enormous bird's demise, the last English birds dying in Norfolk in 1845. Though extinct in NW Europe, it survives on the Asian steppes. The wheatear, now found here in small numbers, was trapped in thousands by downland shepherds in the 19th C. The birds were packed in fat in barrels and sold for roasting.

Other downland birds (faring better than the wheatear) include skylarks, corn buntings, red-legged and common partridges, and cuckoos. Open, scrubby areas may harbour yellowhammers, whitethroats and linnets; valley floor scrub holds songbirds.

🌼 On the uncultivated slopes, the native downland flowers make a colourful display. Vetches, viper's bugloss, round-headed rampion, orchids and clustered bellflower may be found.

🏰 Bramber has a Norman castle built to guard commerce on the river. Salt heaps have been found nearby, showing that saltpans near the castle were exploited until the 14th C.

🏯 Stretham Manor was originally a moated site – easily seen, though heavily overgrown. It was built in Norman times for the Bishops of Chichester, who were very powerful and kept close connections with surrounding areas. A large medieval timber-lined stone wharf has been found here.

🚂 The railway was part of the London, Brighton and South Coast Railway, opened in 1861, and closed down in the 1950s, a victim of Dr. Beeching's cuts. In Henfield, a new housing estate has been built over the old station site, called, appropriately, The Beechings.

WILTSHIRE REGION

Wiltshire's obvious, and, from the walker's point of view, pre-eminent feature is chalk downland. With the chalk hills of Hampshire and Berkshire, the Wiltshire Downs form the principal chalkland of Britain and it makes first-class walking: the slopes are steep enough to make you pant, but climbs never last too long; mile upon mile of well-defined tracks, worn often as not by prehistoric folk, follow the tops; underfoot the going is, at best, springy turf; at worst, sticky chalk.

But as the routes in this section show, downland walking is not the whole story. There is a lush, well-tended, domesticated landscape to be enjoyed along the Test Valley; the specialized, and receding, grassland habitat of Salisbury Plain and, if you know where to look, some interesting industrial scenery, including the extraordinary giant's staircase of locks lifting the Kennet and Avon Canal nearly 250 feet (76 m) outside Devizes.

Nonetheless, the staple diet of walkers will remain the hilltop tracks. Don't forget that Wiltshire boasts its own exclusive version of The Ridgeway Path: Wansdyke, west of Marlborough, and south of the A4.

A Flight of Locks
4¼ miles (7 km) Sheet 173 977627

Easy A fascinating route centring on the magnificent flight of locks at Devizes, testament to the remarkable skills of 19th-C. canal engineers. *Field, canal-side.*

Start Rowde, 2 miles (3 km) NW of Devizes on the A342. Turn left off the A342, just past the church. **Parking** along minor road N of church, or near ➋ where the minor road widens.

➊ Walk down minor road, away from church and village. Turn left at crossroads ➋ along path signposted Kennet and Avon Canal. Bear right at fork ➌. Where track divides ➍, keep straight on down grassy overgrown path. Turn left to cross stile ➎. Bear right and follow side of field to footbridge and stile ➏ beside canal. Turn right at canal to cross footbridge ➐. Turn left and follow canal towpath for 1½ miles (2.5 km) to the A361 bridge ➑. Cross bridge, turn left and follow road back along canal-side. A few yards after cottage and derelict building (on right), go through gate ahead ➒. Cross field diagonally, bearing right, towards house ➓. Follow lane from house to road. Turn right, and at T-junction, in about ½ mile (0.8 km), turn left to ➊.

🛶 The flight of locks at Devizes enables the Kennet and Avon Canal to climb 234 feet (71 m) in less than 2 miles. There are a remarkable 29 locks in the flight, 16 of these rising like the steps of a staircase up Caen Hill, with side ponds which acted as reservoirs. They prevented the water level in each lock dropping too much every time the one beneath was filled, or overfilling when the one above was emptied. The Devizes locks were the last part of the canal to be finished, and their opening, on 28 December 1810, achieved the completion of the link from Bristol to Reading. Despite the work required of bargees to negotiate this stretch, the canal was very busy, and gaslights were installed by the locks so that they could be used 24 hours a day. After dark, the passage cost an extra shilling. Information about the restoration of the canal and its function can be found at the Canal Centre at Devizes Wharf.

🏠 This 170-year-old lock-keeper's cottage is one of four along the flight.

⸮ Views past the W end of the Marlborough Downs.

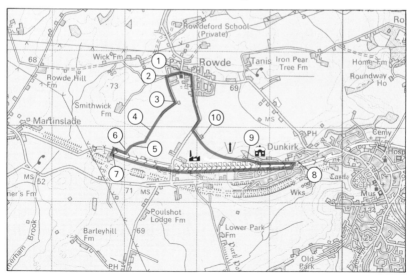

Wiltshire Region
NEAR SALISBURY

Salisbury Plain
7 miles (11 km) Sheet 184
037370

Easy A superb Iron Age hill-fort is the focus for a route through this unspoilt part of the downs. *Open downland.*

Start Steeple Langford, 9 miles (14.5 km) NW from Salisbury on the A36. **Parking** at large clearing on right beside minor road going S to Hanging Langford.

❶ Turn left and walk back up road to Steeple Langford and the A36. Cross over the A36 and take lane opposite ❷. Follow for 1½ miles (2.5 km) to the A303. Turn left and walk down road for ½ mile (0.5 km). Take second track on right ❸ past Yarnbury Castle. At track junction ❹, turn sharply right back to the A303. Take track immediately opposite ❺ which becomes a lane. At fork ❻, turn left along grassy

track. Turn right at crosstracks ❼ and go down to the A36 ignoring tracks on left and right. Take lane opposite ❽, which becomes footpath to road. Turn left to ❶.

🏠 Steeple Langford lies in the lush valley of the River Wylye, which flows on to Salisbury. The river widens here – hence the name Langford, originally Long-ford – and is good for fishing.

⛪ The Church of All Saints is 14th C., although there was a Norman building on the site, and possibly a Saxon church before that. The Purbeck marble font, and the chancel and tower arches, are all that remain of the 12th-C. building.

✹ On both sides of the path the remains of Celtic field systems can be seen.

✹ Yarnbury Castle is an Iron Age hill-fort, covering 28½ acres. An outer fort, built in the 2nd C. B.C., encircles an earlier fortification, dating from the 7th–5th C. B.C. On the SE part of the older fort are remains of the pens of an 18th-C. sheep fair.

🏠 The milestone here indicates the ancient down road from Old Sarum to Bath.

🍺 The Rainbow's End.

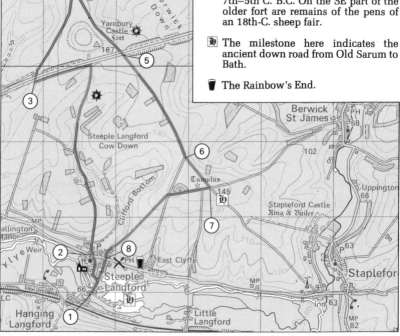

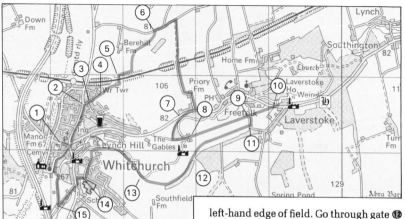

The Test Valley
7 miles (11 km) Sheet 185 461480

Easy The garden-like beauty of this valley is best appreciated in late spring or summer. *Fields, river valley.*

Start Whitchurch, 7 miles (11 km) E of Andover on the B3400. Trains from Salisbury and London. From the station go left and turn right at junction with road bridge. The walk can be picked up from the road on the left signposted Police Station **②**. **Car park** signposted from roundabout in centre of Whitchurch.

① From car park turn right, back to roundabout. Turn left up main street past White Hart Hotel on right. After ½ mile (0.8 km), turn right **②**. Go past police station **③** on right and keep straight on to gate with footpath sign **④**. Follow footpath under railway. Turn right across stile **⑤** and follow path running along right-hand edge of field. At small lane **⑥**, turn right and take first right down good track signposted to the B3400. Cross, turn right, and continue 100 yards (91 m). Take signposted footpath on left **⑦** to small lane. Turn left to bridge. Keep straight on across 2 stiles **⑧** and keep to left side of fields, following river to Freefolk Lane **⑨**. Cross park and recreation fields ahead to Laverstoke Mill **⑩**. Retrace steps to **⑨**. Turn left, then right through gate **⑪** where road bears sharply left. Keep to left-hand edge of field. Go through gate **⑫** and cross small stile on right into field. Keep to left-hand edge of field to cross stile **⑬**. Follow path to road then keep straight on. At junction **⑭** turn right, then take first left, then first right down narrow straight lane to mill **⑮**. Bear right and follow river to church. Take road to centre of Whitchurch and **①**.

🍸 The White Hart Hotel.

🏭 Bere Mill was where the Huguenot émigré, Henry Portal (formerly Henri de Portal), started his paper-making business in the early 18th C. In 1724 he was commissioned by the Bank of England to supply them with paper for banknotes. Portal's still supplies them, from larger premises in Overton.

⛪ St. Nicholas', 19th C., ornate interior.

📖 The second part of Richard Adams's *Watership Down* is set here around Laverstoke Park.

🏭 In the Fulling Mill, wool was made into cloth and bleached.

🏭 The Silk Mill was built in 1815 and is still in use, producing cloth for the robes of the legal profession. (To 'take the silk' means to become the Queen's Counsel.)

⛪ All Hallows Church was originally a Saxon building with additions made in 1190, and in the 15th and 18th C.

SURREY

Here is a key area for approximately eleven million people – the inhabitants of Greater London – and indeed hundreds of thousands of others in the Home Counties. It has an enlightened county council, with a diligent approach to preserving and marking rights of way, and a policy of creating large, sometimes connected, open spaces out of commons and specially purchased land. It is crossed at frequent intervals by train and bus routes out of London. Within the county boundaries lies a substantial section of the North Downs Way, signposted by the National Trust's acorn symbols (in Kent they change to low stone markers). This offers many opportunities to leave London by one public transport route, do a stretch of the long-distance path and return by another public transport route.

The price for all this convenience is the frequent necessity to share the paths with other walkers. However, if you want to take your mind off the twentieth century, there is some ancient history: the top of Holmbury Hill, for instance, is an 8-acre fortified camp dating from the second century B.C., and nearby is the site of a Roman villa.

Godstone and Bletchingley
5 miles (8 km) Sheet 187 350515

Easy A peaceful rural route close to London taking in 2 historic towns. *Pasture, woods, fields; mud. The route after Raby's, between ③ and ④ may be overgrown.*

Start Godstone, 6 miles (9.5 km) E of Redhill on the A25. Buses from Croydon and Redhill. **Parking** on the village green.

① Cross green to children's playground. Bear left down lane. ② Turn left on to Garston Park drive. At last building, cross stile on right. Go over 2 more stiles, finally making for far end of sloping field. Go through woods to road. ③ Cross to turning opposite and go downhill, later turning right on to bridleway just before Raby's. Continue on surfaced lane. When this turns left, go straight ahead on track into trees. Avoid right fork, and at end of woods, cross quarry road to fenced path opposite, turning left on to lane. ④ Turn right on to road. At main road through Bletchingley, turn left and cross to war memorial. Turn right down Church Walk to church. Retrace steps to war memorial. Continue up High Street to Stychens Lane ⑤. To visit Castle Hill, turn left down Castle Square, soon taking signposted path on right around hill to viewpoint seat. Retrace steps to ⑤. Go down Stychens Lane, shortly taking higher signposted parallel footpath on right. Keep same direction. Continue past Brewer Street Farm. ⑥ At junction, turn right, passing Place Farm. When road turns right, ignore first bridleway on left and keep in the same direction on bridleway for nearly one mile (1.5 km). ⑦ At house on left, turn left on to surfaced lane. ⑧ With farm buildings ahead, turn right over stile, crossing field diagonally right. Maintain same direction on hedged path and later over meadow to stile. Turn right on enclosed track to ①.

✗ The White Hart Inn, opposite the green in Godstone, was restored in Elizabethan times and is said to date from considerably earlier.

🏠 Bletchingley is a former market town with a fine Norman parish church. Before the 1832 franchise reforms, the hundred or so electors in the town returned 2 M.P.s – making Bletchingly a 'rotten borough'.

🏠 Brewer Street Farm was originally a yeoman farmer's house dating from 1430. Its roof is of Horsham slates.

🏠 Place Farm is the only remnant of Bletchingley Place, a manor given to Anne of Cleves on her divorce from Henry VIII. It incorporates part of the gatehouse of the manor.

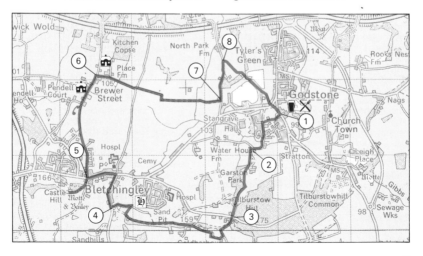

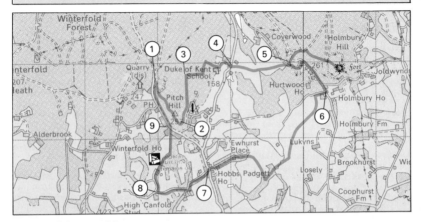

Views of the Weald
5 miles (8 km) Sheet 187 079427

Moderate An ancient fort and the remains of Roman occupation are included in this route, which follows some little-used paths in an otherwise well-trodden area. *Hills, fields, woods; 2 climbs; mud.*

Start Hurtwood, 10 miles (16 km) SE of Guildford. Take the A246 E from Guildford then turn S on to the A 25 and follow to Shere. Turn S on to minor road. **Car park** (Hurtwood Control Car Park No. 3) is 4 miles (6.5 km) down on the left before reaching The Windmill Inn, in the woods.

① From car park take uphill track parallel with road on right (all forks rejoin main path) and continue to top of Pitch Hill. ② Cross open space, passing trig. point, to left-hand side of 2 paths, bearing left round hillside. Keep to main path, continue for ¼ mile (0.5 km), then go over crossing track. ③ At next crossing track, turn right and soon left at T-junction. Take first track on right, continue over crossing track, and go through gap in iron fence. Continue down past school buildings to road. ④ Cross to signposted footpath opposite following it over open valley. Through posts and uphill to stile and crossing track. ⑤ Turn left on track, soon bearing right uphill. Cross road to car park. Take track from far right-hand corner to junction of several paths. Go through old concrete blocks to path on extreme right. Shortly afterwards, turn

right then left again, keeping right at choices till reaching open space and memorial seat on top of Holmbury Hill. Retrace steps to ⑤. Turn right on to track, bearing left uphill and then turning right along road. ⑥ Turn right on to Radnor House drive, then continue on track. Turn left over stile. Cross field to gate in far corner. Make for stile ahead slightly to right. Keep same direction over 2 more stiles, then bear right over footbridge keeping stream on left. Cross stile to path on edge of woods. Shortly afterwards, turn right through second of 2 gates, following fence on right over field. Turn left on to bridleway to road. ⑦ Cross to Coneyhurst Lane. At Shippen Hill bear right on to drive. ⑧ Turn right on to track to Rapsley Farm. Pass house and continue uphill on track, avoiding right fork. ⑨ At road, turn left to ①.

\⼂/ From Pitch Hill, S across the Weald.

❈ On top of Holmbury Hill is the 8-acre site of an ancient fortified camp dating from 150 B.C. The earthworks of double banks and ditches can still be seen in places. In 1930, excavations yielded many flint tools, pottery shards and other items.

🄰 At Rapsley Farm is the site of a Roman courtyard villa of the 2nd C. It had a bathhouse on the E side, an aisled hall to the W, and, on the S side, a timbered building with an apsidal end which may have been a shrine.

Surrey
NEAR HORLEY

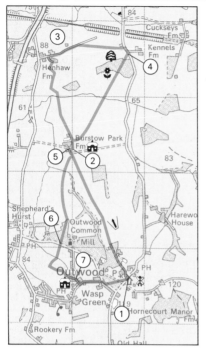

Outwood Mill and Poundhill
5¼ miles (8.5 km) Sheet 187 327456

Easy Some of the best of rural Surrey. *Pasture, woods; mud.*

Start Outwood, 6 miles (9.5 km) SE of Redhill. Take the A23 S from Redhill, and after 2 miles (3 km), turn E to Outwood. **Parking** area opposite Outwood Mill.

① From mill, take Bletchingley road, soon turning left on to signposted footpath. Ignore right turning. After Treetops go straight on to stile, and continue to opening into next field. Keep hedge on right. Cross third and fourth fields, and go through gate, keeping hedge on left. Just before buildings, turn right on to signposted path, bearing left to gate. ② Keep hedge on left. After another gate, fork diagonally left to stile in field corner. Bear left to gate with yellow waymark. Keep along side of field with hedge on

right. After stile, bear slightly left to second stile in hedge. Bear left to third stile. Continue with hedge on right to top corner of field, turning left for few yards to plank bridge and stile. Carry on with fence on right. Opposite Henshaw Farm turn left on to track. ③ At surfaced track turn right, later bearing right then left to road. ④ Turn right and soon go right again on to signposted bridleway downhill through trees to gate. Go round field edge to far right-hand corner. Continue round corner for 30 yards (27 m) to path leading to gate. Go over 4 fields towards house. ⑤ Turn left through 2 successive gates. Turn right, then cross bridleway to gate. Follow cart track over 2 fields. In third and fourth fields keep hedge on left. Bear left on track for few yards before forking right into trees. Continue to road. ⑥ Cross to path opposite. After crossing stile by stream watch for concealed stile on left. Cross stile and keep hedge on left to next stile, then go diagonally right to gate. Go through farm to road. ⑦ Turn right to T-junction, then turn left. Continue past another junction. Just before post box, turn left by telegraph pole on to footpath into trees, soon forking right to road and continuing to ①.

🏵 A post mill built in 1665, Outwood Mill is thought to be the oldest working mill in the country. Tradition has it that in 1666 local people watched the Great Fire of London from its top. It was renovated in 1952, and although privately owned, is open to the public on Sundays from Easter to the end of October.

\/ Nutfield Priory is the large building visible on the skyline to the left during the first part of the walk. Although built in a Tudor style, it dates from the 1870s.

🏠 Burstow Park Farm dates from the 18th C.

🌲 Poundhill is an area of mixed wood-
🌱 land in which scrub has been removed leaving only larger trees with plenty of clearings where wild flowers grow, including primroses and orchids.

🏠 The Old Farmhouse, formerly Wasp Green Farm, was built in the 16th C.

Surrey
NEAR GUILDFORD

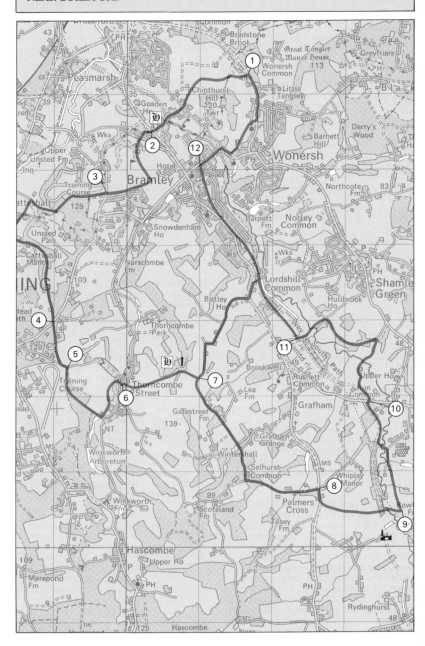

Surrey
NEAR GUILDFORD

Thorncombe Street and Bramley
9 or 12½ miles (14.5 or 20 km)
Sheet 186 017463

Moderate A choice of walks (or one very long route for a midsummer day), covering substantial stretches of rolling downland and tracing the route of a disused railway. *Fields, woodland, canal-side, disused railway; one climb; mud.*

Start Wonersh, 3½ miles (5.5 km) SE of Guildford. Use Chinthurst Hill **Car Park** on the N side of the village.

① Go through trees at far end of car park, turn left and continue for a few yards; then turn right on to bridleway. At road, cross and follow road opposite leading to Gosden Green. Keep to right of green. ② Cross road to path opposite, soon turning left on to drive. Enter golf club at visitors' car park. Bear right uphill, then turn left alongside fairway and pass conifer clump on right to kissing gate into bridleway. Turn right to road.③ Cross to bridleway opposite. Continue until bridleway meets crossing path, then turn right. At junction of paths take second on left. Ignore left turning and continue to outskirts of Godalming. At Ram Cider House turn left and continue for nearly one mile (1.5 km). ④ Cross road to path opposite. Go over crossing path and turn left on to road. ⑤ Turn right on to signposted footpath. Cross stile into meadow and continue with trees on right. Just before house, cross stile on right and turn left. Immediately after passing house, turn left under holly arch to stile. Keep fence on right for over ¼ mile (0.5 km). Cross stile in field corner and go forward to bar stile into next field. Turn right and soon cross stile on right. Follow same direction to road. Turn right to T-junction at hamlet. ⑥ Turn left and 20 yards (18 m) beyond phone box turn right. When track turns right, maintain same direction uphill. Go over bar stile to top of hill. Cross stile, and keep fence on left to next stile in field corner. Continue with fence on right. Later, at gate on right, continue for few yards into woods, then turn right on to downhill path and leave woods by gate. At bottom of field bear right on to track. ⑦ For 9-mile (14.5-km) walk, go left for few yards, then left again. Turn right on fenced track. At house, turn left to road.

Turn left and continue for 250 yards (229 m), then go right on to bridleway. Go under bridge, then turn right up path to old railway. Follow railway for one mile to road at ⑫. For 12½-mile (20-km) walk, turn right. After ¾ mile (1 km), turn left on to road to crossroads. ⑧ Turn right on to A281 for 150 yards (137 m), then turn left on to signposted footpath. At field, continue with hedge on left. At next field bear left and continue in same direction with hedge on right, later with hedge on left. At corner of field, cross stile and bridge. Turn right on to path leading to bridge over River Wey, then bear diagonally right to stile on to old railway track. Cross to another stile and continue up to wooden barrier by crossing path ⑨. Turn left and follow path when it turns sharply right. Just before farm buildings, turn left through gate into field and cross bridge over river. Turn diagonally right over field to fence beside old canal. Follow fence on left to waymarked stile on to towpath. Continue to road. ⑩ Cross to track opposite with canal hidden in trees on left. Avoid right fork, then bear right and pass barns. Go through gate, cross river, and bear diagonally right over field to gate into path. Turn left round cottage on to bridleway and continue for ½ mile (0.5 km). Turn right on to crossing path. About 50 yards (46 m) beyond cottage on left, turn left on grass track to waymarked gate. Continue straight ahead to bridge. Cross river and immediately bear diagonally right up to waymarked gate. Go straight ahead to bridge over old railway track. ⑪ Take gate and stepped path on far right side of bridge to old railway path. Turn left and continue for 1¾ miles (3 km) to road. ⑫ Turn right and shortly right again at T-junction. Just before house, turn left through kissing gate. At road, turn left to ①.

🏏 A plaque on Gosden Green sports pavilion tells of the first women's cricket match, played here in 1745.

📖 In his *Rural Rides*, William Cobbett describes the topography of the area as "in the form that the surface-water in a boiling copper would be in, if you could make it still".

🚣 Completed in 1816, the Wey and Arun Canal provided the final link from the Thames to the south coast.

THE WEALD

The name means 'wild', and until quite recent times it was just that: acres of dense, shadowy woodland, crouched in the hollow that separates the North Downs from the South. Iron ore, mined and smelted here even before the Romans, gave an economic value to the trees, which provided charcoal to power the kilns. Consequently, a great deal of ancient woodland was carefully managed and replanted, and some, indeed, has survived.

At the heart of the Weald lies Ashdown Forest – not really a discrete parcel of land, but a patchwork of small commons, remnants of the royal hunting forest. They offer open vistas across bracken and heather moorland, punctuated by the craggy outlines of old Scots pines. There. is plenty to occupy the walker here, and the paths tend to be well-trodden, if not well-marked.

Bodiam Castle
7¼ miles (11.5 km)
Sheet 188 or 199 798283

Easy Dominated by Bodiam Castle. *Farmland, grassland, hop gardens.*

Start Sandhurst, 3 miles (5 km) SE of Hawkhurst on the A268. **Parking** in lay-by on S side of Lower Green, near Old School.

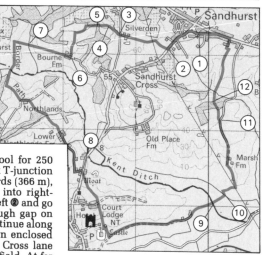

❶ Walk uphill past Old School for 250 yards (229 m), then turn left at T-junction by Upper Green. After 400 yards (366 m), turn right through iron gate into right-hand field. Follow hedge on left ❷ and go to far end of field. Pass through gap on left to cross stile on right. Continue along field-edge path, then go down enclosed pathway to metalled lane ❸. Cross lane and go through gateway into field. At far side ❹, go over stile into wood. Cross small footbridge and continue across orchard, through boundary trees, to cross footbridge over stream ❺. Past ruined building on left, cross stile in fence into large field. Go diagonally across field, aiming for top corner of neck of woodland. Turn left around woodland to field corner and climb fence. Go right down edge of field for 55 yards (50.5 m), then turn right and immediately left on to track. Pass through gate to Bourne Farm, past farm buildings, then through gap into hop garden. Turn right along field edge then through gap and across stile 15 yards ahead ❻. Turn right, then left to cross stile in far corner of hop garden. Proceed along top edge of next field, crossing bridge ❼ (beware of holes). Continue uphill in same direction passing through 2 narrow fields. After second field, turn left along field edge with hedge on left. At bottom of field, pass through gap on left, then bear right to reach footbridge over Kent Ditch. Cross and go up track to Northlands Farm. Turn left and, just past buildings, right downhill. Follow track to road ❽. Turn right and in 20 yards (18 m), turn left. Cross field diagonally, making for solitary oak tree on brow of hill ahead. Cross stile to right of tree and keep on across next field to stile ahead. Cross stile and concrete road, then proceed in same direction, passing

behind old Oast House to go through gateway. Go downhill, crossing stile to enter enclosed path and, at foot of hill, cross another stile to enter Bodiam Castle grounds. Go round left of castle and join cart track below. Turn left and continue along track for one mile (1.5 km) to footbridge over Kent Ditch ❾. Cross, then turn right and climb gate on top of dyke bank. Turn left and follow side of ditch to reach another footbridge ❿. Cross, then turn left and go around 3 sides of meadow to cross a stile in line with footbridge. Continue uphill, passing through Marsh Quarter Farm and after 650 yards (594 m), at footpath crossing ⓫, turn left into field by concrete footpath signpost. Then turn right and follow field-edge path around a curve for 100 yards (91 m), then strike off diagonally left uphill to corner of wood. Continue in same direction along side of wood for 25 yards (22 m), then follow track into wood. Beyond wood, cross bridge and stile to reach field ahead ⓬. Maintain direction to find stile in thicket on far side of field which leads to a footbridge. Cross and aim for right-hand side of 2 tall trees on hill brow to find stile into next field. Keep in same direction, crossing stile beside iron gate, then another stile on to a track leading to main road. Turn left to ❶.

🏰 Massive 14th-C. Bodiam Castle.

The Weald
WEST SUSSEX

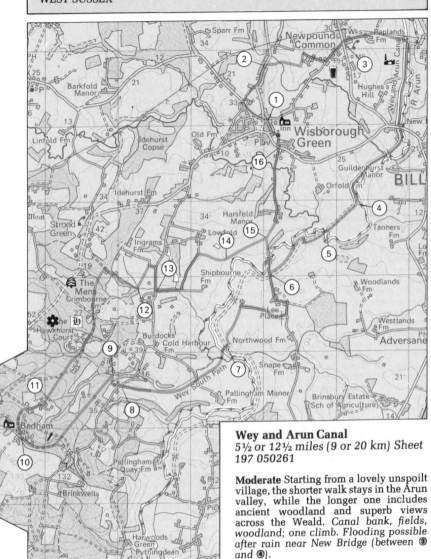

Wey and Arun Canal
5½ or 12½ miles (9 or 20 km) Sheet 197 050261

Moderate Starting from a lovely unspoilt village, the shorter walk stays in the Arun valley, while the longer one includes ancient woodland and superb views across the Weald. *Canal bank, fields, woodland; one climb. Flooding possible after rain near New Bridge (between ③ and ④).*

Start Wisborough Green, 7 miles (11 km) SW of Horsham. Take the A28 W from Horsham then turn S on the A264 to Billingshurst. Follow the A272 to Wisborough Green. **Parking** around village green, N of the A272.

The Weald
WEST SUSSEX

① Start along road, signposted Kirdford, on N edge of green. Just beyond Park Lodge, turn right along green lane. At road, turn left. ② Beyond row of houses turn right by post box and head across field. At end of first field, turn left and immediately right, through bridle gate, then across large field. Just short of farm buildings, turn left along field edge and right on bridleway and farm road to lane. Turn left, cross B2133 ③ and follow access drive to Paplands Farm. Continue ahead beyond farm to reach disused canal. Cross bridge by lock and turn right along canal bank, for 1½ miles (2.5 km), crossing the A272 at New Bridge. ④ Where canal disappears altogether at corner of large field, cross wooden footbridge and continue along hedge, parallel to canal trace. Cross stile into wooded area with nettles. Then cross sluice and river ⑤, and go *slightly* right (not along river bank) soon with hedge and canal remnant on right. Cross plank bridge and continue beside old canal, shortly swapping sides via bridge in poor repair. ⑥ For 5½-mile (9-km) walk, turn right at path junction and follow path to next junction ⑮. For 12½-mile (20-km) walk, turn left at track junction recrossing canal. Bear left then right on main track past Lee Place. At meeting of 4 ways, go ahead along access road. In 200 yards (183 m), turn right on to rutted track following sharp turn left. ⑦ Turn right and cross canal, river and ditch before bearing right to follow hedge and bank. Cross private road, keeping right of Furnacewood House. Follow hedge and then tree-lined track. At road, turn left. After 100 yards (91 m), turn right (signposted Foxbar ⑧. Beyond house, take path on right. Enter wood and just short of footbridge in dip, turn back sharply left. ⑨ Follow straight woodland path, crossing access road after about ½ mile (0.8 km). Go another ½ mile (0.5 km), then turn right along road. ⑩ Opposite Bedham Farm, fork right on to signposted bridleway. By ruin of Bedham church, fork right downhill. At T-junction, turn right, soon bearing left on to driveway. ⑪ After 200 yards, turn left, keeping building on right and follow path back into woodland. At road, keep left on signposted bridleway. Join metalled drive by stream crossing. Pass Hawkhurst Court to road. Take path opposite through nature reserve (may be overgrown in summer).

At T-junction, turn right, soon entering woodland path. ⑫ After ½ mile, just beyond footbridge, turn left and recross stream. Go over stile and climb slight gradient to go through gate ahead. Head slightly right to signpost visible on other side of field. Turn right along drive to road and right again. ⑬ A few yards after crossing stream, turn left on access road to Shipbourne Farm. After ¼ mile turn left, and in another 500 yards (457 m), go right through gate and along field edge. ⑭ Soon after second gate, turn left through bridle gate and skirt edge of 3 fields. Turn left at T-junction ⑮. Keep left of buildings at Harsfold Farm and follow access road to the A272 ⑯. Cross and go ahead into Glebe Way, immediately forking left into churchyard. From main churchyard gate, road bearing half-right leads back to ①.

🏛 Wisborough Green's church has a 14th-C. shingled spire, and impressive 13th-C. wall paintings.

🍺 The Bat and Ball.

🛶 The Wey and Arun canal is currently being restored as part of a long-term plan to reopen London's lost canal link with the sea. Rowner Lock has been fully restored with new lock gates. Further S a new lift bridge has been constructed. Between Rowner and Newbridge the canal has been partially dredged and cleared.

∨ Views over the Weald.

🏛 Bedham Church, built in 1880 by a local benefactor, now a ruin, lost in the woods.

✿ Hawkhurst Court gardens are open on occasions in summer months. A plaque on a building near the path tells of the ill-fated raid on Dieppe in August 1942 which was mounted from here.

🍃 The Mens is a rare piece of ancient woodland, probably never clear-felled, though undoubtedly managed and exploited for wood in the past. In such primary woods, a much greater variety of small plants grow beneath the trees than in secondary (planted) woods, even long-established ones.

The Weald
EAST SUSSEX

Pooh Bear's Forest
8½ miles (13.5 km) Sheets 188 and 198 466240

Easy This forms either the first section of a weekend walk through A. A. Milne's Sussex, a peaceful rolling landscape including parts of Ashdown Forest; or it forms part of a one-day circular route. *Lanes, farmland, pasture, woodland, disused railway; mud after rain.*

Start Maresfield, 11 miles (18 km) E of Haywards Heath on the A272. Buses from Uckfield, Haywards Heath and East Grinstead. **Parking** opposite church. **Return** One-day walk: follow route to Nutley Mill ⑧, then turn to next walk (page 102) and pick up route from ⑦ back to Maresfield. 2-day walk: stay overnight in Hartfield, then return on foot to Maresfield (see next walk). See accommodation note.

① Between Chequers and a milepost, 30 yards (27 m) from church, take narrow lane, 100 yards (91 m) to road junction. Turn left, past link road to the A22, and on to Reedings Farm ②. Go through farm entrance (signstone) to gate, then along side of fence to another gate. Turn left to field corner and then half-right to a point about 50 yards (46 m) to right of furthest corner of field. Continue into copse and to footbridge. Carry on diagonally across pasture towards single oak tree. Enter enclosed track to Hendall Manor, at left of oak tree. Turn left at junction with the Wealdway ③. Go past manor, bear right and go over stile at side of farm gate. At field, turn left and continue to large chestnut tree and gate. Go through this, and turn right following yellow waymarks, track indistinct ④. Continue down short, steep section through fir plantation, cross forest ride and carry on to footbridge. Turn immediately right over stile and follow left side of pasture to gate and stile, then follow drive to road ⑤. Cross into drive opposite. After 100 yards turn left on beaten path opposite largest oak tree, beside garage of The Cottage. Turn left at junction with broad ride. Cross the B2026 and maintain same general direction for ½ mile (0.8 km) on distinct track to ford. Leave more obvious track, turn right between 2 streams and walk 150 yards up to Airman's Grave ⑥. Continue to car park then turn left along track

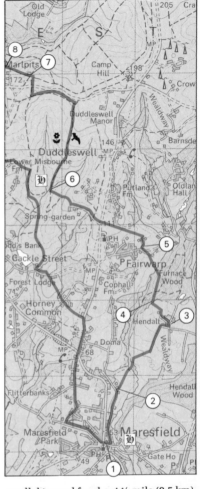

parallel to road for about ⅓ mile (0.5 km). Turn right through one car park, cross road through another. ⑦ Turn left along ride, and bear left after about ¼ mile (0.5 km) along track with field on left and wood on right. Go through 5-bar gate to Nutley Mill ⑧. For one-day walk, turn to page 103. For 2-day walk, bear right, away from mill, over stile back to forest, along path under oak and holly trees at first. Cross 2 distinct rides, then make for right-hand side of valley (do not cross the

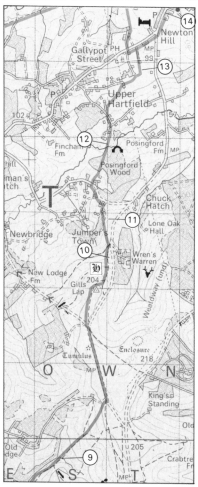

dylow), then take drive to road. Turn left and fork right after 50 yards. Just past next bend, find bridle gate on right, alongside field gate (signstone). Keep to this bridlepath down to Pooh Bridge ⑫. Follow path slightly uphill. After 300 yards (274 m) go through field gates on right to field (signstone). Keep round left side to stile and climb diagonally towards the furthest corner. Climb stile to narrow path (signstone) inside a wood at first, then continuing into field in front of large white house. Go round to stile by bridle gate at end of garden ⑬. Turn left down narrow field and go past small barn to road. For Hartfield, turn right. Stairs Farm (see below) is opposite Post Office ⑭.

🏛 The A22 through Maresfield, built in 1752, was one of the turnpikes, the first new roads to cross the Weald since those that the Romans laid.

🏛 The 'Airman's Grave' monument.

🌱 In August a superb display of marsh gentians can be seen by the path. Also found here are the sundew and a great variety of mosses and liverworts.
🦅 Birds include the stonechat, linnet, nightjar, meadow pipit and curlew.

🔭 To the SE is Camp Hill, one of several clumps of pine planted in the 19th C. as a landscape feature and to encourage game birds to breed.

🔭 Gill's Lap is the highest hilltop in the forest at 671 feet (205 m), and commands views over Five Hundred Acre Wood to the NE.

🏛 To the left of the path is the Enchanted Place, with a plaque in memory of A. A. Milne and Ernest Shepard.

🐇 Rabbits were 'farmed' at Wren's Warren for centuries.

⌒ Old friends of Winnie the Pooh will be pleased to find that Pooh Bridge – where the game of Pooh-sticks was invented – is just as A. A. Milne described it, having been renovated, but not changed.

🏨 Stairs Farmhouse, recommended for a night in Hartfield: (089277) 793.

valley towards a stone-gabled house, Old Lodge). After about ½ mile, turn left down short track to cross side stream (often dry), and continue, with valley on left, up to another ford and waterfall ⑨. Continue in same direction up to road at drive for Old Lodge. Cross to ride parallel to road and turn left up to road junction. From car park follow distinct track up to Gills Lap and down to Enchanted Place ⑩. Continue downhill and where track veers to right ⑪, follow path past house (Win-

The Weald
EAST SUSSEX

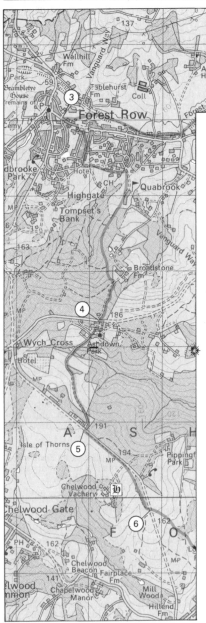

Forest Windmill
12½ miles (20 km) Sheets 187, 188 and 198 477356

Easy Here is the second part of the 2-day outing starting from Maresfield (the first day is covered in **Pooh Bear's Forest**, pages 100–1). Alternatively, you can make it a one-day circular walk by following the special instructions. Both are delightful. *Rough track, woodland, parkland, lanes, farmland; mud after rain.*

Start Hartfield, 6 miles (9.5 km) SE of East Grinstead. Take the A22 from East Grinstead, and in Forest Row turn left along the B2110 to Hartfield. **Parking** on roadside in village. **Return** One-day walk: follow route to Nutley Mill ⑦ then turn to previous walk, picking up route at ⑧ to return to Hartfield.

① Facing Post Office, turn left and walk about ½ mile (0.8 km) along road, going about 200 yards (183 m) past the point where you joined it yesterday. Turn right to Culvers Farm (look for concrete sign, Bridlepath). Go down drive past Culvers Farm. Take enclosed bridleway to dismantled railway ②. Climb steps, turn left and follow railway for just over 3 miles (5 km) to Forest Row. Head for large car park just E of the A22/B2110 junction ③. From car park go past school to small green on right side of the B2110. Cross on tarmac path to corner, then follow enclosed path at corner of garden of Firbank. Continue to road and turn right. Opposite a post box, leave road on path forking left to metalled track. Turn left, then take left fork to house called Shalesbrook. Take rough track for 100 yards (91 m) then fork left and cross ford. Turn right on metalled track and continue, past row of houses, keeping straight on into beech woods of Broadstone Warren, to reach the surfaced drive to Forest Rangers

Depot at road ④. Cross to stile and sign-stone, then follow series of signs down and through grounds of Ashdown Park to enclosed track. Continue to stile by gate. Cross directly to some rails and go on to building visible in the furthest corner of these fields. Then take track to the A22 ⑤. Cross to ride some 50 yards (46 m) into forest. Turn left on this, and follow for almost one mile (1.5 km), to car park on the A22 ⑥. Cross, and from centre of picnic area go past sleeper post, making straight for Nutley Mill on other side of valley ⑦. To continue two-day walk, at Nutley Mill, go on drive to road for 2-day walk. (For one-day walk, turn to page 100.) Cross and continue on track past cottages, then, just after second brick cottage, turn right on path down to drive. Follow to the A22 by Shelley Arms ⑧. Turn left past church, then go left down Clock House Lane. Where drive bears right, keep straight on down to stream and up to cross ride. Bear right, keeping field hedges to right all the way down to ford. Follow stream down to junction with another and almost immediately turn left over bridge. Go straight on uphill for 100 yards (91 m), and turn right on less prominent path. Gradually descend, parallel to fields on right, to gate near road at Booring Wheel Mill ⑨. Turn left on to road and just past second house on right, take narrow enclosed path to some rails into field. Turn left along edge to corner, then go round to right, down to a stream. Cross bridge and at gate, go over step on left, turning right to road. Cross to well-used path by house and follow to the B2026 ⑩. Turn right and continue 300 yards (274 m) to cross the A22 at junction, to drive almost opposite. Follow for about ½ mile (0.8 km), and bear right, then left, on surfaced private road, emerging through gateway of Maresfield Park opposite Maresfield Church ⑪.

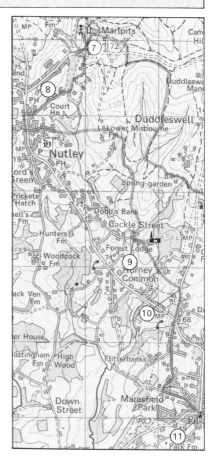

🕮 Just N of the railway line at Lower Parrock is a very early forge and furnace which supplied cannon balls to the army of Henry VIII.

⚐⚜ A hill-fort, the most important archaeological site in the forest, can be seen to the E of the path.

🕮 At Chelwood Vachery the monks of Michelham Priory raised cattle.

🛠 Nutley Mill is the only trestle-post windmill in the country.

🕮 Nutley was just within the medieval boundary of the royal hunting grounds – the forest pale – marked by a high bank.

🕮 Booring Wheel Mill once powered machinery for boring out cannons. A Kipling poem recalls the importance of the Weald's iron industry:

> Out of the Weald, the secret Weald,
> Man cast in ancient years
> The horse-shoes red at Flodden Field,
> The arrows at Poitiers!

CHILTERNS AND THAMES VALLEY

These modestly dramatic chalk hills are a borderland
between some strongly contrasting landscapes and regions.
They are the first taste of real country outside the north-
west suburbs of London; walking among them, you might
almost, in the right conditions, hear the murmur of traffic
from the city; certainly they can enable you to walk what
seems like remote, secluded country when suburbia is just
a valley or two away. The northern end of the range leaks
over the Buckinghamshire county boundary into
Hertfordshire and Bedfordshire, so that here, close to
Dunstable, you are approaching the south Midlands –
where identity and allegiances are different to those of the
prosperous south-east. Travel to the south-western end of
the range, and you are uncompromisingly in the south-east,
for here the hills tail off into the Thames Valley between
Reading and Goring.

As typical chalk hills, the Chilterns have well-defined
patches of beech woodland growing usually on or near
their tops. These hangers provide the open, airy woodland
walking which so many people prize: the canopy formed by
beech trees is dense, and their roots grow near the surface,
monopolizing nutrients in the topsoil and thus creating
unfavourable conditions for undergrowth.

Combined with an intensive footpath system, maintained
by the Chiltern Society, these features make as valuable
walking as any within a day's reach of London.

Dunstable Downs and Whipsnade
4½ miles (7.5 km) Sheet 166 008198

Easy With superb views over open downland, this walk reveals the essence of the Chilterns. *Remote valley, heath, downs; one climb; mud on bridleways at points* **⑭** *and* **⑮**.

Start 2 miles (3 km) SW of Dunstable. From the centre of Dunstable, take the B489 W, then turn S on to the B4541 and follow it for nearly one mile (1.5 km) to **car park** at the top of the Downs. Regular bus service to Whipsnade from Luton and Dunstable (start walk at **⑬**).

① From public lavatories, take the B4541 S, then, by an obelisk, fork left. **②** Just past house, turn left through hedge gap, soon entering fenced path. **③** Go straight on downhill to 2 trees. **④** Bear half-left into lane and continue towards Kensworth Quarry. **⑤** Turn right through a copse. **⑥** At far end of copse, go straight on, over stile. Follow bottom of steep bank to second stile, then continue straight on over 2 further stiles. **⑦** Turn right and follow hedges uphill. **⑧** In garden, turn left across neighbouring garden to reach road, then turn right. **⑨** After end of pavement, turn left over stile, cross field and continue to crossroads at Whipsnade Heath. **⑩** Take Studham road. **⑪** Before left-hand bend, turn right through gate and head for church. **⑫** At Whipsnade Green, turn left and take road to Whipsnade Tree Cathedral. **⑬** At car park, go through kissing gate and follow left-hand hedge to reach a bridleway. **⑭** Turn right on to bridleway to top of Whipsnade Down. **⑮** Turn right along top of Downs to reach belt of scrub. **⑯** Go through gate, turn left, then turn right through scrub to **①**.

※ The five Knolls is perhaps the finest prehistoric burial ground in England. There are 8 sites in all, with remains dating from the early Bronze Age to the pagan Anglo-Saxon period. Neolithic and Beaker pottery has also been found here.

✎ Kensworth Quarry is the only active chalk quarry in the Bedfordshire Chilterns.

🍺 The Chequers serves food.

🌲 Whipsnade Tree Cathedral is made up of 25 different tree and shrub species. It was not deliberately laid out in the form of a cathedral, but services are held there nonetheless.

👁 The White Lion on Whipsnade Down can be seen SW of here. The lion, 483 feet (147 m) from nose to tail, is one of many figures carved into these chalk downs.

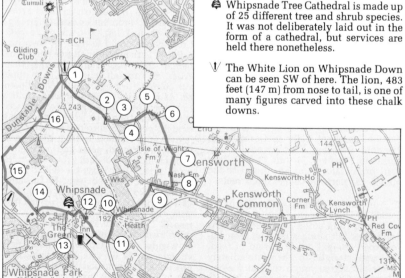

Chilterns and Thames Valley
BERKSHIRE/OXFORDSHIRE BORDER

The Goring Gap and Woodcote
9 miles (14 km) Sheets 174 and 175
603806

Moderate The views from the escarpment and the quiet woodlands of this route have a surprisingly rural feel, rare in the increasingly urban Thames Valley. *Fields, woods, upland plateau; 3 climbs; mud in field at ⑲. Route ill-defined at ⑪, ⑲ and ㉚ – follow directions carefully.*

Start Goring, 9 miles (14.5 km) NW of Reading. From Reading, take the A329, towards Oxford. At Streatley, turn E along the B4009 to centre of Goring. At the far end of the railway bridge, turn right and follow the railway to Goring and Streatley Station. Frequent trains to Goring from London, Reading, Didcot and Oxford. Buses to Streatley, ¾ mile (1 km) from start from Oxford and Reading. Use the station **car park**, or village side-streets.

① From Goring Station, walk towards the B4009. ② Opposite road bridge over railway, turn right along access road. ③ At bend, fork left along alleyway, then follow road straight on. ④ At end of road, take path straight on, then immediately turn right across rough road and along alleyway. ⑤ Go straight on across field. ⑥

A view to Wittenham Clumps.

After climbing stile, fork right on to path behind gardens to road. ⑦ Cross road diagonally, and take narrow hedged path into woodland, bearing right to junction of paths. ⑧ Turn left on to fenced bridleway. ⑨ Turn right on to track, later a road. Take second farm track on left ⑩. In High Wood ⑪, fork left off track on to path. Cross narrow field to road ⑫, then turn right. ⑬ Turn left through gate and follow hedge, then turn right through Dean Wood. ⑭ Turn left on to road, then opposite church, turn right along fenced path. ⑮. At road, go straight on, then follow round left-hand bend. ⑯ Turn right into Wood Lane, then take left-hand footpath straight on. ⑰ At entrance to wood, fork left. ⑱ Turn right on to B471. ⑲ At bend, turn right through gates and pass left of 2 old chalkpits to distant gate. ⑳ Turn left on to drive, then cross the B4526 and a field to reach fenced path. ㉑ In valley bottom, take path, later lane, straight on ㉒ Turn right on to road. ㉓ Turn left over stile, then bear half-right to gate by tall tree. ㉔ Turn left along lane. ㉕ Turn right on to road. ㉖ By cottage, fork right. ㉗ At a wiggle, take narrow sunken path straight on. ㉘ By gate, turn right, then fork left along farm road. ㉙ By sheds, turn left at junction. ㉚ Just past farm, turn

Chilterns and Thames Valley
BERKSHIRE/OXFORDSHIRE BORDER

right through gate, cross paddock diagonally, then 2 stiles. Bear half-right past corner of barn and go across field to stile into Great Chalk Wood. In wood, go straight on to T-junction **31**, then turn sharp left. **32** On leaving wood, cross 2 stiles, then turn right and follow top edge of 2 fields. **33** Turn right across recreation ground to estate road. Turn left then right to join the B4526 and turn left to crossroads. Turn left to **1**.

St. Thomas of Canterbury Church (just off the map) was built by Robert D'Oilly soon after the Norman Conquest. Following their victory at the Battle of Hastings, the Norman armies passed through Goring, on their circuitous journey to London.

Goring was built where the Icknield Way crossed the River Thames. Named after the Iceni tribe which inhabited Norfolk, the way is thought to be pre-Roman and follows the chalk escarpments from East Anglia to Stonehenge.

A sweeping view of the Berkshire Downs, Thames Valley, Didcot Power Station and Wittenham Clumps (a hill topped with trees to the NW).

Over the Goring Gap to the Berkshire Downs. Here the Thames breaks through the chalk bank that stretches across southern England from Salisbury Plain to the Wash. The gap looks as if it was caused by a fault in the rock, but in fact it was created by the river cutting its way through, at a time when the clay plains of Oxfordshire were higher than the chalk to the E. This made the Thames a much faster and more powerful river than it is today, and as it flowed over the Chilterns it eroded a gorge. The clay later sank, leaving a gap in the ridge.

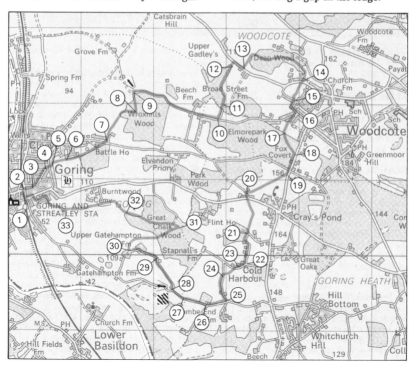

Bledlow Ridge and Radnage
4 or 7¼ miles (6.5 or 11.5 km) Sheet
165 799975

St. Lawrence's Church, West Wycombe.

Moderate/strenuous Rapidly changing
scenery and a sense of rural remoteness
characterize this walk through ridge-and-
bottom landscape typical of the central
Chilterns. *Fields, hills, woods; 3 or 6
climbs; mud.*

Start Bledlow Ridge, 5 miles (8 km) NW
of High Wycombe. From High Wycombe,
take the A40 towards Oxford. After passing through West Wycombe, fork right
and continue for 2½ miles (4 km) to the
junction with Haw Lane in Bledlow Ridge
village. Buses from High Wycombe and
Thame (no evening or Sunday service).
Parking in service road by the junction
of Chinnor Road and Haw Lane. Please
do not obstruct.

① For 4-mile (6.5-km) walk, take road
towards Chinnor to The Boot ⑬ and turn
left into hedged path to ⑭. Follow route
back to start. For 7¼-mile (11.5-km) walk,
take Chinnor Road towards High
Wycombe. ② Turn left into Scrubbs Lane.

At end of lane ③ go straight on downhill.
④ Turn left into Slough Lane, bearing
right, round bend. ⑤ Just past pond, turn
right over stile and climb hill diagonally
to sunken way into woodland. ⑥ At top of
ridge, turn sharp left down to road. ⑦
Cross, and continue over Slough Hill. ⑧
Turn left along road. ⑨ Turn right on to
bridleway and follow to Lodge Hill Farm.
⑩ Turn left up farm drive, then go left
over stile and straight across field to go
through gate. Bear half-right to cross stile.
⑪ Go straight uphill to stile under tallest
tree in hedge. ⑫ Follow left-hand hedge,
later a drive, to road ⑬. Cross and take
hedged path straight on, across road. ⑭ In
wood, fork right, then follow right-hand
edge of scrubby field downhill. ⑮ By
stile, turn left to climb second, concealed
stile, then go straight across field to stile
by power line. ⑯ Turn left on to road,
then, at junctions, fork right then left. ⑰
By Elbow Knapp, turn right over a stile
and climb to Andridge. ⑱ Take drive
through farm ⑲ At right-hand bend, go
straight on over 2 stiles, then turn left
along track to gap in hedge ⑳. Go through

this and follow left-hand hedge to reach second power line, then turn right to far corner of field. ⑳ Turn left along road and after left-hand bend, turn right on to fenced bridleway ㉒, soon climbing through wood. ㉓ Just past large house, turn left through village. ㉔ Turn right into Green End Road. ㉕ Opposite Hill Green Farm, turn left on to footpath, downhill. Go straight across minor road and then uphill to Bledlow Ridge. Turn left along road to ①.

👁 The golden ball that crowns the tower of St. Lawrence's Church at West Wycombe can be seen from here. Originally the church for the lost village of Averingdown, it was completely remodelled in the mid-18th C. for the eccentric Sir Francis Dashwood (later Lord Le Despencer), Chancellor of the Exchequer and founder of the infamous Hell Fire Club. There is a room seating 10 people in the church tower where the members of the club are said to have practised black magic. The motto of the club was *Fay ce que voudras* – Do as you please.

🌳 Some very old yew trees can be seen in the woods and hedges here. Yews are exceptionally long-lived, but they grow so slowly that it is difficult to estimate their age. Some alive today are believed to be over 1,000 years old.

👁 The view to the SE includes Bradenham Manor, birthplace of Disraeli.

👁 Lacey Green Windmill, seen on a hill to the NE, was built in 1650 and is the third oldest smockmill in the country. It was originally built at Chesham, and was only moved to Lacey Green in 1821. Once in a ruinous condition, it has now been fully restored by the Chiltern Society.

⛪ Radnage Church dates back to the 13th C. and contains medieval murals. The Saxon font was unearthed in a nearby field.

🏠 Beneath its paintwork, the unusual herring-bone pattern of the brick infill (or nogging) of this timber-framed cottage can be seen.

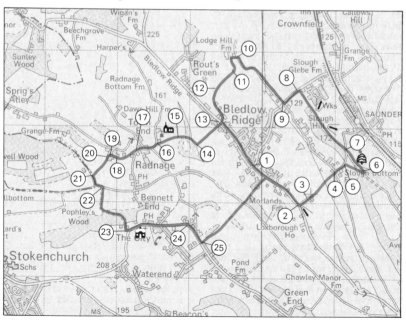

Chilterns and Thames Valley
MID BUCKINGHAMSHIRE

Chiltern Beechwoods
7¾ miles (12 km) Sheet 165 892101

Moderate Starting from Aston Hill, this walk passes through the picturesque villages at the foot of the Chiltern escarpment. *Fields, canal towpath, woods; one climb; mud in field at ⑧. Lane at ⑩ very muddy. Route ill-defined at ⑨, ⑭, ⑰, ⑳ and ㉕.*

Start Aston Hill, 5 miles (8 km) SE of Aylesbury. Take the A41 from Aylesbury towards Tring and turn S on to the B489. Turn SW on to the A4011, and then turn left on to road signposted to St. Leonards, Cholesbury, Chesham and Chiltern Forest Golf Course. At the top of the hill, turn left into the **car park** and picnic site.

① From car park entrance, take track opposite Aston Hill Lodge. ② After 150 yards (137 m), turn left, then left again following sunken gulley. ③ Go straight on along edge of golf course, then between fences to the A4011. ④ Turn left along the A4011. At road junction ⑤ turn right over stile and descend to canal. ⑥ Turn right along towpath and follow, crossing to left-hand side at second road bridge, to Drayton Beauchamp church. ⑦ At first bend in 'dry section', turn left up a steep bank into churchyard. ⑧ Pass left of church to kissing gate, then cross field diagonally to far corner. ⑨ Go straight on across 3 fields to road, left of Rothschild Arms. ⑩ Turn right, crossing the B489 into Buckland. ⑪ At bend by Church Leys, turn right then immediately left to Buckland church. ⑫ Pass right of church to gate, then continue straight on to road. ⑬ Bear slightly right on to path between gardens, then continue across fields to road by Partridge Arms ⑭. Turn left then right along Twitchell Lane to main road ⑮. Cross, and take Church Lane past church and farm. ⑯ On reaching stream, turn left, then at end of lane, turn right and go straight on to edge of airfield. ⑰ Turn left and follow edge of airfield at first, then continue straight on to canal bridge. ⑱ Do not cross bridge, but turn right and follow canal to road. ⑲ Turn left, then left again to Halton church. ⑳ At far side of churchyard, turn left into trees, then right on to stony track. ㉑ Turn left on to a private road. ㉒ At sharp bend, cross rails and continue along adjoining track. ㉓ Turn left on to road, cross the A4011 and continue into Aston Woods. Turn sharp left up flight of steps ㉔ beside flint wall. ㉕ Cross road and continue 150 yards or so, then turn right up steep bank, crossing track to stile. ㉖ Bear half left past trig. point to stile and ①.

🐾 Aston Hill at 852 feet (260 m), forms the northern end of the highest ridge in the Chilterns.

🚶 The Wendover Arm of the Grand Union Canal was constructed in the 1790s to supply additional water to the main canal. It was a failure almost from the start. Notorious for its leaks, it often drained water out of the main canal instead of replenishing it. Eventually, a stop-lock had to be built near Tring to prevent this. Commercial

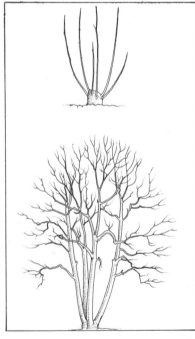

Top, slim stems sprout from the base of a coppiced beech; bottom, a coppice allowed to grow into a standard tree.

Chilterns and Thames Valley
MID BUCKINGHAMSHIRE

traffic on the arm was deterred by the leakages and most of it was closed in 1904. Bucklandwharf, as the name suggests, was a loading point for the barges.

🏠 Drayton Beauchamp Church was built in the 15th C. and contains 2 14th-C. brasses, a memorial to the Cheyne family (of Chelsea fame), and a rare creed window.

🔟 The main road here follows the route of Akeman Street, the Roman road that linked Cirencester to London. For a change, the Romans were not pioneering a highway, but following in the footsteps of others: for a short distance, this was also part of the ancient Lower Icknield Way.

🏠 Viscount Lake, who captured Delhi in 1803 during the Mahrotta War, is buried in Aston Clinton Church.

🏨 Halton House, visible through the trees in winter, was a late 19th-C. Rothschild mansion modelled on a French château. It is now the headquarters of the RAF.

🌲 The beeches here have been coppiced – cut off at the base to produce thin, straight stems from the stump. This was the time-honoured method of managing woodland to produce a steady supply of wood for fencing poles and firewood. In the early 19th C., most of the Chilterns' beech coppices were allowed to grow into standard trees to supply the furniture industry developing in High Wycombe, so this patch is a rare remnant of an earlier age.

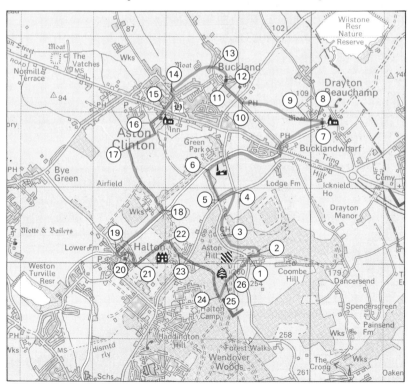

WALES

BRECON BEACONS AND BLACK MOUNTAINS

MID WALES

NORTH WALES

BRECON BEACONS AND BLACK MOUNTAINS

These hill and mountain ranges, facing each other across the valley of the Usk, and united under the management of the Brecon Beacons National Park, are the playground of city dwellers from South Wales and the Bristol area, and, indeed, of many who come from further afield. They are increasingly under pressure from walkers and motorists alike. There is erosion of paths, and, in summer, some of the valleys of the Black Mountains (notably Llanthony Valley) get blocked with cars, bumper to bumper.

A particular aim of this section is to reduce pressure on such sensitive areas; some of the country covered outlies the Beacons and Black Mountains. There is a fine walk at Blaen-y-glyn, on the eastern edge of the Beacons; and there is an excellent short walk near Llangynidr, taking in some of the Usk Valley and an outlying hill of the Beacons. The route exploring the Blorenge plateau, south-west of Abergavenny, is almost on the edge of the coal country. Naturally, you will find some classic hill walking here; treat all the uplands with the same respect, regardless of differing heights.

Partrishow Church
4 miles (6.5 km) Sheet 161
285212

Moderate Panoramic views from Crug Mawr are the highlight of this short walk, at its best in late March when snowdrops encircle Partrishow Church. *Farmland, open hillside, ridge; 3 climbs. In high summer bracken may obscure the tracks between ⑨ and ⑩. If inexperienced in hill walking, do not attempt in poor visibility.*

Start near Forest Coal Pit, 4 miles (6.5 km) N of Abergavenny. From the war memorial in Abergavenny take the old Hereford road (signposted Forest Coal Pit) to Pantygelli, and turn left just past the Crown Inn. At Forest Coal Pit, descend into valley to junction of 5 lanes, at entrance to Grwyne Fawr valley. **Parking** on verge near telephone box at 5-lane junction.

① Walk S along the road a few yards. Turn right to cross a stone bridge over River Grwyne. Go up the hill to reach a junction ②. On the right-hand side of the junction, go through a gate to follow a track across 2 fields. This leads to a gate below a ruined farmhouse ③. Turn right, and at the end of the field turn left to follow a track beside a stone wall. Cross 2 fields and head towards a waymark on a stile, near a wall beside a white cottage. ④ Go over the stile and turn right along the road. Ignore a left turning and follow the road around into a narrow valley. The holy well of St. Patricio may be seen on the right at foot of a steep dip in the lane ⑤. Continue up the hill to reach the church ⑥. Keep on up the hill, and then bear left up a stony track ⑦ between 2 stone walls. Go through a gate ⑧ and head straight up hillside, keeping to the right of a fence, and ascend the spur of Crug Mawr to reach the summit ⑨. Head S towards the Sugar Loaf and follow ridge around over Partrishow Hill overlooking the valley of Nant Mair. At the E end of the ridge, descend to a gate in a stone wall ⑩. Go through the gate and follow a wide path down to road junction ⑪. Take road opposite, past a farmhouse, then keep left at the next road junction and continue to ①.

🏮 In the 6th C., a saint named Issui lived near St. Patricio's Well. He was murdered by an ungrateful traveller who had received hospitality in his humble cell. Later, the well became a place of pilgrimage and was said to possess healing properties. There is a stone with an incised cross beside the road, where steps lead down to the well.

🏠 Partrishow Church, situated 1,000 feet (305 m) above sea level, dates back to 1060. The beautiful carved rood screen was erected at the end of the 15th C. Also in the church is a picture of a skeleton, depicting death, with spade, scythe and hourglass, and a 'dug out' chest. This was hewn out of a solid tree trunk in response to Thomas Cromwell's orders of 1588, that all churches should have a stout chest for the parish valuables. This chest is unusual in having 3 locks – the rector and the 2 churchwardens each held a key, so they all had to be present before the chest could be opened.

⩗ A fine view from here of the southern part of the Black Mountains and the Sugar Loaf.

Pen Allt-mawr and Table Mountain
8½ miles (13.5 km) Sheet 161
234228

Strenuous Taking in one of the best ridges of the Black Mountains and including a visit to an Iron Age hill-fort. *Mountain ridges, open hillside; one long ascent; mud. If inexperienced in hill walking, do not attempt in poor visibility.*

Start Cwm Banw, 3 miles (5 km) N of Crickhowell. From Crickhowell (on the A40, NW of Abergavenny), take the Llanbedr road which leads into the Grwyne Fechan Valley. Ignore the turning to Lanbedr and drive on for almost 2 miles (3 km) to reach a small parking area where the road makes a very sharp bend in Cwm Banw, near old quarry on left.

❶ From the car park, turn left and follow the road up the valley. At a sharp bend in road, turn off to the left, up a farm lane **❷**. Continue past a farm and follow a cart track to a metal gate **❸**. Then go on between 2 stone walls to reach another gate **❹**. The track ascends a long spur passing old quarries to reach more open hillside above. Carry on climbing to reach summit of Pen Twyn Glas **❺**. Continue heading SW and follow path around to reach a steep ascent to Pen Allt-mawr **❻**. Keep on path to summit of Pen Cerrigcalch **❼**. Then continue to the edge of plateau and descend in a SSE direction to reach Table Mountain **❽**. Follow track which skirts the edge of the hillside in NE direction. After about ¾ mile (1 km), drop down to gate in corner of a stone wall **❾**. Go through it and follow a path down to join the road by a cottage. **❿** Turn left and follow road back to **❶**.

Brecon Beacons and Black Mountains
SOUTH POWYS

Not gravestones, or ancient monuments, but 19th-C boundary stones on the summit of Pen Twyn Glas.

The rock slabs on Pen Twyn Glas summit are not gravestones as most people assume, but 19th-C. boundary stones which recorded the estate limits of 2 local landowners.

Pen Allt-mawr gives excellent views of the surrounding hills, including the Beacons. Mynydd Llangynidr, Mynydd Llangorse and Mynydd Llangatwg.

Pen Cerrig-calch – Head of the Chalk Rock – is an outlier of Carboniferous limestone, the only such rock N of the Usk. At 340 million years old, it is 60 million years younger than the old red sandstone of the surrounding hills. Laid down in shallow seas, it was formed, like other limestones, from the chalky bodies of shellfish. Later it was lifted clear of the sea by earth movements. Once exposed, rain eroded much of it, and, in the last million years, glaciers scraped the rest away, revealing the ancient sandstone

beneath. For some reason, the limestone of this isolated peak proved more resistant and survived erosion.

Table Mountain's original name was Crug Hywel (the 'crag of Hywel', a Welsh hero) and Crickhowell is a corruption of this. The hill has an early Iron Age hill-fort of a simple design with a rampart, a single ditch, and counterscarp bank outside the ditch. An indentation on the western side marks the entrance. Small hill-forts like this were probably used as refuges for local farming people living in the valleys below, and were not permanently occupied. Most Iron Age hillforts were improved over the centuries, and a second rampart added, but this one is unusual, in that it was left unchanged by its later users.

117

Brecon Beacons and Black Mountains
GWENT

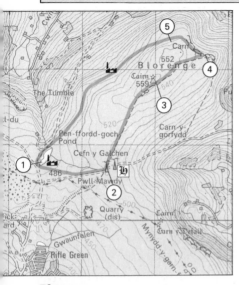

Blorenge
3 miles (5 km) Sheet 161 254108

Easy This area, which once rattled with industrial activity, now offers peaceful moorland walking and superb views. *Open moor. If inexperienced in hill walking, do not attempt in poor visibility.*

Start 4 miles (6.5 km) SW of Abergavenny. From Abergavenny, drive across the River Usk to Llanfoist, then take the B4246 which ascends the western slopes of the Blorenge. Stop at large pool on left-hand side, near highest point. **Parking** beside the B4246, near Pen-fford-goch pond.

① From the pond, follow a track across the open hillside towards 2 tall radio masts. On reaching a road near the masts, turn left and walk along the road to the Foxhunter Car Park ②. From the car park, follow a track across the moorland NE, to reach the Blorenge summit ③. Follow a path that runs to the right of the large cairn to reach the north-eastern escarpment ④ for impressive views. Keeping at the same level, follow the lip of the escarpment round to the NW. On seeing a shallow cutting to the right ⑤ descend slightly to go through the cutting and then follow an old tramway which contours the hillside and brings you back to point ①.

🔼 Pen-ffordd-goch pond was constructed in the 19th C. to supply 2 smaller ponds at Garn-ddyrys forge, once situated on the slopes below. It is featured in Alexander Cordell's novel *Rape of the Fair Country*, which describes life in a hard-working community during the Industrial Revolution and tells the story of the Chartists' uprising.

🔟 The grave of a famous show-jumping horse gives this car park its name. The skin of the horse was buried here by its owner, Colonel Harry Llewellyn, one moonlit night in 1959. A plaque lists the horse's achievements.

🔼 The Blorenge escarpment commands an impressive view over the Vale of Usk and Abergavenny to the Sugar Loaf, Skirrid Fawr and the Black Mountains. Watch out for buzzards soaring on the up-currents of air created by the steep escarpment. Hang-gliders use the same air currents as the birds, launching themselves from here, to land in a field beside the Usk, near Abergavenny.

🔼 This tramway, dating from the early 19th C., was one of those linking the iron-smelting works at Garn Ddrys with the limestone quarries of Pwll-du and, on the far side of the Blorenge, the Monmouthshire canal. The canal was opened in 1799 and by the 1840s was carrying 800,000 tons (813,000 tonnes) of coal a year to Newport. Coal and pig-iron both came across the Blorenge in trams that were pulled up slopes by horses, and down them by gravity. A man would run beside the trucks and control their speed with a pole (known as a sprag), which acted as a brake on the wheels. The pole often broke and runaway trucks were a constant hazard. Above Llanfoist, at the point where the tramway met the canal, (grid reference 285129), the old wharf and warehouse can still be seen, though they are private. In Blanaevon, the tramworks and the Big Pit mining museum are well worth a visit.

The Chartist Cave
4¾ miles (7.5 km) Sheet 161 157171

Moderate Through remote moorland with much history – both industrial and political. *Open moorland. If inexperienced in hill walking, do not attempt in poor visibility.*

Start Blaen Onneu 9 miles (14.5 km) due W of Abergavenny. From Abergavenny, follow the A465 towards Merthyr Tydfil. After 8 miles (13 km), turn on to the B4560 and follow it for 3 miles (5 km) to **car park** at Blaen Onneu on left side of the B4560.

① Walk S along the B4560 for about ¾ mile (1 km) and then turn on to gravel track on right ②. This leads to a small abandoned quarry ③. (Cave entrance and pot-hole – beware of steep drop.) Scramble up a steep track to the left of the cave to the open moorland above and then continue along line of quarry track, WSW, to reach a trig. point ④. From here, follow a path towards Garn Fawr – a hump on the ridge about 1½ miles (2 km) away. ⑤ From a grassy cairn walk N (passing on your right the small pools of Llyn y Garn-Fawr, generally only there after periods of heavy rain) and then NE to reach a low cliff and the Chartist Cave ⑥. Continue NE to reach the edge of Cwm Claisfer ⑦

and skirt around the hillside to meet the base of a limestone escarpment ⑧. Keep straight on and follow a track beside a stone wall above the forestry plantation; at the end of this don't follow path downhill, but keep up at the base of escarpment, joining an old tramway leading back to ①.

There is a small cave in a quarry face and also a pot-hole in the quarry floor where a 12-foot (4-m) drop leads to further passages. Don't enter.

As in many limestone areas, there are numerous swallet holes: cone-shaped depressions in the ground caused by the roofs of underground chambers collapsing. It has been claimed that there are more swallet holes to the square mile in this national park than in any other area of Britain.

The entrance to the Chartist Cave is under an impressive rock arch set in a depression, so it is easily missed. The Chartist movement, whose members met and stored their ammunition here, was a 19th-C. organization which demanded electoral freedom, as set out in its People's Charter.

Horse-drawn trams once carried limestone, quarried from the escarpment at Blaen-Onneu, along this tramway.

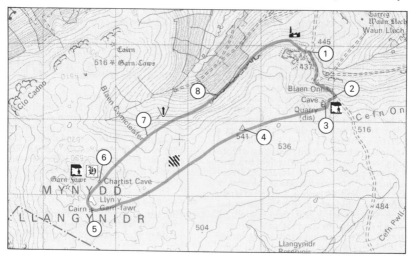

Brecon Beacons and Black Mountains
SOUTH POWYS

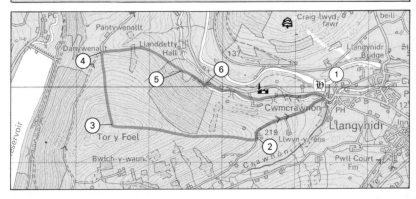

Tor y Foel
4½ miles (7 km) Sheet 161 144198

Moderate Short, but with plenty of variety, taking in the picturesque wooded valley of the Usk and an outlying Brecon peak. *Canal towpath, quiet road, mountain ridge, farmland; one climb; mud.*

Start near Llangynidr, 9 miles (14.5 km) NW of Abergavenny. From Abergavenny, follow the A40 to Crickhowell, then turn on to the B4558 and follow to Coach and Horses Inn, one mile (1.5 km) beyond Llangynidr. Large **car park** at inn.

① Just below the inn, gain access to the canal towpath and follow it for 400 yards (366 m) to a bridge (no. 134). Leave the towpath and follow the road over the bridge towards Tor y Foel. A steady ascent leads up to a point where the road flattens out. Near a house, turn right through the second gate ② to follow a track on the left side of a sunken lane. A well-beaten path (not shown on O.S. map) follows the crest of the ridge to reach the summit of Tor y Foel ③. From here, head down in a northerly direction to meet a road by a cattle-grid ④. At this point, turn right on to a track which leads past a fence to a gate. Go across a sloping field towards a wood. Cross a small stream and bear slightly right to reach a gate at the edge of the wood. Follow path through the wood and across the next field to join a rutted track. Go through a gate, then straight on beside a hedge to another gate. Cross a stream and go through a gate at the corner of the wood ⑤ directly ahead. Bear right,

to cross a stile beside a tree and then go on to join a track which leads down to the canal ⑥. Turn right and follow the canal towpath back to ①.

One of the most beautiful canals in Britain, the Brecon and Abergavenny now lies entirely within a national park. Construction took place between 1797–1812, under the direction of Thomas Dadford, who was also responsible for the Monmouthshire Canal. This canal joined the now-abandoned Monmouthshire at Pontymoile, S of Abergavenny. There are only 6 locks on the full 33-mile (55-km) run of this canal, thanks to a remarkable piece of engineering, which kept the canal level for most of the way, by means of many bends, aqueducts and embankments. Only at Llangynidr was Dadford defeated by the topography, and it is there that 5 of the 6 locks are found.

The 17th-C. mystical poet, Henry Vaughan, described the waters of the Usk as "fresh as the air and clear as glass". He was born and he died in this part of Wales and celebrated the Usk valley in many of his poems. His nickname, The Silurist, refers to the tribe of Silures, who inhabited South Wales and the Welsh borders.

On Buckland Hill, Colonal Gwynne Holford, a veteran of Waterloo, had trees planted to represent squares of infantry and troops of cavalry at the battle.

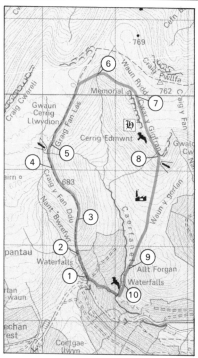

as the path becomes steep, leading up to the ridge of Craig y Fan Ddu. ③ Walk on along the ridge, keeping the valley on your left to reach some rocks on the right ④. From here, strike NE to reach the escarpment of Craig Fan Las and follow a good path around the edge. ⑤ Cross the rocky gully of the Caerfanel. Skirt around the head of the valley ⑥ and, on reaching the edge of Cwar y Gigfran cliffs ⑦, continue to the southern end of the escarpment to reach the 'Balcony' (a depression behind a large block) ⑧. Descend the ridge towards Blaen-y-glyn and follow an old quarry track going down into the valley ⑨. Keep to the left bank of the stream (Caerfanell) and then follow the path across the stream, beside a large block in mid-stream, to reach a series of waterfalls. Just below the first waterfall, cross the stream on a footbridge and then follow the track to the left, over a stile, and past ruins of farmhouse ⑩. Where a stream tumbles down on the right, follow a track marked with red rings on posts and trees, up a narrow valley, passing several waterfalls to steeply ascend to ①.

⑴ NW to Pen y Fan, the highest point of the Brecon Beacon range.

⑲ A Wellington bomber crashed here in 1941. Remains of the aircraft can still be seen.

⚲ Cwar y Gigfran means Raven's Quarry, and these huge black birds are still frequently seen in this area. They can be distinguished from crows by their diamond-shaped tails, and deep, croaking voices.

⑴ 'The Balcony' – a useful place to stop for a picnic – with views across to the Black Mountains and the Sugar Loaf.

⚒ This track was built for the removal of stone from Cwar y Gigfran. The stone was dragged down the hillside on sledges drawn by ponies and used for building houses in Merthyr Tydfil.

⚲ In the vicinity of the Blaen-y-glyn falls, look out for pied flycatchers, tree pipits and whinchats. You may also hear wood warblers, with their distinctive quavering song.

Blaen-y-glyn Circuit
5 miles (8 km) Sheets 160 and 161
056176

Moderate An introduction to the eastern Brecon Beacons, passing rocky escarpments and impressive waterfalls. *Ridge, moorland, escarpment, ridge, valley; one steep ascent; mud.*

Start Blaen-y-glyn, 7 miles (11 km) S of Brecon. From Brecon take the A40 going E for a few miles, then turn on to the B4558. In Talybont-on-Usk, turn right, and continue, past the reservoir, to reach Abercynafon. About 2 miles (3 km) further on, at a sharp bend in the road, is Blaen-y-glyn **Car Park**, on the right.

① Near the entrance to the car park, follow a track in a northerly direction on the left-hand side of a stream, crossing the stream at the top of a waterfall. ② Walk on past the remains of a stone wall, and continue

MID WALES

Most define Mid Wales as the country between Cardigan Bay and the rolling hills overlooking the English border, but excluding most of the old county of Pembrokeshire. The northern boundary is the southern edge of the Snowdonia National Park; and the southern border, the barriers formed by the Brecon Beacons and Black Mountains. It is a landscape relatively empty of humans, the spoiling touches of tourism few and far between.

The long river valleys that run down to Cardigan Bay are some of the most beautiful in Europe, with flowing Welsh names like the Rheidol. Among the most spectacular sights of the area are the multiple waterfalls at Devil's Bridge, where the Rheidol crashes through gorges hung with gnarled, moss-covered oaks. Its damp, secluded pathways are best explored on a peaceful spring or autumn morning, or an autumn afternoon.

One of the most distinctive features is the group of steep, wooded valleys near Rhayader, which were flooded to make reservoirs. Further north, Lake Vyrnwy, another man-made lake, makes an energetic day's circuit.

To the east is the high ground overlooking England. Here are distant views, rolling hills, and wild ponies.

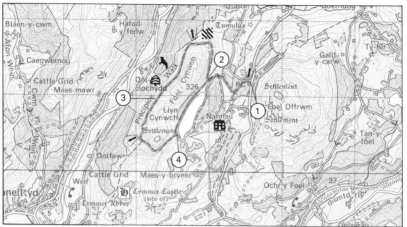

Precipice Walk
3½ miles (5.5 km) Sheet 124 746212

Easy A characteristic variety of Mid Wales scenery, plus panoramic views. *Woods, open hills, lakeside; mud. The going can be rough: stout boots or shoes are recommended.*

Start 3 miles (5 km) NE of Dolgellau. From Dolgellau, take the A470. After 1½ miles (2.5 km), just before the new river bridge, turn right on to lane signposted Llanfachreth and Abergeirw. Follow lane for one mile (1.5 km), then go left, passing Nannau Hall. Shortly afterwards a large Snowdonia National Park **Car Park** is reached, at junction with a lane to the left, signposted Hermon.

① From car park, walk down lane signposted Hermon. After 100 yards (91 m), turn left on to marked track through woods. ② With lake visible up on left, walk across grassy meadow and up hill over stile. Follow clearly marked path around hillside. ③ At precipice, take some care. Although path is safe, there are deep gulleys and the hillside is steep. Follow path as it curls round hill (Foel Cynwch), eventually reaching lake ④. Go along left-hand edge of lake through woods to ②. Retrace steps to ①.

From the car park the Arennigs can be seen to the N.

As the path curls around Foel Cynwch, the deep valley of the Mawddach comes into view, with pine forests in the foreground and range upon range of hills running N to the Rhinogs. This deep valley was scoured out by glaciers which finally disappeared about 10,000 years ago.

The extensive oak, ash and beech woods of the Mawddach valley are the home of buzzards, pied flycatchers, redstarts, and wood warblers. The Vaughan family, owners of the Nannau Estate, laid it out as a 'rustic paradise', planting many trees, especially oak, in the 19th C.

At the far end of the precipice, the Mawddach estuary can be seen winding down to the sea, and beyond, the great mass of Cadair Idris.

Nannau Hall, a fine example of local 18th-C. architecture, stands near the site of Cymmer Abbey. A small Cistercian monastery, built in the early 13th C., it had far more influence in the area than its size would suggest. After being granted a charter in 1209, it held estates stretching from Barmouth to Dolgellau and further inland. At the Reformation it was the only abbey in Meirionnydd and had control over all local mammals, birds, fish, woods and minerals.

Mid Wales
MID POWYS

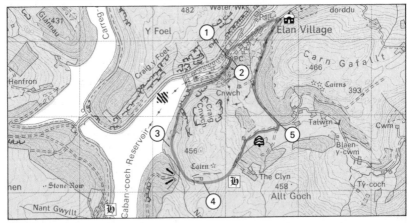

Elan Valley
4 miles (6.5 km) Sheet 147 930648

Moderate The Elan Valley's vast man-made reservoir system is deservedly one of Mid Wales's beauty spots. Flooded valleys contrast with high hills. *Lakeside, moorland, country lane; some short stretches with mud after rain.*

Start at the B4518, going SE from Rhayader. 5 miles (8 km) out of the town, stop at the Elan Valley Visitor Centre with picnic tables and an ample **car park**.

➊ From the car park, turn right and cross the suspension bridge. Go through the gate straight ahead and follow track to the right, through the wood. ➋ The track zigzags; at the top, follow the right-hand track, which leads to the edge of Caban Coch Reservoir. Follow the clearly visible path along the side of the lake, over slaty rocks. On reaching inlet ➌, follow the path as it veers inland. Continue up the edge of the wood, climbing steeply. At the end of perimeter fence, where it turns right, keep straight on up the hill towards the brow, where a large clump of pines comes into view. Follow down the right-hand side of the clump and turn left at the far end, to the cart track. Pass ruined farmhouse ➍ and carry on until reaching a gate. Go through and follow the lane downhill as it winds across a marshy valley. Where it joins another lane ➎, turn left and walk back through village to ➊.

The Elan Valley is one of many flooded Welsh valleys whose water supplies the cities of England – a point on which many Welsh people feel strongly. The series of lakes, created by a total of five dams, dates from 1904; Elan water goes to Birmingham.

The view takes in the whole, long, thin Valley of the Elan; behind the conspicuous dam seen NW is Garreg Ddu Reservoir.

On the far shore of Caban Coch (Red Cabin) Reservoir, just about due W, it is possible, when the water is low, to make out the garden walls of a house, Nant Gwyllt, which was the inspiration for Francis Brett Young's novel *The House Under the Water*.

Out on the hilltops it is easy to understand why the area once had a reputation for brigands and lawlessness; indeed in medieval times, disbanded soldiers congregated here.

The lane displays the now increasingly rare art of hedge laying. As a county, Powys has encouraged the art and the result, a neat, dense, healthy hedge, is very pleasing compared with mangled specimens produced by the almost universal mechanical flail.

It is worth pausing in Elan village, built in the early years of the century.

Mid Wales
GWYNEDD

Cadair Idris
5¾ miles (9 km) Sheet 124 697152

Strenuous Breathtaking views from this famous summit have drawn visitors to the area for centuries. Open hillside, mountain top, scree, wooded hillside; mud. Strong footwear essential. Attempt in clear weather only, not in winter. Path indistinct between ❷ and ❸. Descend scree slope at ❺ slowly, to avoid accidents.

Start Cadair Idris, 3 miles (5 km) SW of Dolgellau. Take the A493 out from Dolgellau, marked to Tywyn. Just past a large chapel, and still in the town, take a smaller road to the left, marked to Cadair Idris and Gwernan Lake Hotel. Follow this road for 2 miles (3 km), passing the Gwernan Lake Hotel on right. Large **car park** in woods ½ mile (0.8 km) further on.

❶ Turn right out of car park over bridge, and follow public footpath sign by telephone box. Climb steeply, in places going up slabs of rock-like steps. Go through gate in wall, then follow path in long zigzag up hillside. After steep climb on long ridge, meeting of paths ❷ is seen. Turn left and follow path upwards. Go past sheer cliffs ❸ to highest point of Cadair Idris, a short way beyond. ❹ On the way down, follow line of small stone cairns which run left across flat, grassy top of mountain. This is start of the Fox's Path. Cross scree slope ❺, taking great care as slope is steep and rocks are very uneven. At bottom of scree slope, continue downwards, bearing right, past end of small lake ❻. Cross river ❼, then walk along bank to gap in wall. Follow clear path down through more wooded country, reaching road by Gwernan Lake Hotel ❽. Turn left along road to ❾.

🔱 A view of the Mawddach Estuary and Barmouth, with Barmouth Railway Bridge.

⛰ Cadair Idris forms part of the rock mass known as the Larlech Dome. Much of this has been eroded away over millions of years, but in areas of the harder volcanic rock, some peaks remain, including Cadair Idris and Snowdon.

🔱 On a clear day, Snaefell on the Isle of Man, 110 miles (177 km) distant, can be seen from Penygadair. The Irish coast is also easily visible.

🏚 The small shelter at Penygadair was built by the mountain guide, Richard Pugh, in the 1830s. Cadair Idris was a popular tourist attraction at the time, and Pugh provided the visitors with all convenient refreshments in the hut while they sheltered from the elements. In 1856, Tennyson came here, and before him, Pennant, Defoe and Camden.

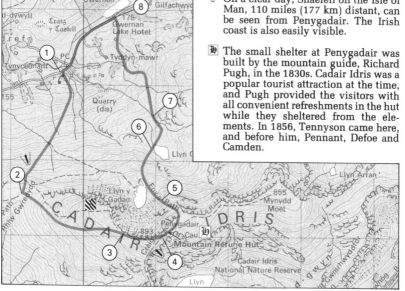

Mid Wales
MID POWYS

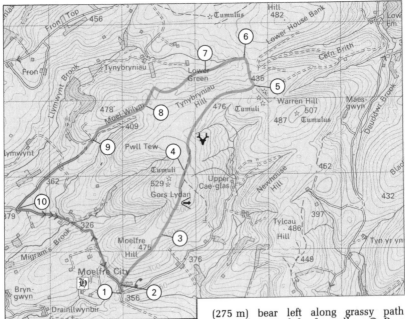

Moel Wilym

7¼ miles (11.5 km) Sheet 136
119754

Moderate Smooth, rolling hills, grazed by sheep and semi-wild ponies. *Open common, moorland, hills, valleys; one climb; mud.*

Start Moelfre City, 15 miles (24 km) S of Newtown, Powys. **Parking** on the common land by telephone box.

① Walk past telephone box, cross cattle-grid and walk up farm entrance road to right ②. After 100 yards (91 m), at farm entrance, go through gate on left on to common land. Follow line of wall/fence along poorly defined track through bracken. When fence turns sharp right ③, continue along leftmost grassy track close to summit of Gorslydan. ④ The track becomes a clearly defined cart track leading past the head of a shallow valley. Continue for just over a mile (2 km) to a grove of pine trees. ⑤ Turn left down track, downhill. ⑥ after about 300 yards (275 m) bear left along grassy path descending on left of a valley. ⑦ Pass along upper side of fenced-in field. Take the track through bracken to a small gorge. Cross stream and climb side of gorge. Follow path left, along line of stream, then bear right on wide curve through heather and bilberry. Turn left on to well-used cart track, ⑧, and carry on a short way to meeting of several tracks. Take right-hand one over hill until fence is reached. Follow fence downhill on left-hand curve. In valley bottom, go through gate and along farm track. At junction turn left ⑨ and follow lane to road ⑩. Turn left to Moelfre City and ①.

🏠 Moelfre City is an old name appearing on many local maps from the 17th C. onwards.

⚑ Beacon Hill and the hills around Ludlow can be seen in the distance.

🦌 Herds of Welsh ponies graze on the unspoilt common land known as the Cefn (translated literally as 'back' and referring to the shape of the rounded hills).

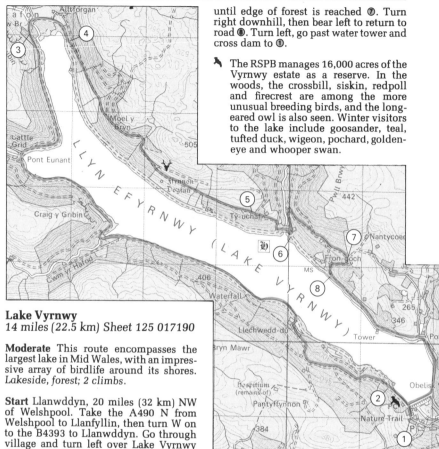

until edge of forest is reached ⑦. Turn right downhill, then bear left to return to road ⑧. Turn left, go past water tower and cross dam to ①.

🐦 The RSPB manages 16,000 acres of the Vyrnwy estate as a reserve. In the woods, the crossbill, siskin, redpoll and firecrest are among the more unusual breeding birds, and the long-eared owl is also seen. Winter visitors to the lake include goosander, teal, tufted duck, wigeon, pochard, golden-eye and whooper swan.

Lake Vyrnwy
14 miles (22.5 km) Sheet 125 017190

Moderate This route encompasses the largest lake in Mid Wales, with an impressive array of birdlife around its shores. *Lakeside, forest; 2 climbs.*

Start Llanwddyn, 20 miles (32 km) NW of Welshpool. Take the A490 N from Welshpool to Llanfyllin, then turn W on to the B4393 to Llanwddyn. Go through village and turn left over Lake Vyrnwy dam. **Car park** on the S side of dam.

① From car park take road straight along lakeside. Do not cross dam. On right-hand bend, take forest track to left uphill ②. Keeping to right, follow track down to road. Turn left and keep on road past Pont Eunant and go over Rhiwargor Bridge ③. Go past head of lake, then take forest road leading uphill to left ④. Keep on forest track parallel to lake. After 2½ miles (4 km), take right fork downhill past Ty-uchaf ⑤. Rejoin road and cross bridge over Afon Cedig. Take track to left past old barn ⑥ up hill. Turn right along forestry road, and keep on upper track

🦊 As well as hares and foxes, the red squirrel is known to inhabit this stretch of the plantation – one of its last strongholds in the British Isles.

🏚 Lake Vyrnwy, a flooded valley, supplies water to Liverpool along a 68-mile (109-km) aqueduct. The dam became operational in 1888. Near where the River Cedig flows into the lake lies the drowned village of Llanwddyn: when the level is low, outlines of the houses can be seen. The reservoir was used as the setting for the film *The Dambusters*.

127

Mid Wales
NORTH POWYS

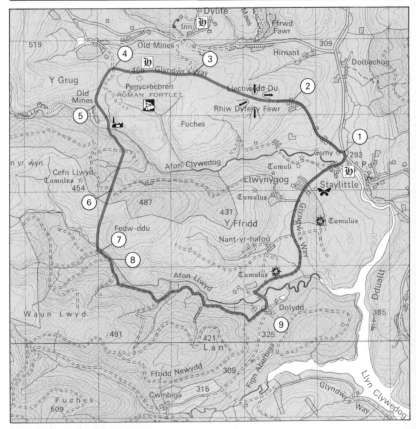

Staylittle and Gallows Hill
7¾ miles (12 km) Sheet 135 884925

Strenuous Fine country in the Clywedog Valley and Hafren Forest area, with some panoramic views of rolling hills as far as the eye can see. This is, however, a generally exposed upland route, with boggy ground in parts: recommended for the drier months only. *Upland hills, river valley, forest; pay particular attention to directions between ⑤ and ⑦; be prepared for wet ground at any season; 2 (theoretically dry) river crossings; 2 climbs.*

Start 12 miles (19 km) SE of Machynlleth: take the A489 from Machynlleth in the direction of Newtown, turning right on

to the B4518 at Llanbrynmair, continuing to Staylittle (alternative approach from Machynlleth is on the mountain road via Dylife). Before entering Staylittle from the north, **park** on the right where the old road has been blocked off (cul-de-sac sign at entry to side road).

① From parking, walk up the single-track drive, past small graveyard. The route passes close to Rhiw-defeitty-fawr Farm ② where there are a couple of gates. Pass through them and follow the track climbing out on to the top of the hills. At the point where the main track appears to bear left alongside a wire fence, go straight ahead through gate – following the older track. Continue, passing

Mid Wales
NORTH POWYS

through several farm gates – the course of the track is clear. The hamlet of Dylife eventually comes into view across the valley; keep left, ignoring a cart track ❸ which runs off to the right downhill towards Dylife. Further on, the track passes the highest point of the hills, Penycrocbren – in English, Gallows Hill. At the junction of the track with a modern one ❹, turn left, uphill. Follow this road as it curls around the hill and, where it bears left past some disused mine workings, keep straight on along a less well-defined track ❺. This reaches some more mine workings on the edge of a deep valley. Locate the path running down the side of a fairly steep gulley and some spoil heaps, and follow it, working down to the river, which is to the left. (Old mine buildings and plant are just above the river.) Cross the river using the stepping stones on one of the shallower stretches. Follow the wire fence running along the edge of the forest until, after 100–150 yards (92–137 m), a track is seen running diagonally up the hillside through the forest. Climb the low fence and follow this public right-of-way up through the trees. Continue, crossing a forestry road, and then go straight along the firebreak gap in the trees. Cross a second forestry road and follow the track through the trees to a gate ❻, which leads on to moorland. Strike straight out across the moor, following an indistinct track which leads to the side of a valley running down towards Hafren Forest. Cross the stream running down the valley where it joins the Afon Llwyd, the mountain river running parallel with the edge of the forest. Continue along the river to where some old sheep-pens can be seen on the far bank and cross the river at this point: there are several places where the banks are close enough to jump across, or there is a ford ❼ which can be used when the river is low. Close by, a Forestry Commission road can be seen coming down to the sheep-pens; follow it into the forest and soon turn left. At the next T-junction ❽, turn left. At the next T-junction take the left-hand road and continue through the forest to the forest offices close to the public road. Turn left here, ❾ cross the common and continue to Staylittle and ❿: it is a single-track road, with plenty of verge on which to walk in case of oncoming traffic.

🏠 The name Staylittle is said to originate from the skill of the village blacksmiths: they worked so fast that their forge was known as the Stay-a-Little Forge. This was a lead-mining community which had its heyday 150-300 years ago.

👁 Panoramic 360° views of this remote country, signs of human habitation confined to the few isolated farmhouses.

🏠 Dylife (Place of Floods) was the old district name hereabouts. It was a lead-mining community in its heyday during the 17th to 19th C.

🏛 The grassy ramparts right beside the track, about 25 yards (22.5 m) square, are all that remain of the Roman Fort: it would have dominated the area, and its function was probably to protect the lead mines.

🏠 In 1938 a gibbet cage was found close to this point; inside was a skull. It is likely to have been the remains of Sien-y-Gof (John the Smith) who worked in the local lead mine around 1700 and murdered his wife and children by throwing them down a mine shaft. A map of 1738 marks the gallows on Penycrocbren, so the likes of Smith were probably still being hung in this lonely spot in the mid-18th C., perhaps later.

⚒ Industrial archaeologists think that the peak of activity in the lead mines here was probably in late Stuart and early Georgian times: in those days, the area looked very different, for the coniferous forest is a recent development, planted in the 1920s. The river provided power for the mining machinery, and for settling out the crushed lead ore from base rock.

❋ The area is rich in prehistoric tumuli; it is possible that Bronze Age people mined here. Look for further tumuli from the road nearer Staylittle.

🦋 In late summer the large green-and-gold caterpillars of the emperor moth can be found by the side of the road leading across the common.

Mid Wales
NORTH DYFED

Devil's Bridge
13¾ miles (22 km) Sheet 135
768742.

Strenuous Centred on a noted beauty spot, this route makes a fine introduction to the great variety of scenery in this part of Mid Wales. It is a fascinating walk at any season, different sections all have an individual character which alters with the time of year. *Wooded valley, hill pasture, river valley, oak woods; soft patches at all times, and one ford to cross – water can rise to 12 inches (30 cm) after heavy rain – take appropriate footwear; three climbs, one very steep.*

Start Devil's Bridge, 12 miles (19 km) E of Aberystwith on the A4120. From the A4120 turn on to the B4574 and locate large **car park** in 150 yards (137 m) up the hill.

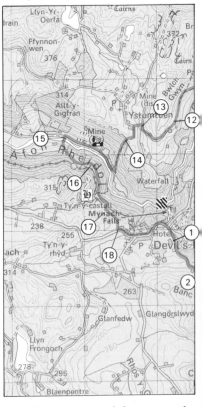

① From the car park turn right uphill along the B4574; after about ½ mile (0.8 km), just past a small cottage on the right, take the track to the left, through the gate ②. Follow it down past a couple of cottages and over a footbridge. At the fork ③, take the lower track and cross bridge into forest. Continue along this forestry road until a farm is reached; immediately after the second bridge, take the lower, right-hand road ④. Continue on this until reaching a meeting of roads; turn left across the bridge and walk uphill ⑤, bearing right. At the next junction, turn left. (For a shortened walk, turning right here brings you back to the outward route close to the cottages.) Take the upper, right-hand road at the next fork, and follow it uphill past cottage in woods. Soon after the cottage, turn left and follow road through long, right bend, downhill ⑥. Continue on road, heading towards Blaen Myherin farmhouse, seen straight ahead. The road curls left crossing a ford which in normal conditions is shallow; a track to Blaen Myherin branches off here ⑦. Continue on the road as it runs back down the other side of the valley and just before reaching the old farmhouse of Nantsyddion, take the road ⑧ to the right, uphill. Keep straight on, bearing right ⑨ at the next fork. At the brow of the hill, continue with road as it leaves the forest and runs downhill across open country. Reaching Tymawr Farm, carry on

through farm gates and down on to the A4120. Turn left ⑩ and in about 200 yards (182 m), locate church and car park to right, together with signs pointing way to Parson's Bridge. Follow this, negotiating steep descent down rough steps to ⑪ footbridge in gorge. Cross, bear half-left up the small hill, and follow the path alongside the grove of trees. Go through gate into meadow and follow the path around the edge of the meadow until reaching grassy track (blue waymarks help with route here). Turn left and walk along the track to another meadow; across this meadow go through the gate in the far upper corner to the cottage. Go along the old access track to cottage, passing through gate. Soon reach an inhabited farmhouse and ⑫ metalled lane, which curls right; pass through the gate across

Mid Wales
NORTH DYFED

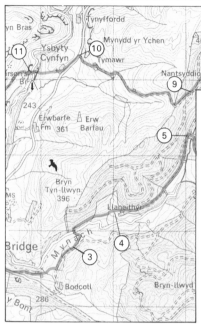

gate; go through and follow route across track, passing through farm gate on far side. Follow path through field for a short distance, and ⑰ enter the woods through a small gate. Continue with path up small hill and then through woods until reaching open field. Follow the edge of the trees, then cross the field making for the gate on to the A4120, close to a bungalow ⑱. Turn left and walk back to Devil's Bridge.

≋ The wooded gorge where the rivers Rheidol and Mynach meet is a great draw: there is a bridge from which to view the rushing waters (fine falls) and various opportunities for refreshment. This is also the terminus of the Vale of Rheidol narrow-gauge steam railway.

🏠 Blaen Myherin is typical of the many remote dwellings in the area; the setting of meadow surrounded by wooded hills is distinctly Alpine.

▨ From Parson's Bridge, exciting views of the torrent below.

⛏ The lead mines in the vicinity were worked into the last century, indeed the railway was originally built to carry their ore to Aberystwyth.

▨ With a gauge of 1ft 11½ ins (0.6 m) the Vale of Rheidol Railway is the only narrow-track system operated by British Rail; the 12-mile, one-hour trip from Aberystwyth to Devil's Bridge is indeed spectacular.

↰ There are sightings of red kites in this area. One of Britain's rarest breeding birds, with only 20–30 pairs nesting in the whole country, it has chosen Mid Wales as a last refuge. Distinguishing marks are the forked tail and white patches on the undersides of angular wings.

the lane and look out for stile ⑬ crossing wire fence on left. Cross stile, and the footbridge soon after; walk short distance across field up to farm on hill; you come out with the path on to a cart track close to one of the farm's stone barns. Here turn *left*, ignoring sign for shop and youth hostel to the right. Follow the cart track for about 150 yards, turn right, and shortly after, enter forest ⑭. At the bottom of the very steep track bear right, past cottages and disused mine workings. Soon reach metalled road and continue along it; shortly after, locate footbridge on left over river ⑮. Cross and take the path up the hill to the left, alongside hedge. Go through gate at top corner and follow the path which climbs steeply uphill through woods. Eventually reach Rhiwfron Halt, on the Vale of Rheidol Railway – which is simply an open space by the track. Climb under the wire fence (where it has been wired up) and walk left beside the track for about 150 yards; climb the stile ⑯ back into the Goed Rheidol woods and follow the path parallel to the railway. This leads to a swing

NORTH WALES

The boundaries of this region – a nation in miniature – practically draw themselves. The southern fringe is a line drawn eastwards from the Dovey estuary. The eastern boundary is the border with England. The northern and western boundaries, not forgetting Anglesey, are the sea.

This selection of routes looks beyond the most obvious feature of North Wales – the famous mountain ranges of the west and north-west – and concentrates on less typical, but equally rewarding localities. For hill-walking there are three main alternatives, two in the east of the region, well away from the crowds of Snowdon. Of these, one is in the Clywdian Range, running west and north of Ruthin. It can be very lonely here indeed; but your solitude could be relieved by a sighting of the uncommon merlin, smallest of the European falcons. This walk also introduces a section of The Offa's Dyke Path which actually follows the raised earthwork – for not all of this unofficial long-distance route does so. Across the Vale of Clwyd from the Clywidian hills is a route in Clocaenog Forest. You won't find grandeur – but there is a fair chance of having it to yourself.

There are two walks on Anglesey, and this is a deliberate emphasis: it really is worth taking the trouble to discover the island's timelessness and privacy. Another hill walk is sited, again away from the mainstream, in the hills behind Llanfairfechan, with sensational views over the Menai Strait towards Anglesey. For a gentle, pastoral day out, try the Elwy Valley route, based on Llanfair Talhaiarn.

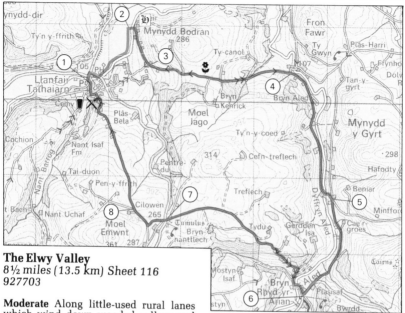

The Elwy Valley
*8½ miles (13.5 km) Sheet 116
927703*

Moderate Along little-used rural lanes which wind down wooded valleys and across rushing streams: tranquillity and timelessness. *Riverside, hedge-lined lanes; 4 climbs; mud between ① and ②.*

Start Llanfair Talhaiarn, 5 miles (8 km) S of Abergele. From Abergele (between Rhyl and Colwyn Bay) take the A548 S for 5 miles to Llanfair Talhaiarn. Buses to Llanfair Talhaiarn from Abergele and Llanrwst. **Car park** at entrance to village.

① From car park, cross main road and follow public footpath beside River Elwy. ② At footbridge, cross the river and climb short, steep hill to lane. Turn right, and at junction ③ bear left up hill. ④ After 1½ miles (2.5 km), bear right at road junction. (A short detour is worth making to the left to visit the old bridge at Pont yr Aled.) Follow narrow lane beside River Aled, to the new bridge ⑤. Turn right just after crossing the bridge on to a small road. Follow this to where it joins the B5382. ⑥ Keep on along this road for several hundred yards, then turn right on to lane. Just over an old iron bridge, turn right up a steep hill. Follow lane to road junction. ⑦ Cross the A544 and bear right uphill.

At brow and junction of lanes, turn right. Follow lane to next junction ⑧ and bear right again. Follow the lane back to ①.

🍺 The Swan and the Black Lion both ✕ serve food; good bakery in village.

🏛 From 1874–7 the Catholic priest and poet, Gerard Manley Hopkins, lived at nearby St. Asaph and spent many hours by this river, fishing and writing his verses. His sonnet, 'In the Valley of the Elwy' lyrically describes the local countryside;

*Lovely the woods, waters, meadows,
    coombes, vales,
All the air things wear that build this
    world of Wales . . .*

🌸 The hedges here are all about 200–300 years old. The age of the hedge can be gauged by taking a 30-yard (27-m) stretch and counting the number of well-established woody species such as hazel, holly and elder. Each woody species is reckoned to represent a hundred years of growth.

133

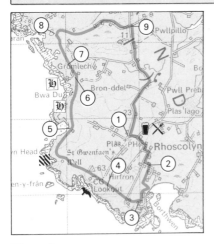

Rhoscolyn
4½ miles (7 km) Sheet 114 268756

Easy The spectacular sea cliffs of Holy Island are as much part of the scenery as its sandy beaches, although not as much visited. *Fields, cliff tops, marsh, meadow; waterproof footwear essential.*

Start Rhoscolyn, 5 miles (8 km) S of Holyhead. Approaching Holyhead on the A5, turn left in Valley (signposted Trearddur Bay). At Four Mile Bridge, turn left down the lane marked Rhoscolyn. Locate the church about 2 miles (3 km) down this lane on a hill to the right. Limited bus service from Holyhead and Trearddur Bay to Rhoscolyn. **Parking** by Rhoscolyn church (except on Sunday mornings).

① From church, walk down lane to the right, and after 100 yards (91 m), turn right down lane past White Eagle Inn. Follow road as it zigzags, and after about ¼ mile (0.5 km) take path through stone wall to right ②. Cross field to stile, then cross next field to Public Footpath sign in middle of field. Turn left here and follow path through 2 gates in walls. ③ At second gate, bear half-right across meadow, past old well and grave. Cross concrete slab bridge over stream, and follow signposted footpath. At top of rough ground, turn right along path between low walls ④. Climb on to open grassland and bear slightly left uphill to

set of concrete steps bridging stone wall. Walk behind the coast-guard look-out, and carry on along cliff top. ⑤ Take care at point where deep chasm is seen on seaward side, as the dip on the inland side of the path is very deep and sheer. The path is over a bridge of rock. ⑥ Climb wooden stile and bear half-right across low-lying ground. Follow path up hill through gate and between low walls. At driveway to house on cliffs, pass through gateway and turn immediately left along wall. Follow this wall for a short distance, then, where it turns seawards ⑦, cut across grassland in direct line with chimney of smelter at Holyhead, 4 miles (6.5 km) away. ⑧ After several hundred yards, stone steps are reached. Go up steps, then walk past rocky inlet and follow stone wall on right-hand side. Take cart track through old stone gateposts. Go past reedy pond and turn right, following marker arrow on post. Walk away from sea, passing occasional marker arrows. Path joins stony track past a cottage. ⑨ At stile on to lane, turn right and walk one mile (1.5 km) to ①.

⍾ The White Eagle Inn serves bar meals ✕ and has a fine view of Snowdon.

🐦 Choughs – black, glossy, crow-like birds with red beaks and legs – are a familiar sight on this stretch of coast. This is an uncommon bird, surviving in only a very few places in Britain.

〰 Much of the rock is Pre-Cambrian – over 600 million years old.

🅱 At Bwa Du (Black Arch) there is a memorial to Tyger, a dog. On 17 September 1819, a ketch sank ¾ mile (1 km) offshore in thick fog. The crew of 4 swam ashore, guided by Tyger, who led the way to land through the fog, barking as he swam to guide the men. He dragged the cabin boy on to the rocks; plunged in again to help the captain ashore; then collapsed and died of exhaustion.

🅱 Rhoscolyn Bay once had a small but thriving oyster fishery. The decline in the industry began about 150 years ago and still continues, despite the dedication of the Ministry of Agriculture scientists.

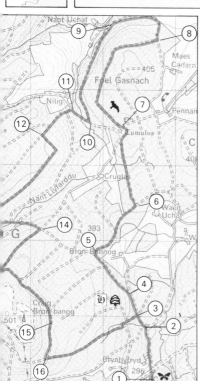

running under road. Go straight across at next crossroads. ❸ At the following junction ❹ carry straight on uphill across recently felled area. (Bron Bannog farm can be seen on right.) At next junction ❺, go straight on again, then follow track as it curves to the left. Bear right at next Y-junction, just over a small stream. A wide fire break is passed with a telegraph line running up it, then another area of clear felling is reached, with Waen Uchaf farm visible on the right ❻. Turn left here. After a long straight stretch, bear right at track junction, then follow track round to the left, soon reaching another junction with a single-track road, close to an ancient tumulus (not easily visible). ❼ Take the forestry track diagonally opposite, across the road. Follow this track around the hill, bearing left at a junction ❽, to come out on the side of a steep valley. At bottom of hill, with Nant Uchaf far on the right, take left-hand fork ❾ and follow the track along the valley to road ❿. Turn right along road, going over bridge; 100 yards (91 m) beyond picnic site, turn left on to forestry road ⓫. Continue for 500 yards (457 m), then take forestry track to the left ⓬. Turn left at next T-junction ⓭. Go straight on at the next 2 junctions, but at third ⓮ turn right. After ½ mile (0.8 km), turn left and follow track as it passes by the open ground of Craig Bron-banog Rock, on high hillside, and bears round to the right ⓯. At next T-junction ⓰, turn sharp left and carry straight on until original track is reached ❸. Turn right and return to ❶.

❤ The lakeside picnic site at ❶ is a good area for seeing dragonflies, butterflies and newts.

🏛 Clocaenog Forest was part of the huge expansion in afforestation after the First World War, which, in the words of Lloyd George, "we came closer to losing for lack of timber than for lack of food".

🪶 The forest is a stronghold for lesser redpolls and crossbills; once only seen on passage, they now breed here quite often.

🐾 Polecats are quite common here. On a brief sighting, they look like short-legged black cats dashing for cover.

Clocaenog Forest
10½ miles (17 km) Sheet 116
037512

Moderate Clocaenog Forest is part of the Mynydd Hiraethog, or Mountain of Longing, an area of upland which was heavily settled in prehistoric times and still has an air of mystery, remoteness and space. *Coniferous forest, open country, hills; 2 climbs. It is important to follow the directions carefully, as Forestry Commission roads can be confusing.*

Start Pont Petryal, 6 miles (9.5 km) SW of Ruthin. Forestry commission **car park** at Bod Petryal, just off the B5105.

❶ Cross the B5105 and take lane marked Cyffyliog. Take the second forestry road to the left ❷ just beyond small stream

Jubilee Tower and Offa's Dyke Path
7¾ miles (12 km) Sheet 116 162605

Strenuous Taking in some of the finest country in Clwyd, and offering first-rate hill walking, with superb views of the whole of northern Wales, from the coast to Snowdonia and southwards. *Forest, high moorland, gorse common; 3 climbs; mud. Sections ③ and ⑦ need to be carefully followed. Parts of the route are very exposed and adequate clothing and boots must be worn in winter; compass needed.*

Start 4 miles (6.5 km) NE of Ruthin. From Ruthin follow the A 494 (Mold) road for 4 miles, passing through the village of Llanbedr-Dyffryn-Clwyd. Just outside the E side of the village is a lane marked Lon Cae Glas. Drive 1½ miles (2.5 km) up this steep lane, to brow of hill. The Ruthin–Mold bus stops at Lanbedr-Dyffryn-Clwyd. Large **car park** at Bwlch Penbarra, on hilltop.

① Cross cattle-grid from car park and go on to Forestry Commission road. At bottom of valley take track to right, then bear left. ② Follow forestry road around long right-hand bend to where a more overgrown track goes uphill to the left ③. Follow this and continue to Jubilee Tower ④. From the tower take Offa's Dyke path ⑤ in a NW direction across the moors. Pass a small lake on the right (Pwll-y-rhôs) and after about one mile (1.5 km), a crossing of tracks is reached ⑥. Go left, downhill. (At bottom of hill, a smallholding, Fron-haul, is seen on right.) Directly opposite 4-barred gate (bearing signs Private and Fron-haul) ⑦, turn left straight up hillside. At brow of hill, bear half-right across small area of gorse, following sheep tracks. The route gradually comes down to a stone wall marking the boundary of cultivated land from common, and a track. Follow contour of hillside for ½ mile (0.8 km). ⑧ Follow the path which runs along wall, and later crosses streams and small valleys. After one mile, a building (marked 'Teiran' on map) is seen on right. Just beyond, there is an old cart track bearing left, between grassy walls ⑨. Follow this back to ①.

🌱 Fine views from the car park, E towards Cheshire and W to the vale of Clwyd. Across the valley the patch-work of different conifers used by the Forestry Commission can be very clearly seen. Larches, brown and leafless in winter, but light green in summer, contrast with the darker green of Douglas firs and the bluey-green of spruce. Each species is chosen for particular conditions. Douglas firs grow well on steep, rocky hillsides, and can tolerate shade. The Sitka spruce survives damp conditions and will grow up to altitudes of 1,400 feet (427 m).

🏛 Jubilee Tower was built in 1820 to commemorate the diamond jubilee of George III (1760–1820). The original tower was blown down shortly after being built. The massive base still remains and is used as a viewing platform, with sighting plaques set in the walls. A wild place, well worth the steep climb to reach it.

🏛 Offa's Dyke Path, opened in 1971, runs 168 miles (270 km) from the coast near Prestatyn to the Severn Estuary. About 60 miles (96.5 km) of this route follows the ancient earthwork, known as Offa's Dyke. This earthwork – consisting of a ditch to the W and a ridge up to 20-feet (6-m) high behind it – was built to mark the boundary, agreed in the late 8th C., between the Celtic princes of Wales and Offa, the Saxon king of Mercia. The dyke was built piecemeal, under the aegis of local rulers, and is therefore rather patchy. There was an apparent lack of enthusiasm for the project locally: the dyke should have run to the E of the Clwydian Hills, but this section was never completed.

🦅 On the remote moors, merlins and ravens can be seen. The merlin, now quite rare, was once highly prized as a small hunting falcon for ladies. It is in fact the smallest of the European falcons – but nonetheless a dashing and extremely agile predator.

🦅 At the edge of the common land and on the farmed areas redstarts are often seen.

🏛 The track running back to Bwlch Penbarra is an ancient drover's way.

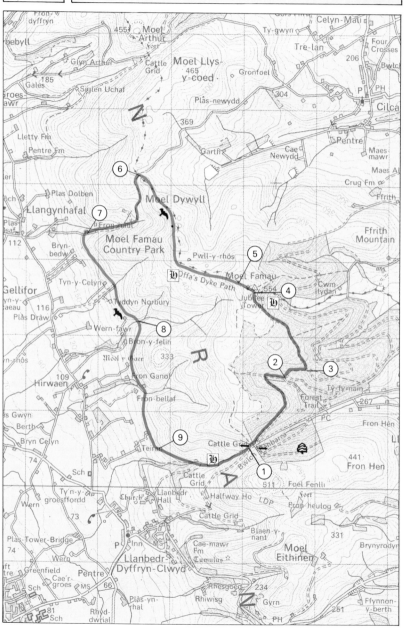

North Wales
ANGLESEY

Red Wharf Bay
8¼ miles (13.5 km) Sheet 114
530810

Easy/moderate This walk samples Anglesey's timeless atmosphere, its varied scenery and superb views. The great sweep of Red Wharf Bay is magnificent, with the headland of Llanddona at the far end and the strange hill, Castell Mawr, at the other. *Sandy seashore, meadows, forest; one climb. Path may be overgrown between ① and ②.*

Start Red Wharf Bay, 7 miles (11 km) N of the Menai Bridge. From the Menai Bridge, follow the A5025 NW towards Amlwch. 2 miles (3 km) N of Pentraeth take the signposted road to Red Wharf Bay. **Car park** on front of Red Wharf Bay.

① From car park, go past Ship Inn and take signposted public footpath. On reaching road ② turn left and follow it down to beach. Keeping above high tide level, turn right along beach and follow shoreline. (It is inadvisable to take a short cut across sands here as there are several quite deep channels to cross: on a rising tide these can be dangerous.) About 2½ miles (4 km) along shore is a bungalow called Ger y Mor ③. Take sandy track inland and follow lane uphill. ④ At stony

At low tide the exposed sands of Red Wharf Bay extend about 10 square miles. In addition to the Ship Inn (see below) the Min-y-Don Hotel is popular for meals.

track called Forest Lane turn right, past a scattering of modern houses. Follow track into the forest, using stile on left of forest gate. At left turn, carry straight on along forestry road. Keep left at junction and continue along road for 1½ miles (2.5 km). At far end ⑤ turn right along the B5109. After ½ mile (0.8 km), just beyond the Georgian mansion Plas Gwyn ⑥, turn right down side road, and right again towards the sea. After 1 mile (1.5 km), a telephone box is reached ⑦. Turn left here along narrow lane and walk back to Red Wharf Bay.

The Ship Inn is 18th C. and recalls the days when Red Wharf Bay was a ship-building village. Brigs of around 100–50 tons (102–3 tonnes) were built here, mostly for the copper-ore traffic from Amlwch.

Castell-mawr, the large limestone block behind the village, is the site of an early British fort (500 B.C.–100 A.D.). Roman coins have also been found there.

North Wales
ANGLESEY

Red Wharf Bay is where the submarine *Thetis* was beached after sinking, with nearly all hands, off the Great Orme, just before the Second World War. The event was in the news for some time, as the submarine had sunk while on sea trials. The crew were trapped and in spite of great efforts over several days, the rescuers could not reach them in time.

The meadows surrounding the bay are unimproved – largely untreated by artificial fertilizers and weedkillers – and boast a wealth of plants and insects.

A coven of witches once lived at Llanddona, and were often said to be seen flying across the bay. They were supposed to have come here from Ireland after being expelled by St. Patrick. A more likely story is that they came from a wrecked Spanish ship. The women were dark, foreign and adept at conjuring tricks, which created suspicion in local minds.

Plas Gwyn (White House) is a Georgian mansion, built in the 18th C. In a nearby field, 3 stones can be seen. These commemorate the 3 leaps – a traditional Celtic contest between 2 lovers for the hand of a girl – in this case the daughter of Einion. Howel won the contest by leaping furthest, and the 3 stones mark his efforts. The loser died of a broken heart.

George Borrow passed by here on his journey through Wales. *Wild Wales*, published in 1862, is an account of his travels, and in it he commented on Traeth-coch: "I thought I had never beheld a more beautiful and tranquil scene".

It is still peaceful here, even 100 years later.

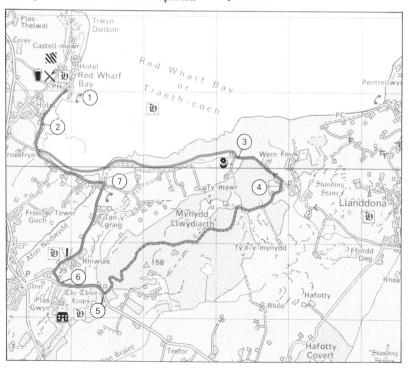

North Wales
GWYNEDD

The Roman Road and Druid's Circle
12½ miles (20 km) Sheet 115 692742

Moderate A step into prehistory: the whole area abounds in standing stones, tumuli, stone circles and cromlechs. It also offers fine, open hill walking with magnificent views of Anglesey and the Menai Straits. *Open hills, meadows, high moors; 2 climbs; mud. If inexperienced in hill walking, avoid in poor visibility. Directions between ⑦ and ⑧, and ⑭ and ⑮ must be followed carefully.*

Start Llanfairfechan, on the north coast, half-way between Llandudno and Bangor. Travelling W along the A55, turn left at traffic lights in Llanfairfechan. Go through village and take road on left marked Mount and Valley Roads. Follow Valley Road until a large green is reached on the right. Buses or trains to Llanfairfechan. **Parking** in bay at far end of green.

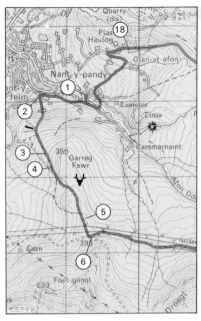

① From green, walk up road and cross bridge. Turn right at junction. About ¼ mile (0.5 km) along lane at fifth gate ②, immediately past bungalow on left, take path to left, with second public footpath sign. Follow track uphill and over several stiles to the top. At wall on brow of hill ③, carry straight on across gorse-covered pasture. When a stone wall is reached ④ follow track diagonally left over brow of hill (don't follow wall). At base of pylon fork left and about **100 yards (91 m)** further on, the Roman road is reached ⑥. Turn left and follow for 4 miles (6.5 km). ⑦ About 200 yards beyond the Youth Hostel at Rhiw, climb small stile on left and follow indistinct track diagonally uphill across meadow. Pass by a stone sheep-fold and follow the stone wall uphill. After a steep climb, a wooden stile over the wall will be seen half-left. Go over wall, then cut across pasture to broken-down wall ⑧. Stepping through the stones, turn right and follow line of wall along indistinct cart track. This eventually leads to a well-used cart track ⑨. Go left and follow it downhill. At the bottom, take the path to the left ⑩, which almost doubles back on the earlier track. Walk across to wall, where a small stream runs down between high stone walls ⑪.

Take track up short hill from here, then, at top of hill, go right, across open ground. After about ¼ mile turn right on to well-made cart track ⑫. Go past large sheepfold then turn left ⑬ uphill. At brow of hill ⑭, go straight along grassy track. The paths here are very indistinct. Walk towards line of pine trees seen clearly across the valley. A fast-flowing stream has to be crossed (Afon Gyrach). There are also stiles over the walls which help to guide the way. At Bryn Derwydd ⑮ take track to left, which shortly afterwards turns sharp right and goes through gate. Go left to reach the druid's circle ⑯ and follow signposted path. Beyond druid's circle, carry on and rejoin wide trackway heading W. ⑰ Pass through farm ⑱ and at T-junction, turn left and follow lane downhill to ①.

\!/ View of Menai Straits, Puffin Island and Anglesey. At low tide, Lavan Sands can be seen stretching almost to Anglesey. In Stuart times, travellers crossed to Anglesey over these sands, taking a short ferry journey across the narrow channel.

North Wales
GWYNEDD

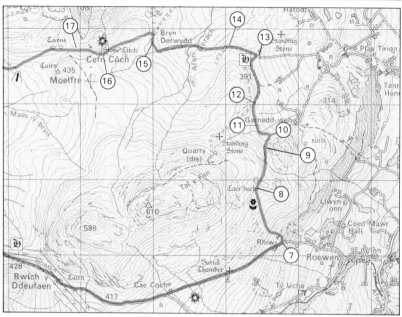

♈ Welsh mountain ponies – a tough breed – graze over these hills in a semi-wild state.

ⓗ The Roman road, built around 100 A.D., has the communicating link between Chester (Deva) and Caernarfon (Segentium). This stretch across the high hills must have been, and still is, particularly bleak. The road passes through Bwlch y Ddeufaen (Pass of Two Stones). The 2 stones can be seen, and there are several cairns in the vicinity – ancient even when the Romans built their road. The large cairn on the right is known, intriguingly, as Barclodiad y Gawres – the Giantess's Apronful.

✹ The road runs past Cae Coch, and, about 300 yards (274 m) further on, behind a wall on the right, there is a large standing stone. On the left is a massive oval stone and, a short way on, is a well-preserved cromlech, consisting of a capstone and upright pillars. Most of these were probably erected between 2000 and 3000 B.C.

About 50 yards (46 m) E of the cromlech is a stone cist – a type of burial chest, which superseded the cromlech.

♣ The meadows passed through after crossing the little stile hold many unusual plants.

ⓗ The multi-celled sheep-pens are a feature of this locality.

✹ The druid's circle, one of many in this area, was probably used for ritual purposes. The remains of several adults and one child have been found buried here, dating, like the stones, from the Bronze Age.

↯✹ Approaching Llanfairfechan, the rounded hill ahead is Dinas, an Iron Age hill-fort built a few hundred years before the Roman occupation. It had a central area, 120 feet (36.5 m) across, containing at least 14 huts and ringed by walls 9 feet (3 m) thick. The remains of a terraced field system can be seen outside the walls.

MIDDLE ENGLAND

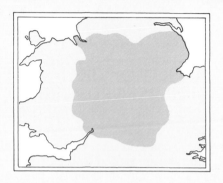

FOREST OF DEAN AND HEREFORDSHIRE

These two areas account for the southern end of the Welsh
Marches, and they are united by the River Wye. In the
Forest of Dean it cuts an often dramatic path, with many a
tourist trap, including the famous double bend at Symond's
Yat, hellish on summer bank holidays. Further north, in the
relatively flat, but by no means level pastoral landscape of
the old county of Herefordshire – which is now called
Hereford and Worcester – the river runs in graceful
meanders towards Hereford. Many are, with justice,
passionately fond of this countryside and an outstanding
walk in the section is situated by the river shortly before it
reaches the county town of Hereford.
The Wye is a major geographical feature of the Forest of
Dean, but not responsible for its unique atmosphere. This is
woodland sited on top of a coal field; it has the fascinating,
often touching marks of long-standing human habitation
and activity. The mining community here was as fiercely
close-knit and independent as any, especially the 'free
miners': those who invoked the ancient privilege of mining
in the Forest. To do so, they had to demonstrate that they
had a free-mining father; that they were over 21; and that
they had been born within the parish of St. Briavels, the
village on the B4228 in the heart of the mining area.
(Note: for the sake of brevity, 'Hereford and Worcester' is
given as 'Herefordshire' in this section.)

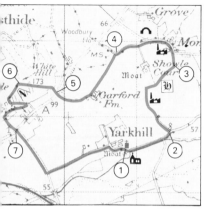

Frome Valley
6 miles (9.5 km) Sheet 149
608426

Easy Includes a variety of landscape, accessible rights of way, panoramic views from Shucknall Hill and a section of the Herefordshire and Gloucestershire Canal. *River bank, hop fields, meadows, lanes, woods; one climb; mud. If field at ④ is cropped, follow right-hand edge to end of farm drive ⑤.*

Start Yarkhill, 7 miles (11 km) NE of Hereford. Take the A438 from Hereford towards Ledbury. At Stoke Edith turn left at crossroads (signposted Yarkhill). After one mile (1.5 km), turn right to hamlet of Yarkhill. **Parking** on grass verge outside church.

① Facing church, turn right along Watery Lane beside River Frome. At Little Yarkhill Farm ②, turn sharp left, and pass cottage before bearing right through hop fields and meadows. Carry straight on at junction with farm track. At next junction ③, turn left along track and continue for 200 yards (183 m) to join tarmac lane, which bears left over 2 canal bridges at Monkhide. After the second bridge, continue for 500 yards (457 m) to right-hand bend ④. Go straight on through gate, and continue across huge field to enter gate. Follow track ahead to Garford Farm. Keep to right of buildings and follow drive to cross main road ⑤. Go through gate opposite. Keep right of small reser-

voir, then bear right uphill towards woods. After 150 yards (137 m) cross stile on left, and go through woods to young plantation. Climb steeply across plantation, then go through gap in hedge, over cultivated hilltop to trig. point. Continue in same direction, keeping right of a tree clump to meet bridleway ⑥. Follow this to the left, and at derelict cottages follow path descending left through woods. Before reaching road, turn right along track to cottages. At first whitewashed cottage on left, turn left down narrow path, cross stile and go left across field to gate. Go through this and cross main road ⑦. Follow tarmac lane opposite for one mile, turning left at junction to return to ①.

🏛 Yarkhill has a Norman church, much restored by the Victorians, with an early 13th-C. door. Remains of a homestead moat can be seen 50 yards (46 m) S of the church.

🏚 Hop kilns, with their cowled towers, are a distinctive feature of the farms here. The hop fields and orchards of SE Herefordshire once attracted many city-dwellers coming from the Midlands and South Wales for hop-picking holidays. Mechanical pickers are now used.

ᵇ The path here follows a green lane, one of the ancient byways which are sadly disappearing rapidly in Herefordshire.

🏚 The Herefordshire and Gloucestershire Canal linked the Wye with the Severn, a distance of 34 miles (55 km). Construction started in the 1790s, but difficulties delayed the completion of the section between Ledbury and Hereford until 1845. Even then, its usefulness was rather short-lived. The Gloucester–Ledbury Railway was opened in 1885, following the bed of the drained canal in places. There are many remains of the canal to be seen, including bridges, aqueducts, tunnels and short stretches of water.

⌒ Monkhide's unusual Skew Bridge was built at an angle of 60° to avoid altering the road where it meets the canal.

⩔ Over the Frome Valley.

Forest of Dean and Herefordshire
NEAR HEREFORD

Ballingham Hill
8 or 12 miles (13 or 19 km)
Sheet 149 568347

Easy Along a delightful stretch of the River Wye. *Riverside, winding lanes, fields, parkland; one climb.*

Start Holme Lacey, 6 miles (9.5 km) SE of Hereford; in the village, take the road opposite College of Agriculture to Ballingham; after ½ mile (0.8 km) **parking** outside the church.

① Facing church, turn right between church and old vicarage. Cross paddock, stile and footbridge, then bear left around fields to River Wye. Turn right along riverside path for 1¼ miles (2 km) to road ②. Follow this, then turn right opposite Fisherman's Cottage. Go through gate, then ascend steeply across paddocks to path. Follow this, bearing left past Mountain Ash Cottage to chapel. Take tarmac lane to road, cross, then follow lane opposite to Ballingham Church ③. Turn right along road and carry straight on at junction to Carey ④. Keep right in village, cross brook, then turn right over footbridge into field. Path is indistinct here. Bear right, up bank and follow left-hand side of adjoining field to hidden stile. Climb stile and go through field to another stile, between houses. Turn left along road and follow for 200 yards (183 m), then turn left through field-gate. Keep to right-hand side of fields to green lane, passing converted barn before joining tarmac lane ⑤. Turn right and continue for ¾ mile (1 km), bearing left, then turning right past Bolstone Church. After 250 yards (229 m), turn left, climb gate, cross orchard and go over stile into woods. Step over brook, and leave woods at narrow gate ⑥. (For shorter walk, turn sharp right along ill-defined path, keeping to right-hand side of fields, to Hollington Farm. Turn left along road and, at junction with track, turn right, cross disused railway track, then head diagonally left across fields to the gate and ⑦). For longer walk, continue with path ahead through fields and over stiles to gate. Climb gate and go across field to pool. Join farm track straight ahead and follow it for one mile (1.5 km) to road ⑦. Turn right through Holme Lacey, go over railway bridge, then turn left to follow footpath through field

to riverside ⑧. Follow banks of Wye to right for 1¾ miles (3 km) to road bridge ⑨. Cross road, then keep to riverside for 1¼ miles. As river bends left, bear right to field-gate. Turn left along lane to ①.

🏰 Holme Lacey church and vicarage stand in an isolated position near the site of a deserted medieval village. The church dates back to the 13th C. The unusually tall vicarage, built in the 17th C., is raised above the flood level. Near the house stood a huge pear tree which, according to an 1870 guide book, produced enough fruit to make 12–16 hogsheads – 600–800 gallons (2,730–3,640 l) – of perry.

📖 Before the building of the bridges, there were no less than 7 ford or ferry crossings along this short stretch.

🚂 The Hereford–Ross–Gloucester Railway, opened 1855, closed 1964.

🏰 Ballingham Church is dedicated to St. Dubricius, a legendary local saint.

🍺 The Cottage of Content Inn was formerly called, more prosaically, the
✕ Miner's Arms.

📖 In his *English Hours*, the American writer Henry James described the "copse-checkered slopes of rolling Hereford, white with the blossom of apples" and it still rings true.

🏰 Bolstone has a tiny Norman church standing in the middle of a farmyard, locked and redundant.

🏛 Holme Lacey House was built by the Scudamore family in the 17th C.

📖 In 1811, a great storm caused the River Lugg to flood to a depth of 20 feet (6 m), drowning 4 people.

🚂 Before the Herefordshire and Gloucestershire Canal, or the Hereford–Ross–Gloucester Railway were built, goods were conveyed by barges on the Wye. Navigation was never easy due to the variable water level of the swift-flowing river, but these stone remains are probably the foundations of the wharves.

Forest of Dean and Herefordshire
NEAR HEREFORD

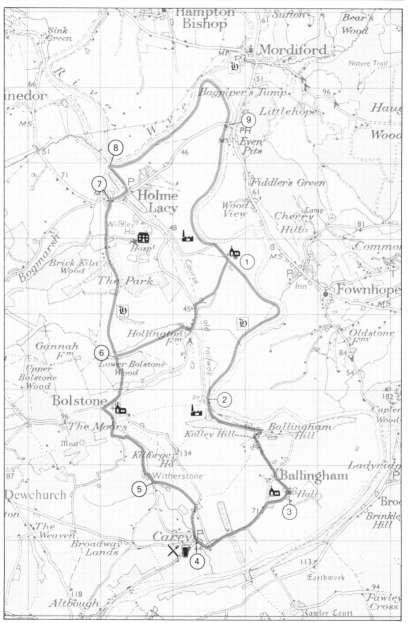

Forest of Dean and Herefordshire
NEAR CINDERFORD

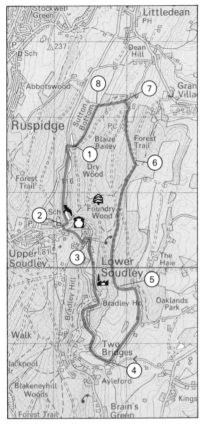

Soudley Ponds and Foundry Wood
4½ miles (7 km) Sheet 162 663116

Easy Varied walking through the historic Forest of Dean. *Wooded slopes, valley, pasture, hillside; one climb; mud after rain between hamlets after* ③.

Start Blaize Bailey Car Park, 12½ miles (20 km) SW of Gloucester. Take the A48 from Gloucester, then at Elton Service Station turn on to the A4151 to Littledean, In village, follow second turning left (signposted Soudley) for one mile (1.5 km) to Forestry Commission **car park** near ponds. (Do not follow signs uphill to Blaize Bailey viewpoint.) Gloucester to Cinderford buses stop at Littledean; walk down road signposted Soudley for one mile to car park.

① Return to road, turn left, then after 50 yards (46 m), bear left alongside pond, and continue to road. Turn right, and after 100 yards (91 m), cross to lane opposite, turning sharp left down cinder path alongside fence ②. Keep on path above mill pool to reach road. Turn left, cross bridge and turn right at telephone box ③ and follow lanes and bridleways for 1¼ miles (2 km), bearing left in hamlets. ④ Cross stile adjoining gate on left just past Ayleford Farm. Keeping hedge on right, cross 4 fields and turn left uphill. Cross stile ⑤ into forest, taking track to right after 20 yards (18 m), shortly joining clearer track straight ahead (beware of oncoming cars). After ¼ mile (0.5 km) take first track bearing right and follow for ¾ mile (1 km) to junction ⑥. Bear left and go past stone-built viewpoint to cottage ⑦. Follow garden fence to left and take well-defined path downhill, turning left after dip ⑧ to follow track to ①.

Soudley Ponds, a man-made haven for water birds, once supplied nearby Camp Mill, now the Dean Heritage museum.

The Haie Hill railway tunnel was part of a goods line that linked the mining town of Cinderford with ports such as Bullo Pill and Newnham on the Severn Estuary. The tunnel was built by the Bullo Pill Railway in 1809, and later widened by the Great Western Railway. The industrial activities of the Forest of Dean attracted early railways, even before the invention of the steam engine. In 1817 a tramway for horse-drawn trucks was opened between Monmouth, on the Wye, and Coleford, in the western part of the Forest.

The name Foundry Wood recalls the use of charcoal in early iron smelting. (Camp Mill, now the museum, was originally a foundry.) Until 1612, the foundries ran on muscle power, with men pumping the bellows for up to 14 hours a day. Then the introduction of water power stepped up production and greatly increased the demand for charcoal.

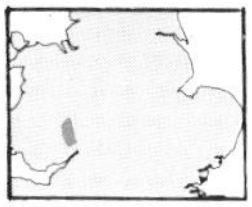

Forest of Dean and Herefordshire

NEAR CHEPSTOW

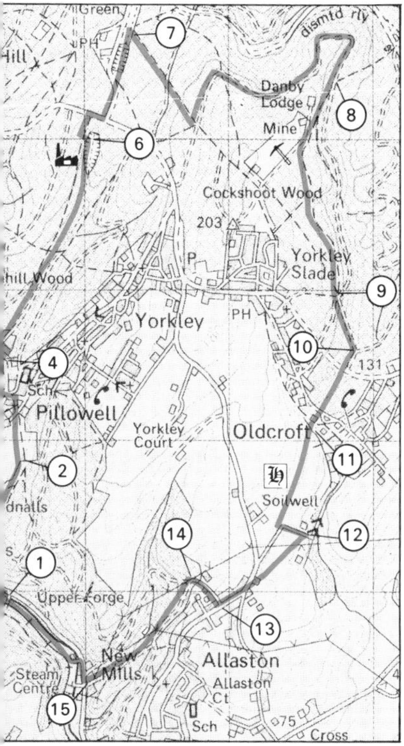

The Miner's Forest

7½ miles (12 km) Sheet 162 625050

Easy The atmosphere of the once-industrial Forest of Dean. *Forest, disused railway, pasture; one climb; mud after rain.*

Start Lydney, 9 miles (14.5 km) NE of Chepstow. Take the B4231 for 1½ miles (2.5 km), passing Norchard Steam Centre, to forest track entrance on right. **Parking** at track entrance, not blocking access.

① From entrance, cross stile and ascend track through woods, keeping straight ahead when main track veers right after ¼ mile (0.5 km) and when path joins from left. At derelict gate, keep right of gate-posts to stile into recreation ground ② and cross lower edge, leaving by downhill track between cottages. Turn left on to second tarmac road ③ and follow downhill. Before sharp left bend, take track to right of cottage ahead ④. Follow well-worn track left, round gardens, and turn right on to old railway track at wooden barrier ⑤. Follow track for one mile (1.5 km) to bricked-up tunnel ⑥, climbing steps to left and bearing left along track to road. Turn right, then take road on left, signposted Mosely Green. At left bend, take track straight ahead, crossing open ground to meet track ⑦. Turn sharp right through conifer plantation and ascend for ½ mile (0.8 km), turning left at cross-tracks, where ground levels out. Follow this track around hill for ¾ mile (1 km) until it descends to junction of paths ⑧. Take right-hand path uphill to barn. Turn left, then take left-hand of 2 tracks for ¾ mile, ignoring track on right, to junction of tracks ⑨. Take path on left 100 yards (90 m) to track in line with pylons ⑩. Turn right and continue across road on to grassy path. Cross minor road, turning left at next minor road, and, shortly, right, round pig enclosure ⑪. After 20 yards (18 m), cross stile on left and go across field to further stile. Cross, and follow green lane to next stile. Climb and turn left along road. At sharp left turn, cross stile on right ⑫ and bear right across field to gate and stile. Cross and keep to left of next field, then go through gate to stile and road. Follow road opposite for 200 yards (183 m), turning right at telephone box ⑬. Go down lane to stile into woodland, cross, and after 50 yards (46 m), turn left on to wide track ⑭. Bearing right at junctions, continue downhill to road near Steam Centre ⑮. Turn right and cross road to right of cottage opposite. Follow path beside cottage, turning right immediately before reaching railway line, and follow this path for ½ mile to meet track from woodland. Turn right, cross stream to road, then turn left and cross road to ①.

The line of the former Severn and Wye Railway 'mineral loop'.

Throughout the Forest, abandoned 'free mines' are visible, but Danby Lodge is one of the 11 still working.

The evidence of kerbing here indicates that the track follows the route of the Roman road from Lydney to Ariconium, near Ross-on-Wye.

COTSWOLDS

A great limestone belt loops across England from Dorset to Humberside. It is especially prominent between Bath and Chipping Camden – the area known as the Cotswolds. You do not have to look hard to see that the limestone is everywhere: in the dry-stone walls, lying loose on ploughed-up fields and, of course, in the buildings. The stone comes in a range of subtly varying shades of grey and gold, and gives the towns and villages a comforting uniformity that brings visitors in their thousands. The beauty does depend largely on the building, but don't undervalue the country itself. The tops are bleak to many people's taste, but the valleys and bottoms are charming, with exquisite rivers. The routes in this section explore those aspects of the Cotswolds, not forgetting a taste of two typical Cotswold towns, centres of the woollen trade that once made the area rich.

Cotswolds
SOUTH GLOUCESTERSHIRE

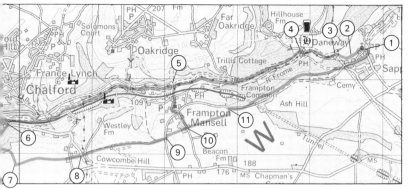

Golden Valley
3½ or 7¼ miles (5.5 or 11.5 km)
Sheet 163 947034

Easy/moderate An attractive valley, cut deep into the Cotswold plateau. *Canal towpath, valley edge; one climb.*

Start Sapperton, 5 miles (8 km) W of Cirencester. **Parking** by church or inn.

① From church, walk down path to left of churchyard on to road. Turn left and, in 100 yards (91 m), go right, past cottage, to stile ②. Turn half-left down field to another stile which leads to canal tunnel ③. Follow towpath, crossing road at Daneway ④, and later crossing footbridge to towpath on opposite bank. For the 3½-mile (5.5-km) walk, turn left over stile to right of cottage at second brick bridge ⑤. Go up hillside, over railway, to join lane at junction. Take lane straight ahead, turn right beyond church at Frampton Mansell, then fork almost immediately left. Rejoin main route at stile 250 yards (229 m) on left ⑩. For 7¼-m (11.5-km) walk, cross bridge ⑤ and continue along towpath for 1½ miles (2.5 km) until the A419 is reached ⑥. Turn left uphill on to road. Immediately after crossing railway line, take track on right, up through wood. At first main crossroads, turn right and then left. At next junction, go straight ahead and climb to top of wood. Keep left in field and at top ⑦, turn left, keeping right of wall. Follow this to gate, which leads to path between hedges. At road, go straight across, down lane, for 250 yards to the A419 ⑧. Cross road and lane and continue

on bridleway. At junction, go straight ahead on track to road ⑨. Turn left for 75 yards (68 m), to stile on right. Climb, and keep to left of field, to another lane. Cross and take signposted stile opposite, ⑩, and follow path on unploughed strip between crops, to stile at corner of wood. Turn left beyond this to lane ⑪. Turn right and continue 300 yards (274 m), then go left down track through wood. After 100 yards, fork right off main track, under large tree. In large clearing (containing telephone poles), where track swings left, fork right on to path, which eventually joins road. Go up road and turn left to ①.

🍺 The inn near the canal at Daneway 🍺 was built for the workers, many of them Irish immigrants, who constructed the canal. Their capacity for alcohol and strong language often scandalized locals, so separate drinking places were established for them.

🚪 The Thames and Severn Canal was opened in 1784 to link the Severn Estuary with the Thames at Lechlade via the Stroudwater Canal. Architecturally, it is a highly individual waterway, with circular cottages for the lock-keepers (one can be seen to the W of Chalford) and grandiose classical entrances each end of Sapperton Tunnel. This 2-mile (3-km) long tunnel is one of the obstacles to reopening the canal: the cost of restoring it has been put at £2 million.

🚪 Chalford was the centre of the woollen industry in Golden Valley.

151

Cotswolds
SOUTH GLOUCESTERSHIRE

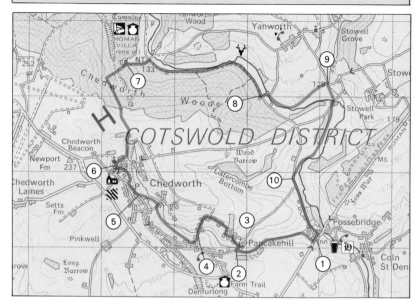

The Roman Cotswolds
7¼ miles (11.5 km) Sheet 163
079111

Easy Fine countryside, and an opportunity to visit the superb Chedworth Roman villa. *Fields, valley, woods, riverside.*

Start Fossebridge, 7 miles (11 km) NW of Cirencester on the A429 (Fosse Way). Buses from Cirencester stop at Fossebridge, 3 times weekly (not Sundays). Use the inn **car park**, by arrangement, if intending to visit pub. Otherwise **parking** on verge of the A429, up lane beside inn, or down lane beyond bridge (in direction of Coln St. Dennis).

① From inn, walk uphill, away from bridge. Pass lane on right, then go through first gate on right, just past cottage. Continue on right of field, up valley to reach road at Pancakehill ②. Turn right, then first left. At road junction, turn left through gate and go down track. At gate below barn, join tarmac track. Turn right to road, which turns left into farm drive ③. Turn left at end of farmyard, downhill along lane. Climb up to green ④. Cross this on right to road then turn right beside

conifer hedge, down grass track. After 35 yards (32 m), turn left over stile. Aim for gate in far corner of field, then continue through fields to lane. Turn right and continue 35 yards, then left over stone stile. Carry on up valley over 3 stiles, then turn half-left uphill to gate ⑤. Turn right at road, and pass old railway bridge to stone stile on right. Follow path to reach road alongside Seven Tuns ⑥. Cross road from inn and take path beside cottage, turning right past church. At first corner, go straight ahead on path which follows old railway. Aim for stile near right-hand end of wood. Pass through wood and carry on in same direction through gate and beside wall. Go straight ahead to stile into Chedworth Woods. Follow path for ¼ mile (0.5 km), keeping left at fork. Go straight ahead at crossroads, and right at another fork to meet track in valley. Turn right to Roman villa ⑦. Continue down road from villa for ¼ mile to road junction. Turn right on to track marked Private Road, footpath only. Follow for 1¼ miles (2 km) to lane ⑧. Turn left over bridge, then immediately right through gate. Follow path through riverside fields, swinging gradually away from river to reach lane at sharp bend ⑨. Turn

Cotswolds
SOUTH GLOUCESTERSHIRE

right across meadow, aiming just left of house, to reach stone stile on to lane. Turn right over bridge and, just beyond farm, go through gateway on left. Follow edge of wood on right until it ends, then follow river bank to reach stone stile. Go straight on to gate into lane ⑩. Turn left, and after ¼ mile, opposite house dated 1844, take footpath on left to ①.

The Fosse Way was the Roman road from Bath to Lincoln. Now the A429, it leads S from here to Cirencester, the Roman town of Corinium. The ancient crossing of the River Coln here has had an inn beside it for centuries.

The Farm Trail is worth a visit.

Chedworth's houses are scattered along the sides of the valley on a spring line. The village has an excellent church with a Norman tower, and fine gargoyles, font and pulpit. It

Mosaic on view at the famous remains of Chedworth Roman Villa.

shows a mixture of styles, as the original 12th-C. church was rebuilt in 1461 with the proceeds of the wool trade. The manor house is medieval in origin, but the present building dates from the 17th C.

The Roman villa here was discovered in 1864, when an unco-operative ferret was dug out of a rabbit burrow along with pieces of mosaic. It is the best exposed Roman villa in the W of England, with a central heating system, elaborate baths, and a shrine to the water goddess of the nearby spring. Open March–October, Tuesday–Sunday, plus Bank Holidays, 11–6. In November and February, open 11–4.

The Coln is a noted trout stream, with a high lime content. Such streams have very clear water and characteristic plant and animal life. Look on the river bed for the larvae of caddis flies which cover themselves with tiny stones neatly fitted together.

Wotton-under-Edge to Tetbury
13 miles (20.5 km) Sheet 162
756932

Moderate The first part of a 2-day route, or a one-day linear walk, with a bus journey back to the start. Through one of the most picturesque parts of the Cotswolds, with marvellous views. *Farmland, woods, dry valley; 3 climbs; mud. Should not be attempted in winter. For one-day walk, check bus times by ringing Stroud (045 36) 3421.*

Start Wotton-under-Edge, 19 miles (30.5 km) NE of Bristol. From Junction 14 on

keeping left, into wood. At track junction, turn left to edge of wood. Go across field to gate and on along track. At lane ❺ turn right, and at bottom of valley, go left through old metal gate, to follow path at edge of wood. Leave wood on path and follow bed of stream for 30 yards (27 m) to old gateway. Take track up wooded valley, passing below Lasborough House, to drive ❻. Cross this, climb half-right up hillside ahead and continue to small gate. Pass castle mound, enter lane and turn left. Just beyond church ❼, go through gate on right and keep right. Follow track through wood to gate. Turn left along edge of field and, cutting across corner,

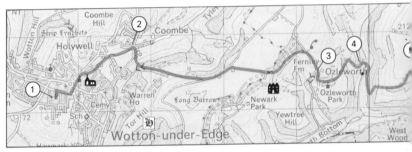

the M5, take the B4059, then to B4058 E. Use the Chipping **car park** (signposted off the B4058). **Return** One-day walk: bus from Tetbury to Nailsworth, then from Nailsworth to Wotton-under-Edge (no Sunday service). 2-day walk: overnight in Tetbury (see note below), and continue next day using route on pages 156–7.

❶ Leave bottom left-hand corner of car park, to reach Long Street. Turn right, then left at Falcon Inn. At roundabout, take Stroud Road, then second right (Valley Road). At stream, go ahead on footpath beside it. Cross lane and continue beside stream to reach lane in Coombe ❷. Turn right uphill and after 150 yards (137 m), go left up drive. In 20 yards (18 m), turn right up steep footpath to lane. Turn left and continue ½ mile (0.8 km), then fork right. Keep right to gates of Ozleworth Park ❸. Walk up drive to left of house, pass church and go through farmyard. Descend valley to reach London Bridge ❹. Turn left through gate to conduit 200 yards upstream. Cross and return along far bank. Follow track down valley,

pass through gate on left. Continue up track to another gate. Keep to left of next field to reach inn ❽. Go down lane opposite inn, through Kingscote, keeping right past church. 50 yards (46 m) beyond first farm on left, go ahead through gate and cross field to stile. Continue in same direction on track, and 150 yards (137 m) before wood, turn right to stile in hedge ❾. Go straight ahead for 100 yards (91 m) to fence, then keep left along fence. Cross stile by gate, and aim for left-hand pylon ahead. Drop into head of valley to reach stile in fence near pylon. Walk to pylon and carry on in same direction to gate, just left of small wood. Keep right beside wood to lane ❿. Turn right uphill to the A46 ⓫. Cross and go up farm road opposite. Just beyond farm-house, fork right along side of field, then drop down into Ledgemore Bottom. Pass under power line and carry on through several gates. Cross concrete farm road ⓬ and continue. Leave valley on track passing back under power lines. Beyond pair of farm cottages, fork left at Chavenage Green, through avenue of trees. At road

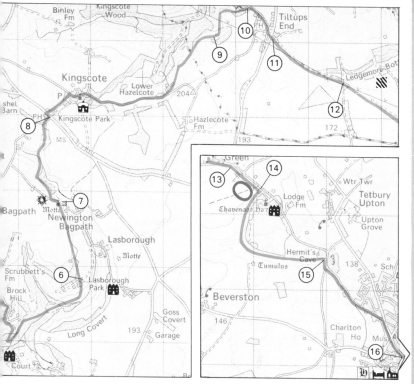

turn left. At junction, go straight
ahead. Just before manor house entrance
gate, turn right through farmyard ⑭.
When tarmac ends, go ahead on track
between stone walls. At end of wood, go
straight ahead, keeping to boundary wall
on left. Take track to gate at bottom of dry
valley. Follow wall to left, then go along
bottom of valley. When gate on left gives
entry to planted area, pass through and
go down valley bottom, keeping left, to
lane ⑮. Turn right, and go left at road
junction. Follow lane into Tetbury to
main road. Turn right and follow road to
junction. Turn right, go past Tourist
Information Office, and keep left on Long
Street into town centre, to Market Hall ⑯.

Wotton (pronounced Wootton)-under-
Edge was one of the centres of the
Cotswold woollen industry from the
16th to the 18th C. It has a magnificent
Perpendicular church.

Isaac Pitman lived in Wotton from
1836–9 and began to develop his
shorthand system here.

Newark Park, open to the public.

Boxwell's manor house dates from
Elizabethan times. It was used as a
refuge by Charles II after the Battle of
Worcester. The 40-acre wood of box
trees (the largest in the country), plus
a medieval well dedicated to St. Catherine, give the place its name.

Lasborough Park, erected in 1794.

The mound beside the path is the site
of an early Norman wooden castle.
Around it runs a ditch – the moat.

Hunter's Hall, once a coaching inn.

Ledgemore Bottom is a typical limestone dry valley. The water sinks
down into the permeable rock in summer and springs flow in winter only.

Chavenage House is Elizabethan.

Tetbury: ring the Tourist Information
Centre (0666) 53552.

Cotswolds
MID GLOUCESTERSHIRE

Tetbury to Wotton-under-Edge
11¾ miles (19 km) Sheet 162
891932

Moderate The second part of a 2-day route starting at Wotton-under-Edge, or a one-day linear route. Starts on the Cotswold plateau, then dips to the lovely Ozleworth Valley. *Fields, woods, valley. Route ill-defined between ⑩ and ⑪. Follow directions carefully. Track at ⑭ is always wet. Should not be attempted in winter. For one-day walk, check bus times on Stroud (045 36) 3421*

Start Tetbury, 9 miles (14.5 km) SW of Cirencester on the A433. Large **car park** near Town Hall. **Return** One-day walk: bus Wotton-under-Edge–Nailsworth–Tetbury (no Sunday service).

① From the Market Hall, follow Church Street and beyond church turn right into West Street. Take first track on left under viaduct. Go over stream beside old ford and up to the A433. Continue and take first right, then turn left into Longfurlong

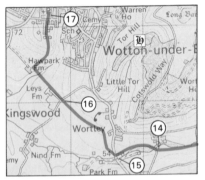

Lane ②. At end of houses on left, cross stile into field, aiming left of big trees to another stile. In a few yards, turn right and follow waymarked route to lane. Turn left to reach lodge ③. When drive swings right, go straight ahead to gate and on to second gate at right-hand edge of wood. Continue in same direction, heading for left-hand edge of small wood. Cross fence near wood into paddock. Cross wall on far side. Keep to left-hand side of next field and go through gap on to grass track. Follow to stone stile on left. Cross next field diagonally to another stone stile, then turn right to gate. Aim for far left-hand corner of next field, to small gate. Beyond this, follow fence round corner to stile by gate. Cross next field to small gate by belt of trees. After 20 yards (18 m), go through another gate to reach the A433 at crossroads ④. Go through small gate opposite and head for gate on left of wood. Continue in same direction to drive junction. Go ahead on drive to lane ⑤. Turn right through village past crossroads. Cross the A433 and follow track which eventually reaches drive ⑥. Go straight on through gate and walk up valley. Keep left to gate in top left corner. Follow main track through wood, walking straight ahead to gate on to grass track ⑦. Follow this, keeping left, to go through right-hand of 2 gates. Turn half-right up field until wall is seen ahead. Aim for left-hand end of this, then follow wall in same direction, keeping right, through 3 fields to gate into track. Turn right for 50 yards (46 m) to lane, then turn left into Leighterton. Turn left at inn ⑧ and immediately fork right. After 150 yards (137 m), go through gate on right and straight across field to wall junction. Follow left-hand wall and in field corner go through gate; continue in same direc-

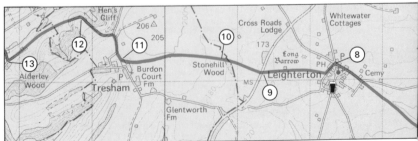

156

tion on other side of wall. Turn left through gate into second field before road. Walk on right-hand side of fields to small gate on to the A46 ⑨. Cross and go through wall gap immediately opposite and walk ahead across field, aiming slightly right of wood to another wall gap. Aim for far right-hand edge of wood, crossing field to wall junction and stone stile. Keep left around field and beside wood. At end of Stonehill Wood ⑩, cross remains of wall and go straight ahead over field to junction of fences. Follow left-hand fence, and turn left, then right. When fence ends, continue straight ahead, until right-hand end of hedge is reached. Continue in same direction across big field. When buildings come into view, aim for bell tower, to reach stile in fence. A few yards further, on left, another stile leads to path in garden. Follow to stile beside cottage, then walk down garden path to lane at Tresham ⑪. Turn immediately right through gateway, then go left between house and barn. Walk round far end of barn. Cross field to gate on to farm track. Turn right and fork left to follow track descending steeply into Ozleworth Valley. Near bottom, where track turns sharply right ⑫, go left over stile and across field to another gate. Walk on across large field to far right corner. Take track past house for farm buildings ⑬. Turn right down farm track. Just before stream, cross stile on left, and follow stream on right. Go through gate on to track ⑭. Turn right, cross stream and keep left to stile into large field. Keep to left-hand side of field and cross further stiles to reach road ⑮. Cross and go through gate opposite, turn half-right and walk across field to gate in far corner. In next field, keep right to top corner, then turn left along top edge. Climb gate in far corner

and keep left in next field to climb another gate beside lane ⑯. Go straight ahead up farm drive, but go through gate on right just before house. Walk beside house, in same direction, to another gate. Go ahead down field, through gate and carry on in same line to cross stream. Just before next farm, turn right over stile. Walk up field, keeping right, to another stile. From here, turn left up hill to stile. Keep right through recreation ground to lane. On far side, pathway leads into The Chipping car park ⑰.

ⓣ Tetbury probably got its name from the Abbess Tetha, head of a nunnery established here in the 7th C. In the 17th and 18th C. the town was second only to Wotton as a centre of the woollen industry. The grand pillared Town Hall, built in 1665, was once a wool market.

🏛 Westonbirt Arboretum has a superb international collection of trees.

❚ Leighterton, an unspoilt village, with an old inn and a 13th-C. church.

OXFORDSHIRE

On its long journey through mid-Oxfordshire, the Thames
gathers strength from a host of smaller rivers that rise far
away in the Chilterns, the Berkshire Downs or the
Cotswolds. These hills surround Oxfordshire's heartland,
composed mainly of undistinguished clay country, which
is, however, rich in winding river valleys offering
unexpectedly secluded corners in a densely populated
county. There is also plenty of easy-going walking along
the Thames towpath: arguably its chief delight is in the
open expanse of Port Meadow above Oxford.
In Oxfordshire, as elsewhere, the Thames has rich
cultural and historical associations. The Wittenham
Clumps, the tree-topped relic of an Iron Age hill-fort beside
the river near Abingdon, is visible for miles around and is
easily climbed for views to Oxford and the Chilterns.

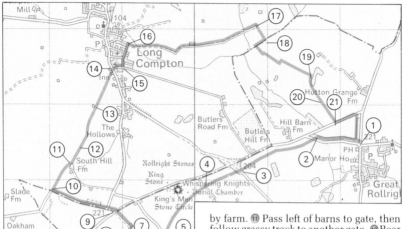

The King's Men

4¾ or 7½ miles (7.5 or 12 km)
Sheet 151 323315

Easy/moderate High on the Cotswold escarpment: superb vantage points; spectacular standing stones. *Hills, fields; 2 climbs; mud.*

Start Great Rollright, 20 miles (32 km) NW of Oxford. **Parking** on wide grass verges at crossroads N of Unicorn pub.

❶ From crossroads, take the Long Compton road. ❷ After dip in road, fork left through white gates on to track, continuing to steps down to the A34. ❸ Cross, climb bank, then keep right of hedges through 2 fields. ❹ Cross farm road and continue straight on across 3 more fields to road. ❺ Cross and head for gap to right of barn, to reach road into Little Rollright. ❻ Turn right and follow road to church. ❼ Just past church, turn right into field and make for hedge gap between 2 barns on hilltop. ❽ Go through the gap and turn right on to track, then turn left by barn to road. ❾ For the 4¾-mile (7.5-km) walk, turn right and follow road signs back to Great Rollright. For the 7½-mile (12-km) walk, go straight on along the Little Compton road to sharp left-hand bend. ❿ Turn right over stile and head for trees

by farm. ⓫ Pass left of barns to gate, then follow grassy track to another gate. ⓬ Bear slightly right across second field after farm to cross stile in bottom corner. Head for large tree to reach corner of hedge. ⓭ Go through hedge gap, pass right of barn and keep left of hedge to gate at far end of field. Continue straight on to the A34. ⓮ Cross and take side road virtually opposite. ⓯ By farm, turn left and follow a road to sharp left-hand bend. ⓰ Turn right through iron gate and follow track passing farm buildings until it turns uphill to barn. ⓱ Turn right and follow right-hand hedge downhill to cross bridge over stream. ⓲ Turn right to corner of field, then go left and follow hedge uphill through 3 fields. ⓳ On reaching tree belt, turn right through gates and skirt trees to third gate. Follow hedge uphill. ⓴ Go through gate and turn right, then left into field. Bear slightly right to gate at hilltop. ㉑ Cross road and go through fence gap. Turn left and follow 2 sides of field to gate leading to ❶.

✸ The Rollright Stones, thought to date from the Bronze Age, between 2500 B.C. and 2000 B.C., are on 3 sites straddling the ancient ridge-top road. Only the 'Whispering Knights' – the remains of an old barrow which resembles men, heads bent together in conversation – are visible from the route (between ❹ and ❺). A detour on to the top road gives access to these remains, and to the 'King Stone', and the 'King's Men' standing stones.

Oxfordshire
NEAR OXFORD

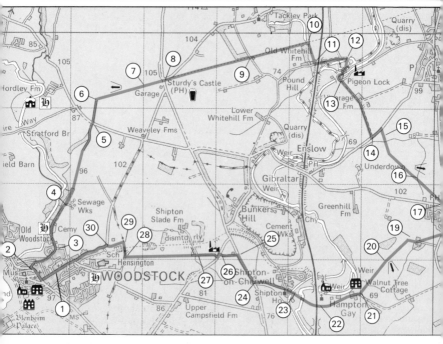

Woodstock and Blenheim
10 miles (16 km) Sheet 164 447168

Moderate Lost villages; the historic town of Woodstock; Blenheim Palace; Akeman Street; the River Cherwell and The Oxford Canal: with so much to see, it is worth allowing a whole day. *Valley, fields, plateau; 2 climbs; mud. Route ill-defined or may be overgrown at* ④, ⑤, ⑦, ⑨ *and* ㉙, *and between* ⑭ *and* ⑳. *Follow directions carefully.*

Start Woodstock, 8 miles (13 km) NW of Oxford on the A34. Regular buses from Oxford, also from London and Birmingham. **Car park** in town centre.

① From car park, return to the A34 and head N to Queen's Own pub ②. Turn right into Upper Brook Hill, then continue along Brook Hill. ③ At fork by Cedar Gable, keep left and follow road to sewage works. ④ By sewage works entrance, take bridleway straight ahead, to reach the B4027. ⑤ Cross, and take bridleway straight on. ⑥ At first track junction, turn right, then continue straight on to junction with bridleway. ⑦ Take path between hedges straight ahead to reach the A423. ⑧ Take Tackley road opposite, then, at bend, go straight on through gates and follow hedge. ⑨ Cross road and continue in same direction until reaching second footbridge. ⑩ Cross, then turn right and head just left of cottage. ⑪ Turn left into lane, later a track, and continue to 2 bridges. ⑫ Cross bridges and a meadow to stile, then cross series of bridges to reach Pigeon Lock. ⑬ Go over bridge by lock and turn left, then right, through gate, on to a fenced track past Vicarage farm to the A4095. ⑭ Turn left, then right through first gate and go straight downhill to footbridge at end of hedge. ⑮ Continue uphill to gate, then bear half-left to gate in far corner of next field. ⑯ Go straight on across further field to stile, into plantation to left of far corner of field. Continue to the B4027. ⑰ Go straight on along the B4027 past Bletchington Green, then, at crossroads, turn right. ⑱ Opposite last house in village, turn right over stile and pass just right of some barns to gate. ⑲ Go through gate and head just right of 2 trees to further gate. ⑳ Keep left, then make for centre of farm ahead to reach road. ㉑ Turn right and at end of road, continue straight on to railway crossing. ㉒ Cross railway and bear half-right to footbridge. Go straight on to canal bridge. ㉓ Carry straight on up village street, then at fork, keep left. ㉔ At the A423, turn right and follow it to hilltop. ㉕ Under power line, turn left on to metalled track to the A4095. ㉖ Cross and take road ahead. ㉗ At right-hand bend, go straight on through gates past house, then follow hedge straight on. ㉘ At junction, turn right into lane. ㉙ After crossing former railway bridge, turn left over stile and go straight across field to gate on to road.　　Carry straight on to ①.

🏘 Woodstock has had royal associations since Saxon times. Kings hunted from the royal manor here, which was walled in the 12th C. to contain the deer. Henry II built a bower near Woodstock Palace for his mistress, Fair Rosamund. In 1704, the estate was given by Queen Anne to the Duke of Marlborough in gratitude for winning the Battle of Blenheim. Nothing remains of Woodstock Palace, but in its place stands the grandiose Blenheim Palace, commissioned, of Vanbrugh, by the Duke and paid for mostly by Parliament. The architecture was not to everyone's taste. Alexander Pope wrote of it: "I never saw so great a thing with so much littleness in it". Capability Brown laid out the park in the 1770s, damming the River Glyme to create the lake.

⛪ Woodstock Church was originally Norman, but has been altered, its tower dating from the 18th C. The town hall was built by Sir William Chambers in 1766 at the Duke's expense.

🏘 Dornford Lane is an ancient green lane, dating from at least 1100, which linked the royal Manor of Woodstock to the royal demesne farm at Steeple Barton.

👁 Hordley Farm, built about 1500, can be seen to the W. It marks the site of the lost village of Hordley, which, in 1279, had a chapel and 19 households. It is one of several local lost villages.

🍴 Sturdy's Castle Inn; food.

🚣 Oxford Canal, first laid out by Brindley, was completed in 1790. It improved transport between Oxford and the Midlands, and made coal much cheaper in the Oxford area.

👁 Bletchingdon church and park.

👁 Oxford and surrounding hills.

🏛 The Jacobean manor house in the lost village of Hampton Gay has been a ruin for many years. The nearby church was largely rebuilt in the early 19th C. but still has a 15th-C. tower.

🚣 Here the walk runs parallel to the old Woodstock Branch Line, built in the 1880s. Its cuttings have long since been filled in and the line is marked only by a hedgerow, a field's length to the right.

Plan of Blenheim Palace and Park, with Capability Brown's lake. Marked by a square near the top edge is the column in honour of the great duke – a conspicuous local landmark.

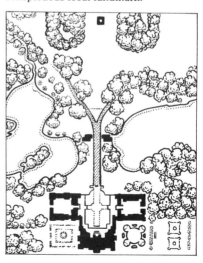

Oxfordshire
ABINGDON

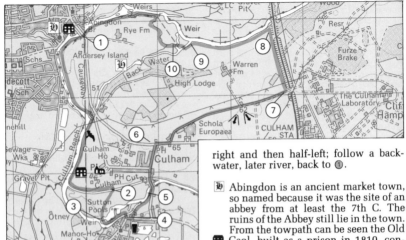

Mid-Thames
7 miles (11 km) Sheet 164 500968

Easy From Abingdon's interesting river front the walk follows the Thames Valley to picturesque Sutton Courtenay. *Riverside, fields; marshy in places. Should not be attempted when Thames is in flood.*

Start Abingdon, 6 miles (9.5 km) S of Oxford. In the town centre, take the A415 towards Dorchester. **Car park** at far end of Abingdon Bridge, on the left.

① From S end of Abingdon Bridge, go through gap in wall and follow towpath downstream to first bridge over Culham Cut. ② Turn right over bridge and go across island. ③ Cross series of weirs and islands to reach the B4016, then turn left. ④ Opposite The Fish, turn left on to concrete drive to stile. Follow hedge, later river, to kissing gate on to road. ⑤ Turn left and follow road straight on to the A415. ⑥ Turn right, then left into Thame Lane and follow it straight on to bridge over railway. ⑦ Just before bridge, turn left on to track along field edge and follow railway to river. ⑧ Go left and follow riverbank to Back Water. ⑨ Turn left and follow Back Water, later turning right over 2 bridges and bearing half-left. ⑩ Cross another bridge, then turn half-

right and then half-left; follow a backwater, later river, back to ①.

🏛 Abingdon is an ancient market town, so named because it was the site of an abbey from at least the 7th C. The ruins of the Abbey still lie in the town. From the towpath can be seen the Old Gaol, built as a prison in 1810, converted into a corn mill in 1867 and now the Arts and Sports Centre.

🏛 The Back Water marks the original course of the Thames. The monks diverted the river in 1060 to supply the Abbey with water.

🏹 In recent years, much of the reed bed along the banks of the Thames has been eroded by heavy boat traffic. Here a section remains, but is being encroached upon from the land side by ploughing. Boat traffic is highly disruptive to river wildlife and is thought to be partly responsible for the decline in swan numbers – along with anglers' discarded lead weights, which poison the birds if swallowed.

⛪ Culham church and manor house are visible from the towpath. The former's tower dates from 1710. The manor house is partly Jacobean.

🏛 Inhabited since the Stone Age, Sutton Courtenay was given to Abingdon Abbey in 687. Sutton Courtenay Abbey dates from the 14th C. Asquith is buried by the 12th-C. church.

🍺 The Fish Inn; food.

🔭 E to Wittenham Clumps, S to Didcot Power Station and Berkshire Downs.

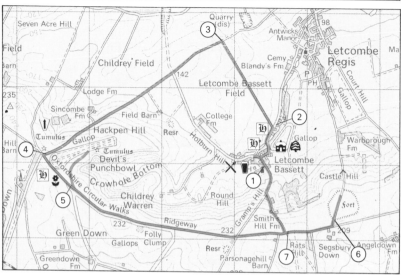

Letcombe Bassett
8 miles (13 km) Sheet 174 374849

Moderate A delightful route through the southern part of the county, including a section of the ancient Ridge Way. *Fields, high downland, woods.*

Start Letcombe Bassett, 2½ miles (4 km) SW of Wantage. Take the B4507 W from Wantage. After ½ mile (0.8 km) turn left for Letcombe Regis. At Letcombe Regis follow the road signposted Letcombe Bassett – about one mile (1.5 km). **Parking** by church, in Church Lane, and at ④.

① From church, walk down Church Lane to road. Turn left to Yew Tree pub and then right. Opposite thatched cottage ② take path marked Public Bridleway. Turn left at track junction ③ to the B4001. Follow the B4001 to top of ridge ④ then turn left on to Ridge Way. Cross huge stile on left ⑤ and walk for ¼ mile (0.5 km) for a better view of Devil's Punchbowl. Retrace to Ridge Way and turn left. Follow Ridge Way for 2½ miles, then take well-defined track on left ⑥, opposite large cluster of farm buildings. Continue ¼ mile along track to Castle Hill before going back to Ridge Way ⑥. Turn right, then take first right ⑦, leading to ①.

🏠 The old rectory, a Queen Anne house, has a 300-year-old mulberry tree in its
🌳 garden, under which Jonathan Swift sat when he visited the local rector in the summer of 1714. Here, too, he wrote *Verses on Himself* and entertained Alexander Pope.

🍺 The Yew Tree pub serves snacks.
✗ Attached to it is a working smithy. Strings of racehorses are a familiar sight in the village and on the downs.

📖 Letcombe Bassett was used by Thomas Hardy as a model for Cresscombe in his novel *Jude the Obscure*.

📖 Letcombe Brook farmhouse is famous for growing watercress. "Bassett cress" was one of the street cries of early 19th-C. London.

🔭 N over the Vale of the White Horse.

📖 The Ridge Way is an ancient E–W route, established when thick, impenetrable forest made it impossible to make lowland routes. Today it forms The Ridgeway Path – an official long-distance route. Along this section,
🌷 members of the primrose family are particularly abundant.

SHROPSHIRE HIGHLANDS

Long Mountain, Stiperstones, Long Mynd, Wenlock Edge: parallel ridges of weathered rock that stretch like crooked fingers across Shropshire's otherwise gentle countryside. Some of these hills can look quite like mountains when seen towering above a deep dale like Cardingmill Valley, or viewed at a distance from near Bridgnorth. And the views from the tops can give the walker the impression of having scaled great heights, though the two highest hills, Brown Clee and Titterstone Clee, do not quite reach 1,800 feet (550 m). The wildest parts of the Shropshire Hills are in the west, starting with Long Mountain on the Welsh border. Here is an area of open, barren moorland, rocks and heath, interspersed with some mountain pasture. Further east, a ridge of quartzite stands out among the rest: the Stiperstones. There are views to the Welsh Hills from the tops of these rocky crags; Devil's Chair is a popular spot. To the east again lies the Long Mynd, a 6-mile (9.5-km) wide plateau of preCambrian rock clothed in bracken, heather and spear grass. Running along its spine is the Portway, once used by Neolithic traders and now an exhilarating upland path. Steep ravines (called batches locally) plunge down from The Long Mynd to Church Stretton, a former spa town with a welcoming village atmosphere. The land rises quickly again, this time to the lava and ash ridges of Ragleth, Lawley and Cair Caradoc. From here there are marvellous views of Wenlock Edge, that long, straight line of well-wooded limestone, immortalized by A. E. Housman in *A Shropshire Lad*.

Shropshire Highlands
NEAR LUDLOW

Brown Clee Hill
6¾ miles (10.5 km) Sheet 137
568835

Moderate The highest hill in Shropshire.
Moorland, pasture; one climb; mud.

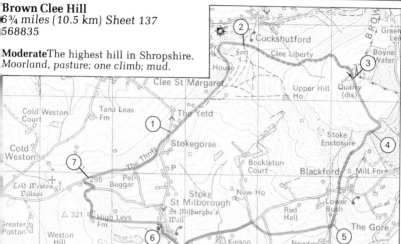

Start Clee St. Margaret, 8 miles (13 km) NE of Ludlow. From Ludlow, take the A4117 E for 1½ miles (2.5 km), then turn on to the B4364 in the direction of Bridgnorth. Turn at sign to Stoke St. Milborough, and from there follow signs to Clee St. Margaret. **Parking** in lay-by on the right at top of steep hill descending into Clee St. Margaret.

① Go through gate at end of lay-by and follow track across open moorland. At gates, remain on open moorland and head for earthen ramparts of Nordybank hill-fort in near distance. ② From hill-fort, join surfaced road heading up to lower summit of Brown Clee (marked by 2 radio relay masts). ③ Go through gate at rear of relay station (at right-hand end of copse). Head across marshy moorland towards woodland on near horizon. The path is near the line marked by occasional fencing. At wood, turn right and follow path to corner of woodland. ④ Go through gate and follow hawthorn hedge to end. Pass through further gate and turn right, following track. At cottage, bear left along bridleway, not through farm gate next to cottage, but on next level up. Go through gate and head down to minor road. Cross road by telephone box and continue down bridleway. ⑤ Pass Newton Cottage on left, then after 130 yards (120 m) cross stile on right. Go over footbridge and head

half-left up through trees to metal hurdles in fence. Go over hurdles and follow hedge, keeping it on left. After crossing two stiles, enter field with wire fence on left. Go half-right across field to gate in corner. Go through gate and follow hedge on right to iron hurdle in corner of field. Go over stile (or nearby fence) and follow right-hand hedge to stile. Go over stile and turn left to field gate on to farm drive. Turn right to stile opposite holly tree, then bear half-right across fields to minor road. Bear left down road for ½ mile (0.8 km), then turn right into Stoke St. Milborough. ⑥ Go through kissing gate in the NW wall of churchyard and follow path along valley to High Leys farmyard. Turn right along farm road and follow to main road, then turn left. ⑦ At top of hill, turn right over right-hand field gate and, keeping hedge on left, follow path to gate in hedge on left. Go through gate and immediately go over stile. Follow hedge on right to stile. Cross stile on to farm track leading to minor road. Then left to ①.

✸ The hill-fort of Nordybank is the most complete survivor of a number on the Clee Hills range.

↖ Clee Burf, the lower of the 2 summits of Brown Clee Hill, was once a local centre for quarrying dolerite.

Shropshire Highlands
NEAR SHREWSBURY

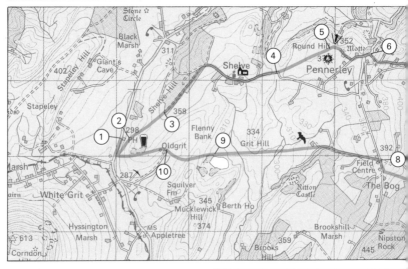

The Stiperstones
7 miles (11 km) Sheet 137 321982

Moderate Industrial archaeology, superb views, and a striking jagged skyline make this a fascinating and atmospheric walk. *Woodland, moorland, fields; marshy in places. Care is needed following the line of stiles across the fields between ⑧ and ⑨. Small spoil heaps between ③ and ④ have been obscured by felling.*

Start The More Arms public house, 14 miles (22.5 km) SW of Shrewsbury on the A488. **Parking** opposite the More Arms.

① Facing the More Arms, walk down road to right. After 100 yards (91 m), cross wooden stile on left just before field gate and turn sharp left. Follow path close behind pub. ② Cross wooden fence and bear half-right across fields. Pass through gate in fence and then follow line of stiles to corner of plantation on hilltop. ③ Cross stile at woodland corner and follow forestry road into wood. Where road turns right before small spoil heaps, continue along track in same direction to minor road. Pass through gate on to road. Turn right and follow road through Shelve. ④ At sharp right-hand bend, go through gate on left and bear half-right, following fence/hedge up hillside. Go through next

Devil's Chair, major feature of the craggy chain of Stiperstones Ridge.

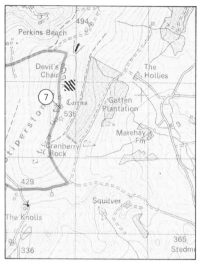

and head for small wood straight ahead, across 3 stiles. ⑨ Skirt right-hand side of small lake, cross stile at end and go half-right up hillside. Go straight over next stile and across 3 fields towards farm buildings. ⑩ At farmyard turn right, then go left around last barn and up past new house. Cross stile and head for fir trees. Follow left-hand edge of these and go downhill to road. Turn right to ①.

🍺 The More Arms serves bar snacks.

⛪ All Saints Church, Shelve, dates from around 1839, but is built on the site of a 13th-C. church. At 1,150 feet (350 m) above sea level, it is one of the highest churches in England.

⚜ Two pre-Roman burial mounds survive on the top of Round Hill, both easily visible from the walk. The white areas seen in the trees to the N are spoil heaps from old lead mines.

⚑ From Devil's Chair, 80 miles (129 km) in any direction: N over Cheshire (look for Jodrell Bank Radio Telescope) to the Lancashire moorlands; W to Cadair Idris on the West Wales coast; S to the Black Mountains above Cardiff and SE to the Malvern Hills.

⚜ Great crags of Ordovician quartzite (550 million years old) on Stiperstones Ridge form a jagged skyline in the otherwise well-rounded uplands of Shropshire. Each group has a name: Scattered Rock, Devil's Chair, and Cranberry Rock. Many legends surround the name Devil's Chair. One suggests that the Devil took a particular dislike to Shropshire and that he jumped on his chair, gradually forcing it downwards to sea level to be submerged.

🦅 On the marshy area listen for the curlew's haunting call.

⚒ The ruined building on the right of the road housed the beam engine which pumped water out of the lead mine here 70 years ago. The walk passes many such relics of lead and zinc mining, which flourished here from Roman times until 1950.

gate on left and go diagonally right, across field to further gate, about 200 yards (183 m) before small copse. Pass through gate and bear half-right across field to stile. ⑤ Go over the stile, and bear half-right to pine trees. Cross stile on right, immediately past caravan. Go half-left downhill to dirt road. Turn left, then left again along minor road. ⑥ After 65yards (60 m), turn right up dirt road, pass old lead workings and chapel on right, and continue uphill. Bear left at T-junction and walk uphill to field gate. Pass through this and walk up to summit ridge N of Devil's Chair. Turn right and follow ridge-top track. ⑦ Pass trig. point right and take distinct path down to left to car park. Go over stile into car park and turn right to minor road. Turn right along it and at T-junction, bear right, cross road and, after 50 yards (45 m) take stile on left. Turn half-right to next stile then go half-right downhill to old mine buildings and Field Studies Centre. ⑧ At crossroads, take unmade road, passing Studies Centre to right. Follow rough road, cross stream at far end and go through gate up drive towards Ritton Farm. At next gate, cross stile marked with yellow arrows 10 yards (9 m) to left. Go slightly left across field to another stile. Cross, and bear slightly left to further stile. Follow yellow arrows across 3 further stiles to small stream. Cross this

Shropshire Highlands
NEAR LUDLOW

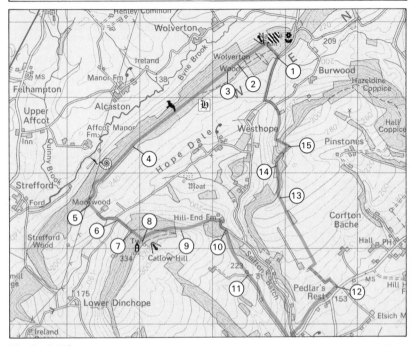

Wenlock Edge
8¾ miles (14 km) Sheet 137 479876

Moderate Contrasting with the other walks in this section, this route takes in mature woodland along the steep scarp slopes of the Edge. *Woodland, fields; one very steep climb at ⑦; mud. Route ill-defined between ⑨ and ⑩.*

Start Edgewood Picnic Area, near Westhope, 8½ miles (13.5 km) due NNW of Ludlow. From Ludlow take the A49 NW to Craven Arms, then turn E on to the B4368 towards Much Wenlock. After 3 miles (5 km), turn N down minor road to Westhope, and follow signs to picnic area and **car park**.

① Turn right out of car park entrance down minor road. After 75 yards (68 m) take path along edge of mature woodland on left. Bear left at end and follow path along top edge of steep scarp slope. ② At junction of paths take second right. ③ Bear right at fork, then go left. ④ At wooden

gate posts bear left uphill and follow woodland edge along overgrown path. ⑤ On reaching forest track bear left up to pylon, then go left down lane beside pylon to tarmac lane. Bear right to junction. ⑥ Bear right again and at right-hand bend go straight up forestry track to clearing. ⑦ Take grassy footpath straight up hillside, keeping to right-hand path through wood. ⑧ At top of slope, at sharp right-hand bend, turn left. Follow woodland track to end of wood. ⑨ Cross wooden fence and stay on left-hand side of field to far end, keeping woodland on left. Turn left through gate, then go right through second gate with red diamond painted on it. Follow ill-defined path to farm drive (farm is on your left) and turn right. ⑩ After 100 yards (91 m) take right-hand fork up into woods. Follow rough track through wood, then go across field, keeping woodland immediately on left. Cross new stile and follow path to end. ⑪ Turn right, then immediately left and follow surfaced lane over ½ mile (0.8 km) to stile on left. Follow yellow arrows

down bridle path to main road. Turn left and follow road for about ½ mile (0.8 km). ⑫ Turn left, and following line of bridleway, go up farm lane towards Elsich Barn Farm. At lone pine tree turn right through gate. Go to end of field and turn left up near side of hedgerow. Follow this right, uphill, beyond small copse. ⑬ At top of field cross fence on right and bear left across field to gate into woodland. Go through this gate and down to barn. ⑭ Turn right immediately before barn. Do not go over stile into new plantation, but continue in field with plantation on left. ⑮ Bear sharp left at top of hill and follow rough road around bend and down to farm drive. Bear left here, go left again at first junction, then sharp right at next junction back to ①.

🐾 The route follows part of the Edgewood Nature Trail, described by the information board at the car park.

⚠ The view NE along Wenlock Edge is spectacular.

〽 The Edge has 2 distinct levels: Wenlock limestone, forming the lower edge, dates from the Silurian, 500 million years ago, when the area was a reef in a tropical sea. The upper edge is of the slightly more erosion-resistant Aymestry limestone.

Flounder's Folly, marking the summit of Callow Hill: wide views.

🦅 Birds of the deciduous woodland of Wenlock Edge include jays, green woodpeckers and buzzards. The wood is charming in spring when the bluebells are in flower, but it changes character in autumn and winter, as Housman described in *A Shropshire Lad*:

> On Wenlock Edge the wood's in trouble;
> His forest fleece the Wrekin heaves;
> The gale, it plies the saplings double
> And thick on Severn snow the leaves.

⛏ Several small quarry faces are to be found in the woods immediately adjoining the path. These limestone exposures are rich in the fossils of marine animals, largely shell fragments, sea lilies (crinoids) and the woodlouse-like trilobites.

♟ Callow Hill marks the highest point of the upper edge, crowned by a folly erected in 1838 by a local eccentric, B. Flounder. The internal staircase has long rotted away, but views from the tower's foot are extensive. To the SE, Ludlow is visible, dominated by its castle and church.

Shropshire Highlands
NEAR CHURCH STRETTON

Across The Long Mynd
5½ or 10½ miles (9 or 17 km)
Sheet 137 441948

Moderate Follows quiet pathways into the heart of the Long Mynd, with excellent views. *Ridge, valley; 2 climbs; mud.*

Start Cardingmill Valley, 13 miles (21 km) S of Shrewsbury. Take the A49 S from Shrewsbury and after 11 miles (17.5 km), turn W on to the B4370 to All Stretton. Follow signs to Cardingmill Valley. Trains run to Church Stretton; from town centre walk to Cardingmill Valley, follow signs. N.T. car park at ①.

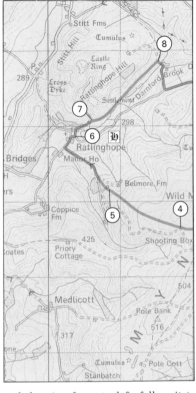

① From car park follow brook upstream, keeping, where possible, to left-hand bank. Where valley divides, take right-hand fork, following path up to ridge. ② Fork left where path divides, and follow distinct path to wooden signpost ③ at ridge top. (For 5½-mile (9 km) walk, turn right at signpost and follow wide track to minor road. Veer right on to this and rejoin the longer walk at cattle-grid sign ⑪.) For 10½-mile (17-km) walk turn left towards Pole Bank. At junction of several tracks and paths, take second right, a narrow cart track which heads directly for summit of Corndon, in the middle distance. ④ Bear right on to minor road, and at sharp left-hand bend, continue straight ahead, following signposted path towards Ratlinghope. Keep to fence to left of house. ⑤ Bear left down farm track to minor road and turn right, crossing cattle-grid. Follow road downhill to T-junction. Turn right towards Darnford. ⑥ Take second track off to left and follow it to stream. Cross footbridge to left of, and just beyond, cottage. Turn right at far end, following path uphill above stream. ⑦ Bear right through farm gate below hawthorn trees and remain in main valley, following level path around hillside. ⑧ Bear right over footbridge in front of barn and right again in front of farmhouse. Follow farm drive up to minor road. Turn left on to road and follow it for about ½ mile (0.8 km). ⑨ Cross cattle-grid and take path off to left, just past National Trust Long Mynd signpost. Cross stream at bottom and climb straight up valley side to fence at top. Cross stile in fence, then walk to hilltop. ⑩ Bear half-right to 2 farm gates. Pass through right-hand one

and, keeping fence to left, follow it to another gate. Go through this, then follow track around to left and up to minor road by cattle-grid sign ⑪. Go straight across minor road and along rough track, keeping fence to left. ⑫ About 50 yards (46 m) after fence turns a little to the left, take a wide, grassy track following the previous line. As you come over the brow, the track bears right towards a white-painted house. Turn right at fence just before house and follow path down into deep valley. Keep to left-hand slope. Cut left, well above chalet-bungalow, and head for valley bottom downstream from it. Follow flow of stream. ⑬ At bottom end of car park, cross stream on right and turn left to stile. Cross and go half-right, following lower field boundary to kissing gate. Go through this and head straight across road after 300 yards (274 m), along

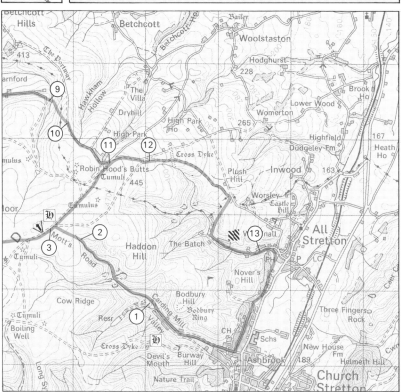

narrow holly-lined path. Go through next gate and bear right, uphill to rough track. Follow yellow arrow through gate opposite and go down tarmac road. Turn right at end and follow valley floor road back to ①.

🏠 Cardingmill Valley owes its name to 'carding' – the process whereby wool is combed out ready for spinning.

🏠 The Portway is a medieval road, once used by pack ponies carrying lead ore and salt between England and Wales.

👁 Views from near the signpost are immense – as far as Snowdon in North Wales. The gliders and hang gliders often seen here take advantage of updraughts of air from the precipitous sides of Long Mynd.

🏠 In her novels of Edwardian rural life, Mary Webb modelled the village 'Slepe' on Ratlinghope (pronounced locally as "Ratchup"), with its tranquil waterside meadows, farmsteads and little-used byways. 'Hope' is Anglo-Saxon for wooded valley, and the remaining pieces of woodland here only hint at its former extent.

〰 Streams have cut deeply into the eastern edge of Long Mynd here, exposing some of the most ancient rocks in Britain: slates and sandstones dating from the pre-Cambrian era, 1,000 million years ago. This Uriconian sandstone is particularly resistant to erosion, resulting in the sudden rise of the Long Mynd from the flatter Shropshire plain which is made up of younger, softer rock.

WEST MIDLANDS

The inhabitants of Britain's second largest city,
Birmingham, know that it requires some open-mindedness
and ingenuity to get the most out of walking their
metropolitan county; indeed the same goes for those who
live in Birmingham's satellites, such as Solihull, Halesowen,
Walsall and West Bromwich, whose urban and suburban
sprawl takes up much of the rest of the available countryside.
Yet some areas considered by outsiders as built-up, or
industrialized beyond recall, offer pleasant surprises, and the
many canals provide instantly easy and accessible strolling.
In fact, you can walk right round Birmingham on the
162-mile (260-km) West Midland Way, which ingeniously
links public footpaths and bridleways at an average
distance of 12 miles (19 km) from the Birmingham
conurbation's outer edge. And a worthy walk it is, too, for
here is what the novelist Henry James described as
"midmost England" – the essence of Englishness as
expressed, at any rate, by the landscape. Actually, only one
walk in the section lies within West Midlands the county;
the other two are in Staffordshire.
There is plenty of more than passing interest, too: strange
houses hewn out of rock at Kinver Edge; haunting
reminders of the First World War on Cannock Chase; the
landscape of the potteries, especially if viewed from the
hills nearby. Arnold Bennett, one of their most famous
sons, described how "the vaporous poison of their ovens
has soiled and shrivelled the surrounding country 'til there
is no village lane within a league but what offers a gaunt
and ludicrous travesty of rural charms". Since then,
economic recession, combined with clean-air acts, has, at
least, done much to improve the environment.

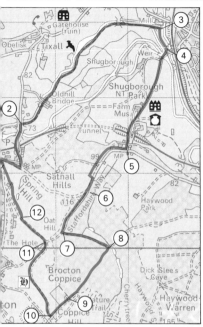

Shugborough and Milford
7 miles (11 km) Sheet 127 973211

Easy In the heart of the industrial Midlands, here is peaceful walking through the great woodlands of Cannock Chase. *Canal towpath, parkland, woods; one climb.*

Start Milford, 4 miles (6.5 km) SE of Stafford on the A513 to Lichfield. Buses from Stafford and Lichfield (not Sunday mornings). Alight at Milford Common. Use Milford Common **Car Park** off the A513. Turn right opposite Barley Mow.

❶ From car park, cross common to the A513 then turn right. Fork left just past garage, then take second turning left (Tixall Road). Cross railway and river bridges and turn right along the canal towpath ❷. Continue for about 2 miles (3 km). On reaching junction with Trent and Mersey canal ❸, cross 2 bridges, then turn right and follow the canal to bridge no 73. Immediately leave canal and turn right, then left, on track over Essex bridge ❹.

Continue along bridle path for about one mile (1.5 km) and turn right on reaching main road ❺. Carefully follow footpath beside road, passing entrance to Satnall Hills, and enter Cannock Chase at picnic area ❻. Follow track beside fence on left. Turn left where fence turns left ❼ into valley and continue to the stepping stones ❽. Do not cross stepping stones but turn right and climb up to Coppice Hill on metalled road to car park ❾. Continue through car park and take first track on right (signposted Mere Pool) ❿. Continue along track to junction of many tracks, in about ½ mile (0.8 km) ⓫. Follow disused railway track through cutting. At far end of cutting ⓬ continue in same direction as disused railway, along one of many tracks back to Milford Car Park. Keep in same general direction as railway track, to return to ❶.

🦆 Tixall Wide, an open basin of the canal, is a favourite place for birdwatchers. The great crested grebe can be seen here; in spring breeding pairs engage in elaborate courtship displays. Rising high out of the water, they face each other, break to beak, and move their heads from side to side. The male is sometimes seen passing food to the female.

🎲 Tixall Gatehouse can be seen from this point. Mary Queen of Scots was detained here for 17 days in 1586, while her home at Chartley was searched for evidence of her involvement in the Babington Plot.

🏛 Shugborough Hall (National Trust) is the ancestral home of the Anson family, and is still used by Lord Lichfield at weekends. The house is open to the public, as is Shugborough Park Farm, which specializes in rare breeds. The County Museum is also here.

🎖 The route here is part of 'The Great War Trail': it follows the Tackeroo Railway, which brought coal up to a huge army encampment during the First World War. For many soldiers destined to die in the trenches, this cold, windswept spot was the last they saw of England. The Information Centre at Milford has leaflets on the trail; open 2–5.30, weekends.

West Midlands
NEAR STOURBRIDGE

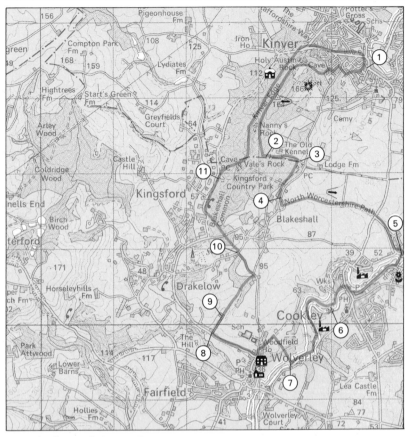

Kinver Edge and the Rock Houses
10½ miles (17 km) Sheet 138
845834

Easy Striking canal architecture, the open heathland of Kinver Edge, and cave dwellings, inhabited as recently as 1950. *Heath, fields, towpath; 2 climbs; mud.*

Start Kinver, 3½ miles (5.5 km) W of Stourbrige. Take the A458 W from Stourbridge and after 3 miles (5 km) turn S on minor road signposted to Kinver. Infrequent buses from Stourbridge. Several **car parks** along the village main street.

① Leave the village along Vicarage Drive

in centre of main street. Turn right at footpath signpost, on unsurfaced drive, to gate. Continue, through metal wicket, between garden fence and hedge, to lane. Turn right to T-junction at The Compa. Turn left and after 100 yards (90 m) take drive on right. At Brackendale, go left of gate and follow garden wall out on to the open slopes of Kinver Edge. Take path bearing right to level grassy plateau at NE end of Edge. Use path with log steps to reach crest of Edge. Walk along Edge to trig. point. Continue along path, later descending gently through scrub to barrier and signpost marking junction of Staffordshire Way and North Worcestershire Path ②. Turn left on to North Worcs.

174

Path, continuing along bridleway to Blakeshall Country Park ③. Leave park on North Worcs. Path, turning right to Blakeshall Lane. Continue right along lane for 100 yards (91 m) to footpath sign. Follow unsurfaced lane on left ④. Turn left shortly (waymark on fence post) and drop gently downhill. Follow narrow path between wire fence and overgrown hedge for roughly ½ mile (0.8 km) to lane. Take narrow lane opposite to Caunsall, turning left at T-junction in village to The Anchor pub ⑤. 20 yards (18 m) past pub, go through kissing gate to footpath sign-posted Wellfield. Follow path across wet meadow to cast-iron footbridge over brook. Join canal towpath at Austwick Bridge. Turn right along towpath and continue through Cookley tunnel to lock at Debdale Bridge ⑥. Follow towpath to Wolverley Forge Bridge ⑦. Leave canal by path on right, 100 yards past bridge, doubling back to go between white cottage and outbuildings to bridge crossing brook. Cross stiles, then enter coppice. Leave wood and cross field to unsurfaced lane. Turn left to meet road on outskirts of Wolverley. Turn left then right along Drakelow Lane to Bay Horse Farm ⑧. Take bridleway signposted Blakeshall Lane. At Solcum House ⑨, go through field gate and follow line of wire fence. Cross broken stile to field. Keep in same direction to reach wicket gate where path enters Solcum Coppice. Follow well-defined track through pine trees uphill to Blakeshall Lane. Turn left along lane and shortly afterwards fork left to meet T-junction in ¼ mile (0.5 km) ⑩. Take path opposite, marked by faded signpost Kingsford ¼ mile. Follow path along field boundary to gate leading into wood. Start of path is unclear, but once inside wood, path becomes well-defined. Descend steeply to wide sandy forest ride. Continue across ride on same line. Soon afterwards, waymarked trails on Blakeshall Common cross the path. Follow red waymarked trail to car park at Kingsford Country Park ⑪. From car park, take path to Vale's Rock (marked by blue arrow on post) and continue to Kinver Edge. Follow wide bridleway below Edge, past Nanny's Rock to Holy Austin Rock. From there, turn right along road to High Street and ①.

✳ The NE end of Kinver Edge was occu-

pied by an Iron Age hill-fort, covering an area of 11 acres. The steep slopes of the Edge formed the defences on 2 sides, while the other approaches were guarded by a bank and ditch.

〽 Extensive views across N Worcestershire to the Malvern Hills, and across the Severn valley and Wyre Forest to the Abberley Hills. To the W are the Titterstone and Brown Clee Hills of Shropshire.

〽 The view ahead is dominated by the Clent Hills, made up of fragments of scree and rising to 1,035 feet (315 m).

⚘ In summer the banks of the brook are covered with Himalayan balsam – a tall plant with pink, helmet-shaped flowers. Although an introduced plant, it does remarkably well in Britain. The green seed pods spring open if touched, flinging seeds in all directions.

🚢 The Staffordshire and Worcestershire Canal was built by Brindley to join the River Severn to the Trent and Mersey Canal. Red sandstone cliffs rise up at the side of the canal for much of its run, and at Cookley it passes through them in a tunnel.

🚢 Beside the lock at Debdale Bridge, the sandstone crag has a large chamber cut into it with stone seats running around its walls.

🏠 Wolverley Church, perched on a rock at the S end of the village, was built in 1772. The 18th-C. houses at the other end include Knight House, an elegant brick mansion built around 1760.

🏠 Many of the soft sandstone outcrops on Kinver Edge have been carved to provide dwellings. Although deserted now, some of these were quite sophisticated, and, in 1851, no less that 12 families were housed in Holy Austin Rock, including those of ironworkers, beesom makers, farm workers and a mole catcher. The earliest records of the rock houses date from the 18th C., and the last inhabitants were rehoused around 1950. The threat of vandalism has made it necessary to fence the caves off.

West Midlands
STAFFORDSHIRE

Churnet Valley
6½ miles (10.5 km) Sheet 128
053446

Moderate Despite the proximity of Alton Towers, this beautiful stretch of the Churnet Valley is not overcrowded. *Disused railway, parkland, mixed woodland; 2 climbs; mud between ❸ and ❹. The path through the dense woodland between ❸ and ❹ is ill-defined – follow directions carefully.*

Start Oakamoor, 3 miles (5 km) E of Cheadle on the B5417. **Parking** at the Churnet Picnic Place, Oakamoor.

❶ From car park, cross bridge over River Churnet and turn right along disused railway siding, past remains of Oakamoor Station. Join main Churnet Valley track way at a gate and stile. Follow line for one mile (1.5 km) to Lord's Bridge ❷ and continue for ¾ mile (1 km) to Alton Station. Pass under road bridge and continue on disused riilway for a further ¾ mile to start of path up Park Banks. ❸ Leave railway at dilapidated kissing gate on left to join unsurfaced road climbing gently uphill. Walk along road to power line. Climb steeply on path through

Churnet Valley and Alton Castle (foreground).

woods from wooden pylon to join another wide track contouring Park Banks at higher level. Go right on track to large sandstone outcrop. Look uphill for rustic handrail which marks line of crude steps. Climb steps and continue steeply up left through rhododendrons to stile in chain-link fence of Alton Park ❹. Walk straight ahead across park to farm and continue in same direction through small plantation beyond farm. Keep on across open parkland to stile in wooden fence. ❺ Cross stile and drop downhill to stone wall where stile and gate give access to road. Turn left along lane for ½ mile (0.8 km). ❻ Go through gap in fence on right marked by signpost. Follow metal rail fence downhill to unsurfaced estate road and large cattle-grid. Go through metal wicket gate directly across park to Cote Farm. An identical wicket gate gives access to metalled estate road. Follow through farm buildings to bend near landscaped pool ❼. At bend in road, find 2 gates on left. Take the right-hand one and climb uphill between metal rail fence and wood. Cross bracken and scrub, then enter mixed woodland. Take care not to

176

climb too high out of woodland. Just before open grassland, cross brook to another metal wicket set in fence ➑. Cross estate road and make for cottages at Ramshorn. Go through wide metal field-gate on left to green track which joins unsurfaced cottage drive. Follow drive to road ➒. Turn left, and after one mile reach caravan/camping site at Old Star ➓. Look for stile on left, cross, and follow low stone wall to road. Take farm drive a few yards to left. At end of drive, go over stile to wide grassy lane leading downhill. At end of lane, go over stile in wall into pasture overlooking Oakamoor. Continue downhill to another farm drive and look for stile in hedge. Cross into field leading steeply down to the B5417. Turn left to ➊.

🏚 The huge stone gateposts near the bridge are relics of a large copper works. Industrial activity in the Churnet Valley dates back to around 1730 when the area became important for copper production, the ore coming from Ecton, 10 miles (16 km) to the N.

In 1866, the wire for the first successful transatlantic telephone cable was made here.

✕ The Rambler's Retreat café.

🚉 The fine building opposite the station is one of the gatehouses of 19th-C.

🏛 Alton Towers, a residence of the Shrewsbury family, famous for its spectacular landscaped park; open to the public.

🏰 Alton Castle, which dominates the skyline S of the valley, was intended to imitate the castles along the Rhine. A. W. Pugin, exponent of the Gothic Revival, designed the castle for the 16th Earl of Shrewsbury, and it was built between 1840–52. The buildings now house a school and hospital. In the grounds are the remains of a medieval castle, built by a crusader in 1150.

✳ Beelow Hill, seen to the left, is the site of a Stone Age burial chamber.

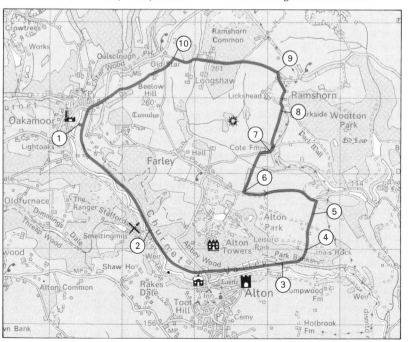

EAST MIDLANDS

Despite industrialization and intensive cultivation of mainly low-lying land, Nottinghamshire and Leicestershire are worthy of the walker's attention: there is much quietly beautiful countryside.

Nottinghamshire still has several large tracts of woodland, including remnants of Sherwood Forest and the great parks of the Dukeries. Leicestershire has the wooded, hilly Charnwood Forest, which in turn contains Bradgate Park. In the east of the county is gentle, undulating countryside with villages built of the local ironstone. Both counties offer pleasant riverside walking in the broad, lush valleys of the Trent and the Soar.

In the less popular parts, the state of the footpaths tends to be poor. They can cut boldly across the neat, planned pattern of the fields left by enclosure, but all too often this means they are ploughed out or cropped over.

Intensively cultivated Lincolnshire has similar problems. The relatively few public footpaths vanish all too often under vast expanses of barley or potatoes. And the fields are long and rolling, daunting even to those confident they know the line of the right of way.

In the north-east and the south of the county lie the melancholy Lincolnshire marsh country and the Fens. The atmosphere of the Lincolnshire Wolds and of Lincolnshire Heath is brisker: these two modest features are part of the twin belts of chalk and limestone which swing right across England from Dorset to Yorkshire. Slightly elevated above the surrounding flatlands, they give surprisingly dramatic views – "big sky country" is what the locals call it.

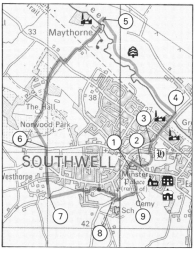

Southwell

4¾ miles (7.5 km) Sheet 120 701538

Easy Explores a minster town and its attractive setting. *Riverside, parkland, meadow, alleyways.*

Start Southwell, 8 miles (13 km) W of Newark. Take the A617 W from Newark and after 4 miles (6.5 km) the A612 to Southwell. **Car park** on Church Street.

① From car park, turn left along Church Street as far as South Muskham prebend (priest's house). Take tarmac path left of prebend ② to Burgage Lane. Turn left, then right to reach The Burgage ③. Turn right down The Burgage and Station Road. Pass end of Southwell Trail and Cauldwell's Mill and turn left ④ to follow River Greet for one mile (1.5 km) to Maythorne. Cross river and millstream ⑤ to pass between mill and former workers' cottages. Cross Southwell Trail again and continue to Lower Kirklington Road. Turn right, then left, after 100 yards (91 m), into grounds of Norwood Park. At crossroads, follow broad grassy path slightly left between fruit trees to Halam Road ⑥. Cross road, and climb a stile. Head across field towards right-hand end of brick building nearly opposite. Cross Oxton Road and go down ginnel (alleyway) opposite, leading into Westhorpe.

Bear right to another ginnel, leading into meadow. Go down edge to stream in steep-sided valley. After crossing footbridge ⑦, turn left and follow stream to Halloughton Road. Turn right and continue for 100 yards, then go left into the access road to nos 37 and 39. Take narrow ginnel on right which winds to a football field. Cross this to rejoin stream where it passes under the A612 ⑧. Cross road and follow tarmac path to school buildings. Turn left and walk across school playing fields, keeping stream on left. Cross footbridge ⑨ and walk past tennis courts and bowling greens to Memorial Gates. Go along Bishop's Drive, but where it bends left continue past Bishop's Palace to ①.

Southwell Minster has been the cathedral church of Nottinghamshire since 1884. The church is mainly a 12th-C. Norman building, but the chapter house is late 13th C. Paulinus, Archbishop of York, founded a church on this site around 630 ". . . having preached to the people of the country round, and baptized them in the River Trent . . .", according to Daniel Defoe, who visited Southwell in the 18th C. Among the surrounding buildings are the Bishop's Palace and Manor, and several prebends, each being named after the village which supplied the priestly inhabitant's income.

Burgage House was the home of Byron's mother, and the poet stayed here during vacations from Harrow and Cambridge in the early 19th C.

Here the route crosses the Southwell Trail, previously the Midland Railway's branch line from Southwell to Mansfield, opened 1871 to carry coal, milk and passengers, closed 1968.

Cauldwell's Mill was rebuilt in 1895 with a tower holding 6,000 gallons (28,000 l) of water: a precaution after 2 disastrous fires in 1867 and 1893.

Along the Greet are old willows, one colonized by wild rose and bramble.

Maythorne Mill was built as a cotton mill, but converted to produce silk and lace-thread in 1832. Now it has been converted again, into flats.

East Midlands
LEICESTERSHIRE

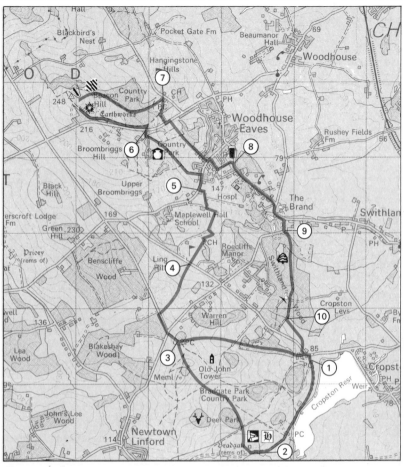

Charnwood Forest
3 or 8 miles (5 or 13 km) Sheet 129
542113

Moderate/easy Explores a singular pocket of country and links 2 of the highest hills in the county; excellent viewpoints. *Open parkland, pasture, heath, woodland; 2 climbs; Swithland Woods, between ⑨ and ⑩, can be very muddy, but side paths may be used.*

Start Cropston, 5 miles (8 km) NW of Leicester. From Leicester, follow the B5328 to Cropston. At village, bear left alongside reservoir, then turn left on to the B5330. After ⅓ mile (0.5 km), turn left to gated entrance into Bradgate Park. Buses to Cropston from Leicester. **Car park** close to entrance of Bradgate Park.

❶ From car park follow drive through park for one mile (1.5 km) to ruins of Bradgate House. ❷ About 20 yards (18 m) past the ruins, turn right along track by wall and follow it to wood. Walk along right side of wood, then take track bearing left to tower. Descend broad slope from tower to gate in wall ③. For 3-mile (5-km) walk, turn right at the gate, and follow path by perimeter wall back to ①. For 8-mile (13-km) walk, go through wood and car park to T-junction. Follow the road opposite for 250 yards (229 m) to sign-posted footpath and stile on right. Walk down right-hand side of first field, then left-hand side of next 2 fields to road. ④ Cross road, go over stile and footbridge, and follow waymarks across golf course to stile into field. Go round right-hand side of field, then on to track which leads to road, ignoring track on right. ⑤ Turn right and follow road for 200 yards (183 m) to gated entrance to Broombriggs Farm. Enter first field on left and follow waymarked path along right-hand side of fields. Bear left in third field to track, then turn right to road. ⑥ Cross and go through gate, then along path into wood. After 75 yards (68 m), turn left along broad track. Follow track right round Beacon Hill, descending through wood to car park. ⑦ Just before car-park barrier, turn right along path to picnic site. Follow path by wall to road and car park for Broombriggs. Take path from car park through middle of field, along edge of wood, and down lane to crossroads. Go straight over, up steep hill, then take path on left at top. Follow path to road. ⑧ Turn right past Wheatsheaf Inn to T-junction. Turn right to next T-junction and bear right again. ⑨ At sharp right bend, bridle track enters Swithland Wood ahead. Follow track into wood for 350 yards (320 m). In clearing by iron railings, ignore main horse ride, and take track bearing left. Follow this straight ahead for ½ mile (0.8 km), ignoring all paths to left and right. ⑩ At stone embankment over stream, take small path on left by fence which leads to stile into field. Cross, then bear right across field to corner and road. Cross road to return to ①.

Bradgate House was built as a hunting lodge by Thomas Grey, 1st Marquis of Dorset, in 1490. It was unusual for its time, being constructed from bricks, rather than stone, and not fortified. The most famous member of the Grey family was Lady Jane Grey, born at Bradgate. Following the death of Edward VI, she was placed on the throne by her scheming father-in-law, the Duke of Northumberland. Her reign lasted 9 days: she was deposed and beheaded on the orders of Mary Tudor. The house fell into decay in the 18th C. and now only the chapel remains intact.

Bradgate Park has been a deer park since the Middle Ages; fallow and red deer still graze. The land has never been cultivated, and has changed little over the centuries. The pollarded oaks are probably the last remnants of the ancient Charnwood Forest. The Park was bought in 1928 by a wealthy local industrialist, Charles Bennion, and presented to the City and Country for "the quiet enjoyment of the people for all time . . .".

This tower was built in 1786 by another of the Grey family, the 5th Earl of Stamford, supposedly to commemorate the accidental death of his miller, 'Old John'. It was used as a hunting lodge for many years. The column on the hill to the S is a war memorial to the Leicestershire Yeomanry.

Broombriggs is a working farm with an interesting 'farm trail'. Visitors should keep strictly to the concessionary footpaths.

Beacon Hill is one of the finest viewpoints in the county. There is a topo-scope 100 yards (91 m) E of the summit. The jagged rocky outcrops are some of the oldest rocks in the country, volcanic granite about 700 million years old. Half-way up the E slope of the hill are traces of the ramparts of an Iron Age hill-fort. Interesting Bronze Age finds, including axes and spearheads, have also been made on the hill.

The Wheatsheaf Inn.

Swithland Wood is an ancient, deciduous wood which contains old slate pits and flooded quarries. The attractive blue-green slate was used for roofs and tombstones in the county from the Middle Ages until the end of the last century. The main quarry pool (near ⑩) is very deep and dangerous; it can be viewed safely from behind the perimeter fence.

East Midlands
LEICESTERSHIRE

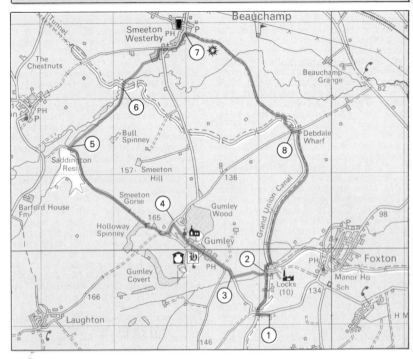

Foxton Locks and The Grand Union Canal

6½ miles (10.5 km) Sheet 141
692892

Moderate The highlight of the walk is a fascinating piece of canal engineering, best seen in summer, when a great many boats are negotiating the locks. The rest is a pleasant ramble through pasture and attractive villages. *Towpath, fields; mud under canal bridge ⑥. Fields between ⑥ and ⑦ are sometimes ploughed.*

Start Foxton, 12 miles (19 km) SE of Leicester. From Leicester, follow the A6 towards Market Harborough. After 12 miles, take minor road to Foxton, following signs through village for Foxton Locks **car park**. Parking at Foxton Locks car park.

① From car park follow signs to canal. Go over footbridge to towpath on left bank of canal, and follow to locks. ② At bottom lock, cross canal by footbridge, then recross, turning right over brick bridge. Go through gate, then along track into field, and bear right to field corner and road. ③ Turn right to Gumley, and go through village to sharp left bend. Follow footpath by left of church into field, then bear right across field to road ④. Turn left to triangular road junction. Take track on right and follow for one mile (1.5 km) to reservoir. ⑤ At dam, cross footbridge over stream on right, and follow waymarks to path junction sign. Ignore paths to right and left and take path ahead for next 3 fields, keeping between stream on left, and feeder channel for canal, on right. ⑥ Go under bridge and follow track into second field. Cross stile in hedge on right, and go across middle of next 2 fields towards village to join lane. Follow lane to main road, then turn right through village and continue ¼ mile (0.5 km) to Debdale Lane, on right. ⑦ Follow lane, which soon

becomes a track, and continue this for 1¼ miles (2 km) to canal, crossing bridge to join road at Debdale Wharf. ⑩ Go over bridge and take towpath on left bank for 1¼ miles, back to locks and ①.

Foxton Locks are a remarkable flight of 10 locks which raise the level of the canal by 75 feet (23 m). Originally built in 1812, the canal eventually formed part of the Grand Union Canal, linking Midland coalfields with London. It took vessels nearly an hour to negotiate the locks, so, to speed up traffic, an ingenious lift system was built at the end of the last century. This could raise or lower boats in 12 minutes, but it proved uneconomic to operate and was abandoned in 1911. The lift site, now being partly restored, is on the Foxton side of the locks. The canal and locks were virtually disused by 1945 and were nearly closed, but they are now enjoying a revival.

Bottom Lock at Foxton Locks – lowest in the flight of 10, formerly scene of long queues of well-laden barges.

Gumley has a Victorian Village Butchery Museum along the main street on the left (not open on Saturdays). An Italian-style bell tower and hunting stable block are now all that remains of Gumley Hall, the home for many years of the Murray-Smith family. It had literary connections in 18th C., when playwrights such as Goldsmith wrote and performed dramas in a private theatre here.

The oldest part of St. Helen's Church is 12th C., but the tower and S aisle were built in the 14th C.

The King's Head.

The pronounced ridges and furrows in the fields are remnants of medieval ploughing strips.

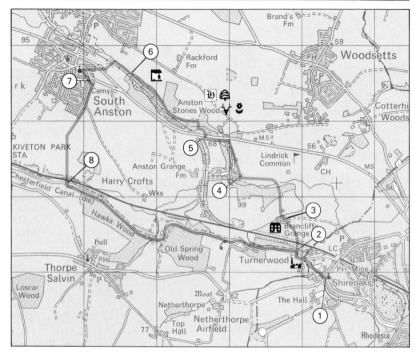

The Chesterfield Canal
6¾ miles (11 km) Sheet 120 553809

Easy The combination of an interesting canal and an abundance of wild flowers makes a pleasant route. *Meadow, woodland, fields, towpath; 2 climbs; mud.*

Start Shireoaks, 2½ miles (4 km) W of Worksop. Take the A57 N from Worksop. After 2 miles (3 km), turn S on to minor road signposted to the church. **Parking** opposite the church.

❶ Take narrow road opposite church and immediately turn right along a lane signposted Public Footpath to Turnerwood ½. Go along bank of Chesterfield Canal, cross bridge and stile straight ahead. ❷ Go half-left to another stile. Take stile and steps straight on across railway embankment, and follow path across field to left of white house. Alternatively (by permission of Mr. Sidda of Brancliffe Grange), pass under railway 100 yards (91 m)

further along, then go across meadow to grange, but *please close all gates*. Pass behind grange ❸ and turn left through gate and go up hill. Pass through wood to reach Monk's Bridge, just after crossing a feeder stream. Turn left to cross fourth and fifth fairways with due care. Follow yellow posts marking footpath along edge of golf course, ignoring a track dropping away left into Lindrick Dale. ❹ Follow hedged lane to the A57. Turn left along verge and continue for 200 yards (183 m), then cross to enter Anston Stones Wood ❺. Go down to stream and follow wide path passing under railway viaduct and along stream before gradually climbing out of valley. (Alternatively, cross stream by footbridge and tackle steep path ahead, turning left along top of wood.) Paths converge at wide grassy area ❻. Near end of grassy sward, bear left, down into valley. Cross footbridge and railway line, then climb to join the A57 beside South Anston service station. Cross road and follow narrow lane opposite to South

184

Anston church. Turn left, and after passing small housing estate to right, take the bridleway ⑦ on right, signposted Thorpe Salvin. Ignore farm road to left, and continue downhill, crossing railway to reach canal ⑧. Turn left to follow towpath to ⑨.

🚤 The Chesterfield Canal was surveyed by James Brindley and completed in 1777 to carry lead and coal from the Chesterfield area to the Trent. It was bought by the Manchester and Lincoln Union Railway in 1848, and thereafter traffic declined. Though the section from Worksop to the Trent is still navigable, the walk passes 22 locks barely used this century, following the collapse of the Norwood tunnel (to the W) in 1908.

🏚 Brancliffe Grange was held by the Cistercian monks of Roche Abbey until claimed by the Crown in 1538. The house and old barn opposite have roof beams thought to date from the

Red squirrel, declining since the advent of the North American grey squirrel.

mid-16th C., but the buildings could be much older.

🔟 Anston Stones Wood was, around 1900, the subject of acrimonious discussion between the Duke of Leeds and local people over rights of way. A court case resulted in victory for the Duke, but in the 1930s the woods were acquired by Anston Parish Council, who continue to maintain them. The wood has a fine mix of trees, including beech, oak, birch and yew, and is said to harbour red squirrels. Flowers include wood anemones, betony, cowslips and bee orchids.

Easily accessible from the upper path is a cave where excavations have revealed brown bear and reindeer bones, and some flints from a Palaeolithic and Mesolithic culture.

185

East Midlands
NOTTINGHAMSHIRE

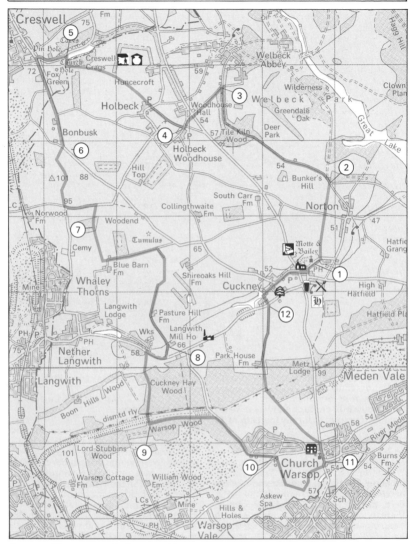

Cresswell Crags and Three Mills
12¼ miles (19.5 km) Sheet 120
567714

Easy Ancient cave dwellings and attractive old mill buildings give this walk historic interest. The locality is still largely unspoiled. *Fields, meadows, woodland; 2 climbs; mud.*

Start Cuckney, 7 miles (11 km) S of Worksop on the A60. At village, turn left along the A616, then first left to church. Use the church **car park**.

① From church, walk along Norton Road to stile on left, just past River Poulter. Continue, parallel with river, to stile on steep wooded bank on right. Enter field and follow hedge on right to road. Cross, and continue with fence now on left. Go through ornate kissing gate and pass lodge and wrought-iron gates to enter gated Private Road bordered by lime trees ②. Ignore first road on left, but take the second ③ to the A60 and cross to Holbeck Woodhouse. Take right-hand road at village ④. At Holbeck turn left, then right into narrow lane. Follow straight course along edge of 2 fields and across meadow. Continue along 2 more field edges, then go straight up hill to join woods on right. Follow edge of woods around to right to reach Cresswell Crags ⑤. Turn left along road and left again at the A616. Follow footpath along the A616 for ½ mile (0.8 km) to Bonbusk ⑥. Do not enter bridleway on right, but go over stile by nearby gate and cross field to end of hedge opposite. Enter field on left and follow hedge along 2 fields to road. Turn left for 200 yards (183 m), then right through a gate and head for end of wood. Take narrow hedged path leading to path along edge of wood ⑦. Continue to old stone stile into meadow below Blue Barn Farm. Go left to a kissing gate and on along track past wood. Take hedged lane right, climb gate and turn right to cross field diagonally. After crossing stile, walk along field edge and then lane to Langwith Mill ⑧. Join the A632, turn right and continue for 200 yards, then go left along signposted lane. Go straight on through Cuckney Hay Wood, and through tunnel under disused mineral railway ⑨. Turn left and follow path near track to road. Turn right along road (or take path just inside Collier Wood to avoid walking on road) to T-junction ⑩. Cross road ahead to enter hedged lane. Take left-hand fork to sports field, then go left around edge to Church Warsop church ⑪. Turn left through churchyard, and continue along the A60 for 100 yards (91 m). Cross stile on left, go diagonally over field and continue to far corner of next field. Go past telegraph pole to corner of plantation. Follow path down edge of wood, veer slightly right, then go left along forest ride to join Park House Farm's access road. Follow this to the A632 ⑫. Cross road, go over Mill Hill, and pass along School Lane. Go straight

along Cresswell Road to reach point ①.

🗓 Caves lining the gorge bear evidence of occupation by Neanderthal man (about 43000 B.C.) and Modern man (from about 30,000 years ago). They probably hunted herds of migrating animals passing through the gorge. Later inhabitants (from 13,000 years ago) appear to have hunted horses. Stone tools found in the cave known as Mother Grundy's Parlour resemble those of the Creswellian – a late Palaeolithic culture in France. Examples of the finds from the caves, including carved bones, can be seen at the Visitor Centre at the eastern end of the crags (open Tues–Sat, 10–5, May–Sept and 10–4.30 Nov–Feb; restricted hours at other times of year.

🚣 Langwith Mill, powered by the River Poulter, was built in 1760 as a cotton mill. In the 1930s it was converted to grain, but is now a crumbling shell, despite being a listed building. Traces of a substantial hamlet can be seen in the adjoining fields, but only the attractive Mill House survives intact.

🏠 Old Hall Farm, adjoining the church in Church Warsop, is a 14th-C. manor house which underwent numerous changes in Tudor times. Just S of the church is a mill pond, separated from its mill by the A60. The mill is dated 1767, but it is clearly older; there are Norman records of a mill here.

🌳 The Mill Hill, created from the waste when Cuckney mill pool was dug, is crowned by many fine beeches.

⛪ The churchyard of Cuckney's mainly 13th-C. church extends over the site of a fortified manor house.

🍺 The Greendale Oak Inn is named after the oak tree in which an arch was cut in 1724, so that the Duke of Portland could drive a coach and 2 horses through and win a bet. An inlaid cabinet was made from the wood cut out of the tree, and was kept at Welbeck Abbey. Despite attempts to prop it up over the years, the tree, which once stood a few miles away, is no longer to be seen.

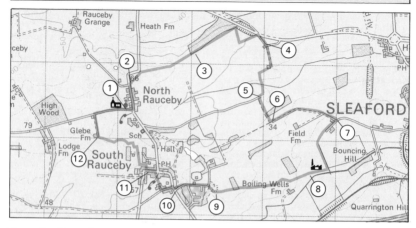

Rauceby Round
7½ miles (12 km) Sheet 130 021465

Moderate Through attractive villages and along the Slea. *Fields, woodlands.*

Start North Rauceby, 4 miles (6.5 km) W of Sleaford. **Parking** on verge by church.

① From church, walk towards war memorial and turn left along Main Street. ② Turn right through field gate 100 yards (91 m) past the last house on right, then head diagonally left, uphill across field. At end of field, turn right, with hedge on left, go through gate and continue to wood. ③ At edge of wood, keep along edge of field with wood on left. At far end, by telegraph pole, turn right, with hedge on left. In 150 yards (140 m) turn left with hedge on left to reach A17. ④ Turn right into lay-by then branch right again up track (signposted Bridleway Sleaford 1 mile). At farm buildings, turn right and then left behind barn. Turn right along edge of field and follow good track down hill to join drove lane. ⑤ At first hedge on left, turn left off drove lane on to track towards wood. ⑥ At T-junction turn left and continue on track bearing right after 200 yards (180 m). ⑦ Turn right, and, after 150 yards (137 m), proceed straight on when track leads to left. Continue straight on at end of hedge with dyke on right. At

grass bridge turn left with ditch on left. On reaching River Slea turn right and follow field boundary towards Boiling Wells Farm. ⑧ Turn left with fence on left and continue past quarry. Keep straight on to end of quarry then turn right, then left, with hedge now on right. ⑨ Turn right over stile and go left uphill around quarry edge. Take clear track through plantation to signpost and stile. Turn left along Pinfold Lane. ⑩ Turn right at T-junction and left into Cliffe View. After 250 yards (229 m) turn right into Beech Rise. Go through kissing gate between nos 6 and 7 and follow footpath uphill to another kissing gate. Turn left at road. ⑪ Turn right off road through metal gate immediately beyond Mill entrance. Bear diagonally left to edge of wood and maintain same direction across field, aiming for right-hand end of wall. Turn left at wall and walk towards farm buildings and metal gate in corner, then follow green lane. ⑫ Turn right through metal gate with farm and hedge on immediate left. Turn right at road to ①.

🏠 North Rauceby's church had a remarkable incumbent at the end of the 18th C: John Pugh, who made his parishioners pay public penance if they had offended his moral sensibilities.

🧺 A traditional industry along the banks of the River Slea was osier gathering.

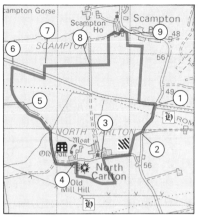

Viewpoint on a Roman Road
5 miles (8 km) Sheet 121 954784

Easy Setting out from a historic cross-roads on Lincoln Cliff, the route takes in open farmland and two interesting old villages. *Arable countryside, escarpment; mud on spring line between ❷ and ❸. There may be some crop obstruction between ❾ and ❿.*

Start Till Bridge Lane Viewpoint, 4½ miles (7 km) N of Lincoln on the B1398 at junction with Till Bridge Lane. Buses from Lincoln and Scunthorpe stop near North Carlton and at Scampton. Walk to Till Bridge Lane Viewpoint to join walk. **Car park** at viewpoint on N side of Till Bridge Lane.

❶ From viewpoint walk towards Lincoln on the B1398 for ¼ mile (0.5 km). ❷ Turn right through field gate (signposted) and bear diagonally left on path across the cliff edge to join North Carlton Lane. Turn right and opposite the village hall ❸ turn left on to track. Turn right at the first hedge with hedge on your left and follow headland to stile. Turn left over stile and go straight forward to stile and signpost on farm track. Turn right to road. ❹ Turn left along lane at grass triangle and right on to signposted green lane. ❺ Where farm track turns left, continue straight on with hedge on right. ❻ Turn right along Till Bridge Lane, continue for 400 yards (366 m), and then turn left on

to signposted track. ❼ After 150 yards (137 m), turn right across ditch and walk straight ahead along ill-defined path in first field, but with dyke on right in second field. At lane ❽ walk straight across to diverted path and follow way-marks to Scampton village. Turn right on to main road through the village. ❾ Turn right off the road to follow diverted path (signposted). Turn left along dyke and then right on waymarked path back to Till Bridge Lane; turn left, uphill, to ❿.

🔟 Till Bridge Lane was a Roman road leading to a crossing of the Trent. King Harold and his troops marched along here on the way to Hastings in 1066, after defeating Harald Hadrada at the battle of Stamford Bridge. Middle Street, now the B1398, is a far more ancient road. It was a trackway linking all the spring-line villages along the cliff edge.

〰️ This is the western escarpment of Lincoln Cliff, a narrow strip of limestone that runs N–S for almost 50 miles (80 km), being broken only at Lincoln. On either side there is impervious clay, so water soaking down through the permeable limestone emerges as springs at the base of the escarpment. Villages like North Carlton and Scampton were established along the spring line. Their parishes are narrow E–W strips, each taking in a section of cliff edge, lowland fen to the W, and upland heath to the E – uncultivated common land until the early 19th C. This offered each parish a variety of agricultural land.

🔟 There was once a Middle Carlton here, midway between North and South Carlton, but it disappeared with the depopulation of the countryside after the Black Death. The outline of the village can be seen, in a certain evening light, from the cliff.

✳️ The mounds of this North Carlton field are probably the remains of the village's medieval fishpond.

🏛️ In 1541, Henry VIII stayed in the manor house at North Carlton on his way to Lincoln. He honoured his host, John Monson, by knighting him.

The Spa Trail and the Viking Way
8½ miles (13.5 km)
Sheet 122 256694

Easy Views over the Bain valley and colourful local history *Canalized river, abandoned railway line, woodland; mud between* ③ *and* ④.

Start Horncastle, 21 miles (34 km) E of Lincoln on the A158. Turn on to the Sleaford road at the traffic lights in the town. Almost immediately, turn off the main road down The Wong and continue to the playing field and swimming pool. Buses to Horncastle from Lincoln and Alford. **Parking** by Horncastle Open Air Swimming Pool.

① From pool, cross bridge over canalized River Bain and turn left along the river-

Horncastle: St Mary's Church, built of the greenstone local to the area, can be quite clearly distinguished left of centre.

side. ② At road, turn right, continue for 50 yards (46 m), and then left on to disused railway line (Spa Trail). ③ After 3 miles (5 km), by former railway-crossing gate-house, turn right into Highall Wood to follow clearly marked green lane. Follow edge of wood around to right and continue through pastures to church at Martin. Continue straight on to road. ④ Turn left and follow road for 1½ miles, (2.5 km). Go round sharp left and right bends, and take right fork at junction. At left-hand bend go straight on, to walk diagonally left across field to far left-hand corner by old railway. ⑨ Cross dyke and continue along edge of field to white field gate with bungalow on left. ⑩ At road,

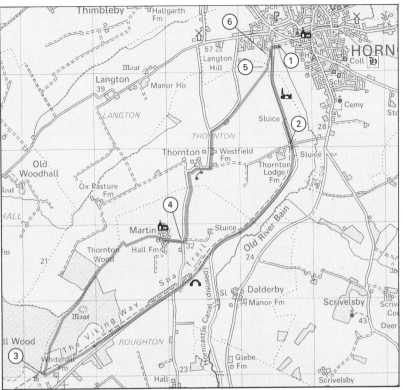

turn right across old railway siding to small path leading back to river and ①.

🏛 Horncastle, standing at the point where the Wolds give way to the Fens and the Bain and Waring rivers meet, was once Bonavallum, a Roman fort. The remains of the fort can still be
🏚 seen in the town. The Church of St. Mary has many mementos of the Battle of Winceby, fought nearby in 1643, when Cromwell came within inches of losing his life after his horse fell dead beneath him. Grabbing another horse, he went on to win the battle. He later arranged for the body of his would-be-slayer – Sir Ingram Hopwood – to be buried in the churchyard.

🚢 The Horncastle Navigation, a canalization of the River Bain, was opened in 1802 to link Horncastle with the River Witham. The cargo was largely agricultural produce such as grain and malt. With the opening of the railway, traffic declined and the canal was finally closed in 1885. (The swimming pool stands on the site of the old dry dock.) The railway line from Woodhall Spa was in turn closed by Dr. Beeching, and is now the bridleway known as the Spa Trail.

⌂ This is the only bridge along the whole 6-mile (9.5-km) stretch of railway. In the flatness of Lincolnshire, level crossings were more usual.

🏚 Martin's Church stands in a farmyard. Its Norman and medieval features have been largely obscured by Victorian rebuilding.

EAST ANGLIA AND REGION

HERTFORDSHIRE AND ESSEX

SUFFOLK

OUSE VALLEY AND FENS

NORFOLK

HERTFORDSHIRE AND ESSEX

This section sets out to complete the circle of good walking withing easy reach of London that starts with the North Downs and Surrey to the south, and continues, on the city's west and north-west flanks, with the Thames Valley and Chilterns. It is not particularly easy to find attractive routes on, or just outside London's northern boundaries; indeed some say that the best of north London walking is found within the city limits; that an early morning stroll across Hampstead Heath can offer a real feeling of tranquillity. Just on the city's north-eastern boundary is Epping Forest, with miles of footpaths – but it is thronged at weekends. The old pollarded hornbeams are perhaps the most impressive feature of these ancient woodlands. Further out from the city, you have to be prepared to take the countryside as you find it. Pre-war ribbon development, new housing estates, light industry and intensive agriculture have all taken their toll. As in any over-populated area, hills are the best chance of enjoying the illusion of distance from urban sprawl; the flatter parts make the reality inescapable.

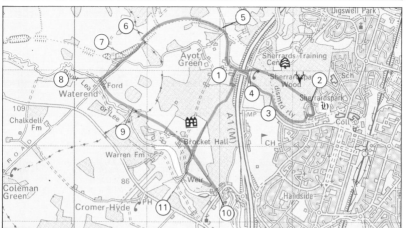

Sherrardspark Woods and Brocket Park
6 miles (9.5 km) Sheet 166 222138

Easy Rural landscapes within easy reach of Welwyn. *Mixed woodland, old railway, parkland; mud. The path after ❽ is occasionally flooded. Keep strictly to marked footpaths in Brocket Park.*

Start Ayot Green, one mile (1.5 km) W of Welwyn Garden City. Take Bridge Road from Welwyn Garden City centre, turn left on to Valley Road, then N on to the B197 and after one mile, turn off towards Ayot St. Peter and Ayot St. Lawrence. After crossing motorway, turn left into Brickwall Close, where there is **parking**.

❶ Walk back over motorway and cross the B197. Turn left and walk 40 yards (37 m) to stile into wood. After 150 yards (137 m), join wider ride and follow this to edge of wood ❷. Leave wood and go straight ahead on joining Roundwood Drive for 100 yards (91 m). Turn right into Reddings, and take path between nos 9 and 11 into wood. Turn right, following disused railway embankment on left for ½ mile (0.8 km). ❸ At cross-track, turn left over old level crossing and climb hill. Turn right at golf course and continue with course close on left, ignoring turnings on each side. ❹ Leave wood, recross motorway and continue into Ayot Green, bearing right downhill. ❺ At foot of hill,

climb steps on left, on to Ayot Greenway and follow for ¾ mile (1 km). ❻ At signpost Bridleway Link, descend on right, go under bridge, and turn right at once (yellow arrow). Keep left of old railway for 330 yards (302 m), then bear left to lane ❼. Turn right, descending to ford at Waterend ❽. Take path on left, just before river, and continue to enter woodland ❾. Follow path, signposted Lemsford, and waymarked with yellow arrows to Lemsford Mill ❿. Double back into park, forking left on alternative path, marked by yellow arrows, descending towards lake. ⓫ Just before drive, turn right and follow path, always with yellow arrows, signposted Ayot Green. Cross stile by cottage and return to ❶.

🦌 Sherrardspark Wood is an unusually varied patch of woodland. Tracks of the shy muntjac deer may be seen.

🏘 Garden cities, where people could enjoy modern facilities and still live and work in country surroundings, were the dream of philanthropist Ebenezer Howard, whose book, *Garden Cities of Tomorrow*, was first published in 1898. Letchworth (founded 1903) was the earliest, followed by Welwyn Garden City, whose first bricks were laid in 1920.

🏛 Splendid Brocket Hall, built by the Georgian architect James Paine.

Hertfordshire and Essex
NEAR HATFIELD

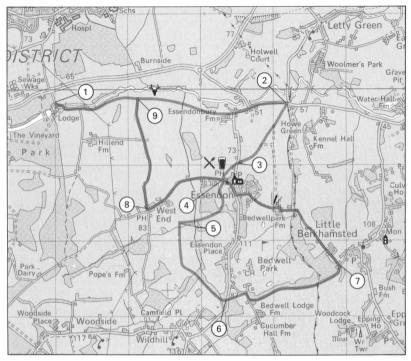

Essendon
4½ or 8½ miles (7 or 13.5 km)
Sheet 166 250098

Easy Remarkably secluded countryside, with gentle hills and valleys typical of Hertfordshire. *Farmland, woodland; mud. Path after ⑥ may be overgrown with nettles. If so, turn left along road, then right at first junction to rejoin route at next junction.*

Start Cecil Saw Mill, one mile (1.5 km) E of Hatfield. Follow the A414 E from Hatfield and turn right ¾ mile (1 km) after junction with the A1000. The lane is marked No through road for motor vehicles, and Lewis Tyler and Son. **Parking** off lane beyond saw-mill entrance, or in lay-bys on the A414, under power line.

① Continue along lane, crossing River Lea. Where lane turns right, uphill, follow bridleway (marked by blue arrow), remaining close to river, ignoring right turns. At the B158, continue along road in the same direction for ½ mile (0.8 km). ② Just before second turning on left, cross stile on right and double back uphill (signposted Public Footpath Essendon ¾). As Essendon village becomes visible, continue to right of a field boundary (broad track bearing left is not right of way). At field corner, go under power line, over stile on right, and straight across field to gate between houses. ③ Cross road and go over fence at broken stile opposite, bearing left uphill. Head for the last house on right. For the 4½-mile (7-km) walk, turn right at road, and descend to cross brook. Continue along lane for ¾ mile to junction with bridleway ⑨. Follow directions from ⑩ to start. For the 8½-mile (13.5-km) walk, turn left at road ④ and almost immediately turn right on to signposted footpath behind Salisbury Crest inn. After stile at corner of churchyard, cross 3 small fields, fol-

Essendon Church, Victorian restoration, with an unusual black basaltware font.

lowing footpath signs. Turn right on to track running downhill to wooden plank bridge over Essendon Brook. Cross, and continue through kissing gate, uphill to green lane. ⑤ Turn left into lane, passing signpost (Bridleway to Wildhill). After ¼ mile (0.5 km), take path on left indicated by yellow arrow on post. After stile, follow hedge downhill to enter woodland at bottom. Ignore left fork, cross stream, and continue ahead on the right of another stream for ¼ mile. Cross foot-bridge and ascend slope to road. ⑥ Cross road and stile to footpath between fences. Emerging at road junction, take road opposite for just under one mile, to reach lodge on left at right-hand bend. ⑦ Turn into drive (signposted Public Bridleway) and continue, passing through gateway and descending gradually to strip of wood. After crossing stream, go straight

uphill to Bedwellpark Farm. Go over stile into yard, turn right between first 2 out-houses, then go left on to farm road, continuing uphill to Essendon. Turn left at road, then right along the B158, and in 50 yards (46 m) fork left (signposted West End), to return to Salisbury Crest. Continue down the lane, descending steeply to cross the brook. Continue for ¾ mile along lane. ⑧ Take bridleway on right signposted with blue arrow and figure 1. Follow this for about one mile until bridleway by the Lea is reached ⑨. Turn left back to ①.

꙼ This stretch of the Lea, Hertfordshire's major river, is now well-stocked with fish, including barbel, chub, bream, gudgeon, perch, pike, rudd and carp.

🍴 The Salisbury Crest is a 17th-C. coaching inn serving real ales and food. The name is a reminder that Hatfield House, 2½ miles (4 km) to the W, has been a residence of the Cecil family since it was built by Robert Cecil, 1st Earl of Salisbury, in 1608. Essendon Church is a Victorian restoration of 1883, but has some ancient monuments and a remarkable ceramic font, one of the few in Britain. It is made of black basaltware, a special clay formulated by Josiah Wedgwood in 1779. Manganese and iron-bearing ores were combined with fine Devonshire clays to give the dense black effect.

🏛 Stratton's Folly, a circular brick tower, was built by John Stratton in 1789 with the reasonable purpose of observing the passage of his ships up and down the Thames, 17 miles (27.5 km) to the S.

🔭 Views to the NE, and later to the NW, across the Lea Valley are mainly of fields and woods: surprisingly little is seen of the nearby urban areas. This is the unchanged landscape described by John Betjeman in his poem *Hertfordshire*:

*Colour-washed cottages reed-thatched
And weather-boarded water mills,
Flint churches, brick and plaster patched,
On mildly undistinguished hills . . .*

197

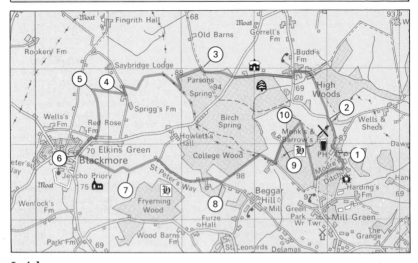

Jericho
6½ miles (10.5 km) Sheet 167
641019

Easy Through peaceful villages, including a section of St. Peter's Way. *Woods, fields, meadows; mud; wire across the path between ❹ and ❺ (easily climbed).*

Start Mill Green Common, 6½ miles (10.5 km) NE of Brentwood. From the A12 take the B1002 to Ingatestone. At second crossroads in town, turn left to Fryerning, then turn right towards Mill Green. Fork left past The Cricketers pub, and continue for one mile (1.5 km) to the Viper pub. If using public transport, take bus to Blackmore from Brentwood and join walk at ❻. (From bus stop go past green on right. At T-junction, turn left then go right to join route.) **Parking** on Mill Green Common opposite The Viper.

❶ Facing the pub on left, turn right along road then fork left for ¼ mile (0.5 km). On left-hand bend ❷ go straight ahead on bridle path to wood. Keep wood to right on track which leads left between houses to T-junction. Turn left, then right along Metson's Lane. Pass coppiced wood on left to road. Cross and take path opposite, through wood. At crossing track, turn right to end of wood. ❸ Turn left, following wood, then hedge on left along wind-ing field-edge for one mile to road. Turn left and continue for 100 yards (91 m), then right on to signposted footpath at New Farm ❹. Pass between buildings and go on with hedge on right. This leads to a track. Follow this and at end, keep hedge on left to field corner. Go through, crossing hedge to power-line pole. ❺ Turn left over ditch and follow ditch on right round bends, then turn left to hedge corner. Turn right over bridge and stile. Follow hedge on left, then track to road. Turn right and just before third road on right ❻, turn left on to signposted path across field. Pass through, crossing hedge and turn left. Do not take the defined path ahead. Keep hedge on left and 75 yards (68 m) before wood ❼, turn left on to track. At hedge, fork right and continue for ½ mile (0.8 km) to wood. Go over crossing track, and 75 yards beyond wood ❽ turn left on to track. After ½ mile, turn right on crossing track and beyond buildings turn left on another track. When track bears left towards farm ❾, turn right on to track on edge of, and through, wood. On far side, bear right, then cut back sharp right through wood ❿. Do not follow path out of wood. At Woodside House cross road on to track beside Moore's Ditch. When path divides, keep ahead following waymarks to pass to left of Rumplestilt-skin Cottage. Follow lane ahead then go left, back to ❶.

Church at Jericho: pagoda-like belfry.

The Viper claims to be the only pub of that name in the country. During the Second World War, local soldiers simply addressed their letters to the landlord at 'The Viper, England'.

This is a coppice wood, where trees – largely oak and hornbeam – are cut almost to ground level so that they sprout bushy growths of thin poles, used for fencing, stakes, and, increasingly, wood-burning stoves. The poles are harvested every 16–20 years, depending on the species of tree and the proposed use of the wood. After a long absence, this type of tree culture is again becoming a feature of woodland management in Essex.

In an attempt to ensure the preservation of the attractive old barns in the area, Essex County Council is undertaking a survey. Many have been restored or converted into houses, a good example being the barn at Barrow Farm, with its half-hipped tiled roof and 2 midstreys – projecting porches.

The present Jericho Priory stands on the foundations of a building frequented by Henry VIII. His courtiers would say, "He has gone to Jericho" – the origin of the expression meaning to disappear. The original priory was later pulled down at his command and a few stones in the grounds of the present house and some parts of the present church are all that remain of it. The pagoda-like timber belfry of the church was built in the 15th C.

St. Peter's Way, which the route follows for a section here, is one of a number of long-distance footpaths in Essex. It links Ongar with St. Peter's Chapel in Bradwell-on-Sea, a distance of some 45 miles (72.5 km).

Fee banks were medieval boundaries to mark common land limits, especially between adjoining manors. The banks are particularly well-defined here. Commoners' rights varied from manor to manor, but could, in woodland, include *cartbote*: to take wood to make or repair carts; *foldbote*: to take wood to make sheep-folds, and *hedgebote*: to take wood to make or repair fences.

The purpose of Moore's Ditch has long been a puzzle to historians. One explanation is that it served to partially conceal troops, and was positioned to give an extensive view to the SE.

Hertfordshire and Essex

Railway Trail
11½ miles (18.5 km) Sheet 167
762228

Easy The first part of a 2-day circular route, or a one-day linear walk, following an attractive disused railway track. *Fields, disused railway, riverside; 2 climbs; may be very wet between ⑤ and ⑥. Walking on the railway is by permission of Essex County Council.*

Start Braintree, 11 miles (17.5 km) N of Chelmsford on the A131. Trains from Chelmsford, Colchester and London (change at Witham). Buses from Bishop's Stortford. Use the Blyth Meadow **Car Park** off Coggersall Road. **Return** One-day walk: bus from Great Dunmow to Braintree. Check bus times by ringing Braintree (0376) 21415. 2-day walk: overnight in Great Dunmow (see note below) and continue next day using route on pages 202–3, starting the walk at point ②.

① From Braintree station or car park, turn left, curving right to main road. Turn left and right up Fairfield Road. Cross Manor Road bearing left and turn right along Leather Lane (to right of Fosters). Turn left and right along Bank Street. (From car park return to main road; turn left, then right into Panfield Lane.) At T-junction turn left and continue a few yards, then right along Panfield Lane. Beyond Coldnailhurst Avenue, on right, lane turns sharp right, and opposite nos 170–2 turn left on to footpath beside barns ②. Follow path towards wood. At end of second field, bear right and left to stile and track to left of posts, not track leading ahead. Continue past track joining from right and, at top of hill, bear right towards Panfield Hall. 30 yards (27 m) before Hall fence and just before track joins from right, turn left with hedge on right. Cross

track and go over field to bridge. Turn right and follow hedge past house to gap to road. Turn left and continue for 400 yards (366 m), then, 70 yards (64 m) past Little Harpers ③, turn left on to signposted footpath and follow stream for ¾ mile (1 km). When hedge turns right, go half-left to bridge near field corner. Turn right to field corner, then go left round bend. In 30 yards, cross plank bridge on right and turn left into green lane. Follow lane ahead uphill and through farm to road. Turn left and fork left at junction. Just before thatched cottage on left ④, turn right on to signposted footpath. Turn left to field corner, then right following track over fields to main road. Turn left and almost immediately right, with hedge on left, to old railway track. ⑤ Turn right and follow dismantled track for 5½ miles (9 km). Just before factory ⑥, bridge is missing, so descend steps on right and go left to main road. Cross and climb steps on far side. Go over station approach and

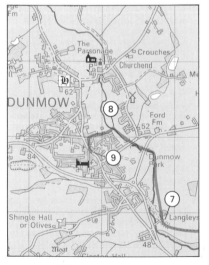

Hertfordshire and Essex
BRAINTREE

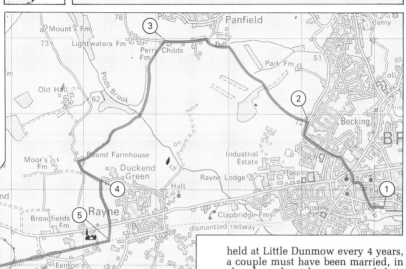

through small gate. In 40 yards (37 m), turn left down steps over goods yard, then go up steps to rejoin old track bed. At end of track descend steeply to river. ⑦ Turn right with river on left and follow main river with plank bridges over side streams to bypass. Cross to footpath opposite, then follow this through white gates to road. Follow river ahead to bridge on left. ⑧ Go ahead up track and follow Mill Lane to junction. Turn left and bear right to main road. For Tourist Information Centre and buses to Braintree turn left ⑨.

🏠 Braintree is at the junction of 2 important Roman roads, Stane Street and the Chelmsford–Sudbury road. Pilgrims, passing through the town to Bury St. Edmunds, brought early prosperity.

🚶 The path here follows the line of the Braintree–Bishop's Stortford railway. It now has an abundance of wild flowers and trees, including dog roses, poppies and white campion. The Great Eastern Railway opened the line in 1869; it was closed in sections from 1966–72.

🏠 To be eligible for the Dunmow flitch of bacon, presented in a ceremony held at Little Dunmow every 4 years, a couple must have been married, in church, and not have regretted their marriage, for a year and a day. 4 couples are required for the ceremony, which was instituted in the 13th C. by Robert Fitzwalter, the lord of the manor. It was a well-known custom, and in 'The Prologue' to the *Canterbury Tales*, the Wife of Bath noted:

The Bacon was not fet for hem, I
trowe,
That some men han in Essex at
Dunmowe. . .

The records of the awarding of the flitch in the 18th C. are hung on the church walls. Also in the church is the chair in which the person who grants the awards sits.

🏠 The name Dunmow is derived from the Anglo-Saxon, meaning 'meadows on a hill'. In 1253 Great Dunmow was granted a market by Henry III and became a prosperous wool town. The market became famous for its toy fairs, but was closed in 1968. St. Mary's Church is 14th C. and has a fine E window and an interesting 15th-C. wooden balcony. In 1785 the first lifeboat was tested on Doctor's Pond, near the square.

🛏 For accommodation ring the Tourist Information Centre, (0371) 0371.

Hertfordshire and Essex
GREAT DUNMOW

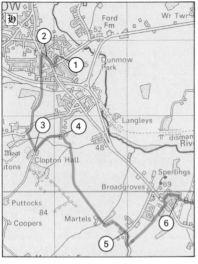

Start Great Dunmow, 9 miles (14.5 km) E of Bishop's Stortford on the A120. Turn left to town centre, but before reaching it turn right in to Chequers Lane and follow signs to **car park**. Buses from Bishop's Stortford and Braintree. Return **One-day** walk: bus from Braintree. Check bus times by ringing Braintree (0376) 21415.

❶ From car park, turn left, walk through further car park and go down Angel Lane. Turn right to war memorial ❷, then turn right again. When lane ends, keep left of Hasler House, following fenced path over bypass and on to road. Turn right then left beside hedge. In field corner, turn right through hedge then go left over ditch. Bear left to road to right of house ❸. Turn left and continue for ¼ mile (0.5 km). At left bend ❹, turn right on to grassy strip to left of house. (If the track is overgrown, divert left into field.) In field corner, turn left and continue for 30 yards (27 m), then go right over bridge. Keep

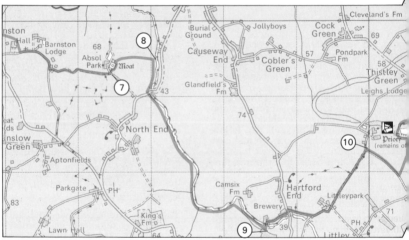

Dunmow
14¾ miles (23.5 km) Sheet 167
628219

Easy The second part of a 2-day route, which can also be a one-day linear walk: an interesting ramble through some picturesque villages. *Arable fields, low hills, disused railway; mud. If field at ❸ is cropped, walk round edge.*

hedge on left. In field corner, turn left over bridge and right over ditch. Turn right, and in field corner, left. Beyond buildings, bear right into drive, following it to road ❺. Go ahead for 100 yards (91 m), then turn left beside house. Beyond house, turn right through gap in hedge and go left. Pass left of barn to road. Turn left, then right, along Berners End. Turn right down Watts Close, bearing left to

footpath to left of no. 19 ⑥. Cross recreation ground, stile, bridle path, field and bridge, aiming about 10 yards (9 m) left of field corner. Continue past buildings, turning right with hedge. Pass to right of church to road. Turn left and continue for ¼ mile. Turn left, following road and track to crossing drive at Absol Park ⑦. Turn right then left between hedge and fence. At end of moat, turn left to join track at end of field. Turn right downhill to stile ⑧. Cross and turn right, following hedge to road. Turn right and continue 30 yards, then go left through gap. Follow river for 1½ miles (2.5 km). Cross plank bridge in undergrowth and bear left with river for further ½ mile (0.8 km). At bridge on left ⑨, cross and pass in front of mill, following drive ahead to road. Enter lane almost opposite. When lane turns sharp right, at Littleypark Farm, go ahead on signposted bridleways to road ⑩; turn right and continue about ¼ mile. Take the signposted footpath on left beside hedge to field corner. Turn left beside

hedge and river. At track, turn right over bridge beside ford, following track to chalet on right. Turn left uphill past barn, then left and right between buildings to road. Turn right, go over crossroads and follow lane for one mile (1.5 km). ⑪ At houses, turn left on to track. In field corner, turn left and continue 30 yards, then right beside hedge and along track to road. Turn left, continue 50 yards (46 m) and, beyond house on right, turn right beside hedge. Go over field and continue, with hedge on left, to road. Turn left and, at junction, keep ahead. At slight right-hand bend ⑫, turn right on to green lane. After ½ mile, lane turns sharp right and shortly left. Follow it for 30 yards, then turn right through gap. Go ahead for 5 yards (4.5 m), then turn left beside hedge. At field corner, cross ditch to crossing track. Turn right and almost immediately left, later passing to left of barn. Go ahead into field and turn right beside hedge to drive. Turn left to road. Turn right and at right-hand bend, go ahead past Gatewood Farm. Bear left, then turn right on old railway track ⑬. Continue for 3 miles (5 km) to Braintree and car park ⑭. Go through car park, then left to road for station. For buses to Dunmow, continue ahead to T-junction, turn left, then right up Fairfield Road. Turn right into Victoria Street for the bus park. For car park continue past Victoria Street and Manor Road. Turn right in School Walk and left to Blyths Meadow.

🄱 See entry on p.201.

🄰 Leez Priory was founded by Augustinian canons at the end of the 12th C. It was dissolved in 1536, when its net annual value was over £114, and was granted to Sir Richard Rich. Using part of the priory and its church as materials, he built a great house; much was demolished in the 18th C.

SUFFOLK

The haunting atmosphere of Suffolk's coast can stay with you long after you have left. Wide, empty horizons are broken here and there by massive churches, many of them abandoned. They were built on the proceeds of wool for the spiritual needs of once-populous villages, now tiny hamlets. At Dunwich, the remains of a busy medieval port lie drowned beneath the encroaching sea. During winter storms, so they say, big waves can make the old church bells ring. Few other places in Britain convey this feeling of man in retreat, and of Nature reclaiming her own.

The opportunities for walking are many. Paths are extensive, and the shore itself offers miles of straightforward going. Even in summer you can soon leave the holiday-makers behind, and in winter, with only the hardiest fishermen for company, it is desolate, windswept and beautiful. Allow plenty of time for walking the beaches: the shingle can halve your usual speed.

Western Suffolk is closer to the twentieth century, and the desolation of the coast contrasts extraordinarily with its safe, rural scenes and well-kept villages. Fields of oil-seed rape make vivid, and sometimes enormous, splashes of yellow on the gently undulating land, and the opulence once brought by the wool trade makes both secular and church architecture something special.

Suffolk
NEAR HADLEIGH

Constable Country
4 miles (6.5 km) Sheet 155 988363

Easy Perhaps the best of the lush, undulating countryside near the Stour Valley which inspired Constable, Gainsborough and many lesser-known artists. *Arable farmland, woodland, meadows. If route just beyond ③ is overgrown, walk around edge of field. Route ill-defined at ⑤ – follow directions carefully.*

Start Stoke-by-Nayland, 6 miles (9.5 km) N of Colchester. Take the A134 from Colchester towards Sudbury. Turn on to the B1087 at Nayland. Stoke-by-Nayland is about 2 miles (3 km) from junction. Buses from Colchester. **Parking** in streets between the church and the junction of the B1087 and the B1068.

① From the crossroads, take the right-hand turn, signposted Ipswich, and after 300 yards (274 m) turn left along path beside the hedge. At bottom, turn left to lane, then turn right through hamlet of Scotland Street. Just beyond River Box ②, turn left into meadow opposite Scotland House. Go straight across meadow to stile. Cross and continue in same direction through thicket, over stile and next meadow. Cross stile to enter woodland and continue up slope and then by left-hand fence for about 50 yards (46 m) to stile ③. Climb, and follow tree-lined path bending right and later left up to gravel road. Walk up hill to turn left along path just before road. Turn right on to track, then left across field. Climb stile, then turn right to crown of pasture, bearing left, down to junction. Go straight ahead to end of garden, then take fenced path on right ④ to Polstead village green. Turn left down road to pond. At junction, take path opposite, bearing left over field to houses. Keep ahead along lane and turn right, along Mill Lane. About 150 yards (137 m) beyond converted mill, opposite thatched cottage ⑤, turn left up side of field. At farm buildings, go right, then left along grass track into field. Go on up left side of field, then across it past oak tree to road. Turn left past school, then right at junction along Butts Road. At end of row of bungalows on right, take path on left and turn left at path junction towards church. Go through churchyard to point ①.

Stoke-by-Nayland's 15th-C. church is featured in several of Constable's paintings, although not always in its actual surroundings. He was not the only artist of renown to immortalize East Anglia and during his exploration of the area, he said that he felt Gainsborough "in every hedge and hollow tree".

This thatched cottage was the home of Maria Marten until she was found murdered in the infamous Red Barn in 1827. After a year of searching, her would-be husband, and murderer, William Corder, was found, and a sensational inquest, trial and execution followed. The case became a *cause célèbre* and an account of the trial, bound in Corder's skin, is kept at Bury St. Edmunds' museum.

Polstead means 'a place of pools' and takes its name from 2 ponds which once existed between the village and the church. One pond remains today.

A hall was recorded at Polstead in the Domesday Book. The present hall was built in the 18th C. and the title to the land was passed down in an unusual manner called 'Borough English', whereby the youngest son, rather than the eldest, inherited all.

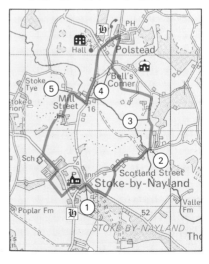

Suffolk
NEAR WICKHAM MARKET

Framlingham and Saxtead Green
8½ miles (13.5 km) Sheet 156
285634

Easy On relatively high ground: a gently undulating clay plateau, delightful in spring when there are splendid displays of wild flowers. *Fields, meadows; mud in fields in winter. Route ill-defined between ④ and ⑤; path may be cropped over.*

Start Framlingham, 15 miles (24 km) NE of Ipswich. Take the A12 from Ipswich towards Lowestoft and turn on to the B1116 to Framlingham at N end of Wickham Market by-pass. **Parking** on Market Hill or near castle.

① From Market Hill, go through covered alleyway in SW corner of square. Turn right over bridge and take the B1119 (Stowmarket road). Opposite Danforth Drive ②, turn left and follow path straight over field to road. Turn left downhill and, just before junction, turn right along green lane. On leaving long field ③, take track to right zigzagging across fields to Saxtead Green. Turn left at road, then right at junction. At bends sign ④, turn left and follow hedge ahead. Cross stile and railway sleeper at end of field on left and walk to right-hand end of small

The post mill at Saxtead Green has been cared for by the Department of the Environment since 1951, and is still in working order.

meadow. Turn right through gateway and continue beside, then beyond, hedge to road. Turn right, and just past Perry Cottage ⑤, turn left to cross field, then continue with ditch on your left. Turn right at end of ditch to follow stream along left side of fields to road junction. Turn left uphill and pass junction before entering field through gateway on right. Follow hedge round to left. As hedge straightens towards wood ⑥, turn right across short length of field to join and follow ditch. Turn left along grass track ⑦ beside next hedge on left and turn diagonally right through gap by wood corner ⑧. Join hedge on left and follow it between farm buildings to road. Turn right and continue to sharp right-hand bend ⑨. Just round bend, turn left down side of field and 40 yards (37 m) before bottom, go left through hedge to cross corner of meadow, and field beyond, to left corner of wood. Follow track straight ahead to metalled private road and turn right. Turn left, uphill at junction and at top ⑩, take path on right beside hedge. Fork right where hedge bends left and

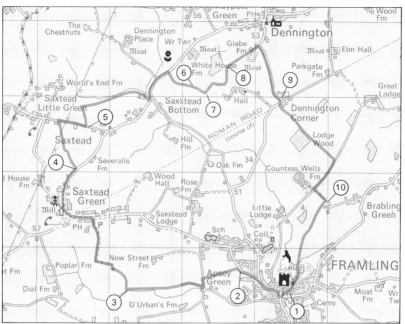

descend towards castle. Cross footbridge into castle grounds and bear left up to bridge at entrance. The street from the castle leads down to ①.

🏚 The post mills of E Suffolk were the finest of their type. The mill at Saxtead Green was probably built in the late 18th C., and produced flour until 1914. Then, like many country mills, it was used to grind animal feed, finally ceasing operation in 1947. It is called a post mill because the body of the windmill (containing all the machinery), rotates around a large post which rests on the stationary base. This meant that the sails always turned to face the wind, propelled by a fantail at one side. The mill is open to visitors in summer.

🌷 An example of 'prairie farming' where hedges and ditches have been removed to create huge fields; but without these 'wildlife highways' farmland becomes devoid of hedge-row birds and mammals. There are

practical disadvantages too – strong winds are not broken by any barriers and can quickly erode the soil.

🏛 St. Mary's Church, Dennington, is a fine Perpendicular building. Most of the church, including the 82-foot (25-m) tower, was built in the 14th C. Lord Bardolph, the man who provided Shakespeare's character of the same name in *Henry IV, Parts I* and *II*, is buried here.

🐦 Framlingham Mere is the haunt of a large variety of birds, including snipe, and the smaller, shorter-billed jack snipe, a winter visitor from Europe. The mere is occasionally visited by garganey, ferruginous duck and Bewick's swan.

🏰 The walls and towers of Framlingham Castle date back to the 13th C., although the ornamental chimneys are Tudor additions. Mary Tudor was staying here in 1553 when she learned that she was to be queen.

Suffolk
LAVENHAM

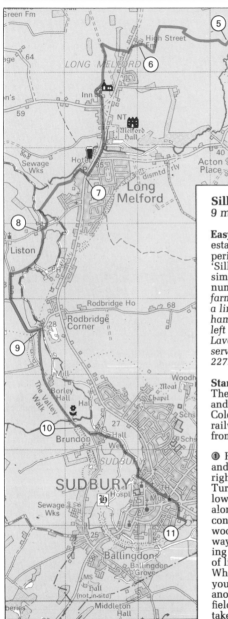

Silly Suffolk
9 miles (14.5 km) Sheet 155 913489

Easy Links 3 small but impressive towns established at the height of Suffolk's prosperity, when the county earned the name 'Silly Suffolk' ('silly' then meaning simple and pious) on account of its numerous churches and abbeys. *Arable farmland, river valley, meadows. This is a linear route designed to start at Lavenham, returning to one's car, previously left at Sudbury. Buses from Sudbury to Lavenham run in the mornings only, and services are infrequent: ring Bures (0787) 227233 for times; no Sunday service.*

Start Lavenham, but leave car at Sudbury. There are bus services to both Lavenham and Sudbury from Bury St. Edmunds and Colchester. Large **car park** by Sudbury railway station; buses to Lavenham leave from bus station nearby.

① From bus stop, walk back to church, and take path past W end. Go diagonally right down meadow, then up to road. Turn left, then right at junction and follow lane to former railway line ②. Go left along this, passing under bridge ③ and continue along cutting and through wood. Take path beside field where railway track has been removed. After crossing track ④, keep on along another length of line and on left side of field beyond it. When fence is reached, the track takes you right to cross the stream and joins another track along lower edge of sloping field ⑤. Turn left to follow this and then take next path to right uphill. The path

208

bends right then left as you climb. Go through hedge gap at top and turn left. Turn right at bottom of slope towards farm. Cross into adjacent field on reaching buildings ⑥. Locate and continue through gap between houses to road. Cross, turn left, then right beside allotments after 100 yards (91 m). Go right at belt of trees, then left over stile and pasture to Kentwell Hall Drive. Turn left and climb metal stile 100 yards on right, then head over pasture, aiming just right of church. Climb 2 stiles on either side of copse and turn left at end of paddock into churchyard. Go down side of green and along Hall Street as far as Cock and Bell Lane ⑦. Turn right, then left at end, behind gardens. Bear right beyond playing fields, and go straight over meadows, aiming for Liston church, to concrete dam by River Stour. Cross this and 2 footbridges, to reach road by Liston Mill ⑧. Turn right, then left after 80 yards (73 m), along narrow earth path. Beyond garden fences, continue along left side of 2 fields, then pass through gate and go straight on to road. Bear left and keep straight on at junction. Just after sharp left bend, turn right along further stretch of old railway walk ⑨, passing Borley Hall and Mill. Immediately past bridge over stream ⑩, bear left along bridleway to Brundon Mill. Bear right in front of cottages opposite mill and keep wall on left before entering paddock. From left-hand corner of this, walk on over meadows towards nearest church towers. Cross river bridge and road by St. Gregory's Church, then keep ahead to Market Hill. Walk through town to station ⑪.

🏰 In the 15th C., Lavenham was one of the richest villages in England. Its prosperity was founded on the wool trade and displayed in large, ornate buildings, including a church with a 141-foot (43-m) tower. Today, the medieval street plan and many half-timbered buildings – notably the Guildhall – remain.

⛪ Holy Trinity Church was designed by the royal mason, Cornelius Cure.

🏛 Melford Hall was built by William Cordell in the 1550s. Cordell went on to become Speaker of the House of Commons and Master of the Rolls, and in 1578 he entertained Elizabeth I at the mansion. It is said that she was welcomed by 500 young gentlemen and 1,500 serving men.

🍺 The 16th-C. Bull Inn is reputedly haunted. A murder was committed near the dining-room door in 1648; some experience mysterious chills.

🌿 Wild flowers to be found around the old railway include devil's bit scabious, meadow saxifrage, hound's-tongue and wild strawberry. On the extensive water meadows at Sudbury, early marsh orchids can be found.

🏰 Gainsborough was born in Sudbury and now has a street named after him. He only worked in the town for 4 years, but he produced some of his most famous work here, including the portrait *Mr. and Mrs. Robert Andrews*.

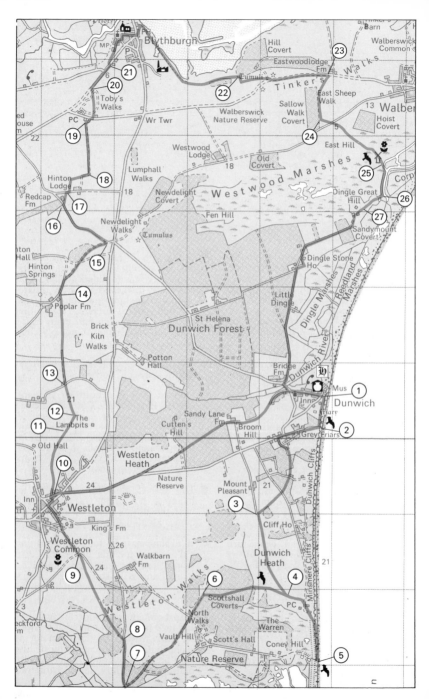

Dunwich and Walberswick
8 or 16 miles (13 or 25.5 km)
Sheet 156 479706

Easy Based on Dunwich, once a prosperous port with a huge abbey, and covering fascinating ground for historians and bird-watchers; binoculars are recommended. *Cliffs, mixed woodland, heath, farmland, tidal marshes, conifer forest. A detour to Minsmere Reserve adds 1¼ miles (2 km) to route. Route liable to be overgrown at ③, between ⑩ and ⑫, ⑰ and ⑲, and at ㉑.*

Start Dunwich, 15 miles (24 km) S of Lowestoft. In village where continue straight to beach; **car park** on beach.

① From car park, go back to junction by The Ship and turn left along path to cliff top, then right along cliff edge. At fence ②, turn right along path under tiny arch, then along track. This joins road at a bend. Follow past Little Grey Friars, then turn left along access drive. From house, continue along grass path which bends to the right and crosses track before reaching road. Go right and immediately left along narrow bridleway. Go straight ahead on track, and where it turns right ③, go left along path through heath towards cottages on Minsmere Cliffs. (Continue past path junction ④ to beach, to visit hides ⑤.) Retrace through car park and at ④, bear left along track beside overhead cables. This bends steadily left and dips to enter woodland. At T-junction ⑥, turn left to follow path beside long clearing. Cross gravel road and keep going ahead on grass track between fields. Track joins earth road at entrance to Minsmere. Soon afterwards, turn sharp right up gravel road by house ⑦. When road bends down to left, fork left in dip through gap beside gate ⑧ to woodland path. Follow path to join lane at bridleway crossing ⑨. Keep on along lane, forking right to descend into village. (For shorter walk, take Dunwich road from top of green. When road bends right, go straight on along sandy road through forest to rejoin lane into Dunwich.) For longer walk, cross street and turn half-right over long triangular green to opening between red-brick wall and row of cottages ⑩. Go through opening and follow lane. After it has crossed open field, keep on along narrower path on left side of 2 fields. Bear left across the field ⑪ towards overhead cables. Follow them to a culvert ⑫ then up to barn on roadside ⑬. Continue ahead down track and up further slope, then on along green lane to road by cottages ⑭. Bear right to road junction and turn left ⑮ towards Wenhaston. As soon as near side of wood on left is reached ⑯, go right over ditch, then left up short side of field to cross another ditch. On reaching track ⑰, turn right along it, soon turning left along grass track at end of field. Continue through gap and turn right to follow field boundary. At end of hedge/fence enter field ahead ⑱ and turn left. Follow hedge beside 2 fields to reach road ⑲. Turn right and continue about 50 yards (46 m), then go left over hump, to cross Toby's Walks Picnic Area. Leave by the posts towards left-hand end ⑳ and continue down verge on right side of the A12. Take care – busy road. Turn right, and just past junction, opposite house called Hillside ㉑, turn left down path. After 20 yards (18 m) go right over stile and along lower field edge. At cottage, cross stile into lane and continue to the A12. Walk round to left until safe to cross. Go down track beyond White Hart, towards marshes. Turn right at bottom to enter Walberswick Nature Reserve along former railway line. Follow water's edge for just over one mile (1.5 km). After joining fence on left as path moves away from river, you reach start of track for horse riders only ㉒. Turn right here and then bear left along track to join road. Follow this for about ⅓ mile (0.5 km), then turn off to right along bridleway ㉓ over open grassy area, to walk beside pine wood. At bottom of dip ㉔, veer to left to cross road and then turn off to right after 100 yards (91 m), following path as it bends to the left. Continue along raised path and turn right at ruined wind pump. About 100 yards further on ㉕, turn left to follow Old Dunwich River. Turn right at next path junction ㉖ and go round right side of low knoll. Bear left at next low hill ㉗ and continue through area of grass and gorse. Follow track onwards through woodland and between the fields beyond, then bear left on to gravel road beside some houses. Where track joins road, go left, then left again at church to reach ①.

Continued on next page.

Continued from previous page.

The beach at Dunwich.

🔟 Dunwich is a village haunted by its past, the ruined friary walls dominating the remnants of the village. Once a flourishing port, it has largely been 📷 drowned by the advancing sea. Small museum open 2–4.30 in summer, but not Monday, Wednesday or Friday.

🐦 Below the path, sand martins fly to their nests, excavated in the soft, crumbling cliff. A few pioneering fulmars may also be seen – birds familiar from the west of Britain but, as yet, rare here. The species has expanded remarkably since 1878, when its only breeding place in the British Isles was St. Kilda.

🐦 In summer, look out for stonechats on Dunwich Heath, and listen for the deep foghorn-like *oomph-oomph* of the bittern coming from the vast reed beds of Minsmere, seen ahead.

🐦 Minsmere, the RSPB reserve, is best known for its avocets which can be seen from the public hides here. These exquisite black-and-white waders disappeared from Britain in the 19th C., but recolonized the E coast in the 1940s. This is one of several reserves managed in part for their benefit.

⚓ Westleton Common, like Dunwich Common, is a remnant of the once extensive heaths of the Suffolk Sandlings. Agriculture and conifer plantations have both taken much of the heathland, and birds like the nightjar have declined as a result.

⛪ Blythburgh Church has an eventful past. In 1577, it was struck by lightning during a service. The congregation believed that the Devil had paid them a visit, and his fingers are said to have caused the scorch marks, still visible on the north door. The church was rebuilt on a grand scale, but the declining fortunes of Blythburgh as a port, and the dissolution of the nearby priory, left it poor and underpopulated. Savage destruction by Cromwell's men followed, then centuries of neglect, so that by the 1870s most of the windows were bricked up, and parishioners had to use umbrellas in church. A century of restoration has followed, and is still continuing.

🚂 The path here follows the course of the disused Southwold Railway, an unprofitable branch line, with a narrow, 3-foot (0.9-m) gauge. It ran from 1879–1929.

⚓ This extensive area of reed bed is still 'managed' by periodic cutting for thatch. (Without this, woodland takes 🐦 over.) Several rarities may be seen here, including flocks of bearded tits, with their long tails and beautiful apricot-and-black markings. Short-eared owls and marsh harriers hunt low over the reeds.

Breckland
7 miles (11 km) Sheet 144 or 155
800713

Easy Through an unusual, historic, and disappearing landscape, with the chance to see a reconstructed Anglo-Saxon village. *Country park, Breckland, forest.*

Start 5 miles (8 km) NW of Bury St. Edmunds. Take the A1101 from Bury St. Edmunds towards Mildenhall. Just past Lackford, turn right into West Stow Country Park; ample **car park**.

① From car park, head over grass path to Anglo-Saxon village site ②. Descend to river towpath and turn right to follow it to end of Country Park. Climb stile and turn right along shady lane. Cross road and continue up sandy track towards forest. Just past Pear Tree Cottage ③, turn sharp right and follow path along forest edge, then go straight on, between trees, to car park at Forest Lodge ④. Turn left along gravel road past Information Centre and right at next junction, to follow forest edge again. Bear right down slope, to leave forest through gateway and continue along track to Wordwell Hall Farm. Turn right along road towards church and take path along near side of churchyard wall ⑤. Bear half-left over field from end of wall, to stile in field corner and go straight ahead by stream to gate. Continue across field, bearing slightly right to join hedge, and keep this on your left to reach road ⑥. Walk straight on along road and take second turning on the right. Immediately before road bends left ⑦, turn right

through gap in wall and follow path straight across area of grass and bracken, and cross bridge over stream. Follow grass track right, to road, then turn left through West Stow. At end of houses, turn left down track by plantations and continue 100 yards (91 m) before turning right ⑧ to go straight along woodland path. Bear right at end of path to rejoin road. Turn left into Country Park at gate just beyond dip and continue along grass path by pine belt to ⑨.

※ The site of an Anglo-Saxon village was found here in the late 1940s.

⚑ Excavation revealed a complex settlement of huts, halls, pits and ditches, dating from the pagan Saxon period 400–650 A.D.; also everyday objects of the time, such as bone combs, pottery and weaving implements. The village has now been partially reconstructed.

➤ The River Lark is a migration route for many birds.

⛟ The remains of the unusual crescent-shaped Cherry Ground lock.

⛰ West Stow lies in the Breckland area of East Anglia. Because the topsoil drains quickly and the underlying chalk is absorbent, the land is very dry and dusty, and supports a correspondingly specialized vegetation.

❀ Typical flower species: maiden pink, sand catchfly, yellow rattle.

🏰 Little remains of West Stow Hall except a Tudor gatehouse.

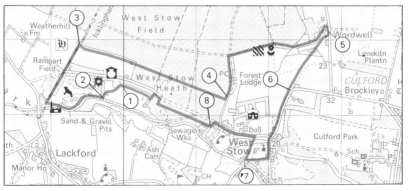

OUSE VALLEY AND FENS

There are few areas in Britain where the eye has such freedom. The huge vistas and uninterrupted horizons can be disconcerting at first, but the quality of the light and the changing moods of the Fens, make it delightful and novel. Waterways divide the landscape; you get to value them as variation in the scenery in much the same way as hills elsewhere in the country. The Ouse and the Nene, which wind their way to the Wash, make a happy contrast to the dead straight courses cut through the rich alluvial soil by the man-made channels.

Before it was drained, this area was wild, inhospitable wetland; most people made their living by catching fowl or cutting reeds for thatch. Villages were few and isolated, and the Fennies had a reputation for inbreeding and witchcraft. Wicken Fen, one of the pockets which side-stepped drainage, has been maintained for reed cutting, offering an insight into life on the original fenland.

Moving south, contours start to appear on the map, and south-east of Cambridge there is some enjoyable walking on the Gog Magog Hills. Legend explains the existence, and the name, of these unexpected hills: the giant Gog Magog became enamoured of Granta, a water nymph, but was rejected and turned into a hill. Romantic associations or not, it would be misleading to give the impression that these hills are anything but tame by normal standards; they are distinctive here, and command extensive views. One walk in the section, *The Cam Valley*, lies south of Cambridge, outside the Ouse Valley and the Fens area.

Ouse Valley and Fens
NORTH CAMBRIDGESHIRE

Old Sulehay Forest
3 miles (5 km) Sheet 142 075991

Easy A short walk through an area rich in plantlife, and with plenty to interest the historian. *River valley, woodland, fields.*

Start Wansford, 8 miles (13 km) W of Peterborough on the A47. Turn off the A47 to village after crossing the A1. Infrequent buses from Peterborough. **Parking** in the wide village street.

① From main street, cross old bridge and turn left along footpath at base of bridge wall ②. Follow through grass fields and along field edges. Look for gap in wall ③ approaching Yarwell, and continue, turning right along main street. Follow to main road, then turn right to bridleway on left ④. Follow bridleway through woods to main ride ⑤. Turn right and continue through wood to road. Turn left downhill to Wansford church, turning right to recross bridge to ①.

🏠 The old stone houses in both Wansford and Yarwell are tiled in Collyweston stone, still quarried in that village, 4 miles (6.5 km) to the N. In Roman times, clay dug at Wansford was transported by river to the pottery at Castor, 4 miles away.

〰 The Nene connects the Wash to an arm of the Grand Union Canal at Northampton, with no less than 38 locks in between. Its course is meandering, and Wansford is on one of its many U-turns.

🍺 The Angel at Yarwell.

🌳 Old Sulehay Forest is one of the last, and most eastern, remnants of Rockingham Forest, which stretched over 33 miles (53 km) in medieval times. This piece of the forest is preserved, although at one time it was under threat from quarry extensions. There are a number of soil types in the area, ranging from limestone to clay and sand. These support an interesting variety of plants, including caper spurge, deadly nightshade, nettle-leaved bellflower, and an uncommon tree, the small-leaved lime. Three species of deer, glow-worms and the land winkle are among the animals found in the wood. The land to the W was also once wooded, but Charles I sold the timber, most of the oak going to the navy for ship building.

Deadly nightshade and berries – two of which may kill a child if eaten. They appear from August to November.

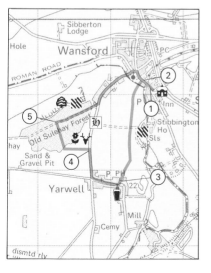

Ouse Valley and Fens
WEST CAMBRIDGESHIRE

The Black Peatlands of Ramsey
5 miles (8 km) Sheet 142 287852

Easy The contrasting landscapes of the flat fens to the north and the uplands of the south create an interesting walk. *Grass and peat drove roads, fields.*

Start Ramsey, 12 miles (19 km) N of Huntingdon. From Huntingdon, take the A141 N to Warboys, then turn on to the B1040 to Ramsey. Turn left in village along Great Whyte. Infrequent buses from Huntingdon and Peterborough; **parking** along Great Whyte.

① From Great Whyte, walk back to junction and turn left along the B1096 towards church. Turn right at first road, to footpath on right **②**. Follow path across golf course, following marker posts, then turn left into overgrown drove road. Follow around right-hand bend, then take next drove road on left. Continue to made-up drove road **③**. Turn right and follow the drove to track going right, **④**, to side of barns. Follow track, turn left at end, and continue to road. Turn right and follow road to footpath through church grounds. Follow path at rear of houses and across golf course on raised bank to old railway **⑤**. Cross, and follow path ahead, then go half-left across fields to track. Turn left, cross bridge, then go right along river

edge to rear of buildings **⑥**. Turn left across common, then go right up lane to road. Turn right, then left along Great Whyte to **①**.

�✉ Ramsey lies at the centre of the black peat farmland which supports lush growth of vegetables such as carrots and celery. The main street, called the Great Whyte, was built over Bury Brook in 1852, and has a Victorian clock and iron column.

Ⓐ Ramsey Abbey was founded in 969 A.D. by Ethelwine, and was among the most influential monastic centres until the Dissolution of the Monasteries in the 16th C. All that remains of it are the 13th-C. chapel, the porter's lodge and part of the gate-house.

�✉ These fens lie below sea level and were some of the last to be drained. Water violet, flowering rush and arrowhead can be found here.

⛪ Bury Church was once the 'mother' parish to Ramsey. The font is 14th C., and there are unusual 13th-C. Sanctus bell-openings on both sides of the chancel. (These bells were originally rung at the Sanctus during Mass.)

🍴 The Angel, in the High Street; food.

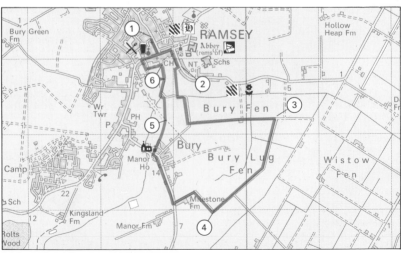

216

Ouse Valley and Fens
NORTH CAMBRIDGESHIRE

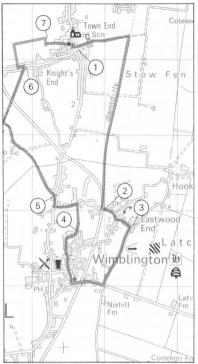

March – and the Fen Heartland
6 miles (9.5 km) Sheet 143
416952

Easy Through eerie fenland landscape, with its rich, black soil and relentlessly level horizons. *Disused railway line, grass drove roads.*

Start March, 10½ miles (17 km) S of Wisbech. Take the A141 S from Wisbech, turning E after 10 miles (16 km) to March. Follow the B1101 from town centre to Town End church. Trains from Peterborough, Spalding, Wisbech and Ely to March. Follow the B1101 S for 1½ miles (2.5 km) to start. **Parking** on the B1101 near the church.

① Almost opposite church, go across main road and down Barkers Lane to old railway. Turn right and follow track to bypass. Turn left at first turn ② and follow

road, keeping left at junction, to drove road just before last house on right ③. Turn right to lane, then right again. Cross bypass and turn right past church. Follow road ahead into Norfolk Street, then bear left into Eaton Estate. Cross green diagonally, and go down track. After 135 yards (123.5 m), cross to other side of dyke ④ and continue to Bridge Lane. Turn left, then right at road to bend. Keep watch for, and go down, drove road on left ⑤, just past cottage on roadside. Follow past farm and on to golf course. Take grass drove, then track, across bypass to Knight's End ⑥. Turn left, then right down narrow footpath beside no. 88. Follow field edge, turning right at top and right at end ⑦, to track. Turn left along track to church ①.

The 15th-C. church of St. Wendreda contains a magnificent double hammer-beam roof. It is adorned with almost 200 angels, carved in oak, and unusual in having open wings.

The fens to the E of Wimblington stretch low and flat to the Bedford Levels and beyond to Ely and Norfolk. A rise in sea level of only 20 feet (6 m) would transform this landscape into a vast bay, dotted with islands. Glaciation and fluctuations in sea level have wrought dramatic changes on this landscape. Once, it was covered by sea, then dense woodland, and, more recently, by a vast swamp. The most recent changes have been man-made. In the 17th C., Cornelius Vermuyden and other Dutch engineers were commissioned by the Duke of Bedford to drain the Fens and so reclaim them for agriculture. Almost 700 windmills were sited, pumping water into natural and man-made channels, and a valuable area of fertile alluvial soil emerged, particularly suitable for growing fruit and flowers.

In the peat field, ancient tree trunks can be seen. These 'bog oaks' (usually oak or yew) are the remains of the original forest cover. Raised, light-coloured tracks across the dark peat are the old river beds, known hereabouts as 'roddens'.

The Anchor at Wimblington; food.

Ouse Valley and Fens
EAST CAMBRIDGESHIRE

Ely's Drove Roads
9¼ miles (15 km) Sheet 143 541803

Easy Dominated by views of Ely Cathedral, this walk follows historic ways between two fen 'islands', Ely and Downham. *Grass drove roads, peat fen; mud.*

Start Ely, 16 miles (25.5 km) N of Cambridge on the A10. Trains from Cambridge and King's Lynn. Entering Ely from the S, take the first right turn for Stuntney, Soham and Newmarket; follow road to **car park** on left.

① From car park, follow signs to cathedral. Facing W door of cathedral, turn left and follow Steeple Row on right to passage on to High Street. Turn right to square and walk diagonally across it to continue down narrow road (Vineyards). At end, turn right and quickly left to another road. Turn left, then right alongside a house and follow field edge to bypass. Turn left, then right along Prickwillow Road. At bottom of hill **②**, keep straight on along grass drove to railway. Cross line and continue to barns **③**. Keep left and follow drove road towards large silos **④**. Turn left at main road, then take first right to Chettisham. Turn left past church, cross bypass **⑤** into track. At end of pond, turn right, then left, along grass drove road to bridge. Cross and turn left on to track **⑥** and continue to road. Turn left, then go right at junction to Little Downham. Follow main street to Chapel

Below, bladder campion, and below right, oxeye daisy.

Lane. **⑦** Turn left and follow road, then drove road, all the way to bypass **⑧**, ignoring tracks on left and right. Cross, and follow road to Ely and **①**.

🌾 Ely rises above the silt of the Fens on an island of harder, greensand rock. Before the drainage of the Fens in the 17th and 18th C., it was literally an island, approachable only by boat or causeway. Legend has it that Hereward held out against William the Conqueror here. The cathedral was founded by St. Ethelreda in 673 and is remarkable for its long nave – 537 feet (164 m) – and its octagon and lantern. This must have been an invaluable navigation aid to early travellers to the city. The Old Fire Engine House, across the green, serves excellent teas and snacks.

🌿 The verges of the wide drove roads are havens for wild flowers, including oxeye daisy, field scabious, bladder campion and yellow rattle. Once widespread, they are now largely absent from the fields because of spraying. Butterflies, including ringlet, gatekeeper, small skipper and Essex skipper are attracted by the verge flowers, and in the hedges, goldfinches, linnets and yellow wagtails are seen.

🏛 The medieval church at Chettisham has interesting Norman carvings on the vestry wall.

🍺 Turn right at ⑦ for the Plough.

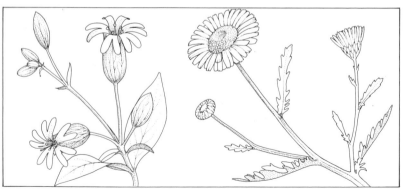

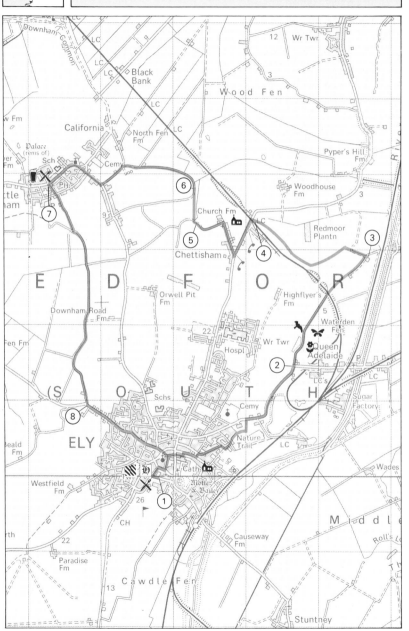

Ouse Valley and Fens
NORTH CAMBRIDGESHIRE

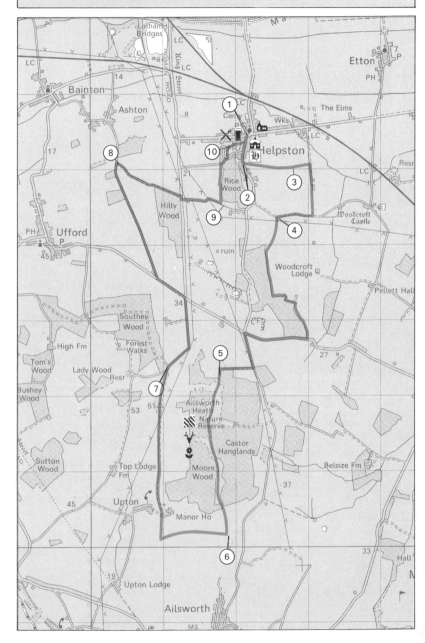

John Clare's Country
11¼ miles (18 km) Sheet 142
122055

Easy Some of the peaceful spots that inspired Clare are still to be found along this route, despite encroachment by intensive farming. *Fields, heath; mud in winter.*

Start Helpston, 8 miles (13 km) NW of Peterborough. From Peterborough, take the A15 to Glinton, then turn W along the B1443 to Helpston; infrequent buses from Peterborough. **Parking** near Clare Memorial in centre of Helpston.

➊ From Clare Memorial, go down Woodgate Road and Heath Road. Continue past Clare's Cottage to stile in hedge on left ➋. Cross stile and follow waymarks straight on across another stile, field and bridge, to gap in hedge on right ➌. Cross to other side of hedge and follow to dyke. Turn right to bridge, cross dyke and track. Follow dyke and field edges to track, then turn right to bend ➍. Turn left on to track and follow field, then wood edge, to road. Turn right, then take first left to track on right. Follow track to gate of nature reserve on left ➎. Continue straight through reserve, through gates, and into fields to crossing track ➏. Turn right to woods and follow field edge, then go through gates into wood to track. Turn right and follow track past church to road ➐. Turn right and follow road to junction. Turn left, then take first right for one mile (1.5 km), to track on right ➑. Follow track to King Street. Cross, and follow field edge and dyke to wood. Just before wood, turn left ➒, and follow field edge, then go left and right on to track to road. Turn right, then left, along narrow passage between houses, to school fence ➓. Turn right, then walk to left of barns, into yard. Cross to right to stone stile and continue over others to pub. Turn left back to ➊.

🏛 St. Botolph's in Helpston has a 14th-C. chancel and porch entrance. The tower is largely Norman, with some 19th-C. rebuilding. John Clare's tomb is here.

✗ The Exeter Arms, to the N of the church, was formerly a courthouse.

🏠 John Clare, the 'Northamptonshire Peasant Poet', was born in the cottage along Heath Road in 1793 and spent his childhood here. The surrounding countryside was, in his youth, open heath, free for all to use as rough grazing. It was the inspiration for much of his poetry, and in the poem 'I am', his love of wilderness was powerfully expressed:

> I long for scenes where man has
> never trod.
> A place where woman never smiled
> or wept;
> There to abide with my Creator, God,
> And sleep as I in childhood sweetly
> slept:
> Untroubling and untroubled where I
> lie,
> The grass below – above the vaulted
> sky.

📖 In the early 19th C., the Inclosure Acts privatized the land, an event thought to have been partly responsible for Clare entering a mental hospice in 1837. He died in 1864.

〰 Owing to its underlying strata of limestone, estuarine clay, boulder clay, and sand, Ailsworth Heath contains a large number of different soil types in a small area. These provide a range of ✛ habitats for wild life: deer, nightingales, glow-worms and toads all live ❧ here, along with an array of plants. The clay flora includes crested cow wheat and herb Paris.

John Clare's cottage, from an engraving.

Ouse Valley and Fens
SOUTH CAMBRIDGESHIRE

The Cam Valley
8, 10 or 12 miles (13, 16 or 19 km)
Sheet 154 376455

Moderate Views across the valley, nature reserves, and some attractive villages. *Woodlands, meadows, fields; mud.*

Start Meldreth, 11 miles (17.5 km) SW of Cambridge. From Cambridge take the A10 SW to Melbourn. Turn W at the traffic lights to Meldreth Station, just over the railway bridge. Regular trains from Cambridge and Royston (not Sundays). Buses to Meldreth and Melbourn, both ½ mile (0.8 km) from the start, from Cambridge and Royston. Limited **parking** in station yard. **Return** The route can be shortened to 8 or 10 miles (13 or 16 km) by stopping at Foxton or Shepreth, and taking a train back to Meldreth. For train times, ring Royston (0763) 43128.

① From Meldreth Station platform, take narrow footpath N between garden fences to Meldreth village. Turn right on to road, and after 200 yards (183 m), right down Flambards Close ② At end of close, cross bridge over River Mel. Turn left on to path by river, through a wood and meadows. Cross stile by The Mill to meet the road opposite Meldreth Church. ③ Take short lane on left side of churchyard into field. Bear right across field, behind church to bridge. Cross and go diagonally left to far corner into farmyard, then turn left along rough headland, following field boundary, to Malton Road. ④ Turn left, and continue past Malton Farm to 4 cottages and signpost. ⑤ Cross field diagonally to find narrow path by brook leading through 3 fields into Orwell (by garages). Follow estate road to recreation ground, then turn right, up to church. ⑥ Follow signposted path up steps by churchyard to Orwell pits, returning to road on parallel path. Turn left to junction. Turn right towards Malton for 300 yards (274 m). ⑦ Turn left over stile by signpost on path to Barrington. Following large field boundary, look for plank bridge crossing ditch. ⑧ At road, turn right into Barrington. Continue through village to footpath sign on right ⑨. Go down cul-de-sac to footpath and bridge over River Cam. Cross second bridge and take clear track across small field and by hedge on left. Look for gap in tall hedge

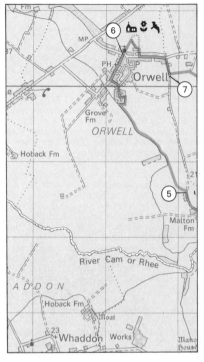

and cross 2 plank bridges in succession, into small field. Veer round right margin of field to find hard track, leading to signpost on corner of road. ⑩ Follow road to Foxton Station. Take path from station into village. Turn right through village to the A10. ⑪ Cross, and immediately opposite, follow signposted path through old pits to Shepreth village. ⑫ Go over level crossing and take road towards Meldreth, visiting Moor End Nature Reserve on the way to ①.

🚉 Meldreth Station is a fine example of a simple Great Northern Line station, built in 1851. The waiting room has its original cast-iron fireplace.

🏚 Malton is the site of an abandoned medieval village.

⛪ Orwell Church is mainly in the Perpendicular style, and has a fine chancel and waggon roof. The chalk (or

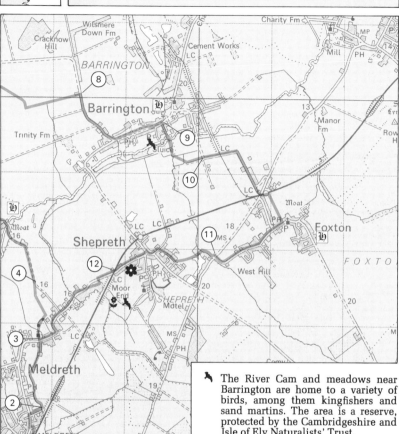

'clunch') pit behind the church may have provided some of its building material, and today has an interesting range of plants, including great broomrape, greater knapweed and scabious. In the blackthorn and hawthorn bushes, the willow warbler and chiffchaff can be found. The pit has been made into a nature reserve administered by the parish council.

Barrington is a Saxon village with a typical plan: a huge green surrounded by houses with the church at one end.

The River Cam and meadows near Barrington are home to a variety of birds, among them kingfishers and sand martins. The area is a reserve, protected by the Cambridgeshire and Isle of Ely Naturalists' Trust.

Perhaps more is known about the social history of Foxton than of any other English village. It is the subject of a fascinating, meticulous study by Rowland Parker, described in his book *The Common Stream*. The archaeologist, Louis Leakey, famous for his discoveries of early man in Africa, lived here for a while in the 1930s.

The cottage by the level-crossing gates in Shepreth is renowned for its garden, to which visitors are welcome.

Moor End Nature Reserve has a fine showing of cowslips in spring. Look for sedge warblers in summer.

NORFOLK

Here is a taste, rather than a comprehensive selection, of Norfolk routes. This is fitting, for the pleasures of walking this county are rather specialized. The Brecks, for example, are a mixture of sandy land, somewhat reminiscent of Surrey commons, with some dense foresty plantation and some arable and wetland. Many find this a curious mixture; on the other hand, the juxtaposed habitats have a character of their own, reflected in the bird life, flora and fauna.

A route on Cley Marshes introduces one of the most atmospheric stretches of the Norfolk coast, and one of the most famous bird-watching sites in Britain. Even those with no special interest in birds will find it hard not to appreciate the ornithological riches here. The simple fact that East Anglia juts out into the North Sea means that species which would otherwise pass unseen are arrested by the land; the uncommon and the rare turn up regularly, and thanks to the management of the Norfolk Naturalists' Trust, large numbers of visitors, particularly during the spring and autumn migration, can share the sights and sounds.

Bridgham Field and Forest
6 miles (9.5 km) Sheet 144 982853

Moderate Typical Breckland landscapes, with a variety of woodland. *Open farmland, tree-lined avenue, pine plantation, meadows, riverside, mixed woodland.*

Start near East Harling, 10 miles (16 km) E of Thetford. Take the A11 NE from Thetford and after 7 miles (11 km) turn S on to the B111 to East Harling. In the village, turn SW on minor road (signposted West Harling and Thetford) and at a sharp left-hand bend take the track immediately ahead. **Parking** on left of track, just past cottage.

① Walk down sandy track away from road. Go through fields and woodland to signpost to church ②. Go through churchyard and cross fence. Follow field edge on left to gate. Climb this, then turn right to 5-bar gate ③. Go through and at second electricity pole, turn left through plantation. Emerge at camp site ④. Keep house on left and bear left across field, following power line through plantation. Use series of 3 stiles to cross meadows. Turn right at third, and follow field edge, then signpost to left, passing behind Stonehouse Farm. Turn right up avenue ⑤, cross river bridge and cross stile immediately on right ⑥. Cross field to kissing gate and turn right into Bridgham. Take second left and next 2 lefts to return to road. Turn right and retrace to ⑤. Carry straight on for one mile (1.5 km) to junction ⑦. Turn left on to minor road and soon left again on to road. At junction ⑧, keep straight ahead (not left to The Dower House) to ②. Retrace to ①.

🌸 Leaving a border beside the arable fields here has encouraged flowers, including poppies, campions, clover, cranesbills and speedwells. These in turn attract a range of butterflies, such
🦋 as large and small skippers, browns and whites, small copper, brimstone, small tortoiseshell and peacock.

⛪ Here is a typical Norfolk church, with flint walls and a red-tiled roof. The church registers date back to 1538 (when 13s 4d was paid for a bell frame), but since then the building has been extensively renovated.

🐦 The old outbuildings of the farm are much used by nesting swallows. Young birds line the wires in high summer, waiting for food.

🦋 Crossing the River Thet, you may see
🐦 dragonflies and damselflies, and perhaps, with patience, a kingfisher.

🌲 This is a well-managed conifer plantation, broken up by narrow rides lined with broad-leaved trees, especially oaks, for aesthetic effect. The rides open out suddenly to give wide views where the conifers have
🌸 been felled. The 2 principal conifers planted here are Scots pine (pinkish trunks) and Corsican pine (blue-grey). The range of grassland plants includes the brilliant blue viper's bug

🌲 The superb old lime avenue here is followed by oak, beech, chestnut and
🦋 silver birch. Butterflies include the speckled wood, camouflaged to look like dappled sunlight on trunks.

225

Norfolk
NEAR SHERINGHAM

Cley Marshes
7 miles (11 km) Sheet 133 054441

Moderate Wide sea views and a great range of birds are the principal attractions of this atmospheric stretch of Norfolk coast. *Saltmarsh, shingle beach, heath, farmland; one short climb; mud. If embankment between ② and ③ is overgrown, use road instead. If field between ⑥ and ⑦ is cropped, walk close to field boundary hedge.*

Start Cley next the Sea, 13 miles (21 km) NE of Fakenham. Use the Norfolk Naturalists' Trust **Car Park** ¾ mile (1 km) E of Cley.

① Turn left from car park and walk along grass road verge to Cley village. ② Just past petrol station, turn right through alleyway to Cley Mill. Skirt rear of windmill and follow path on top of embankment towards beach and coastguard station. ③ Turn right along shingle embankment between sea and salt marsh for 2 miles (3 km). ④ Just before grassy hill next to beach, turn right down to track at right angles to beach. Cross road and walk up to Salthouse Church. Turn left through churchyard and right on reaching road. ⑤ Continue over crossroads to follow track up short steep hill to

heath. Cross heath and turn right at road. Go straight over crossroads. ⑥ Where road joins from left, turn right through field entrance. Cross fields, keeping close to field boundaries on left. ⑦ At road, turn left, then cross to small parking area. Follow track at side of road, past public hides to nature reserve, back to ①.

🏠 Overlooking the car park is the Norfolk Naturalists' Trust's Information Centre which has displays and information about the wildlife of the north Norfolk coast. Day permits are available from the information centre (closed Mondays) to visit all the hides on Cley Marshes Nature Reserve. There are also several hides at the side of the A149, open and free of charge.

🏚 Cley next the Sea is now a mile (1.5 km) inland, but before land reclamation in the 17th C., was a bustling port, exporting grain and wool.

✳ The windmill, is open to visitors.

🦅 Cley Marshes Nature Reserve offers many uncommon and rare birds, including avocets and spoonbills in summer, and glaucous gulls and snow buntings in winter. The bittern breeds here, as does the bearded tit.

✻ Salthouse Heath was among the first parts of England to be settled by farmers, as the light sandy soil could be cultivated easily with simple tools.

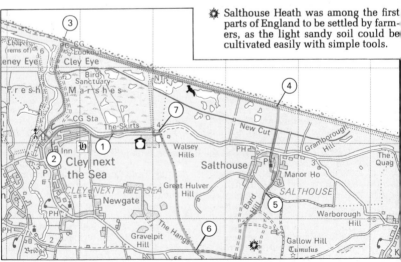

Halvergate Marshes
11 miles (17.5 km) Sheet 134 427055

Moderate Through a beautiful landscape, fast disappearing: one of the few areas of extensive marshland remaining in Britain. *Marshland; mud. Route between ⑦ and ⑧ may be overgrown.*

Start Wickhampton, 8 miles (13 km) SW of Great Yarmouth. **Parking** by church.

① Walk down track to right of church, bearing left at first fork. ② Fork left on to concrete track. ③ At Weaver's Way sign on left, keep right through metal gate with fingerpost. Make for wind pump alongside dyke. ④ Go through gate and head for obvious wooden footbridge. Cross and bear left beside dyke. ⑤ At sheep-pen, cross dyke, and make for double gates across railway ⑥. Continue to Berney windpump, ⑦. Cross stile, then turn left along river bank past shop and pub. Follow bank for 1½ miles (2.5 km) to pump station ⑧. Turn left, cross railway and follow track beside dyke. In 200 yards (183 m), turn left at fingerpost ⑨. After 80 yards (73 m) turn left down to dyke edge. ⑩ At bridge over dyke, turn right. In 50 yards (46 m), turn left through gate. Follow track past wind pumps. ⑪ Keep right towards Manor Farm and follow track round to left. ⑫ Go through gate and turn left immediately through another. ⑬ Turn right through gate and left around edge of meadow. Go through 3 gates in succession and cross to footbridge ⑭.

Cross field to gate between 2 bushes and turn right, to ③. Retrace steps to ①.

🏠 Wickhampton Church is made of the flint characteristic of Norfolk. East Anglia's underlying rock is largely chalk, and pockets of flint within this are the only local source of hard building material. Local clays have been used to make bricks for the cottages, but flint is used for churches. Some interesting examples of brick-and-flint cottages can be seen in the area. The irregular nodules of flint are not ideal for building, but they were often used where other materials were in short supply. Long flints were broken and the tapering tail-ends of the nodules embedded in the mortar of the wall, leaving a flattish, fractured surface showing on the outside.

✘ This derelict wind pump still shows the remains of its working machinery.

✘ Berney Arms wind pump has working sails. Open April–September.

🏚 Land use on Halvergate Marshes has recently been the subject of controversy between conservationists and farmers. Farming subsidies make it attractive for the farmers to convert their land from summer pasture to winter wheat, which entails draining and ploughing large stretches of wetland, at present a haven for breeding lapwings and yellow wagtails.

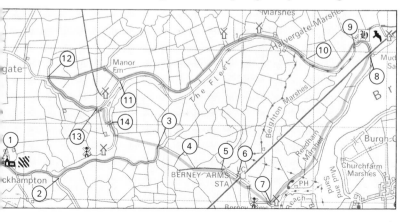

NORTHERN ENGLAND

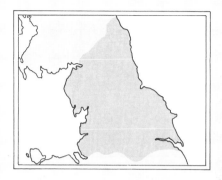

YORKSHIRE PENNINES

THE MOORS AND WOLDS

CUMBRIA

THE NORTH PENNINES

YORKSHIRE PENNINES

The southern end of the Pennine chain is in the Peak
District of Derbyshire; from there the hills march
northwards through South, West and North Yorkshire,
continuing via County Durham and Northumberland to end
at the Scottish border.

The southern end of this section is seamed with canals,
railways and motorways, which link the conurbations on
either side. Close juxtaposition of industry and nature can
create some intriguing contrasts, which ought not to be lost
on the walker. Huddersfield's centre, for example, is within
3 miles (5 km) of the moors, and indeed of the Mollcar
Woods, a sea of bluebells in spring. And from Ainsley Top,
walkers have great views of the Calder Valley and Halifax.

At the northern end of the Yorkshire Pennines come the
Dales. For many walkers, these valleys, cut deeply into
surrounding moorland and fells, are the ultimate. No other
English landscape so closely unites the wild and the
domestic. The sheep and bent grass of the fells immediately
border the enclosed, green beauty of the Dales themselves.

Wessenden Valley
5 ½ miles (9 km) Sheet 110 048117

Moderate Close to civilization, but with the atmosphere of true wilderness, this highland valley offers first-class walking. *Reservoir, rough moorland, fields. Path ill-defined between ⑤ and ⑦.*

Start Marsden, on the A62 between Manchester and Huddersfield; trains from Huddersfield and Manchester, buses from Huddersfield and Oldham. **Parking** near Marsden Station, or in vicinity of church.

① Follow road from church/railway station towards the A62. Go left, under bridge beneath the A62, past playing field to traffic island. Keep straight ahead, bearing left at fork on to reservoir track. ② Follow track past Butterly and Blakeley reservoirs. At Wessenden Lodge (farm) entrance ③, keep right on track below farm towards Wessenden Reservoir Dam. Turn left at dam ④ to locate path above and behind farm to stile. ⑤ Go straight on, bearing slightly right to stile above and ahead. Care is needed following the path here. ⑥ Continue in same direction, con-

touring around hillside, through gaps in ruined walls. Walk along inside of moorland wall towards ruined farm, crossing bridge over stream. At farm ⑦, follow track up to gate. Continue ahead, bearing left along track which descends gully by wall. Cross Rams Clough at footbridge, then climb up to bench and viewpoint. ⑧ Continue along track which becomes narrow lane past farms. At junction of lanes ⑨, take the right fork towards Acre Head Farm. ⑩ As track bends right, go left over stile over electric fence by telegraph poles. Path descends steeply. Go over stile in wall corner into narrow enclosed footpath. Follow enclosed way to farm ⑪ then go down steps into farmyard. Pass through gate, left, on to farm track. Keep straight on to town centre.

Marsden, at the head of the Colne Valley, lies at the foot of several important trans-Pennine routes. An ancient packhorse way leads over to Littleborough and Rochdale, and 18th-C. turnpike roads pioneered routes which are now followed by the A62 through Stanedge cutting. Even more remarkable is the Stanedge tunnel, built between 1798–1810, and, at over 3 miles (5 km), the longest canal tunnel in the country. Boats were 'legged' through the tunnel: the boatman lay on his back on the boat's deckhousing and propelled himself by 'walking' the roof of the tunnel. The whole passage took about 3½ hours. The nearby railway tunnels were connected by air ducts to the canal tunnel, and trains poured acid smoke over the bargees. Information Centre by the tunnel entrance.

The dramatically beautiful Wessenden valley is enhanced by 4 reservoirs, built in the 1880s and 1890s by Huddersfield Corporation. The highest passed on this walk, Wessenden Reservoir, has a capacity of 109 million gallons (496 million l), and an austere and beautiful setting.

Binn Moor is an extensive area of Pennine moorland owned by the National Trust. This is a water catchment area for the reservoirs, and the water conduits along Binn Edge provide interesting walks.

Yorkshire Pennines
WEST YORKSHIRE

Hardcastle Crags
5½ miles (9 km) Sheet 103 988292

Easy A romantic and beautiful landscape, with particularly fine colouring in autumn. *Riverside, woodland, moorland; one climb.*

Start Hebden Bridge, 9 miles (14.5 km) W of Halifax. Take the A6033 road N (signposted Keighley). After ½ mile (0.8 km), bear left on to moor road (signposted Midgehole, Hardcastle Crags). Frequent trains on Leeds–Halifax–Manchester line to Hebden Bridge; 1½-mile (2.5-km) walk from station to Hardcastle Crags, or take bus along Keighley road to lane end. Large National Trust **car park** at entrance to estate.

① From car park, return to main entrance, going right down to bridge. Climb stile beside bridge and follow riverside path. ② Keep along riverside path (nature trail) through woods for 1½ miles to bridge and mill. ③ From mill, continue along main track past crags. ④ At fork, bear right on main track going uphill. Where it joins a second track, go left. ⑤ Before farm take gate sharp right (signposted) to path which bears right through field and follows wall uphill. ⑥ Go through gate to other side of wall, over moorland ridge, and down to enclosed track. Turn right at T-junction and take main track above Grimsworth Dean. To visit Lumb pack-horse bridge and waterfall, take left turn at junction of tracks ⑦ past ruined farm to valley bottom. Retrace to ⑦, turn left, and continue along track to ①.

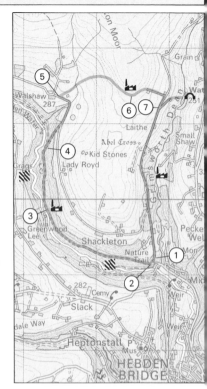

🗻 Hebden Water and Grimsworth Dean are both deep gorges through the gritstone, with fast-flowing streams and superb woodlands – oak, birch, alder, beech and pine. For many years the area was known as Little Switzerland and was popular with many Swiss émigrés working in the Lancashire and Yorkshire textile trades, who held reunions in these valleys which reminded them of their homeland.

🏭 Gibson Mill, an old textile mill with its mill pond.

🗻 Deep in the woods are the rocky outcrops known as Hardcastle Crags. This area was probably well known to the Brontë sisters, and could well have been the Penistone Crags visited by Catherine Earnshaw and Heathcliffe as children in *Wuthering Heights*.

🚶 Limers' Gate is a moorland track that forms part of a route from Lancashire to Halifax. In the 17th and 18th C., pack-ponies brought lime, needed to sweeten the acid soil of Pennine farms, along this route. 'Gate' is a northern expression for 'road'.

⌒ Lumb Bridge is a perfect example of a Pennine packhorse bridge. Nearby is a fine waterfall.

🏭 The bottom of Grimsworth Dean contains remains of old water mills and mill races, again evidence of the early industrial activity in the valley.

Yorkshire Pennines
WEST YORKSHIRE

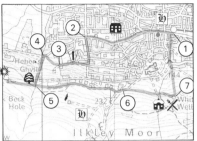

On Ilkley Moor
3½ miles (5.5 km) Sheet 104 118476

Moderate Attractive woodland and a superb viewpoint; a splendid walk for late summer when the heather is out and the bracken turns gold. *Victorian suburbs, woods, woodland paths, moorland; 2 climbs.*

Start Ilkley, 9 miles (14.5 km) N of Bradford. Bus or train from Bradford or Leeds, but no train on Sundays in winter. Large **car park** on E side of railway station.

① From car park turn right along The Grove, then fork left along Grove Road and follow this for ½ mile (0.8 km). At pillar box ② turn left into Victoria Avenue. As road ends, continue on path up steps. At cottage, turn right on to track towards woods. Bear right through stile ③ to path through woods. ④ Descend steps at end of woods into road, but bear left before lavatories to follow path that winds and climbs through oak woods. ⑤ Go through gate at top of woods and cross moor by path. Turn right on to main path to Swastika Stone (look for iron fence around ancient stone). Retrace steps along main path, then continue straight on, keeping above wood, reservoir and houses to join tarmac road. ⑥ Follow road for 150 yards (137 m) then branch right along path through bracken that joins main track to White Wells directly ahead. Take track to White Wells ⑦ and from there follow path and steps downhill to road. Take road downhill to station.

🏛 A former Roman fortress town on a crossing of the River Wharfe, Ilkley remained little more than a village for many centuries, until the discovery of mineral springs in the 18th C. These brought wealthy carriage folk in search of a cure and spawned several hydrotherapy establishments in the 19th C. But it was the coming of the railways, bringing the first commuters, mainly Bradford woolmen, that caused the town's expansion. The town's museum, in an Elizabethan manor house, displays Ilkley's past from prehistoric times.

🏛 Heathcote is a splendid Edwardian house, designed by Edwin Lutyens, in the style of an Italianate villa.

\⅄ Superb views across and along Wharfedale from the footpath through Panorama Woods. The outcrop of Panorama Rock is a notable viewpoint.

🏞 Heber's Ghyll, with semi-natural woodland, a path, bridges and a tumbling stream, has a distinctly Victorian flavour.

🟡 Ilkley Moor is particularly rich in archaeological remains, including strange cup-and-ring marked rocks and stone circles. The Swastika Stone is carved with a crude follyfoot, or swastika, dating from late Bronze Age times, around 1,800 B.C. To those early people it symbolized eternal life.

🏛 Ilkley Moor is one of the most famous in the British Isles thanks to a Victorian popular song – *On Ilkley Moor Baht 'At* – written, sad to relate, by someone from Lincolnshire. It is a fine area of heather and bracken, the heather turning rich purple in late summer. The whole area is urban common and open to the public.

🏠 White Wells is a beautiful little 18th-C. bathhouse, perfectly restored. It was built over an ice-cold moorland spring and allowed wealthy patients, many of them brought up from the town by donkey, to take cold baths in the pure water. It is now open to visitors at weekends and holiday times, and refreshments are served in the adjoining house. Moorland tarns close to the wells were converted in Victorian times to small ornamental lakes.

Yorkshire Pennines
NORTH YORKSHIRE

Entrance to Victoria Cave, perhaps the most impressive of the local limestone caves.

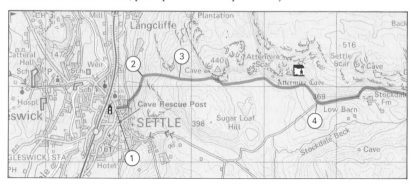

Settle to Malham
6 miles (9.5 km) Sheet 98 820637

Moderate The first part of a 2-day route, or an excellent one-day linear walk, passing through dramatic scenery created by the ravages of water on Pennine linestone. *Pastures, rough fells; one climb.*

Start Settle, 15 miles (24 km) NW of Skipton. To be sure of making the public transport link back at the end of the walk (whether 2-day or one-day), park at Skipton and take the bus or train to Settle. **Car park** off Gargrave Road, Skipton. **Return** One-day walk: take bus from Malham to Skipton (evenings-only service on Sundays). 2-day walk: stay overnight in Malham, continue to Grassington (see walk on pages 236–7) and return from there to Skipton by bus. For accommodation in Malham, see note below. Check Malham and Settle bus times by ringing Gargrave (075 678) 215.

➊ From Settle market-place, follow road up Constitution Hill. Road soon becomes lane. Bear right up track and pass through 2 gates into field. Continue along track to next gate ➋, then turn sharp right uphill. Ascend to gate in top of field. Follow wall to next gate. ➌ Continue along path as it bears right to gate in far right-hand corner of field, continuing to stile. Path veers right below Attermire Scar in long field. Follow wall to lane ➍. Turn left along lane towards Stockdale Farm, then over stile on the left to follow path round the left-hand side of the farm. Continue alongside wall to join main path climbing natural pass through hills. ➎ Go through gate at summit, and follow well-defined grassy lane. This descends to meet lane above Malham village. ➏ Turn right, descending steeply. As lane swings left, go straight ahead through gate on to grassy track which becomes enclosed way to Malham village ➐.

🏛 Settle has a number of impressive buildings, including a 17th-C. folly and the remarkable 2-tier shambles in the market-place.

🗻 The line of the Mid-Craven Fault exposes the superb limestone escarpment of Great Scar, weathered to produce the effect of a miniature Alpine range with several small caves. In the last century, important archaeological remains were found in Victoria and Attermire caves, including prehistoric animal bones, Mesolithic and Neolithic tools and weapons, and Romano-British jewellery.

🏚 Incredibly, the winding grassy path over the ridge was, until the early 19th C., the main road between Settle and Malham. It was used by many travellers, perhaps the most famous being William and Dorothy Wordsworth.

🏔 Around Malham are the most spectacular limestone formations of the Mid-Craven Fault: Malham Cove and Tarn, Gordale Scar and Janet's Foss. Equally interesting are the ancient field systems, some of them Iron Age in origin, which can be clearly distinguished, especially in evening light, all around the village.

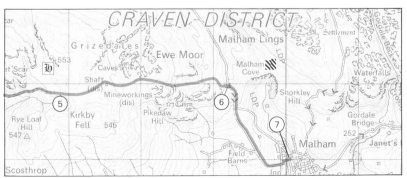

Yorkshire Pennines
NORTH YORKSHIRE

Malham to Grassington
11 miles (17.5 km) Sheet 98 900630

Moderate A fitting climax to an exhilarating 2-day route (see pages 234–5), or a fine one-day linear walk. *Limestone uplands; 2 climbs. Times of buses should be checked before setting off.*

Start Malham, 9 miles (14.5 km) NNW of Skipton. For one-day walk, park at Skipton and take bus to Malham (not on Sundays). **Car park** off Gargrave Road, Skipton. **Return** 2-day route: bus from Grassington to Skipton; check bus times by ringing Harrogate (0423) 66061; one-day route: check Grassington to Malham bus times on Gargrave (075 678) 215.

① From Malham village centre, follow the road S, soon crossing the footbridge on the left, signposted Pennine Way. Follow the path over stiles on the left-hand side of the stream. Just before a barn ②, turn left over ladder stile to follow clear path, marked by stiles, to Janet's Foss. Continue past waterfall to lane, and turn right along it. ③ After crossing bridge, turn left for Gordale Scar, returning by same route to lane. Follow lane uphill, past farm ④, continuing for 1½ miles (2.5 km) as track swings N and becomes unmetalled. At junction of tracks ⑤, turn right along grassy lane. Continue in same direction

into enclosed path which climbs ridge into Wharfedale. Descend into Kilnsey village. ⑥ At Kilnsey, turn left past Tennant Arms. Walk along road for 150 yards (137 m), then turn right through gate by barn. Cross the field, heading for corner of wall ahead. Turn right at corner, and follow wall to stile by bridge. Climb stile into road and turn left for Conistone. From Conistone follow Grassington road, then take signposted path which leads through gate on left ⑦, before last house in village. Follow wall uphill. ⑧ In third field, bear left to gate above. Go through this and the next gate, then veer left uphill by trees and above scar. Cross stile above cliff. Path crosses top of scar then winds uphill to stile. ⑨ Go up slope, then bear left to ladder stile. Follow wall above wood along faint tracks. After a mile (1.5

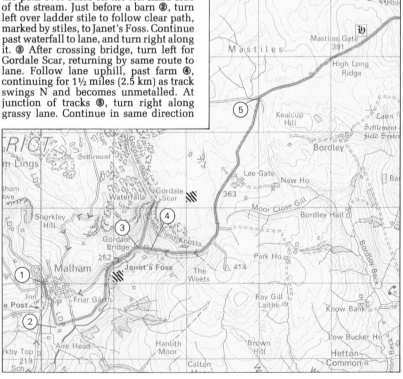

236

Yorkshire Pennines
NORTH YORKSHIRE

km), path descends through line of stiles to farm and along lane to Grassington **⑩**.

※ Janet's Foss is a small waterfall tumbling over an apron of tufa. The curious name is a corruption of 'Gennet', a local fairy.

※ Gordale Scar is thought to be an underground cavern, penetrated and deepened by glacial meltwaters, whose roof has collapsed. It has attracted many artists, including Turner, and has been painted in words as well, notably by Thomas Gray.

▣ Mastiles Gate is situated on Mastiles Lane, a magnificent drove road once used by the monks of Fountains Abbey to bring sheep and produce from their

estates in Borrowdale and Malhamdale to their great grange at Kilnsey.

※ Kilnsey Crag is a huge limestone outcrop, which was undercut by an iceage glacier grinding its way down the valley.

🏠 In front of the 17th-C. Old Hall at Kilnsey is a small outhouse which was once part of the gatehouse of the monastic grange of Fountains Abbey.

※ The footpath from Conistone crosses beautiful limestone pastures and goes close to Dib Scar, a deep, rocky gorge, with impressive outcrops all around.
⚘ There are remains of medieval leadmine workings, and this is also a splendid area for wild flowers.

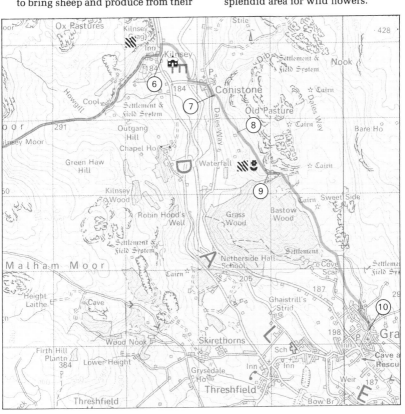

THE MOORS AND WOLDS

The North York Moors and the Yorkshire Wolds, separated by the Vale of Pickering, account for the most popular walking in this part of the North-East, which includes Humberside. The Wolds are represented in this short section by just one route, taking in Londesborough Park, in the county of Humberside. Public footpaths in the Wolds are sparse because the old county council moved slowly when making the definitive map of rights of way; however, Humberside County Council has improved the network.

The two Moors walks show the gentler side of this bleak plateau, swept by icy winds and rain. The heather-clad tops are cleft by some deeply cut dales, and these harbour some attractive hamlets and substantial, stone-built villages. Ampleforth, starting point of one of the routes, is one such. The other route, starting at Newton-on-Rawcliffe, is similarly unspoilt. Nearby is a station on the North Yorkshire Moors Railway, which you can use to approach the start by steam train.

The Moors and Wolds
NORTH YORKSHIRE

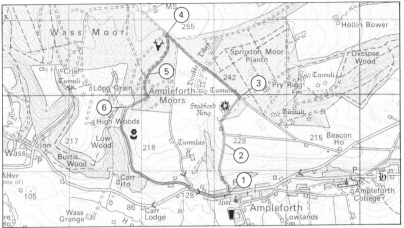

Ampleforth Moors
5 miles (8 km) Sheet 100 581787

Easy Delightful strolling in a relatively unfrequented locality on the S edge of the North York Moors. *Farmland, forest, lane.*

Start Ampleforth, 6 miles (9.5 km) SW of Helmsley on the unclassified road leading W from the B1257 at Oswaldkirk: **parking** in the village main street, or down the road, to the S.

① Take the footpath opposite the telephone box in the main street, following it up drive towards house. At right-hand corner, go left up grass bank to gate and straight up hill to gate at top. Go into field on right. ② In top right-hand corner of field, go through gate, turn sharp left, then right to pass old building on left. Meet lane ③ and turn left. Continue just under one mile (1.5 km) and ④ turn left down forest ride. In about 150 yards (137 m) take the left fork ⑤ and in about 75 yards (68 m) watch out for a narrow path to the right down a small valley. Follow this and ⑥ go through gate on left into lane; turn left. Follow it rather over a mile back into Ampleforth village and ①.

🍺 With its stone houses strung out along the road, Ampleforth is a particularly pleasant village, and there are 2 good pubs; try the local brews and the food.

✳ Studford Ring is an ancient earthwork of uncertain age or use.

🦌 There is a chance of seeing deer in this forestry area of mature pine trees.

🌱 High Woods Lane is a delightful country lane with a range of roadside plants.

🏛 A mile to the E of the village is Ampleforth Abbey and College; monks of the Benedictine foundation teach at the well-known Roman Catholic public school: not open to the public.

Benedictine monk and habit, as worn since the Middle Ages.

The Moors and Wolds
NORTH YORKSHIRE

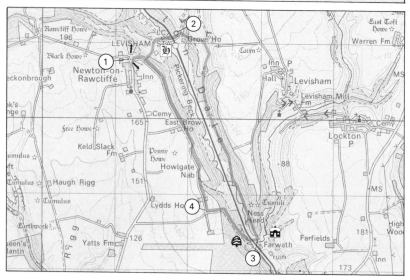

Newton-on-Rawcliffe
5 miles (8 km) Sheet 100 812902

Moderate Not overdeveloped, and certainly not spoiled by tourism, this area shows off the local North York Moors scenery well, with the added interest of a historic steam railway and station. *Steep hillsides, valley, lane; one climb; mud after rain; avoid when there is snow and ice on the ground.*

Start Pickering. Head N on the unclassified road which leads out of town past the railway station. Continue 4 miles (6.5 km) to Newton-on-Rawcliffe; **parking** in the wide village street; trains in summer from Pickering, Goathland or Grosmont to Levisham.

① From the N end of the village, take the lane on the right; soon cross stile on left and go downhill towards Levisham Station. Past the station, go through the white hand gate on right ② and take the path uphill through woods and field. Go over stile, then turn right to follow the valley side above the railway. In about 1¾ miles (3 km) cross the railway near cottages (only place) ③ and the footbridge over the stream. Continue on the broad track, uphill. On meeting the lane, ④ turn

right. It is about 1½ miles (2.5 km) back to ①.

Newton-on-Rawcliffe is a typical North Yorks Moors village, with stone houses and a wide green; the pond is nicely restored. There are unusual views, especially up Newton Dale Gorge, formed by ice-age glaciation.

Levisham Station is a stop on the preserved section of the North Yorks Moors Railway, built by George Stephenson in 1836. Originally it carried horse-drawn carriages, but steam of course took over and you can enjoy a nostalgic ride on a steam train during summer (April–October). It is a wonderful way to see the moors, and the line itself is, as might be expected, a feat of engineering. One of the most impressive sections is the climb through the gorge of Newton Dale.

At Farwath there are 3 railway cottages in a gloriously isolated position: no access road except the rough track up the hill; transport by tractor only.

Modern hill farming co-exists here with 'unimproved land' and forestry with older woodland.

The Moors and Wolds
HUMBERSIDE

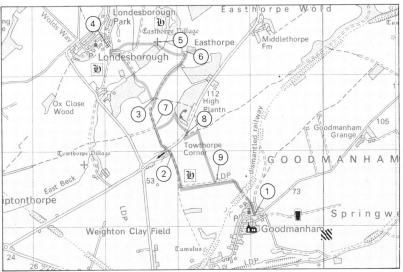

Londesborough Park
5 miles (8 km) Sheet 106 890432

Easy A fine all-year walk in the Yorkshire Wolds, with plenty of interest, from Londesborough Park to Easthorpe deserted village. *Hilly countryside, first arable, then parkland; waymarked.*

Start Goodmanham, about 1½ miles (2.5 km) NE of Market Weighton, which is at the junction of the A1079 and the A1034, about 15 miles (24 km) NW of Kingston upon Hull. **Parking** in N part of village, near church; buses to Market Weighton.

① NE of the church, follow the well-defined track under the disused railway line. Continue about one mile (1.5 km) to the car park and picnic area ② where cross the main road and follow track and farm road. ③ Turn left into parkland across stream and follow tracks to Londesborough. ④ Go through gate and down field to stile and bridge ⑤ where cross stream. Follow the shallow valley uphill to gate. ⑥ Turn right and follow farm road. Where the road turns right ⑦ turn left up the hill to the wood where turn right and continue to the main road where turn right and in a few yards left along the first hedge, ⑧. Soon turn right at first field edge

on right. In nearly ½ mile (0.8 km) ⑨ turn left to follow track back to village and point ①.

🏠 It is thought that Goodmanham's church stands on the site of a Pagan temple, presided over by a heathen priest, Coifi, who destroyed it when he was converted to Christianity.

🏛 Here is part of a Roman road which ran from Brough to Malton, also of the Wolds Way long distance path.

⑂ The Vale of York.

🏛 The remains of Londesborough Hall and estate are relics of bygone splendours: there was a succession of important aristocratic owners, including the Burlingtons and Devonshires and more recently, the Denisons, Earls of Londesborough, who entertained lavishly here.

🏛 Site of a deserted village.

🍺 Goodmanham Arms; real ale; snacks.

⚒ Rifle Butts Quarry is a nature reserve with interesting geological formations (information board).

CUMBRIA

To most walkers, Cumbria means the Lake District; and that, in July and August, means scant privacy. If you want solitude, one approach is to ignore all advice on which are the best bits and attempt to improvise with map and compass; another is to travel outside the central Keswick–Ambleside axis. Two routes in this section point the way; both are located well south of Kendal, are set uncompromisingly in lowland, yet offer satisfying walking, plus the chance to gain a broader picture of the county. Another fine walking area outside the popular central area is the low hills around Arnside on Morecambe Bay; and another is the Howgill Fells, east of the M6.

At any season, the uplands must be treated with respect; the two fell walks make substantial day rambles for which the appropriate clothing and footwear are essential.

Lancaster–Kendal Canal
6½ miles (10.5 km) Sheet 97 496853

Easy A relaxing riverside stroll followed by the towpath of the now-drained Lancaster–Kendal Canal, with its bridges and aqueduct still intact. *Parkland, riverside, canal towpath.*

Start at the junction of the A6 and the A590 near Levens Hall, about 4 miles (6.5 km) S of Kendal. **Parking** in lay-by about 200 yards (183 m) N of traffic lights.

① From the traffic lights, locate stile and footpath signposted Park End. Cross and continue about 200 yards, then take the slightly rising track; keep straight ahead to sign pointing to stile beside steel gate; cross and ② turn right to follow wall to stile. Cross and continue to stile beside house. Turn right along the narrow lane, which leads to a path under a road bridge. Cross the river to join a narrow road. Follow this, turning right to cross a bridge, ③, then turn left on to the road signposted Sedgwick. Follow this 300 yards (274 m), leaving it for the lane marked No Entry. Leave the lane through gate by the footpath signposted Hawes Bridge. Keeping the river on the left, ignore the broad path curving to the right, and pass through a stile. Carry straight on, eventually joining a road. Here ④ turn right and in 300 yards go through a steel gate and under a bridge. Carry on along canal bank, over Sedgwick, The towpath fades after the next bridge. Carry on for another 300 yards, then drop down to the right to join road via stile. Then left ⑤ across bridge, then right to enter Levens Park at footpath sign. Follow the path ahead, running close to the river, to arrive at the main road opposite Levens Hall. Cross the bridge to return to ①.

🏛 Levens Hall is renowned for its extra-
⛪ ordinarily ingenious topiary, open daily. The house, open in summer, is well worth a visit: it is Elizabethan, with fine plaster- and woodwork, leather wall hangings and 17th-18th C. furniture. There is a steam engine display in one of the outbuildings.

Topiary at Levens Hall: the designs in yew and box are claimed to be still largely faithful to the originals of 1690.

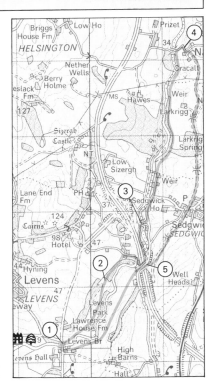

Cumbria
NEAR NEWBY BRIDGE

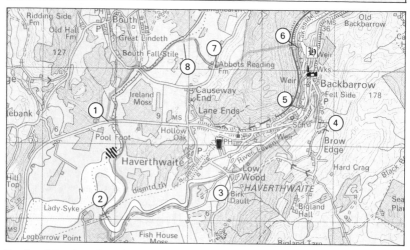

Rusland Pool and River Leven
6½ miles (10.5 km) Sheet 97 328843

Moderate Three quarters of the route is within sight or sound of rivers. *Estuary, woodland, riverside, farmland.*

Start Pool-Foot, on the A590, roughly half-way between Haverthwaite and Greenodd. From Newby Bridge, at the S tip of Windermere, take the A590, signposted Barrow and Ulverston. Nearly 2 miles (3 km) W of Backbarrow, watch out for Dicksons Arms; **parking** by pub in large lay-by, 200 yards (183 m) W of bridge.

① From parking, cross the road and make for the bridge; cross, locating footpath sign on right; through stile, continue on raised embankment beside river for one mile (1.5 km). ② Cross the old railway bridge and enter the woods by the stile on the left. Leave the woods and follow the track to the left for ¾ mile (1 km). Just behind ruined house, cross the beck (stream) to the left and follow the river bank, rejoining the track by a stile. Follow the track to a road where ③ take the narrow road opposite. In 200 yards, enter the woods at the footpath sign. Leave the woods, go past farm, and join road at footpath sign, ④ turning left. Continue to No Cycles sign, and turn left, passing between houses. Follow the footpath

under the road and across the River Leven by a footbridge. At road ⑤ turn right and continue in direction of hotel; but turn left before the bridge, and follow this road as far as ⑥ footpath on left signposted Rusland. Follow path uphill, through woods, and turn right 30 yards (27 m) after crossing a stile. Follow the grassy path downhill until it forks, and go through the gate to the left. Make down the field towards the farmhouse, and join the road, where ⑦ turn left. Continue 15 yards (14 m), then take the track to the right. Follow it to the field and bear left, following the drainage ditch to the river – Rusland Pool – where ⑧ continue, keeping river on right, to road. Cross the bridge; with river on left, carry on to ①.

〰 The fast-flowing River Leven orginates from Lake Windermere, joining the more sedate Rusland Pool.

🍺 Angler's Arms; bar food.

🏭 The White Waters Hotel was formerly a cotton mill, and latterly a 'Blue Mill' – manufacturing the little blue bags that made washing whiter, before modern detergents stole the market.

🚂 Here the route crosses the Lakeside and Haverthwaite Railway, the sole remaining 3½ miles (5.5 km) of the former Furness branch line.

Cumbria
NEAR COCKERMOUTH

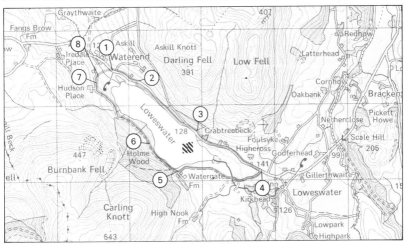

Loweswater
4 miles (6.5 km) Sheet 89 141210

Easy Delightful, all-year walking around a lake which is off the main tourist track; and the bonus of mostly dry paths, with alternatives if it does happen to be wet. *Peaceful roads, lakeside paths and tracks, partly wooded.*

Start the NW end of Loweswater, which is on the unclassified road linking Loweswater village and the A5086 about 6 miles (9.5 km) SW of Cockermouth. Approaching from the W, (ie from the A5086), reach Fang's Brow, the steep narrow hill leading down to the lake; as you approach the lake, there are several lay-bys which provide ample **parking**.

① Identify the lay-by with a telephone box, and from it start walking along the road, lake on right, facing SE. At the next lay-by ② make use of the bridleway on the right to avoid walking the road for a short section. Soon after rejoining the road, the stone wall on the right finishes at some trees and a footpath leaves the road; follow it down the slope to the water's edge, and turn left. Continue on path for about a mile (1.5 km) until reaching stone wall and gate marked Private, Keep Out. Follow the path up the incline with the wall on the right and pass through gate on to the road at ③ Crabtree Farm. Walk

SW along the road for about ½ mile (0.8 km), leaving the lake behind, until reaching ④ a narrow road leading off right. Turn down this and fork right at the next junction; in another ½ mile, reach Watergate Farm and the S side of the lake, ⑤. Follow the farm road which runs alongside the lake; just after leaving the lakeside, it forks. ⑥ (From here, you can make a detour to Holme Force, an impressive waterfull, especially after rain: follow the left-hand track across a beck, then leave it for the footpath up through the woods, running near the beck.) Retrace to ⑥ and carry straight on – by the side of the lake. Continue until passing through gate on to narrow, walled lane; carry on up the hill, soon reaching Hudson Place farm. ⑦ Follow narrow farm road downhill, and about half-way down ⑧ take the track starting from the gate on the right. Follow it down the hillside, cross river by footbridge and, just over it, the stile on the right. Follow the path up the side of the next field on left to gate at top on to road near telephone kiosk and ②.

〰 Loweswater, the most westerly and smallest of the 3 lakes forming the Buttermere valley, is also one of the smallest in the Lake District. Its water flows into Crummock Water, the next lake along the valley. The surrounding fells offer good walking with fine views.

Cumbria
NEAR KESWICK

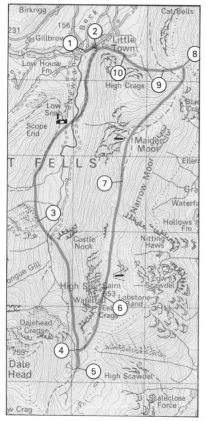

Newlands Valley and Dale Head
8 miles (13 km) Sheet 90 235195

Strenuous One of the finest walks in the Lakes for views. *Fell paths; 3 climbs; not recommended outside April–October: fells may be snow-covered.*

Start Little Town, about 4 miles (6.5 km) SW of Keswick on an unclassified road off the road to Buttermere (Newlands Pass). Mountain Goat buses from Keswick market-place stop at Stair, on the way to Buttermere. Approaching Little Town from the N by car, pass beyond the hamlet and descend hill; **parking** at bottom, before crossing river, on grassy lay-by to the left.

① From parking, walk back up the hill and ② turn sharp right at the top through gate to follow the old mine road. Continue up the valley about 1½ miles (2 km) until the road finishes at the ruins of Castle Nook Mine, ③). Take the footpath which starts here, ascending the fellside with a large waterfall in view on the right. Just above the falls, at the crest of the ridge, ④ join another path and ⑤ turn right. In 20 yards, turn right by small hillock and cross stone wall to reach Dale Head Tarn – an excellent place to pause for a rest or lunch. Return to the path at ④, and follow it N up High Spy. Reach the summit cairn ⑥, and start to descend, still going N. Continue along grass track over Narrow Moor ⑦. The path gradually descends by Maiden Moor ⑧ to a crossing of paths ⑨. For a detour to the summit of Cat Bells, take the path straight ahead. To return to the start, turn downhill to the W. As the path descends, take the next left fork ⑩. Pass another disused mine, and at a stone wall join bridleway. Turn left ⑪, and follow this back to Little Town and ①.

🏭 These are the remains of Newlands Lead Mine, in Tudor times one of the busiest of several mines in the valleys around Keswick. Goldscope Mines, whose ruins are across the valley, were reputed to be among the richest.

〰 As you begin to descend from the summit of High Spy, Helvellyn comes into view in the next range of hills on the right, easily identified because of the sharply pointed peak on its immediate left – Catchedicam, Helvellyn is third highest mountain in the Lake District.

〰 Walking along the ridge of Narrow Moor, enjoy the view down to the left of Newlands Valley, your outward route. As you continue, Langdale Pikes, and several other well-known fells come into view to the rear. Down to the right is Borrowdale; steeply enclosed, and with its flat green floor, this can claim to be one of the most beautiful valleys in the Lake District. It leads out, at its N end, in to Derwent Water, renowned not only as one of the prettiest lakes in Europe, but, among Beatrix Potter fans, as the setting of Owl Island in *Squirrel Nutkin*.

Patterdale and Kidsty Pike
8 miles (13 km) Sheet 90 394162

Strenuous An attractive fell walk, with fine views, and a high-rise section of a former Roman road. *Peaceful roads and fell paths; 3 climbs – one of them severe, though short; not recommended when there is thick snow on heights.*

Start near Patterdale, at the S tip of Ullswater, about 12 miles (19 km) SW of Penrith; buses from Keswick and Penrith. Ample **parking** space NW of the village in vicinity of the village school.

① From the school leave main road on narrow road crossing the valley; follow it until it meets another road ② and turn sharp right. Continue to Rooking Farm ③ and there locate the footpath starting near the farm, to the E. Follow it quite steeply up side of Place Fell by Boardale Hause for rather less than a mile; it levels out at a junction of paths ④ at summit of Boardale Hause. Note one path rising up Place Fell behind you; a second crossing some level ground to the left before dropping down towards Sandwick; and a third across the fells signposted Kidsty Pike.

Follow this last path up an easy gradient just over a mile (1.5 km) until it reaches ⑤ Angle Tarn. Continue on the path to the left of the tarn, as it climbs on for about 1½ miles (2.5 km) to the top of the ridge ahead, reaching ⑥ The Knott. It is well worth continuing left along the path (High Street), then right at the next junction, to climb to the top of Kidsty Pike – approaching 2 miles there and back. The views from the top are remarkable. Retrace to The Knott and descend the track which zigzags down the fellside towards Hayeswater, seen below. Continue down past the lake and cross the beck below it; then follow Hayeswater Gill downstream on a bridleway. Soon after Pasture Beck joins from the left, reach the buildings at Low Hartsop ⑦. Continue about another ⅓ mile (0.5 km) to turn right at the next lane ⑧ by a large house: don't carry straight on to the main road. Continue by Goldrill Beck for about 2 miles into Patterdale and ①.

🏠 Tradition has it that St. Patrick preached at Patterdale; the church is dedicated to him.

🅱 Along this ridge ran the Roman road from Ambleside to Penrith, known as High Street.

〽 The view from Kidsty Pike takes in, among other features, the lake of Haweswater. In the late 1930s its level was raised in order to meet increased domestic demands submerging the village of Mardale.

🏠 On one of the houses on the left has a spinning gallery.

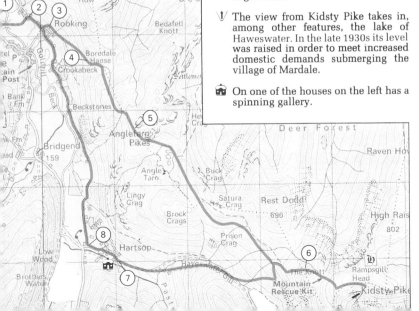

THE NORTH PENNINES

County Durham and Northumberland are covered in this section. Durham is a land of three rivers: bounded by the Tyne and Tees, with the Wear cutting a swathe through the middle. The lowland east, urban and industrialized, accounts for the county's grimy image, but the uplands to the west are one of the best-kept secrets of England's countryside. There are thousands of acres of Pennine moorland where you are more likely to see grouse and sheep than other walkers.

The dales provide a softer alternative to the fells. Weardale is one of the fast-dwindling number of places left in Britain where you can find traditional hay meadows – the ones which seem to grow flowers in as great a profusion as grass. And Upper Teesdale is renowned as a five-star site by botanists. Peaceful as they are today, these valleys were once the scene of a thriving lead industry.

Northumberland is a big county, full of interest for the walker: a rugged coast with splendid cliffs; offshore islands; massive castles; inland, a coastal plain and some dignified river valleys; and an entire national park.

The North Pennines
CO. DURHAM

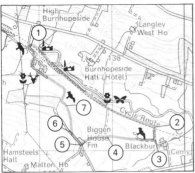

Lanchester Railway
3½ miles (5.5 km) Sheet 88 178464

Easy A walk that shows how nature can fight back: a disused railway line and a former colliery are now peaceful countryside havens for wildlife. This achievement is largely due to the ingenuity of the local branch of Durham County Conservation Trust. Take a field guide for identifying the interesting birds likely to be seen. *Reclaimed railway line, riverside, farmland; mud after rain.*

Start From Durham take the A691 NW for 7 miles (11 km) in the direction of Consett; about ½ mile (0.8 km) outside Lanchester, turn left following the signpost for Malton Picnic Site and **car park**. Hourly bus service from Durham to Castleside.

① From the car park, go through the pines and follow the river downstream. Cross the road and join the disused railway track where it bridges the river. Turn right ② and follow the track. After 1¼ miles (2 km), look out for a large tree on the left and turn through a gate towards a farm with a blue silo ③. In 150 yards (137 m) turn right through the left hand of 2 metal gates. Skirt a small plantation of oaks, go through another gate and turn left. At the end of the hedge, bear left. Cross over into the following field by the lone oak. Aim ④ for the open barn ahead (in theory, the path lies straight ahead across the field; in practice local walkers usually skirt the field). Walk up through Biggin Farm ⑤ and turn right. Go through the gate ⑥ at the top of the lane. Bear right and downhill, crossing 2 stiles

on to a metalled path, ⑦. After about 150 yards turn left on to a broader track. Follow this round past a row of houses, then turn left to return to the car park.

🔍 Look around in the trees for nest boxes for birds and bats. Not only bluetits, but redstarts and tree creepers use the boxes among the pine trees.

🚂 The railway line, a casualty of Beeching's axe.

🚂 The peculiar smell of creosote which you can detect here is a relic of the coal washing plant which was attached to the colliery. Although the slurry lagoon has been capped over, pollution still escapes at this point.

🌿 This more open section of the track is the home of 2 interesting plants: pepper saxifrage and dyer's-greenweed. The latter, closely related to broom, makes a bright yellow dye.

🦋 This is the best section of the walk for butterflies. Look out for the misnamed dingy skipper.

🔍 The marshy field to the left is gradually being invaded by clumps of gorse, an excellent development, since it attracts birds such as whitethroats and blackcaps. Surprisingly, redstarts nest here – they usually choose woodland.

🌿 The route passes areas deliberately planted with trees, and past colliery spoil which has recolonized naturally with birch scrub. In a few places, heather, the natural vegetation, remains. The large open area marks the site of the colliery shafts, and has been given an uneven surface to create sun traps for butterflies and lizards.

🌱 Where the fencing starts on the left, you can make a detour to a pair of ponds, which replace a pond lost during the colliery reclamation. Its larger plants and animals were transferred by hand, the mud at the bottom with a mechanical digger, and the water by pump. As a result, the new ponds have thriving populations of frogs, toads, smooth newts and, most important, the endangered great crested newt.

The North Pennines
CO. DURHAM

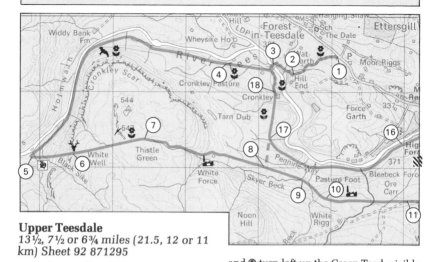

Upper Teesdale
13½, 7½ or 6¾ miles (21.5, 12 or 11 km) Sheet 92 871295

Strenuous Little has been done to introduce Teesdale, internationally famous for its flowers, to interested walkers; this walk redresses the balance. It also offers birds, and some spectacular scenery. For the experienced walker, it is a demanding day out; those who want to take it easy will use the short cuts indicated. Take a plant identification guide. *Rough farmland, moorland, section of The Pennine Way, riverside; several climbs (the start of the Green Trod is a killer); several streams to cross – wear waterproof boots; follow directions with care at ⑩, where the track is poorly defined.*

Start Middleton-in-Teesdale. Take the B6277 in the direction of Newbiggin. About 2 miles (3 km) after Newbiggin, look out for a thick plantation of conifers on the left and High Force Hotel on the right; in about a mile (1.5 km) stop at Forest Methodist Chapel, on the left. **Parking** by the roadside – pull well in and do not block the gates.

① Follow the farm track beside the chapel. Cross the two cattle-grids and where the track forks, bear left and carry on to Hill End Farm ②. Turn right and follow the track to ③ Cronkley Bridge. Turn right and aim for the barn standing below the right-hand edge of ④ Cronkley Goar. Follow the river bank for 2¼ miles (3.5 km)

and ⑤ turn left up the Green Trod, visible as a broad green band against the heather. Continue, following ⑥ the cairns across the fell top past the 2 enclosures. The path dips round to the right of a low outcrop ⑦ but then the Green Trod becomes visible once more. Continue on it, and at a brown nature reserve sign ⑧ go straight ahead. (But to cut the walk short, turn left, go through a gate, and walk up to the black corrugated metal barn on the skyline, where you will rejoin the route at ⑰.) In rather over ¼ mile (0.5 km) ford the streams ⑨ and continue following the Green Trod along the wall to the top of the scar ⑩. The path is somewhat indistinct here, but keep going straight ahead until reaching ⑪ a metalled track. Follow it to ⑫ where it turns left and drops down the scar. Go through the gate to the right and down a narrow valley to ⑬ the road. It is only ½ mile (0.8 km) to the excellent Embleton Arms, Holwick, from here. To continue, follow the road to the left and as you enter the grounds of Holwick Lodge, follow the footpath to the right across the meadow. Join the riverside footpath at Wynch Bridge and Low Force ⑭, turning left to walk upstream. At Holwick Head Bridge ⑮, climb the steps and continue past High Force ⑯. After about a mile, follow the path up through the juniper scrub to a black, corrugated iron barn ⑰. Cross the white-blazed stile in the left-hand corner of the field; turn right and follow the well-worn path beside the wall, crossing back at the next stile. Go through a gap in the low crag seen ahead and follow the path to ⑲ Cronkley Farm, where turn left and follow the track to Cronkley Bridge. Retrace to Dale Chapel.

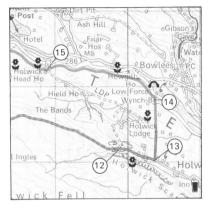

🌸 Heath-spotted orchids beside the track: identify by broad lower lip of flower.

🌸 Wet meadows are rare in England these days. Look for the yellow flowers of rattle: its huge seeds are rather loose in its inflated seed pods, so they really do rattle. Ragged robin – delicate pink flowers – along ditches and low-lying damp areas.

🪶 Ring ouzels among the scree: their song is rather like a blackbird's; summer only.

🌸 Along the river, the insectivorous round-leaved sundew can be found in damp spots. One flush (damp patch) has a large expanse of yellow mountain saxifrage, a very rare plant.

📖 The Green Trod is an ancient drove road, now the preserve of Pennine Way walkers. The sheep are the
🐑 hardy Swaledale breed – black faced, white nosed, white spots on the legs.

✖ The fences are designed to keep sheep, and walkers, off Teesdale's unique rock, the sugar limestone. Its crumbly texture was created by volcanic heat. Many of Teesdale's exciting plants only survive because of

this rock. Look over the fences for hoary rockrose, spring sandwort, autumn felwort and northern bedstraw.

🔨 Look back up Skyer Beck to see the remains of a significant lead mining area. The ruins are of lead miners' 'shop' or lodgings where they lived from Monday to Saturday; on Sundays they walked considerable distances to be at home with their families.

🔨 From here, a view of a modern industry in progress: the whinstone, a kind of basalt, is mined for road stone.

🌸 As you drop down the valley, watch out for the aptly named parsley fern.

🍺 The excellent Embleton Arms is a free
✖ house selling real ale and bar food.

🌸 The hay meadows at Holwick are among the best in Teesdale: fine populations of greater burnet, as well as other hay-meadow plants.

⌒ Wynch Bridge is a Victorian chain bridge; a little upstream is the series of falls known as Low Force.

🌸 Shrubby cinquefoil on the islands of shingle in the river.

🌸 Holwick Head Bridge is a Mecca for fern buffs: species found here include lemon-scented fern, black spleenwort and brittle bladder fern.

🌸 The low, prickly bushes are juniper, whose berries are used in flavouring gin. The yellow spikes of flowers growing in the boggy areas are bog asphodels.

💧 High Force, the highest waterfall in England, was even more impressive before the dam at Cow Green regulated Tees flood water.

🌸 This low scar is another interesting spot for ferns, including oakland and beech ferns.

🌸 Another fine hay meadow, ablaze with rattles, knapweeds and oxeye daisies in early summer.

The North Pennines
CO. DURHAM

Bolt's Law and Rookhope Chimney
15½ miles (25 km) Sheet 87 964504

Strenuous Besides beautiful scenery, an insight into the importance of the North Pennines for minerals, and the harsh lives of the local lead miners. *Rough pasture and moorland; mud; 3 long hard climbs, and several shorter ones; much of the path, across peat, is indistinct – follow directions carefully; do not attempt, for preference, in poor visibility: the 2 high points are liable to disappear in cloud, but the directions enable safe descent.*

Start Blanchland, on the B6306 about 9 miles (14.5 km) S of Hexham. Large **car park** to the N of the village, signposted.

① From the car park, turn right through the village, cross bridge and follow road uphill. Take the first road on the right and follow this round a right-hand bend, then go through the first gate on the left. ② Cross the stile to your left, then follow the fence line up until reaching a gate on the right. Cross, and again follow the fence line, to the top of the ridge. ③ Turn sharp right and aim for the hill top, where ④ walk over to the distinctive square sheepfold to the right, then follow the well-made track down to the road. (For a quick return to ①, turn right here towards Baybridge and follow the riverside back to Blanchland.) At the road ⑤ turn left and follow it over the brow of the hill, cross a cattle-grid and after about 50 yards (46 m) turn right. ⑥ Follow the fence line to Bolt's Law, its summit ⑦ marked by a main point. From the summit take the shooter's track downhill: it starts at the large wooden gate and is visible as a shallow depression. Continue on this track until it turns into a boggy mess, then turn right to reach the road: you should arrive in the vicinity of a double bend. (For a short cut, turn right ⑧ and continue straight ahead to ⑪.) To continue, carry on down to Lintzgarth, taking the short cut straight down to the village when the road doglegs left. Turn right at the T-junction and in about 30 yards (27 m) scramble up the bank to your right to the ruined kilns at the base of Rookhope Chimney. ⑨ Follow the line of the chimney to its summit and ⑩ bear right across the peat hag to regain the road. Look for a large wooden gate ⑪ – about 400 yards (366 m) N of a

cattle-grid. Go through and follow the path that bears left ahead of you. Do not cross the footbridge ⑫ near the dam, but follow the burn and then a track to White Heaps Mine. ⑬ Follow the road through Ramshaw and after about 500 yards (457 m), take the public footpath on the left. ⑭ Go down to the burn, but do not cross the bridge. Follow the path to the right as far as possible, then cross using stepping stones. After a few yards, the path broadens into a sound track which leads to the road on to which ⑮ turn left; in 200 yards (183 m) turn right to follow the riverside path back to Blanchland.

🛏 The shallow pits are the remains of bell-pits used for extracting lead ore.

🔪 Wheatears breed in the ruins of the lead flue.

👁 The view N from Bolt's Law gives an idea of how extensive the lead mining and processing area was hereabouts.

🌱 The flush – boggy patch – contains some interesting wild plants: look for the white flowers of common water crowfoot.

🛏 Since lead fumes are both poisonous and heavy, a tall chimney is needed to carry them away from those working in the vicinity. With some ingenuity, and considerable saving of money, the mining companies built their chimneys resting against the fellside. The fumes emerged over a mile

The North Pennines
CO. DURHAM

and a half away on the fell top; however, the flue also trapped precious lead – so small boys were sent in with hammers to chip away any that crystallized inside the roof.

❦ The top of Redburn Common is an enormous peat hag, an unnerving medium even for experienced fell walkers. Unlike heather moor, it does not support a wide range of wildlife.

🐄 White Heaps Mine is owned by British Steel, who extract fluorspar for use as a flux in steel making. 'White Heaps' refers to the quartz which is often extracted with the fluorspar; there is no market for quartz, so it is just left standing.

🌿 The road by the mine entrance is flanked by fine displays of wild raspberries and wood horsetails, the latter identified by their feathery leaves.

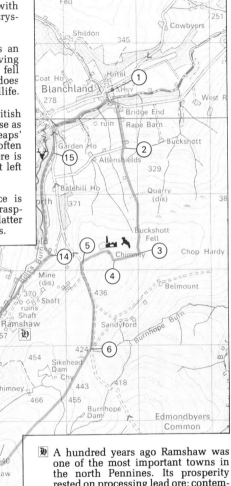

🏛 A hundred years ago Ramshaw was one of the most important towns in the north Pennines. Its prosperity rested on processing lead ore; contemporary accounts paint a picture of 19th-C. County Durham being every bit as wild and woolly as the Yukon or California.

✝ Keep your eyes open for roe deer in Bolts Burn Wood.
All the squirrels in these woods are red: watch for them peering round tree trunks at you.

253

The North Pennines
NORTHUMBERLAND

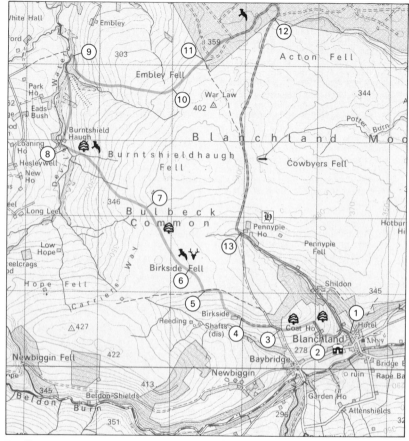

Devil's Water and Blanchland Moor
9¼ miles (15 km) Sheet 87
964504

Strenuous A typically Pennine blend of moorland dissected by wooded valleys, with opportunities to contemplate the role, and the future, of these fine uplands. Best in late spring and summer (the heather blooms in August); may be impassable in winter. *Farmland tracks, open fell, wooded valley, woodland; some sections always wet – use proper footwear; follow directions carefully at Birkside Fell; 2 long climbs.*

Start Blanchland, about 9 miles (14.5 km) S of Hexham, on the B6306; large **car park** to the north of Blanchland, signposted from the village centre.

① Turn left out of the car park, then left again, and follow track through Cote House Farm (marked Coat Ho. on map). ② Go through gate at top and turn left to follow the wall and then a hedge. Keep going until reaching a metalled track ③ lined with Scots pines; carry on up track and round corner, then bear left and take track past Birkside Farm. ④ Follow line of track up the field and go through either gate to find a broad, metalled track. Turn

The North Pennines
NORTHUMBERLAND

left and follow this to its end, ⑤. Bear diagonally right to a large gate in the fence and ⑥ continue straight across moor to a drystone wall – about ½ mile (0.8 km). Cross by stile and ⑦ follow wall down to left. When it meets another wall, turn right and follow this new wall to its end. Turn left and follow the fence, then a beck down the valley, bearing right to skirt Burntshield Haugh. ⑧ Follow the path alongside and into the wood (fairly well-defined, but if in doubt, bear right). Cross the burn, which joins Devil's Water from the right and follow path out of wood on opposite side. ⑨ Turn right and go uphill to the moor. Follow the well-worn track to a post-and-wire fence, where ⑩ turn left and follow fence to gate near south-west corner of Slaley Forest. ⑪ Go through forest, forking left where it opens out. Fork right after about ½ mile ⑫ to follow a well-defined track across Blanchland Moor. Go round by Pennypie House ⑬ and follow left fork through gate back to the car park.

Blanchland is a model village, built from the remains of a Cistercian monastery by Lord Crewe in the 18th C. The monks' dormitory is now the Crewe Arms Hotel.

Some fine trees stand along the roads heading up the fell from Blanchland, planted as windbreaks. The severity of the winter snow dictates pines for this purpose.

Another use of trees is shown here: the remains of an ancient hedgerow, with its tall ashes, beeches and wych-elms. The wych-elms are less susceptible to Dutch elm disease than English elms, and isolated specimens such as these may survive.

Typical moorland birds such as curlew and red grouse; also emperor moths and common lizards.

Look out for old logs wherever a drainage ditch is cut into the peat. These are 'bog oaks', the remains of pines and birches that cloaked the hills until about 4,000 years ago. Sundew may be found in wetter parts of the fell.

The valley of Devil's Water shelters several tree species including gnarled rowans (mountain ash) and silver birches. Watch for dippers and grey wagtails in the stream.

You might be lucky enough to glimpse a pied flycatcher or redstart in Slaley Forest; commoner birds are goldcrests and coal tits. Keep eyes and ears alert for a shower of pine cones, dropped by either crossbills or red squirrels while feeding.

Derwent Reservoir.

Pennypie House takes its curious name from the fact that it really did sell pies for a penny each, especially to lead miners from Shildon, though these days that seems like a long uphill walk for lunch.

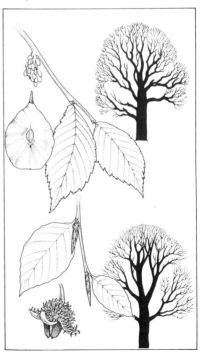

Top, wych-elm, and above, common beech, both outlines showing shape of full-grown tree.

255

The North Pennines
NORTHUMBERLAND

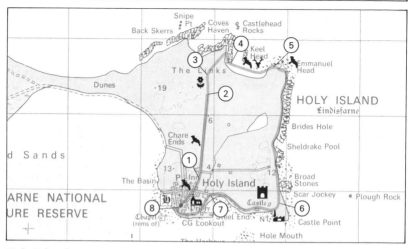

Holy Island
4¼ miles (7 km) Sheet 75 127421

Moderate Many people visit Holy Island, look at the castle, then drive away, missing the wealth of wildlife that makes the place a National Nature Reserve. This route introduces some of the more exciting animals and plants, without neglecting the island's historical interest. Worth a visit at any season: summer for dune flowers, late autumn for Scandinavian migrant birds, winter for wildfowl and waders, late spring for breeding birds. *Rough farmland, dunes, wild coastline; some mud after rain; indistinct path through dunes, but route-finding easy; classed moderate because walking the sand and shingle stretches is hard work.*

Start From the A1 about 8 miles (13 km) S of Berwick-upon-Tweed. Take the turning left signposted Holy Island. Follow the road across the causeway into the village on the island, where the **car park** is clearly signposted. WARNING The causeway is submerged at high tide and the water rises fast. Anyone ignoring the safe crossing times posted at either end of the causeway runs the risk of losing their car. Safe crossing times also available by telephone from the AA's Newcastle office. Buses from Berwick-upon-Tweed (United route 477); times vary with the tides.

① Leaving the car park turn left along the track, passing large wooden farm building on the right. Keep going for about ¾ mile (1 km) and ② follow the track into the dunes at the NCC nature reserve sign. ③ As the dunes flatten out, turn right, following track to the coast. ④ Scramble down on to the beach, turn right and follow the bay round to Emmanuel Head, which is marked by The Monument – a large white pyramid. ⑤ Climb up to The Monument from the beach and continue along the coast using cliff-top path. ⑥ Follow the raised path round past the limekilns to the castle. ⑦ Bear left round the harbour and up on to the sea wall. ⑧ At the church, continue on through the village or priory and village to return to the car park.

🐦 The hedges along either side of the lonnen (lane) are the best places for the migrant birds which draw ornithologists here from far and wide.

🌿 The sand dunes are of national importance. Look out for swards of grass of Parnassus in the dune slacks (damp areas between dunes); also piri-piri burr in the drier areas – an aggressive little plant imported from New Zealand. Its vicious burrs can clog the feathers of ground-nesting birds.

🐦 Look out for waders in this bay, par-

One of many stirring local views of Lindisfarne Castle; the upturned boats are used as storeplaces by fishermen.

ticularly turnstones and purple sandpipers picking among the seaweed. Grey seals often lie out on the rocks at low tide and may also be seen bobbing about in the bay as the tide comes in.

The pyramid at Emmanuel Head is a navigation aid, and also the best place on the island for sea watching. Bird enthusiasts should look out for skuas and shearwaters on passage, and in winter for sea-duck, divers and grebes. Everyone should look out for the rafts of eider ducks. Their 'Roman noses' make even the females unmistakable; they feed on the mussel beds just offshore. Eider down is still used in some parts of the world as a heat insulating material.

The enormous limekilns by the castle were built in 1860 to supply quicklime to Dundee; raw limestone was transported from Keel Head by waggon along the raised causeway.

Lindisfarne Castle, built about 1550 as a coastal defence fort, held, with Bamburgh Castle (down the coast to the SE), a commanding position over the harbour, Budle Bay and Skate Roads.

It was extensively restored in the early 20th C. by Lutyens to make a private house. The plug of rock on which it stands makes a natural rock garden for maritime plants such as sea campion and thrift. Fulmars nest on the water spouts of the castle walls.

The small island with the large cross is Cuddy's Island – Cuddy being an affectionate nickname for St. Cuthbert, bishop of Lindisfarne or Holy Island from 684. By tradition, Cuthbert used the small island as a retreat, but because it was accessible at low tide, abandoned it for Inner Farne (down the coast to the SE) in order to completely avoid worldly distractions. Much of St. Cuthbert's story is told in the church, which is also well worth a visit, if only for the unique carpet in the sanctuary.

The priory, a Benedictine foundation dating from the late 11th C., can be entered from the churchyard, but obtain a ticket first. Don't miss the remarkable Norman 'rainbow' arch.

The flooded area in the field opposite the harbour often rewards a visual search for waders and wildfowl: it is visible from the car park, so you can take a last look at the island's birds before leaving.

257

SCOTLAND

SOUTHERN SCOTLAND

WESTERN SCOTLAND

DEESIDE AND SPEYSIDE

SOUTHERN SCOTLAND

Here is a large region, bounded in the south by the border
and in the north by an imaginary line drawn between
Glasgow and Edinburgh; it also includes the substantial
westwards bulge of Galloway and Dumfries.

The routes in this section show most of its key aspects:
there is an ascent of Merrick, in the Galloway Hills, highest
mountain in southern Scotland. It is not so awesome an
undertaking as it sounds and its locality has some
interesting, if bloodstained, associations on which to reflect
as you pant to the top. In the central hills of the region –
the Lowthers, Moorfoots, Lammermuirs and Pentlands –
there is also plenty of gloomy, and romantic, food for
thought, depending on your disposition: the martyrdom of
Covenanters and the hardships of lead miners, for example.

Not many associate the region with industry, but the
industrial theme returns again on a fine walk within easy
reach of Glasgow, along the Falls of Clyde. And further
along the Clyde Valley, in the orchard country, there is
some underrated, and delightful country to be explored,
again quite close to the two largest cities in Scotland.

Devil's Beef Tub
3¾ miles (6 km) Sheet 78 063125

Easy Here is a famous tourist attraction – which 99 per cent of visitors merely look down into from the roadside. Walking its depths is quite an unusual experience. *Grassy slopes, forest road, open moorland/hill country*.

Start From the centre of Moffat, take the A701 N towards Edinburgh for 5¼ miles (8.5 km); the small but conspicuous Covenanter's Monument by the roadside marks the edge of the Devil's Beef Tub; infrequent bus service from Moffat. **Parking** in disused quarry 200 yards (183 m) E of monument on S side of road.

① From the Covenanter's Monument keep to rim of corrie high above the Beef Tub – numerous sheep tracks. ② Where forestry road leaves main road, bear left through trees. ③ At end of forest turn right (uphill), keeping to edge of trees. ④ At top of forest turn right and follow fence S over tussocky moorland and up easy slope towards prominent trig. point on summit of Annanhead Hill. ⑤ At trig. point (white concrete pillar), turn left and follow wall and fence downhill to col between Annanhead Hill and Great Hill. ⑥ From summit of Great Hill descend S, gradually curving round into base of Beef Tub. ⑦ Climb to main road.

🎟 The roadside monument just off the route commemorates the driver and guard of the Dumfries–Edinburgh mailcoach which became stuck in snowdrifts here on 1 February, 1831. The men shouldered the mailbags and tried to struggle on by foot, but both perished in the snow.

〰 Tweed's Well, the source of the River Tweed, lies in the lower ground just N of the route. The Clyde rises on the slopes of Clyde Law, a couple of miles NW, while the River Annan rises in the Devil's Beef Tub itself: three of Scotland's major rivers rising within a few miles.

〰 The Devil's Beef Tub is a huge, natural, steep-sided hollow, carved out by glaciation; two streams rising high on either side of the hollow merge at the bottom to form the infant River Annan. The Beef Tub has had other names: the Corrie of Annan and the Marquis of Annandale's Beefstand. 'Beef Tub' – and its accompanying reputation – derives from the fact that a couple of centuries ago border cattle raiders, and notably the Johnstone family of whom the Marquis of Annandale was the head, would foray across the border and bring back stolen cattle to the Beef Tub to await disposal. Only the narrow neck at the SE side needed to be closed to make a sizeable cattle pen.

↷ W from Great Hill, over the depths of the Beef Tub.

🎟 The path which climbs the W shoulder of Great Hill was once an important route between Dumfries and Edinburgh. During the 1745 rebellion, a party of captured Highlanders was marched along it; a captive wrapped himself in his plaid and rolled all the way to the bottom, escaping unscathed from his captors, who peppered him with gunfire from above.

🎟 The Covenanter's, or Martyr's Monument, pays tribute to John Hunter, one of the persecuted Covenanters of the 17th C., shot by Government troops.

Southern Scotland
DUMFRIES AND GALLOWAY

The Merrick
9 miles (14.5 km) Sheet 77 414803

Strenuous A safe 'visitor's' route up the highest hill in southern Scotland, followed by exploration of a wilder area on the return journey. As might be expected, the panorama from the summit is sensational; best chance of clear conditions are in spring and summer. *Woodland, upland meadow, forest, hillside, high-level plateau, rocky mountainside, moorland, stream-side path; mud after rain; section between ❹ and ❹ indistinct – see directions (possibility of alternative route); two stiff climbs; do not attempt in poor visibility – the Galloway Hills can be as demanding as the Highlands.*

Start From the A714 (Newton Stewart–Girvan road), branch north at Bargrennan and pass Glentrool Village. Continue to the end of the public road where there is ample free **parking**.

❶ From the car park walk E for about ¼ mile (0.5 km) along the road. ❷ Opposite the Bruce Stone turn left on to path marked The Merrick. ❸ Path is muddy, rocky and indistinct in places. Keep close to the river on the right. (Alternative route indicated by arrow on rock: this leads through forest to Culsharg Bothy). ❹ Keep to the outside of the forest. ❺ On reaching ruined cottage (Culsharg Bothy) and memorial stone, go behind cottage and follow path N through woods. ❻ Reaching forestry road, turn right across concrete bridge, then left on to path signposted Merrick. ❼ Follow wall for first part of walk from Benyellary to The Merrick, then bear right to cross open hillside directly to summit. ❽ Descend E towards shore of Loch Enoch. ❾ Follow shore S until loosely built stone wall is reached. ❿ Follow stone wall SW for ¼ mile. Note Grey Man on a rocky outcrop on the right – map reference 437846. ⓫ Walk SE from the Grey Man, ascend low ridge and turn right. ⓬ Keeping to the high ground, head for the gap between Buchan Hill and the Rig of the Jarkness. ⓭ Follow the path SW beside the Gairland Burn, which leads back to ❶.

🏚 The Bruce Stone commemorates the Battle of Glentrool: Robert the Bruce, newly returned from Ireland, found himself and a small band of followers in the Glen of Trool, pursued by a considerable force of English. Bruce's men spent a day and a night on the hillside to the S of the loch, manoeuvring hundreds of boulders into position above the narrow road. As the English passed beneath, the boulders were rolled down the slope; Bruce's men followed. Hardly an Englishman escaped being hacked down by the Scots guerillas, or swept into the loch by the boulders – or so the story goes. Bruce, who had just had his famous encounter with the spider, felt encouraged to continue with his newly learned lesson of perseverance, and seven years later, in 1314, his campaign for independence culminated in the great victory at Bannockburn. The English were buried in the flat land at the east-end of Loch Trool, still known as the Soldier's Holm.

👁 Views S and SW from The Merrick's summit take in the great wilderness of the Galloway Hills and extend across the Solway Firth to the mountains of the Lake District; you may even be able to make out the Isle of Man.

Northwards there are the Galloway Hills and the long slash of Loch Doon, backed by a sweep of the coast. Moving W, there is the Firth of Clyde, the islands of Arran and Ailsa Craig, the Mull of Kintyre and at 60 miles (96 km), the Antrim coast.

🌊 The Grey Man of The Merrick is a natural rock formation with a striking resemblance to a man's face; many fail to find it, but it is not difficult to locate in clear conditions.

🏚 The inlet on the W side of Loch Neldricken was dubbed 'the murder hole' by S. R. Crockett in his Galloway epic *The Raiders*. It is quite an interesting feature, but unlikely to have been used for concealing dead bodies: the deep mud around the edges restricts access.

👁 The view SW from here is almost Alpine: Bruce Stone far below.

🌱 In summer the hillside here is covered by a pink blanket of tens of thousands of foxgloves.

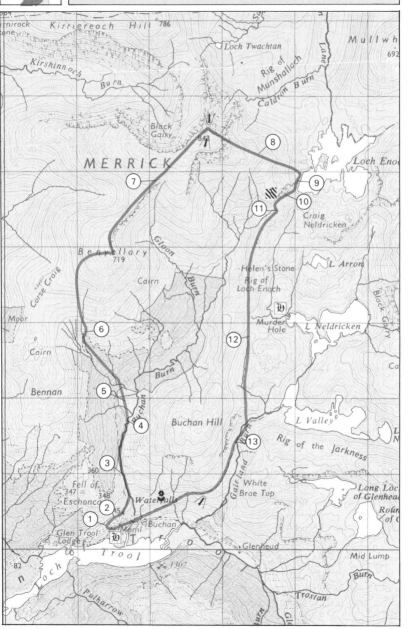

Southern Scotland
BORDERS

St. Abb's Head and Coldingham
3 or 6 miles (5 or 10 km) Sheet 67
906662

Easy From May–July the cliffs are alive with thousands of seabirds, but all year round this is a fascinating walk, along Berwickshire's imposing coastline. *Fields, coastal cliffs, villages; one climb.*

Start Coldingham, 11 miles (18 km) NW of Berwick-upon-Tweed on the A1107. **Parking** in the village streets. Alternatively, turn E on to the B6438 and then right on to minor road to Coldingham Bay and car park. Join walk at ②.

① From village, walk to crossroads on the B6438, then turn right on to minor road towards Coldingham Bay. ② Just past hotel, turn left and follow cliff path. ③ On entering St. Abbs, turn left along left-hand side of first houses. Turn right at end of row of houses to reach village street. ④ Leave St. Abbs on the B6438 and for the shorter route follow this back to ①. For longer route, go to end of walled

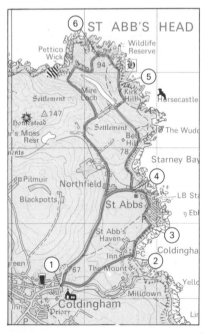

woodland. Turn right immediately, along footpath signposted St. Abb's Head. ⑤ Proceed round right-hand side of loch and go up through gap between low hills. (You can also follow cliff top, but there is no path.) ⑥ Leave St. Abb's Head by lighthouse road and follow for 1¼ miles (2 km) to joint the B6438 to Coldingham.

Coldingham Priory was founded by Ebba, daughter of King Osway of Northumberland, who fled from the wrath of the heathen King Penda of Mercia about 670 A.D. It was plundered by raiding Danes, and later became a Benedictine Priory under the management of Durham Cathedral.

St. Abb's Head is probably the most dramatic headland on the E coast of Scotland. The 300-foot (91.5-m) high cliffs play host to tens of thousands of seabirds each year: gulls, guillemots, razorbills, kittiwakes, fulmars, shags and cormorants.

St. Abb's Lighthouse came into service in 1862, and in 1876 it was fitted with the first siren foghorn in Scotland. The first radar beacon in a Scottish lighthouse was installed here in 1968.

Pettico Wick is much favoured by skin divers on account of the clarity of the water. The rocks here are mainly lavas from volcanoes which were active about 400 million years ago. Looking NW along the coast one can see quite clearly the 2 predominant types of rock – banded and folded sedimentary rocks on one hand, and unstructured lavas on the other.

A prehistoric fort occupies a rocky knoll about a mile (1.5 km) SW of the lighthouse. The fort is D-shaped and about 200 yards (183 m) in diameter, one side being defined by the steep N edge of the knoll. The settlement, dating from before 200 A.D., lies within the walls of the fort, and contains several foundations of circular stone-built houses. There are also remains of 4 other settlements surrounding the fort.

There are 3 pubs in Coldingham.

across S–W shoulder of Stake Hill to meet tarmac road to radar station. ❸ Turn right on to road. ❹ At third bend turn left up marked path. (This cuts out dogleg in road; alternative is to follow road to top of Lowther Hill.) ❺ At radar station, keep to outside of fenced compound and go left to reach road running NE along hilltops. ❻ After telecommunications station on Green Lowther, head directly downhill towards dam at north end of small reservoir. ❼ Cross dam; at far side climb straight uphill on wide track and bear right on to track leading to Leadhills village. There is a maze of tracks and old roads in the vicinity, but the village is clearly visible: keep heading towards it – actual path used does not matter. ❽ Leave Leadhills by main road – B797 – and branch left at Station Road, keeping to left of church. ❾ Follow track bed of disused railway back to start.

Wanlockhead's mining days are evoked in the silver and lead mining trail. Amateurs still pan for gold in local streams – with some success.

Wanlockhead's unusual beam engine (reconstructed in the early 19th C.) pumped water from a lead mine here.

Mining Museum.

The Wanlockhead Youth Hostel is popular with cyclists and hill walkers. Mrs. Isa Young, the warden, belies her name: at over 80 she is the oldest and longest-serving warden of a British hostel.

The Walk Inn.

The summit of Lowther Hill was used as a graveyard for suicides.

Leadhills: Tourist Information housed in Old Miners' Library; see also the Leadhills Bell and the gravestone of John Taylor, laid to rest at 137.

The Brigadoon Tea Room, on a side road to the west of the main street, serves good, reasonably priced teas. But the poster in the window erroneously claims this is Scotland's highest tearoom: those at Cairnwell Pass and on Cairn Gorm are much higher.

Lowther Hills
7 miles (11 km) Sheet 71 876129

Moderate High, lonely country with contrasting features that will give food for thought. Also an opportunity to sample a stretch of The Southern Upland Way long-distance path. *Hill-path, traffic-free tarmac road, ridge, grassy slopes, moorland path, disused railway; one climb..*

Start From the A74 Glasgow–Carlisle road, turn off at Elvanfoot or Abington and follow signposts for Leadhills; stop at Wanlockhead, 1½ miles (2.5 km) further on. **Parking** in the village streets. Make your way to the main road – the B797 – which bypasses the village to the S; here, just below The Walk Inn, locate signpost for Carronbridge via Enterkin.

❶ Take the footpath uphill signposted Carronbridge and Enterkin, keeping to the right side of the inn. ❷ Follow the Southern Upland Way marker posts

Southern Scotland
STRATHCLYDE

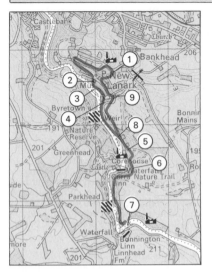

The Falls of Clyde
4 miles (6.5 km) Sheet 72 882427

Easy Spectacular scenery within easy reach of the built-up areas of western central Scotland. The highlight is the dramatic falls, but there is also much interest in New Lanark's restored industrial archaeology. Best in autumn and winter, when rainfall swells the falls and leafless trees give better views. *Restored village, mature woodland, river and gorge; some mud after rain.*

Start From Lanark town centre take the A73 SE. In ¼ mile (0.5 km) bear right on to the unclassified road signposted New Lanark. In just over ½ mile (0.8 km), look out for signs at mini roundabout to **car park** on left in woods. Lanark is served by regular buses and trains from Motherwell and Glasgow; by buses only from Edinburgh.

① Return from car park to main road and turn left, downhill. ② Turn right and cross bridge beside mill building. ③ Turn left and walk along SW side of mill lade – the channel supplying the mill. ④ Cross back over mill lade, and turn right on to woodland path beside river. ⑤ At Bonnington Power Station bear right, away from tarmac road, cross green pipes, and climb uphill on path through trees. ⑥ After viewpoint above Corra Linn climb first set of steps to upper viewpoint, then continue on path through woods. ⑦ From Bonnington Sluice retrace steps to Bonnington Power Station. ⑧ About 200 yards (183 m) past Bonnington Power Station, keep uphill on metalled road. ⑨ At New Lanark, turn left into village. ⑩ Turn right, up steps at church, then continue up path to car park.

⌂ New Lanark is a fascinating village founded in 1785 by David Dale in partnership with Richard Arkwright, inventor of the Spinning Jenny. His machines needed power – and the plan was to harness that of the River Clyde. A 'model' village was constructed along with the mills and in time New Lanark flourished – with excellent labour relations.

⋙ Dundaff Linn is the smallest of the falls – a drop of just 10 feet (3 m). Water is taken from the river upstream of the falls and led through a tunnel 100 yards (91 m) to the mill lade at New Lanark.

⋙ The Clyde Gorge, with its 100-foot (30-m) cliffs, was formed after the most recent ice age (about 12,000 years ago) by glacier melt-water.

⌂ Bonnington Power Station is one of south Scotland's smallest power stations, generating only 16 megawatts compared with the average of 500 megawatts.

⋁ From the viewpoint above Corra Linn there is an astonishing view of the Linn, second of the four Falls of Clyde. With a drop of 85 feet (26 m), it is the highest of the falls and after heavy rain its force is ear-shattering.

⋁ Bonnington Linn: the twin falls are in an awkward bend of the river, giving a less impressive view than Corra Linn, but still awe-inspiring.

⌂ Bonnington Sluice controls the river level, and extracts water for the power station.

✗ Tearoom at shop in main street.

'Tillietudlem Castle'

5½ miles (10.5 km) Sheet 72 806497

Moderate This part of the Clyde Valley SE of Glasgow features often in rambling club programmes, but is neglected by other walkers, probably because of better publicized walking N and NW of the city. *Farmland, moorland, woodland; 2 climbs.*

Start The village of Rosebank, on the A72, about 7½ miles (12 km) NW of Lanark and 6½ miles (10.5 km) SE of Hamilton. Locate the Popinjay Hotel – mock Tudor appearance makes it unmistakable; use the hotel **car park**.

① From the car park, cross the road to the house opposite and take the track on its left. Continue to ② where turn left along the road and continue about ⅓ mile (0.5 km) to join track on left, later turning right ③ with track to rejoin road at ④. Continue on road to Netherburn village and follow Station Road to track bed of disused railway ⑤. Go under bridge and follow railway to gate on left at ⑥ – almost exactly one mile (1.5 km). Go through gate towards old shed to join single-track road to castle. Leaving castle courtyard, turn right at main gateway. Descend path to wicket gate, then go down incline to bridge and ascend opposite bank. Leave path as it veers left and continue along field side of fence above gorge. At gate ⑦ follow path on gorge side of fence to descend down glen and emerge on road ⑧ at Crossford. Follow road left for ¼ mile (0.5 km); locate track on left at Glenside. Follow this track to path on right just before gate ⑨. Follow this uphill, crossing road in rather over one mile and rejoining road at ③. Retrace via ② to Rosebank.

🏨 The Popinjay Hotel, impeccable mock Tudor dating from 1882, is said to take its name from an artificial bird used in shooting practice.

🏚 The site of the house on the opposite hillside was the birthplace in 1726 of William Roy, who rose to Major General and founded the government surveying and map-making service – later called the Ordnance Survey.

🏰 Craignethan Castle, popularly known as Tillietudlem Castle after its fictional name in Sir Walter Scott's *Old Mortality*, was a Hamilton stronghold. Scott was offered it as a residence, but he turned it down.

🍎 The Clyde Valley's orchard country.

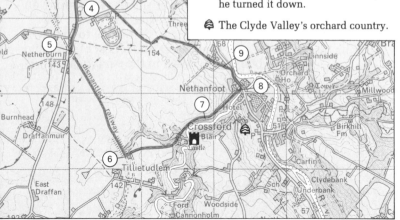

WESTERN SCOTLAND

It is said, fancifully perhaps, that the western coast of
Scotland, with its highlands and islands, is the home of
some of the most bona fide descendants of the ancient
Celts; that when those imaginative and nomadic peoples
were finally confronted with the Atlantic, their long drift
westwards stopped. Confined by this natural barrier, they
settled, and their populations increased. The western
Scotland represented in this section is exactly that Celtic
fringe: beginning just north of Glasgow, it runs in a band
up the west side of the country past Oban and Mull, Fort
William and the Kyle of Lochalsh and Skye up through
Wester Ross and on into the remote north-west. Indeed, you
will find here the most northerly walk either in this book,
or in its companion, the original *Walker's Britain*: Loch
Glencoul, a mere 25 miles (40 km) from Cape Wrath.
Whether or not the west coast is the true Celtic Shangri-
la, you will enjoy some Celtic echoes on these routes. Don't
be surprised to find as much seaside walking as hill
rambling: it is a key part of the experience of the north-
west. With luck, you will happen on a blue August day on
which to do the superb beach walk at Red Point. Your
reward will be crystal clear water, more akin to Pacific
atolls than the cold, wet north-west, the bluest of seas, and
midges to bite you to death in the evenings.

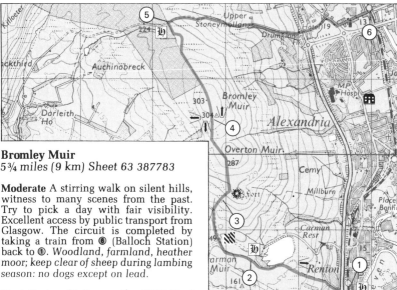

Bromley Muir
5¾ miles (9 km) Sheet 63 387783

Moderate A stirring walk on silent hills, witness to many scenes from the past. Try to pick a day with fair visibility. Excellent access by public transport from Glasgow. The circuit is completed by taking a train from ⑥ (Balloch Station) back to ①. *Woodland, farmland, heather moor; keep clear of sheep during lambing season: no dogs except on lead.*

Start Renton Station on the B857 N of Dunbarton; use the station **car park**.

① Leave station, turning right and soon right again to cross the railway bridge; cross main road by footbridge, descending to side of main road and locating path on left through woodland. At stile turn right, then, in a few yards, left to continue on path to reservoir. Beyond the wayside well, where track veers right, make for the group of tall trees ②. Take the path to the right of the trees, winding through bracken and heather towards ridge. Join road at entrance to former quarry. Take farm road opposite to gate, then follow fence on right uphill to corner post ③. Head for the adjacent wooden power-line posts. Follow path as it climbs over hill, later forking left and descending to stile at fence. Climb to the trig. point at Bromley Muir ④ and continue on path which runs near dyke and descends to Stoneymollan Road ⑤. Follow the road right via footbridge to (former) main road – about 1½ miles (2.5 km). Turn right then left at garage to arrive at Balloch Station ⑥ for trains back to ①.

🏛 The monument by the station is to Tobias Smollett a local man.

\↗ Back over the Vale of Leven, centre of the Scottish calico printing, bleaching and dyeing industry.

🏛 Here is the former site of Carmen Horse Fair, an important local market-place which ceased to function at the time of the First World War.

▨ The older houses in the district are built of sandstone from this quarry.

✴ Remains of an Iron Age fort.

\↗ W and S to the Firth of Clyde; N to Loch Lomond; E to the Vale of Leven and moors N of Glasgow.

🏛 The Cross Stone or Colquhoun Stone was possibly the base of a stone cross and is said to have been used as a clan gathering place.

🏢 The enormous building on the B857 was once the works of the Argyll Motor Company, Scotland's first car manufacturing plant. Subsequently it was a torpedo factory; now it is disused, with an uncertain future.

Western Scotland
STRATHCLYDE

Finlas Water
3 miles (5 km) Sheet 56
344885

Easy A short linear walk near Glasgow and close to Loch Lomond which leads away from the busy lochside into a picturesque glen. *Grazing, wooded riverside, undulating hill country; some mud after rain; keep dogs on leads – sheep grazing.*

Start From Glasgow going N on the A82 signposted Loch Lomond/Crianlarich, go through Arden and past the 2 left turns for Helensburgh, then watch for the next left turn (small signpost) for Shemore. Continue less than one mile (1.5 km) to farm at road end. Check with farmer whether **parking** is acceptable near farm, otherwise use verge further down the road. Numerous buses from Glasgow (Buchan St.) – alight before the Luss at Shemore turning.

❶ From parking continue on untarred farm track: easy to follow. ❷ At Finlas Loch (reservoir) take the small but well-defined footpath on the E shore up to the head of the loch; continue further at will. ❸ Return by same route.

✳ The cup and ring markings on the rock here were probably made by prehistoric man.

〽 A fine view E from here of Loch Lomond and the Highland Boundary Fault – the line which marks the start of the Scottish Highlands.

♨ Rowan and holly grow out of a large boulder: probably an ice-age erratic.

〽 W to the Luss Hills and Coire Cuinne – a corrie or natural depression.

🏭 Finlas Water is a relatively new reservoir supplying Glasgow.

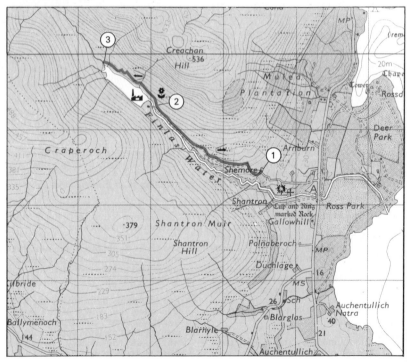

Western Scotland

The Old Post Run
5.5 miles (9 km) Sheet 19 033625

Easy Follows part of the old mail foot-route to the west coast; gentle walking, but grand country; chance to see black houses, fascinating old Highland dwellings. Especially charming in spring, when the colours are fresh. *Alluvial flat beside meandering river; woodland; riverside; loch shore; one wet section of about 100 yards (91 m).*

Start From Kinlochewe, 17 miles (27 km) SE of Gairloch Head on the A832; ¾ mile (1 km) S of Kinlochewe Hotel, turn off at signpost Incheric ½ mile. Continue ¼ mile (0.5 km) to crossroads and turn left; in ½ mile (0.8 km) **parking** at road end before Culaneiler Farm.

➀ Walk past farm on track, passing through gates to reach path, skirting grass bank. Follow the path along the fence and into trees above river; continue following path through birch, alder and oak. ➁ At the open flats go right across the grass — wet section — and join path, continuing behind trees. Pass ruin of black house. Follow lochside path round bay and on to footbridge across burn. Return by same route. Walk can be extended to Lochan Fada by crossing bridge and going up Gleann Bianasdail on rough path: a climb of about 800 feet (244 m) over 3 miles (5 km).

🌱 This is a residential field station for the Nature Conservancy Council's Beinn Eighe Reserve, one of the first nature reserves in Britain. Its main purpose is to preserve and study the 700-acre remnant of Caledonian pine forest at Coillie na Glas-leitire.

〰 Notice the waterfall on the cliff above. The stranded logs and other debris show how high the loch can rise when wind and rain conspire.

🏠 Black houses are aptly named: they had a simple hole in the roof so that smoke could pass through; smoke from the peat fire none the less sooted up the interior. Thatch was the usual roofing material and the dwellings had thick stone walls. They were in regular use up to, and during, Victorian times, and even later.

🏭 Little remains of the ironworks which thrived here in the 17th C. Water and a plentiful supply of wood for powering the furnaces were the basic requirements to set up a foundry — commodities abundant just here.

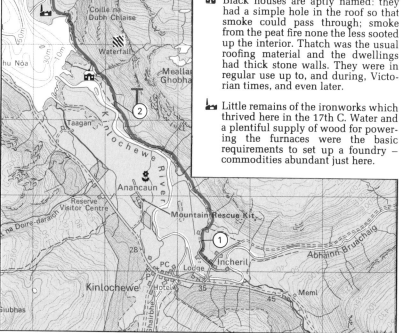

Western Scotland
HIGHLAND

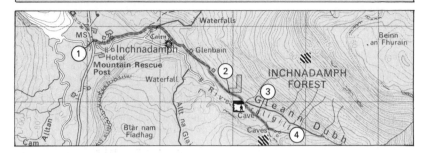

The Caves of Inchnadamph
4 miles (6.5 km) Sheet 15 252218

Moderate Limestone topography is unusual in the Highlands and gives rise to the uncharacteristically lush vegetation on this route, which is quite remotely situated in the north-west near Loch Assynt. A charming glen walk (but snow in winter, and insects July–Sept) with the caves – ice-age bone relics – as a climax of interest. *Well-defined track and path through glen.*

Start From Inverness, take the A836 to Bonar-Bridge and from there head north-west on the A837 for 35 miles (56 km) to the Inchnadamph Hotel, Inchnadamph, which is about 12 miles (19 km) E of Lochinver. **Parking** on verge in proximity of hotel.

① Having crossed the bridge from the hotel, locate side road immediately on right. The private property notice is no problem for walkers: continue along road, following past houses: the last one, Glenbain, is in about one mile (1.5 km). Continue on grassy path, past pinewood, ②. In ¼ mile (0.5 km) reach the River Traligill which disappears into the low cliff at ③. Continue up the glen – way forward is obvious. At ④ the Cleann Dubh Burn flows through an arch and plunges down a cave. In another ½ mile (0.8 km) reach further pot-holes. Return at will along same route.

☀ The ancient cairn possibly marks a burial mound.

⌑ The caves are in Cambrian limestone, of considerable fascination to pot-holers, archaeologists and geologists.

The best caves are near the 2 principal burns, Traligill and Allt nan Uamh. Eminent geologists, Peach and Horne, excavated them in 1917, discovering bones of northern lynx, bear, Arctic fox, reindeer, and two human skeletons dated at 6000 B.C. In one cave there are stalactites: don't touch them – they took thousands of years to form.

☷ Ichnadamph is a National Nature Reserve of interest chiefly for its unique geological formations. Ichnadamph means stag's meadow.

☷ The burn's disappearance down the cave here is just that: its outflow has never been found.

Red Point
3 miles (5 km) Sheet 19
732684

Moderate Open, peaceful walking with a half-mile (0.8-km) stretch along a beautiful beach with white sand. The water is clear, and the bathing safe, so the route comes into its own in summer. *Grass, sand dunes, rocky heath, rocky shore, sand and coral beach, flat grazing land; wet moorland section at start; much of route not on paths, but easy to find way.*

Start About 3 miles (5 km) S of Gairloch, turn on to the B8056 at stone bridge, following signpost Red Point 9 miles. Continue (narrow, twisting drive) to road end, which is ½ mile past Redpoint Viewpoint. **Parking** at road end.

❶ From parking, head roughly W across grass, making for the sand dunes. Cross burn near fence and follow fence to its corner, where there is a gate ❷: cross the fence here and make across the heath towards the prominent rock ❸. From here, follow rising ground to the obvious high point, arriving at the white pillar ❹ about 45 yards (40 m) from the top. Head S across the heath towards the shore and turn left on to the beach. Make for the disused fishing station ❺ at the E end of the beach. (Eilean Tioram, just offshore from the fishing station, is a tidal island, cut off at high water.) From the fishing huts follow the obvious path back across grazing land. Redpoint Farm ❻ is about a mile (1.5 km) further on; take the farm track back to ❶. The walk can be extended about 5 miles (8 km) SE along the rough coastal path to Craig Youth Hostel.

𖣂 Superb ocean views.

𖣂 In one of the most remote and inaccessible parts of the north-west, Red Point beach is beautifully unspoiled. The sand is fine and the water is crystal clear for bathing. Look for the tiny pieces of dried coral in the sand.

𖣂 Seabirds to be seen from the shore include Arctic terns, a speciality of the west coast of Scotland. A pure red beak and tail streamers are the most positive identification points of the adult bird in summer.

𖣂 The fishing station is now disused.

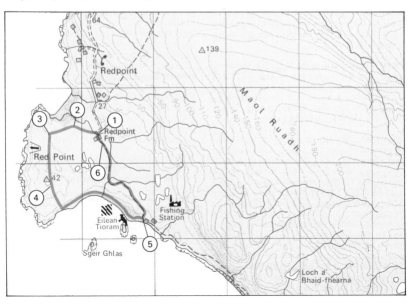

Western Scotland
HIGHLAND

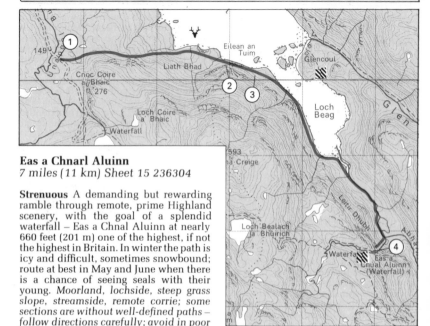

Eas a Chnarl Aluinn
7 miles (11 km) Sheet 15 236304

Strenuous A demanding but rewarding ramble through remote, prime Highland scenery, with the goal of a splendid waterfall – Eas a Chnal Aluinn at nearly 660 feet (201 m) one of the highest, if not the highest in Britain. In winter the path is icy and difficult, sometimes snowbound; route at best in May and June when there is a chance of seeing seals with their young. *Moorland, lochside, steep grass slope, streamside, remote corrie; some sections are without well-defined paths – follow directions carefully; avoid in poor visibility, and take care to keep looking back on way up to falls – this can help in finding the way back if the weather closes in; wear walking boots with pleated soles; allow 4–6 hours.*

Start From Inverness, take the A836 to Bonar-Bridge. Continue on the A837 and A894 NW about 45 miles (72 km) towards Kylestrome; 4 miles (6.5 km) N of Skiag Bridge and 3 miles (5 km) S of Kylesku, look for a bridge; **parking** on verges.

① From the bridge (wet peat at start) make E towards Loch Glencoul, following the wire fence on the left after about ½ mile (0.8 km). No single path to follow, but make use of deer tracks across the rock and heather. Pass lochan (small loch) on left, make towards heather hillside and keep close to bottom of slope as you descend, with wire fence about 50 feet (15 m) to the left; eventually drop to loch shore and cross the bracken knoll towards the crags running down to the shore. Head for the steep grass bank ② running above the shore and traverse upwards on a faint path to reach a grassy gulley at the

level of the top of birch trees on the cliff. Follow the path up the gulley and at top bear left below crag. (This is the easiest route; take care to keep to the beaten path crossing above the birch trees.) Continue on easy, level ground to reach wall ③ and cross it through the large break. Continue on the rough path in the approximate direction of furthest small island on the loch, following the shore to the mouth of the burn. Then make uphill on the left bank of the burn for half an hour to ④ the falls. Return by the same route.

☘ Loch Glencoul is a sea loch – fair chance of seeing grey seals and otters. The latter are increasingly rare.

☘ The Glencoul Fault is much studied by geologists.

⚡ At 1,600 feet (488 m), the Stack of Glencoul is a superb vantage point.

☘ The falls are indeed dramatic; as might be expected. Eas a Chnal Aluinn means the great waterfall of Coul.

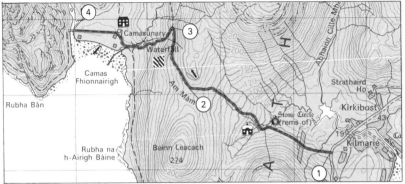

The High Track to the Cuillin
6 miles (9.5 km) Sheet 32 545173

Moderate Perhaps the best approach to Skye's notorious Cuillin Hills for the walker who wants to view them at close quarters, but who wishes to avoid the long climb from Glen Brittle over wet moorland on a path now badly eroded by walkers. A route through prime Highland scenery, well away from the well-trodden parts of Skye. Light effects on the hills at sunrise and sunset can be breathtaking, as indeed are the peaks when snow-capped. *High moorland, glen, shore; one climb.*

Start From Broadford on the Island of Skye, take the A850 in the direction of Portree, soon turning S on the A881 in the direction of Torrin and Elgol. Go round the head of Loch Slapin and in about 4 miles (6.5 km) pass through Kirkibost, then the hamlet of Kilmarie; in a hundred yards or so, stop where the road rises, with a small plantation on the right; **parking** in vicinity of the gate – beware of soft ground, and don't block the road.

❶ Go through gate, shutting it, and follow the well-defined track first through conifers, then across moorland. You pass a picturesque lochan (small loch) to the right, and then climb ❷ over the Pass of Am Màm. Follow the track as it zigzags down the hillside; where it bends sharply left ❸, ignore the smaller path leading off N, continuing on the main track, which heads SW towards the sea. Continue on flat moor and grassland or on the

rocky/shingle beach and return at will from Camasunary ❹ by the same route.

✹ Remains of a Neolithic stone circle: the ground leading to it is usually wet and boggy. Such circles are often found by lochs and lochans.

🏠 Site of an old shieling: these rough structures were used as summer dwellings by crofters who brought their livestock here for summer grazing; hardy as these people were, the hut was probably used simply for shelter and overnight stops.

⋁ From here are the best views to the Cuillin Hills, eroded and dangerous peaks which suffer some of the worst weather in the British Isles. Their pale brown crystalline rock makes compass readings unreliable, and has a magical power to reflect sky colour.

⋙ Fine waterfall.

🏠 The house of Camasunary and the Strathaird Estate belong to Ian Anderson, lead singer and lyricist of Jethro Tull, the folk/rock band.

⋁ A fine view out to the Island of Soay, once owned by writer Gavin Maxwell, famous for his book *The Ring of Bright Water*, and for exploits with otters. His association with Soay, however, pre-dates the otters: it was here that he set up his basking-shark fishery and his experiences of the coast hereabouts are recorded in *Harpoon at a Venture*.

DEESIDE AND SPEYSIDE

Concentrated in this region are more high mountains than anywhere in Britain. They are dangerous, of course, but not so much for their terrain — many climbers find them boringly dome-shaped — as for their sub-Arctic climate. It is not an area for the inexperienced or ill-equipped to roam freely, and many a visitor finds it frustrating not to be able to explore the semi-Alpine uplands at close quarters, for fear of being the cause of a rescue-team call-out. The purpose of two of the four routes in this section is therefore to enable walkers of modest experience to see some serious mountain country, *provided they are well-equipped*. The routes are the Lairig Ghru Circuit, and the two-day Mounth Roads walk. These are substantial, challenging expeditions, and you could well plan a whole holiday around them. Note that the Mounth Roads is *only* a two-day route. It does not offer the option of doing either first or second day as a linear walk on its own: public transport back to the start, or indeed motor assistance from a willing third party, would be impractical.

Deeside and Speyside
GRAMPIAN

Tap o' Noth Iron Age Fort
2½ miles (4 km) Sheet 37 480282

Easy A short but worthwhile walk taking in an exceptional vantage point, a fact not lost on the Iron Age architects of the impressive fort which occupies it. Easy to follow and suitable for any time of year. *Farm track, path, one climb.*

Start From Huntly take the A97 S to Rhynie, turn right on to the A941 and after about 1½ miles (2.5 km) look out for the farm on the right, marked 'Howtown' on the map, but 'Brae Cottage' at the end of the farm track which leads away from the road here; **parking** is possible on the verge without causing obstruction.

① Follow the farm track, which winds NW, then N, reaching ② a gate into plantation where turn right on to the footpath leading up the line of trees. In ¼ mile (0.5 km) reach open hillside and continue to the top of the hill. Return by the same route.

🏞 It is not a particularly high hill, but on a clear day the conical summit commands a nearly uninterrupted view of the whole of NE Scotland.

✳ The builders of Tap o' Noth fort were responsible for flattening off the top of the hill, and to protect their settle- ment they put up the surrounding wall of vitrified masonry. No one knows for certain how the stones were fused together to give the glass-like effect; one theory, recently challenged, is that timber was stacked up against it, then set alight.

Leith Hall and garden, about four miles (6.5 km) E near Kennethmont, is open to the public.

Deeside and Speyside
GRAMPIAN

Lairig Ghru Circuit
12 miles (19 km) Sheet 43 065896

Strenuous Enables the tourist with modest walking experience to see some of the higher Cairngorms. Excellent possibilities for photography, and the River Dee has lovely pools and falls in this area. Perhaps best in early summer when the higher peaks still have some snow, but a superb walk at any time of year, except winter, when do not attempt. *Track, moorland paths, riverside; some mud after rain; one climb.*

Start From Braemar take the Linn of Dee road, following it for about 6 miles (9.5 km); take the sharp right turn across the bridge; once over, turn sharp right again and follow the road up a short but steep hill. **Car park** in ¼ mile (0.5 km).

❶ From the car park it is worth making a detour back down the hill to the Linn of Dee **❷**; retrace to **❸** and turn left through the gate across the track. Continue along track about 3 miles (5 km) to **❹** the White Bridge over the Dee. From here follow the footpath about 4 miles (6.5 km) to a small stream **❺** crossing the path. Here head off towards the lochans (small lochs) – no path – and in less than ½ mile (0.8 km) join the well-defined footpath at **❻**, turning right on to it. Continue downhill on path to **❼** where the path detours left to cross the Luibeg Bridge. It is possible to ford the bridge at **❽** but this is not recommended for inexperienced walkers; make for the bridge, and once across, turn right to follow the path down to where it becomes a track. Continue to Luibeg **❾**, where head left for the bridge over the Derry Burn at **❿**. Cross and go straight ahead, then left up hill at long wooden building, passing Derry Lodge to the left. Go straight on at **⓫** down to the Black Bridge **⓬**. Cross and head up the track, then down to **⓭** where turn right on to the tarred road at the gate. It is another ¼ mile to the car park.

⚒ Though just a few feet wide, the Linn of Dee is a spectacular gorge. The River Dee pours through, over the centuries wearing large 'pots' in the rock. After rain, the water can be seen boiling up in these before flowing out to the peaceful pool below.

❗ A fine view to the W here over the wide flood plain of the Dee. Red deer often graze the grassy sole of the glen.

⚒ The Chest of Dee are two large pools worn by the river.

❗ From here you look straight into the V of the Lairig Ghru itself – probably the most famous pass in Scotland. It cuts right through the main massif of the Cairngorms. On the right is the long

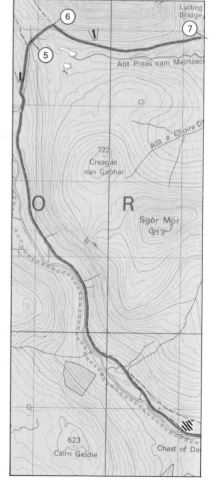

ridge of Carn a' Mhaim, and beyond it Ben Macdui, second highest mountain in Britain. To the left are the 'boiler plate' slabs of The Devil's Point.

Yet another spectacular viewpoint: on the left is the great peak of Cairn Toul, and beyond it Braeriach. It is a useful place to stop and ponder the might of the most recent ice age, which gouged out the Lairig Ghru and, on the left,

the Coire (corrie) an t-Saighdeir (Soldier's Corrie). Devil's Point is seen again to the left, and beyond it Glen Guesachan (Glen of Pines).

On a clear day it is possible to look up from here and see the crags of Coire Sputan Dearg and upper Ben Macdui.

There are remnants in this area of the ancient Caledonian Pine forest. Climatic change, felling by man and browsing by animals account for its gradual reduction.

The flat, grassy bottom of the glen here is a peaceful contrast to the rugged scenery earlier on the route. In the evenings there are usually sizeable herds of red deer grazing by the river.

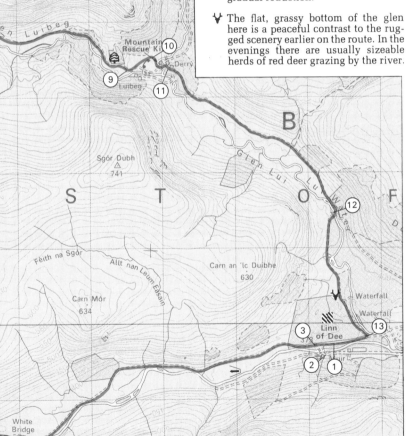

Deeside and Speyside
TAYSIDE/GRAMPIAN

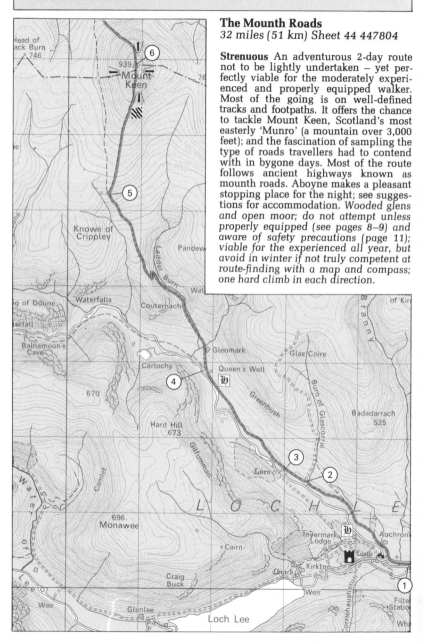

The Mounth Roads
32 miles (51 km) Sheet 44 447804

Strenuous An adventurous 2-day route not to be lightly undertaken – yet perfectly viable for the moderately experienced and properly equipped walker. Most of the going is on well-defined tracks and footpaths. It offers the chance to tackle Mount Keen, Scotland's most easterly 'Munro' (a mountain over 3,000 feet); and the fascination of sampling the type of roads travellers had to contend with in bygone days. Most of the route follows ancient highways known as mounth roads. Aboyne makes a pleasant stopping place for the night; see suggestions for accommodation. *Wooded glens and open moor; do not attempt unless properly equipped (see pages 8–9) and aware of safety precautions (page 11); viable for the experienced all year, but avoid in winter if not truly competent at route-finding with a map and compass; one hard climb in each direction.*

Deeside and Speyside
TAYSIDE/GRAMPIAN

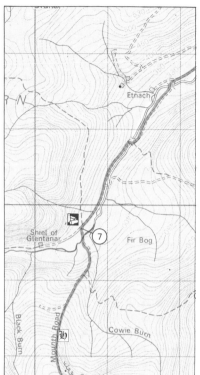

Start From the A94 Aberdeen–Forfar road make for Edzell, and from there continue NW to Tarfside then Invermark, where there is a conspicuous **car park**.

① Leave car park and follow road W about ¼ mile (0.5 km) to bridge; just before bridge, turn right up the road signposted public right of way. Keep to the main track and in about one mile (1.5 km) ② go straight ahead. At the bridge ③ don't turn left; carry straight on and in another mile ④, at Queen's Well, again don't turn left but keep going uphill, through the narrow glen. The going becomes steep for about 2 miles (3 km), but the way is easy to follow; where the track ends, follow the right-hand of the two paths ⑤ directly to the top of Mount Keen: another mile of steep ascent. From the summit ⑥ take the path NW; after about a mile it becomes a track once more. Follow this downhill to

its junction with the track up Glen Tanar ⑦ and turn right.

📖 The upper reaches of Glen Esk have more than their fair share of beauty spots, but in the past they had economic importance, too: iron was smelted here, and there was a profitable silver mine near Invermark. Whisky-making and smuggling have long been local preoccupations; trains of ponies carrying goods, both legal and contraband, were a familiar sight in the glen, trekking S for the Lowland markets.

Macbeth is thought to have fled into the glen after his defeat at Dunsinane.

🏰 Invermark Castle, an impressive ruin, was a residence of the Stirlings.

📖 During a visit to the glen in 1861, Queen Victoria took a drink from this spring, whose water was suitably pure; her host, Lord Dalhousie, built the stone crown over the well and added the inscription:

Rest, traveller, on this lonely green,
And drink and pray for Scotland's Queen.

〰 This very steep section of the route is known as The Ladder, and the stream beside it the Ladder Burn. From the top there is an excellent view back down Glenmark.

↕ Mount Keen tops the 3,000-foot level by 80 feet, making it the most easterly of Scotland's Munros. Marvellous views all round; take care among the boulders on top.

📖 This is one of several mounth roads in the area: they were, of course, the key to local communications. *Grampian Ways* by Robert Smith gives a fascinating account of the roads, and their history.

🏚 Near the sign pointing the way to Mount Keen, Aboyne and Dinnet, are a group of ruins, sole remnants of a once-important inn on the Mounth Road.

Continued on page 282.

TWO-DAY ROUTE

281

Deeside and Speyside
TAYSIDE/GRAMPIAN

Continued from page 281.

Continue down the glen, reaching Half Way Hut in about 3 miles (5 km). Continue on the track about another 5 miles (8 km) to the Home Farm of Glen Tanar ⦿ where you reach the tarred road. Follow it down past Millfield to Bridge o' Ess and ⦿ turn right. Follow the B976 to Aboyne, another 2 miles, where there are hotels and bed-and-breakfast places to suit all pockets.

🏚 Half Way Hut marks the half-way point between Glen Tanar House and Sheil of Glentanar.

∩ This well-made bridge is typical of the diligently maintained Glen Tanar Estate.

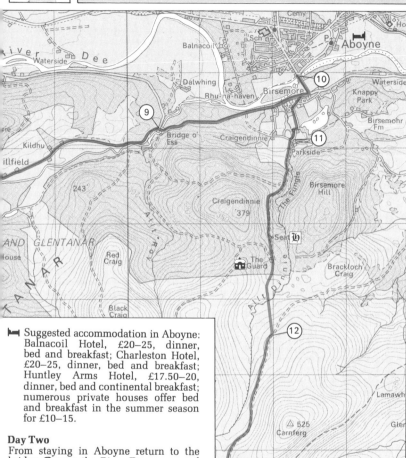

⊢ Suggested accommodation in Aboyne: Balnacoil Hotel, £20–25, dinner, bed and breakfast; Charleston Hotel, £20–25, dinner, bed and breakfast; Huntley Arms Hotel, £17.50–20, dinner, bed and continental breakfast; numerous private houses offer bed and breakfast in the summer season for £10–15.

Day Two

From staying in Aboyne return to the bridge ⑩ over the River Dee; cross and continue to T-junction, turn right and in about 100 yards (91 m) locate the signpost for public footpath by The Fungle to Tarfside. Follow this, keeping to the main track and in about ⅓ mile (0.5 km) ⑪ turn right over the small bridge. Here is a sign for Tarfside; follow it left. It is about one mile of steep ascent to The Seat, from which continue to The Guard. From there go straight ahead into forest and on to a well-defined footpath. Follow this for about ¾ mile (1 km) to ⑫ where it joins a track; turn right on to this and continue, following Scottish Rights of Way Society signs.

⑲ The Seat, an impressive granite structure, was built by Sir William Cunliffe Brookes, one-time laird of Glen Tanar. On one of the granite blocks marking the entrance to the grassy area in front, is the appropriate inscription, 'Rest and be Thankful'.

🏠 The Guard is a private house and its privacy should be respected; but note the fine stained-glass windows in which there are outlines of red deer.

Continued on page 284.

Deeside and Speyside
TAYSIDE/GRAMPIAN

Continued from page283.

The way is clear for about 3 miles until just before Birse Castle ⑬ when turn right down the marked track. Where this joins the well-defined track ⑭ turn right and follow track. In about 2 miles ⑮ this turns to footpath; follow the path about a mile to the watershed ⑯ from where continue down-hill; soon the path becomes a track once more. Carry on downhill through the glen about 3 miles to reach the tarred road at ⑰. Turn right: it is about 3½ miles (6 km) back to ①.

▦ Birse Castle was built in the 1920s, in the style of the original 16th-C. structure, seat of Sir Thomas Gordon.

⑭ This point, known as Meeting of the Paths, is where two of the area's major mounth roads meet and must have been the scene of many a parting and reunion over the years.

⑰ About ½ mile W of Tarfside is a stone with a cross carved on it, said to be an excellent example of Pictish workmanship, and probably carved by a pupil of St. Drostane in about 600 A.D.

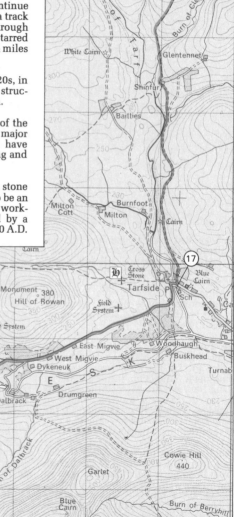

284

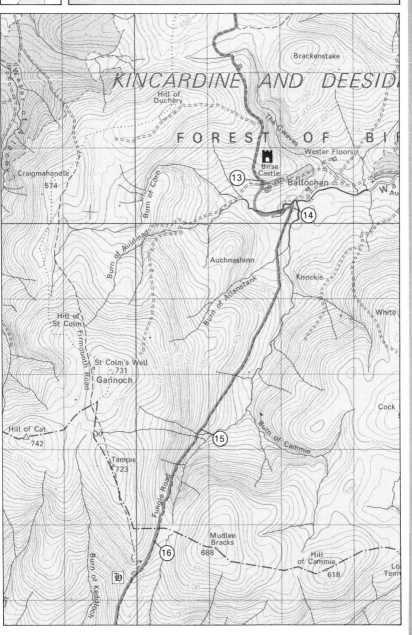

Brackenstake

KINCARDINE AND DEESIDE

Hill of Duchery

The Gwaves

FOREST OF BIR

Wester Floors

Craigmahandle 574

Birse Castle

(13)

Ballochan

(14)

Burn of Corn

Burn of Auldmad

Auchnashinn

W Au

Burn of Allanstank

Knockie

White

Hill of St Colm

St Colm's Well 731

Gannoch

Firmounth Road

Hill of Cat 742

Burn of Cammie

Cock

Tampie 723

(15)

Fungle Road

Mudlee Bracks 688

(16)

Hill of Cammie 618

Burn of Keddloch

Lo Tenn

Deeside and Speyside
GRAMPIAN

Loch Muick Circuit
8 miles (13 km) Sheet 44 311851

Moderate A route that rarely fails to offer some new item of interest, whether wild-life or just the changing mood of the landscape. Impressive views over Loch Muick. *Track and path round loch; do not attempt in winter – the tracks can hold snow for some time.*

Start From Ballater take the B976 about a mile (1.5 km) W to Bridge of Muick, then turn left on to the Spittal of Muick road. Follow this about 7 miles (11 km) to its end where there is a large **car park** at Spittal of Glenmuick.

① Leave the car park, turning right down the hill, and cross the bridge over the stream. Pass the picnic area and lavatories to the left, then on past the Visitor Centre in the conifer wood. A few yards further on ② there is a junction with a road leading off to the right; carry straight on through gate between 2 buildings. In rather over ¼ mile (0.5 km) keep right ③ and walk down towards the loch, keeping left at the junction ④. Continue on the track for nearly 2 miles (3 km) to Black Burn Bridge ⑤, and after crossing, turn sharp right, to leave the track for a well-defined path. After about one mile a path ⑥ heads off uphill; ignore this and walk around the head of the loch. Cross the 2 bridges over the burns and turn right ⑦ towards the lodge marked Glas-allt Shiel on the map. Just before the wood ⑧ follow the sign left, making a detour through the woods. At ⑨ a track leads off left, making

another detour to the Glas-allt waterfall. Soon rejoin the track ⑩ and continue along the loch shore nearly 2 miles to the boathouse ⑪ where turn right to cross the River Muick just as it leaves the loch. Continue on track to rejoin outward route at ⑫ turning left for ①.

Ⓥ The Visitor Centre.

Ⓥ There is a particularly fine view up the loch here, with the lovely rounded form of Broad Cairn rising on the left. You can also see how Loch Muick lies in a deep, steep-sided glacial valley, its sides levelling out to a plateau. The loch itself is exceptionally deep – about 230 feet (70 m).

Ⓦ The Black Burn, crossed here, is so-called because of the dark colouring its water gets from the peat bog through which it runs upstream.

Ⓦ The Glas-allt Waterfall makes a round trip of about a mile. The path is steep – follow it with care – but many will find standing right at the base of the waterfall well worth the effort.

Ⓥ There is often a fine sunset to be seen over the loch from here.

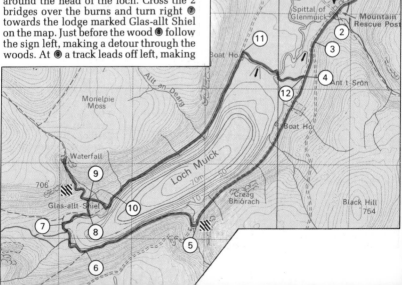

Index

Acknowledgements

David Platten Assessor, Cornwall Moorland and Mountain Training Group; Chairman, Cornwall Outdoor Education Association; *The Outdoor Survival Handbook* (David and Charles, 1979); *Making Camping and Outdoor Gear* (David and Charles, 1981). **Liz Prince** Dartmoor National Park Department); *Walks in the Dartmoor National Park* series (Dartmoor National Park Department). **John Weir** Information Officer for Dartmoor National Park Authority. **Christopher Edwards** Contributor to *In the Steps of Jane Austen* (second edition, Arcady Books, 1985). **Brian Pearce** Assistant Visitor Services Officer, Exmoor National Park; contributor to *Britain on Backroads* (Pan/Ordnance Survey, 1985); *Enjoying Exmoor* (Exmoor National Park, 1985). **C. Trent Thomas**, 25 years in area. **Tom Cairns** Information Officer, Council for Environmental Conservation. **Sheila** and **Peter Burnie** 21 years in area. **John Dent** Retired adult and community education principal; Cotswold warden. **Janet Spayne** and **Audrey Krynski** *Walks in the Surrey Hills* (1974); *Walks in the Hills of Kent* (1976); *Afoot in Surrey* (1979). **John King, George Mills** and **Ben Perkins** Ramblers' Association, Sussex area. **Nick Moon** *Walks for Motorists: Chilterns: Southern Area* and ditto *Northern Area* (Frederick Warne Ltd, 1979); *Chiltern Society Walks: Walks in the Hertfordshire Chilterns* Shire Publications, 1985). **Chris Barber** Originator of the Three Peaks Trail and organizer of the South Wales Marathon walk; *Exploring the Brecon Beacons National Park* (1980); *Exploring Gwent* (1984); *Mysterious Walks* (Granada-Paladin, 1983). **Jim Knowles** County councillor; *Snowdonia Walks for Motorists* (Frederick Warne, 1982); North Wales contributor to *Britain on Backroads* (Pan/Ordnance Survey, 1985); various local guides. **Heather Hurley** *Walking in Wyedean* (Wyedean Tourist Board, 1978); *Country Walks around Herefordshire* (Herefordshire City Council, 1983); *Wyedean Walks* (Douglas McLean, 1983). **Peter Heaton** Chairman of South District, Cotswold Wardens' Service; Chairman of South Gloucestershire Group of Ramblers' Association. **Neil Coates** Partner in Transport for leisure, research and marketing consultancy. **Robert Kirk** Hon. Secretary, Ramblers' Association – Shropshire Area; *The Shropshire Way* (Thornhill Press, 1983); *Walks in the Countryside Around Birmingham* (Foulsham/Ramblers' Association). **David** and **Janet Palmer** The South Staffordshire Group of the Ramblers' Association. **Brett Collier** Ramblers' Association Area Chairman and Joint Secretary of Lincolnshire Fieldpath Association; contributor to: *Ramblers' Ways* (David and Charles, 1980); *Weekend Walking* (Oxford Illustrated Press, 1982); publishes *Plogland* walk leaflets; walk guides for Lindsey Loop (a 100-mile figure-of-eight walk in Lincolnshire). **Malcolm McKenzie** Footpaths Secretary and former Chairman of Newark Ramblers' Association. **Mike Statham** Secretary of Leicester and District Group of Ramblers' Association. **Fred Matthews** Hon. Secretary Essex Group, Ramblers' Association. **Harry Bitten** Illustrator; various guides to walking in Essex and walks for local newspapers; contributor to: *Ramblers' Ways* (David and Charles, 1980); *Walks in the Countryside Round London* (W. Foulsham & Co Ltd, 1985). Co-author of *Walks for Motorists, Essex* (Frederick Warne, 1983). **George Toulmin**, 25 years in area. **John Andrews** Suffolk Ramblers' Association Area Footpaths Secretary; *Discovering Walks in Suffolk* (Shire Publications, 1981); regular contributor to East Anglian Daily Times *Walkers' Way*. **Trevor Noyes** Chairman, Cambridgeshire Area Ramblers' Association; *Rambles with John Clare* (Paul Cutforth, 1978). **John O'Sullivan** RSPB; contributor to *Birdwatcher's Britain* (Pan/Ordnance Survey, 1983). **Colin Speakman** Rambler and freelance writer living in Ilkley, West Yorkshire. Publications include *The Dales Way* (1969); *Transport in Yorkshire* (1970); *Walking in the Craven Dales* (1973); *A Yorkshire Dales Anthology* (1982); *Adam Sedgwick Dalesman and Geologist* (1982); *Walking in the Yorkshire Dales* (1982); *Walking in the Three Peaks* (1983). **Geoff Eastwood** *Walking in East Yorkshire* Geoff Eastwood, 1978). **Betty Hood** Local Ramblers' Association. **Walter Scott** *Inns and Outs in South Lakeland* (Ramblers' Association, 1985). **Dave Forsyth** *Walking in Scotland* (Spurbooks, 1981); regular walking features in *Dunfermline Press* and occasional contributions to *Great Outdoors* magazine. **Bill Brodie** *Walking in Scotland* (Spurbooks, 1981). **Sandy Cousins** Mountaineer and hillwalker; contributor to various outdoor publications and to *Big Walks* and *Classic Walks* (Wilson and Gilbert). **Eilid Ormiston** Geographer, research for Nature Conservancy Council. **Fred Gordon** Mountain rescue team member for ten years. Arranges guided walks or walking holidays in Scotland; details can be obtained by writing to him at 49, Grampian Road, Torry, Aberdeen, AB1 3ED or telephoning (0224) 897758.

PICTURE CREDITS Page 12 Charlie Waite; **19** Robert Estall; **26** Arden; **31** Derek Widdicombe; **38** Derek Widdicombe; **42** Peter Baker; **49** C. Edwards; **47** Charlie Waite; **72** Fotobank; **106** Trevor Wood; **108** Aerofilms; **112** Simon Warner; **117** Chris Barber; **138** Trevor Wood; **142** Peter Baker International Picture Library; **153** George Wright; **169** Neil Coates; **176** Aerofilms; **183** Janet and Colin Bord; **185** Fotobank; **190** Aerofilms; **192** Derek Widdicombe; **197** David Gallant; **199** David Gallant; **205** Derek Widdicombe; **212** Janet and Colin Bord; **228** Derek Forss; **234** Geoffrey Berry; **257** Derek Widdicombe; **258** Charlie Waite.

ARTWORK, EDITORIAL AND DESIGN Artwork by **Tony Graham, Michael Woods** and **Jim Robins**; editors **Linda Gamlin** and **Andrew Duncan**; editorial assistant **Elspeth Boardley**; art editor **Mel Petersen**; designer **Arthur Brown**; additional map artwork **Roger Boffey**.

CHECK WALKING Another group of walkers strode many miles testing the routes; the editors thank them for their work, especially Willa Hancock, Linda Hart, Sheila and Peter Burnie, David Burnie, Mr Reeves Black and Mr and Mrs R. T. Boardley.